# A History of Modern Thailand
## 1767–1942

The University of Queensland Press'
Histories of Southeast Asia Series

*General Series Editor*
Chr. L.M. Penders

Forthcoming
*Prehistory of Austronesia* by Peter Bellwood
*Indonesia in the Nineteenth Century* by Peter Carey and A. Day
*A History of Sumatra* by Christine Dobbin
*The History of Islam in Southeast Asia* by A.H. Johns
*A History of Borneo* by Virginia Matheson
*The Age of Commerce in Southeast Asia, 1400–1680* by A. Reid
*Pre-Islamic Indonesia* by Peter Worsley
*Pre-History of Thai and Indo-Chinese Area* by H. Loofs

WITHDRAWN

# A History of
# Modern Thailand
## 1767–1942

B.J. TERWIEL

University of
Queensland Press

ST LUCIA • LONDON • NEW YORK

© University of Queensland Press, St Lucia, Queensland 1983

Typeset by University of Queensland Press
Printed and bound by The Dominion Press–Hedges & Bell, Melbourne

Distributed in the United Kingdom, Europe, the Middle East, Africa, and the Caribbean by Prentice-Hall International, International Book Distributors Ltd, 66 Wood Lane End, Hemel Hempstead, Herts., England.

*National Library of Australia*
*Cataloguing-in-Publication data*

Terwiel, B.J. (Barend Jan), 1941–.
   A history of modern Thailand, 1767–1942.

   Bibliography.
   Includes index.
   ISBN 0 7022 1892 8.
   ISBN 0 7022 1902 9 (pbk.).

   1. Thailand — History — 1782–1945. I. Title.
   (Series: University of Queensland Press' histories
   of Southeast Asia).

959.3'03

**Library of Congress Cataloging in Publication Data**

Terwiel, B.J. (Barend Jan), 1941–.
   A history of modern Thailand, 1767–1942.

   (The University of Queensland Press' histories of
Southeast Asia series, ISSN 0729-3887)
   Bibliography: p.
   Includes index.
   1. Thailand — History — To 1782. 2. Thailand —
History — 1782–1945. I. Title. II. Series.
DS577.T47     1983          959.3          83-4089
ISBN 0-7022-1892-8
ISBN 0-7022-1902-9 (pbk.)

# *Contents*

Maps and Tables    vii
Preface    ix
Acknowledgments    xi
Introduction    xiii
1.  Backdrop: Society during the Late-Ayutthaya
    Period    1
2.  Siam Under Taksin: Tumult and Reform    29
3.  The First Reign of the Čhakrī Dynasty:
    Innovation in the Guise of Orthodoxy    70
4.  The Second Reign: Peace and Trade    99
5.  The Third Reign: Efficiency
    and Centralization    127
6.  The Fourth Reign: Westernization
    from Above    162
7.  The Fifth Reign, Part I (1868–83): The Regent
    and New Siam    210
8.  The Fifth Reign, Part II (1884–1910): Humiliation
    and the Path to Autocracy    247
9.  The Sixth Reign: The King, Nationalism, and the
    Alienation of the Bureaucracy    290
10. Restoration, Revolt, and the Rise
    of the Military    319
Glossary    350
Reference Bibliography    354
Index    370

# *Maps and Tables*

**Maps**
Thailand (present borders)      xiv
Thailand, showing the approximate boundaries of the six
states that formed after Ayutthaya's destruction      42


**Tables**
Estimated Siamese revenue in 1822, two Crawfurd
accounts      118
Two accounts of spirit tax for fourteen towns in
Siam      119

# Preface

The chief aim of this book is to provide a readable historical narrative, based on a wide range of sources. In style I have been influenced by the Siamese chroniclers, who present events in chronological order and provide information from various perspectives, telling now of a military campaign, now describing a happening in the capital.

For the period before 1850 there were insufficient reliable sources for a wholly satisfactory record, and I have had to attempt to create a consistent picture from incomplete data. For the more modern times, much more information is available, and I have been able to rely with some confidence upon the detailed analyses of previous scholars.

Much space has been devoted to describing the activities of the chief personages, the kings and their entourages. Originally, it had been my intention to devote much less attention to these and to concentrate on the wider social issues, but during the writing of the book I was perforce drawn into discussing personalities in some detail. In the first place this was unavoidable, given the approach of many of the sources upon which this book is based. Secondly, in the case of Siam, with its cultural emphasis upon hierarchy, the chief actors often had an extraordinary influence upon statecraft and policy-making. Thirdly, the space devoted to "personalities" reflects my own dissatisfaction with the "hagiographical" slant of much that has been written previously. In the following chapters it is attempted not to deny those in power their successes but also to sketch their problems and failures. I hope that in this respect I have been able to some extent to set the record straight. The narrative of the exploits of kings and chief ministers is consciously interspersed with discussions of, for example, taxation, corvée, and general economic data. This book is therefore more than a history of kings or an outline of Siamese politics. Throughout the research involved in the preparation of this work I have collected information relevant to the broader framework of Siamese society. Given the relatively undeveloped state of Thai historiography, a history book such as this cannot claim to be definitive or authoritative in all respects. I am aware that some of the interpretations of events in Siamese history are novel, and occasionally my presentation may be regarded as contrary to what hitherto has been widely accepted as the truth. It has not been my intention to provoke controversy; in all instances I reveal the full extent of my sources and thus I hope to facilitate further debate on the more contentious issues.

For the spelling of geographical names I have largely followed that of L. Sternstein in his *Thailand: The Environment of Modernisation* (Sydney: McGraw-Hill, 1976). Some words, such as *baht*, Rama, and Taksin are spelt according to general accepted usage. In all other instances I have attempted to provide the reader with an indication of the actual pronunciation of Thai words by using the Library of Congress system of transliterating Thai, with some minor modifications. In this system *a* sounds as in the first vowel of the French *ami*; *ā* as in English *car*, *ǫ* sounds not unlike the vowel in English *not*; *o* corresponds to the vowel in *note*; and *u* is pronounced like the vowel in English *full*. Among the consonants, *čh* is the unaspirated sound as in Dutch *beetje*, while *ch* is always pronounced as in English *chill*. The *th* is always an aspirated *t* and never the English fricative as in *thin*. Similarly the *ph* is always an aspirated *p*, and never should be pronounced as in *phone*. With these rules in mind it should be possible for the reader who is unfamiliar with the Siamese language to give a fairly accurate rendering of the many Siamese words given in the text. It ought to be understood, however, that Siamese is a tonal language and that for the correct pronunciation one should learn the proper tone of each syllable. A macron over a vowel indicates vowel length.

# Acknowledgments

Much of the preparation of this work took place in Hamburg, at the Abteilung Thailand, Burma und Indochina of the Seminar für Sprache und Kultur Chinas, Universität Hamburg, where I spent some six months under the auspices of a Von Humboldt-Foundation Research Fellowship. With the assistance of the Von Humboldt Foundation I was able to read and reflect undisturbedly and photocopy some essential documents. I am also grateful for assistance received with the checking through collections at the National Libraries of Bangkok and Copenhagen, the Library of the Instituut voor Taal-, Land-, en Volkenkunde at Leyden, the Library of the School of Oriental and African Studies in London, and especially the National Library of Australia and the Menzies Library in Canberra. I thank the editors of Oxford University Press (East Asia Branch) for granting permission to use extracts of S. de la Loubère's *Kingdom of Siam.*

Where I obtained information from fellow-researchers, I mention this in footnotes. One scholar not mentioned in footnotes but who regularly shared items of information and discussed points of view related to the more recent period of Siamese history is Kevin Hewison. I am also grateful to Miss Mary Hutchinson of the Australian National University, and my wife, Fiona Terwiel, for correcting various draft versions.

# Introduction

Considering the crucial importance — both strategically and economically — of South-East Asia to Australia it seems incongruous that hitherto only very few English-language specialized studies of the area have been produced. It is the primary objective of this series to help to fill this gap by providing authoritative scholars with the necessary space to present in some detail their and other scholars' latest findings and analyses in their particular specialty. No attempt will be made to superimpose particular themes and each volume will stand on its own.

The fact that only now for the first time after almost two hundred years of white settlement in this country a project of this kind is considered necessary and viable testifies to the growing realization of Australians that they are a nation in their own right, the destiny of which is no longer solely dependent on European ties but also completely intertwined with the future of our immediate neighbours: the newly independent and vigorous nations of South-East Asia. Indicative of this new spirit of Australian self-awareness is the rapid development of South-East Asian studies during the last two decades and it should be a matter of some national pride that the vast majority of contributors to this project are either Australian or Australian based scholars.

It is hoped that this series will help to provide interested Australians with a deeper understanding and greater appreciation of their immediate neighbours and will help to cement the presently often still tenuous ties into strong links of genuine friendship and fruitful cooperative effort.

*Chr. L.M. Penders*
*General Editor*

Thailand (Present-day Borders)

# 1

# *Backdrop: Society during the Late-Ayutthaya Period*

## The Social and Administrative System in Theory

In the following pages, Siamese society of the late-Ayutthaya period (the late seventeenth and first half of the eighteenth centuries) is depicted in ideal terms. The hierarchy and the rules and regulations are stated without reference to specific instances. The system of administration is described as if each member of the administration actually fulfilled his duties, and as if the king were really guided in every respect by the *Phra' Thammasāt*,[1] the code of laws passed on through the ages.

By far the most important office in the country was that of the king. The person most worthy of this office was the eldest male child from the union of the previous king with his queen.[2] If such a person was not available, or if he was not considered suitable, often the previous king's brother, one who had gained experience through occupying a senior office, such as that of Mahā Uparāt,[3] would be elevated to the position of monarch.[4] When the decision on the succession had been made, this was formalized as soon as possible with an anointing ceremony. If circumstances prevented a full-scale anointment at short notice, it was possible to enact a provisionary installation, which might be followed later by

the full ceremony. As the Thai name for the ritual — *Phra'
rātchaphithī boromaphisēk*, or "royal ceremony of the great
anointment" — indicates, the sprinkling and pouring of
lustral water was the central act.[5] The idea that water is a
suitable medium, which can be pervaded and saturated with
sacred power, was widespread in Siam.[6] The water to be used
for the creation of a new king was collected from various
places around the kingdom, preferably from spots that were
considered sacred in their own right. Siam's chief religious
specialists would further increase the water's spiritual power
by chanting appropriate words over it. The formal installation of a new king included, apart from anointment, a
handing over of the regalia, which consisted of an array of
objects such as the state umbrella, a betel-chewing set, a pair
of slippers, a fan and whisks. Among the insignia of his new
rank, the king would receive a golden plate on which a long
string of royal epithets and honourable names was engraved.[7]
The new king would solemnly declare to rule for the well-
being of the populace, to protect and defend all those who
now fell under his command. Among his first duties were a
procession around the capital city, symbolically receiving the
territory, and the acceptance of pledges of loyalty from all
members of his family and senior state officials.

After a king had been thus formally confirmed in office, he
was very much a being apart. Nobody was allowed to
approach his person; guards were always at hand to prevent
this. His wives, aided by many other women, usually young
females of good family who were presented to serve him,
would supervise the preparation of the king's food. Women
tidied his sleeping quarters and waited on him at table. On the
relatively rare occasions that the king moved outside his
palace, his progress would bring ordinary life to a halt. If his
boat was encountered on the river, all other craft would
move out of the way and the approaching royal boat would
only meet with ships that were no longer propelled, their
rowers having thrown themselves face down.

If the boat passed that of a state official, the official was
obliged to come out of the central high seat with its protective
hood and prostrate himself on the small platform just in
front of it. No one in the boat would stir until the king was

out of sight.[8] If the king proceeded by land, all people close enough to notice his conveyance would instantly fully prostrate themselves and nobody would venture to catch a glimpse of the monarch, either because of genuine respect for that august body passing near by or out of fear of being caught in the act and punished by one of the guards. Such occasions gained immensely in dramatic impact by the fact that absolute silence was maintained when the king moved among the populace.[9]

One of the princes of the highest rank, frequently a younger brother or a son of the king, would be chosen to fill the office of Mahā Uparāt. The Uparāt occupied, at least during late-Ayutthaya times, a palace situated at some distance from that of the king. In accordance with the Siamese notion of the east being the most auspicious direction, undoubtedly because that is the direction in which the sun rises, the palace of the Uparāt was considered to lie "in front" (i.e., to the east) of the king's palace, and therefore in common parlance it was referred to as the Wang Nā, or Front Palace.[10] The prince who was Uparāt was the second highest dignitary in the country, as measured by the attributes of rank and honour that were attached to his office. The holder of this office was the only dignitary excused from having to prostrate himself before the king during royal audiences and council meetings.[11] Although the Uparāt's wealth was not such that he could rival the king's display of power, some of the glamour of the king's office was reflected in the Wang Nā, where a miniature court was kept.

The various members of the royal family each received an allowance from the king. In late-Ayutthaya times, the Uparāt had 40,000 *baht* a year;[12] a prince of *čhaofā* rank[13] would receive 8,000 *baht*; and children and grandchildren of the king not of *čhaofā* rank would annually receive amounts varying between 1,600 and 4,000 *baht* each. The queen, if such a person was appointed, received 24,000 *baht*. The other most important women attached to the king would each be able to maintain their own quarters in the women's compound. They received amounts varying from 400 to 4,000 *baht* each, from a total of 16,000 *baht* annually spent on that section of the royal household.[14]

There is not much known about the women's compound in late-Ayutthaya times. It is certain that young women of rank were presented by their families to serve the king.[15] It is also clear that it was possible for the queen to conduct business and to acquire goods.[16] If we accept the historical reconstruction of Prince Damrong, the women's compound had an elaborate organization in which a complex hierarchial system could be discerned. This was where the king's wives and concubines lived; this was also where princesses were brought up and where they might obtain a good education. Daughters of noble families who had been presented to the court were trained as dancers and musicians. The king could choose whom he liked from among the accomplished women. If a concubine gave birth to a child, her status as mother of a royal child, *čhaočhǭmmāndā*, was higher than that of other concubines. The women's compound was run and organized by women. Mature and experienced ladies would become teachers, or supervisors of other daily activities. It was a place where princesses, by their exalted rank often prevented from marrying, could make a career. The ladies of rank would each have a retinue of women, often drawn from the wealthy families of Ayutthaya, who would gladly assign a daughter to serve a great lady in return for an education and for the prestige and honour of being associated with the royal court.

Some princes, mature and trusted advisers to the king, would receive the nominal headship of an administrative government department. Most departments were called *krom*, and the princes who had become nominal heads would attach the word *krom* as a prefix to their titles and names. The use of the word *krom* as a sign of princely rank probably goes back to the second half of the seventeenth century, to the reign of King Nārāi.

There were many subdivisions among the princes of *krom* rank, the lowest being called *kromamū'n*, a higher rank being a *kromakhun*, and a yet higher one *kromaluang*. In theory it was possible for the king to bestow even higher *krom* ranks, such as *kromphra'* or even *kromsomdetphra'*, but this rarely occurred. The order of the different princely *krom* ranks, ranging from *kromamū'n* to *kromsomdetphra'*, duplicates a range of civilian ranks whereby a *mū'n* would be lower than a *khun*, a *khun* below a *luang* and a *luang* below a *phra'*.[17]

An important part of the palace organization was that of the Mahātlek, or the corps of royal pages. As far as can be determined, all young men in the Mahātlek were drawn from outside the royal family. It was a great honour to be accepted in the corps of pages, for these young men were the personal assistants to the king. Although their rank was not as high as that of many other members of the nobility, these young men were highly respected. In the late part of the seventeenth century it seems that the inner core of the Mahātlek consisted of four groups of ten young men, each group commanded by a young officer holding the rank of *čhamū'n*. Members of this core probably had direct access to the king. The Law of Civil Hierarchy reveals that these sections of the Mahātlek were themselves hierarchically structured, and that within each section there were five different ranks. From de la Loubère's account of Siam published in 1693, it is possible to identify the honorary names of the four *čhamū'n* in 1687. His "Meuing Vai, Meuing Sarapet, Meuing Semeungtchai and Meuingsii" are in fact the *čhamū'n* Waiyaworanāt, Sāraphetphakdī, Samoečhairāt, and Sīsaorak.[18]

The pages entered royal service at the age of fifteen or sixteen. Some of an inner group prepared the king's betel quid; others were responsible for his personal weapons; yet other pages read his documents, helped keep his accounts, or carried messages to provincial officials. The importance of being in the corps of pages lay not only in being near the august presence and being intermediaries between the king and various other people; it also meant having a chance of obtaining acquaintances within the palace and gradually learning the practice of statecraft. After a young page had served some four or five years, the king would have had ample opportunity to assess his character, his intelligence, and his degree of devotion to duty. Upon reaching the age of twenty, it was customary for a page to leave the king's service in order to spend at least one Lenten season as a fully fledged Buddhist monk. Upon successful completion of his season in a monastery, the young man was considered ready to accept responsibilities and could present himself to the king for consideration for an appointment. If he had made a good impression, he could expect to be elevated to one of the middle ranks of the civilian administrative system and to be appointed to his first duties in office. For example, the king could place him in one of the provincial courts as a representative of the central administration.

An interesting feature of the inner Mahātlek at that time is that on certain official occasions when the presence of all forty-four pages was required, they had to arrange themselves in two groups, twenty-two on the king's right-hand side and twenty-two on the left.[19] Each page would know on his appointment whether he belonged to the right-hand side Mahātlek or to the left-hand side Mahātlek. Similarly, members of the king's bodyguard would be either right- or left-hand side guards, and it seems that this gave rise to the custom of tattooing certain soldiers either on the right arm or on the left.[20] The chief state officials also knew beforehand whether they had to range themselves at the king's right hand or at his left. Provincial towns were called right-hand towns or left-hand towns, probably as an indication of whether the provincial governor would have to stand to the right or to the left during audiences.[21] Probably in imitation of the royal court, some government departments would themselves be split up into a right and a left side.[22]

Once a royal page had successfully completed his period of serving the king, he would first be appointed probably at the administrative rank of ǭkluang (also known as luang, because by the late seventeenth century the prefix ǭk was becoming obsolete). He would therefore already outrank administrators who were (ǭk)khun and (ǭk)mū'n. In late-Ayutthayan civil administration, most of the executive officers fell under one of six categories. These six were, from lowest to highest: (ǭk)mū'n, (ǭk)khun, (ǭk)luang, (ǭk)phra; (ǭk)yā, and (ǭk)phayā. While there were a vast number of officials with the rank of khun and mū'n, there were just over a hundred officials mentioned in the laws with the title luang, eighty-eight had the title phra', twenty-four were yā, and seventeen individuals were named as phayā.[23] On solemn ceremonial occasions, when officials appeared with all their signs of dignity, they wore high, white, cone-shaped hats, and it was possible to see at a glance what rank a person occupied, because the protocol prescribed different types of decorative bands round the base of the cone. An officer of *mū'n* rank had a silver-coloured band, and a *khun* a narrow golden one without decoration. A *luang* was entitled to a golden band two inches wide, a *phra'*, gold with leaf decorations, and the two highest ranks had golden bands profusely decorated with rosettes and embroidery.

Among those of *yā* and *phayā* rank could be found the heads of the most important government departments as well as the six chief ministers. These were:

1. The *čhaophayā* Čhakrī, chief of the division known as Mahātthai, which could be translated as Department of Civil Affairs. Near the end of the Ayutthaya period this minister became responsible for control over the provincial towns to the north of the capital. He was president of the king's council and may be regarded as the highest-ranking noble in the country. Like the king and the Uparāt (as well as some other senior ministers) he was allowed to place his personal seal on official documents issued under his command. His seal carried the image of a Rātchasī, the stylized Siamese lion.[24]

2. The *čhaophayā* Mahāsēnābodī, head of the Kalāhom, titular commander-in-chief of the armed forces. During the late-Ayutthaya period he supervised control of the southern provinces. Both the Mahātthai and the Kalāhom devoted much of their attention to organizing and supervising the provincial corvée. The Mahāsēnābodī's seal carried the image of the Khotchasī, a mythical animal representing a lion with an elephant's trunk.

3. The (*ǭk*)*phayā* Thāramāthibodī,[25] head of the Monthienbān Department. This department was popularly known as *krom* Wang (Palace). There is some evidence for the notion that this office once outranked all other ministries,[26] but in late-Ayutthaya times this was certainly no longer the case. The *krom* Wang ministry looked after the upkeep and maintenance of the palace and its inmates. It supervised certain troops attached to the palace and organized the

labour of slaves and freemen who worked for the royal monasteries.

4. The *phayā* Yomarāt, head of the Phra'nakhonbān Department, also known as *krom* Mū'ang (City). Most officials who looked after the peace, order, and safety of the city of Ayutthaya worked in this *krom*. Their tasks included fire prevention measures, police duties, and the maintenance of a criminal court and a prison.

5. The (ō̜k)*yā* Phonlathēp, chief of the Kasēt Department. In popular parlance this was known as *krom* Nā (Department of Lands). The most important tasks performed by this *krom* were the collection of the government's share of the rice crop, the upkeep of a registry of lands, and the settlement of boundary disputes.

6. The (ō̜k)*phayā* Sīthammarāt, chief of the Kō̜t, or Treasure-box. This department was also known as *krom* Phrakhlang, or the Treasury. It was charged with the collection of all taxes on imported and exported goods. As Ayutthaya became a major trading city, the office of the Phrakhlang gained more expertise in dealing with people from many countries. The Treasury became also the storehouse of knowledge of foreign countries, and most of the king's dealings with the world outside Siam took place by way of the palace of the Phrakhlang in a section called *krom* Thā (Harbour Section). Sometime during the late-Ayutthaya period, the chief of the Kalāhom seriously displeased the king, and thereupon the responsibility for manpower control in the southern provinces was transferred from the Kalāhom to the Phrakhlang. As a result, the Phrakhlang's ministry changed character, and many new *kroms* were added to handle the extra work.[27]

During much of the Ayutthaya period, these six dignitaries formed what can be styled the Siamese "inner cabinet", for these chiefs of the six ministries channelled various sources of revenue and controlled most of Siam's manpower. Each year, hundreds of ranking officers would receive a sum of money from the king called *biawat*.[28] In late-Ayutthaya times, a chief minister would receive 4,000 *baht*, while a relatively lowly court official would be given as little as 80 *baht*. The king's expenses on *biawat* have been reported as high as 120,000 *baht*.²⁹ The yearly *biawat* cannot be regarded as equivalent to an official's salary. Salaries derived usually from fees paid for specific services by the populace. It must rather be seen as a sign of the king's largesse, a token of the honour of having been of assistance to the king.

As Ayutthaya grew and developed, the country's administrative system underwent reform and change. New departments were created as the need arose, and occasionally some were merged, or holders of one office were appointed to act as chiefs of a completely different department. For example, in 1687 it seems that the head of the Ecclesiastical Department, an officer carrying the title of (ǫk)yā and the name of Phra' Sadet, held the commission of Phrakhlang.³⁰

From the preceding paragraphs, in which an outline has been given of the system of ranks and titles, it has become clear that the Siamese possessed a quite intricate formal hierarchy. The office to which a person was appointed carried a rank, such as *mū'n*, *phra'*, or *phayā*, and also a formal name, such as Čhakrī, or Yomarāt. For the sake of brevity the names mentioned thus far are not the complete names bestowed upon the holders of an office. For example, strictly speaking, the Čhakrī was known as *čhaophayā* Čhakrī Sǐǫngkharak Samuhanāyok Akhamahāsēnāthibodī Aphaiphiri Barā Kromphāhu, a string of words extolling the minister's role as royal bodyguard, his rank as chief general, and his fearlessness and bravery. It appears that in late-Ayutthaya times it was an established custom to link many positions in the administration with a particular rank and name, so that in the course of time as people moved up in the administrative hierarchy, they would change both rank and name. Officials became known by the ritual name attached to the office they held. To their intimate family and friends, the individuals would naturally retain their given names, those obtained from their parents, although such names may have been but rarely used.³¹

One of the most interesting state ceremonials, with which the king obtained a measure of control over his corps of officials, was the ritual of pronouncing the oath of fidelity.³²

This oath to the king was sworn regularly. The most solemn occasion took place on the third day of the waxing of the moon of the fifth lunar month, in March or April, and was probably connected with the elaborate New Year ceremony. In the morning, Buddhist monks prepared a bowl of water, and all officers drank a cupful while declaring that terrible things might befall them if they were unfaithful to the king. It was carefully watched whether each official drank effortlessly, or if he had difficulty in swallowing. Nobody was exempt from this ceremony. If an official absented himself he could be punished with death, for such behaviour was reckoned tantamount to treason. Nobody was allowed to wear golden rings during such a ceremony, apparently in the belief that such rings might make the wearer invulnerable against the effects of swearing a false oath. Some soldiers, presumably the king's bodyguard, had to take the oath every month, a measure undoubtedly inspired by fear for the king's safety.[33]

Much of the Chao Phraya lowlands was under the direct control of the capital, Ayutthaya. At some distance from Ayutthaya, secondary seats of power were maintained, ruled by an Ayutthaya-appointed governor (*čhaomū'ang*), who would have a council of advisers representing many of the chief departments of the capital. Such secondary seats of power were towns like Kamphaeng Phet, Sawankhalok, Phitsanulok, Nakhon Thai, Phetchabun, and Nakhon Ratchasima towards the north and north-east of Ayutthaya; and places such as Nakhon Si Thammarat, Patthalung, and Pattani in the south. In principle, the governors of such secondary seats of power ruled over all the subsidiary towns immediately surrounding them. These distant regions often sent tax in the form of forest or mining products which the king could export. Each of these provincial seats of power had its own relationship with Ayutthaya; some retained more control over their own affairs than others. Further away on all sides, Ayutthaya liked to be surrounded on all sides by petty states which acknowledged Ayutthaya's leadership in international affairs but who would usually not tolerate the indignity of having representatives of the Ayutthayan government attached to their courts. These petty kingdoms regularly sent a token of allegiance, together with some valuable gifts.

At times when Ayutthaya was powerful and mighty, it might have counted Tenasserim, Chiang Mai, Luang Prabang, Champassak, Cambodia, and some of the states at the southern end of the Malay Peninsula as areas more or less aligned with it, but at no time did Ayutthaya have the administrative apparatus for assuming direct control over these outer regions, probably with the exception of Tenasserim and its subordinate towns.[34]

We have seen how the administrative personnel could be distinguished by ranks, names, and amount of *biawat*. There were other ways in which the differences between one rank and another were ceremonially stressed. High officials would have a state boat, with rowers fore and aft and a seat in the middle. Over the seat a woven bamboo hood (*kūp*) was erected, and not only did the colour in which it was varnished indicate whether the official belonged to a right-hand side department or to a left-hand one (red for the former, black for the latter), but also the hood would carry a decorated band near the edges which showed his rank.[35] As a state official, a man would have the right to travel under a single-tier umbrella, the multi-tiered ones being reserved for the king himself. Special insignia of rank issued by the king were silver equipment with which to prepare betel leaf and areca nut.[36]

Apart from all these ways of distinguishing between one official and another, which were concomitant with the maintenance of an elaborate court and administration, the Siamese were also in the habit of reckoning a person's worth by noticing where someone was placed on the *saktinā* scale. Unlike the insignia of rank and status, the *saktinā* system encompassed, at least in theory, all Siamese. Everyone from the lowliest beggar and the slave to the chief princes had a place according to *saktinā*. The only Siamese who fell outside the system because of his rank and power was the king himself. Originally, the *saktinā* system must have evolved from a custom of allotting plots of land to able people. It is probable that the king gave to his chief advisers a certain number of complete villages, including land and inhabitants, and the peasants thus donated would have had the duty of performing services for their overlords.[37] Some time during the

Ayutthaya period this practice of allotting land to the different categories of citizens developed into the *saktinā* system. By late-Ayutthaya times it was already fully developed, and most Siamese must have known what their position on the *saktinā* scale was. By this time, the system's link with an allotment of land had already been lost, the only remaining trace of this origin being the fact that the units of the *saktinā* scale were still counted in areas of *rai*, each *rai* corresponding approximately to one-quarter of an acre, and that the word *nā*, "arable land", was often used in the proclamations allotting a specific number to a particular type of person.[38] Another feature that undoubtedly goes back to the origin of the system is the exclusion of the king. After all, in theory he is the only one by whom all land is controlled, and if a number were to be allotted to him it would have to be one comprising all the arable fields in the kingdom, which at that time was immeasurable.

In the fully fledged *saktinā* system, the Uparāt is given by far the highest number of *rai*, namely 100,000, by virtue of being a close relative of the monarch and holding the office of head of the Front Palace. A *čhaofā* prince would readily be allotted either 15,000 or 20,000 *rai*, but if such a prince were to be raised to *krom* rank, the *saktinā* position would be increased to an impressive 40,000 or 50,000. Offspring of the king and various middle and lower-ranking mothers would be allotted 6,000 or 7,000, and if they were promoted to *krom* status, their amount would be raised to 11,000. This class of royalty, at that time known as *phračhaolānthoe*, seems to have been the last category in which one was eligible to become a *krom* prince. Members of a further category, *mọmčhao*, offspring of the ranking princes, would obtain 1,500 on the *saktinā* scale, but these were not mentioned as candidates for *krom* rank.

It ought to be noticed that princes reaching *krom* rank range on the scale from 11,000 to 50,000, which means that their places in the *saktinā* scale are all higher than those of the most honoured administrators outside the royal family. The absolute top a commoner could reach was a rank of 10,000, well above many members of the royal family, who ranged usually between 500, and 1,000 *rai*.

At the top of the *saktinā* scale for commoners, at 10,000 *rai*, were found the six most important ministers, the heads of the Mahātthai and Kalāhom, as well as the heads of the Wang, Mū'ang, Nā, and Phrakhlang, and also the governors of some important provincial towns. A few others also rated as high, not necessarily because they wielded immense political power, but because they had the highest standing in ceremonial matters, for example, the Phra' Sadet, principal of the Ecclesiastical Department, and two Mahā Rātchakhrū, the dignitaries heading the Department of State Ceremonial.

The *saktinā* scale may be likened to an ascending system of titles, with distinct "slots" into which a person was fitted. Directly under the 10,000 came the category of 5,000, directly below that were places at 3,000, then followed positions allotted values of 2,400, 2,000, and 1,600. From 1,600 to 600 the places dropped by measures of 200, and then in smaller and smaller intervals from 600 to 500, 400, 350, 300, 250, 200, 150, 100, 80, 50, 30, 25, 20, 15, 10, and 5. Altogether there were twenty-seven steps on the civilians' ladder.[39]

There is no direct link between attaining a rank in the system of *mū'n, khun, luang, phra', yā,* and *phayā* and an exact place on the *saktinā* scale. Though in general the *phayā* may be found among the top stages of the *saktinā* ladder, there were two civil servants with *phayā* rank who stood only at *saktinā* 400, a *saktinā* rank well below many an official of only *khun* or even *mū'n* rank. There is only a vague correspondence between the two systems in so far as that the higher *saktinā* numbers would be allotted to persons in more responsible positions and that often these persons would also be given ranks attached to these positions. Of the two scales, the *saktinā* one seems to be the most accurate in indicating how much responsibility a person carried. Morever, the *saktinā* system covered people who did not qualify for elevation to a rank.

A person who reached the *saktinā* rank of 400 could consider himself a member of the administrative élite; he would have to present himself to the king in a ritual called *thawāi tua* (literally offering, presenting oneself), and from then on was considered to belong to the *khunnāng,* the nobility. Perhaps no more than two thousand persons had *saktinā* of

400 or higher, out of an estimated population of two million.[40] Belonging to the *khunnāng* entitled an official to receive the king's annual gift of money, *biawat*. At the same time, this privilege influenced his legal position regarding inheritance, for the king claimed a share of the *khunnāng's* personal wealth upon his death.[41] The *khunnāng* and their offspring were exempt from corvée without having to apply (and pay) for exemption. *Khunnāng* were allowed to be represented in courts of law by another person. All those of *saktinā* 400 and above were, in principle, eligible to attend royal audiences.[42]

It is not known for certain why the Siamese developed and maintained such an elaborate formal system in which all Siamese were given places on a numerical scale. A possible reason for the continuation of the system in Siamese society lies in the fact that the *saktinā* system became intricately interwoven with the legal system. According to the administration of the law, it made quite a difference to a person whether he or she belonged to a low or a high point in the scale. A high official found guilty of a particular crime might have to pay a higher fine than a commoner. For example, after being convicted of adultery, a man of 10,000 on the *saktinā* scale could be fined 2,000 *baht* of silver, a person of *saktinā* 5,000 could pay up to 1,200 *baht*, while a lowly beggar of a rank of *saktinā* 5 could be fined a maximum of 160 *baht*. The same principle is also true for the laws on compensation. Judges had a table dividing the population into *saktinā* categories ranging from 5 to 10,000, each category subdivided into five lists, setting out the amounts due to an injured party when his dignity only was injured, when he was hurt physically by another person's hand, by a wooden instrument, by a blunt metal instrument, or by a sharp metal one. The latter four types of injury were further subdivided into ten, ranging from simple bodily damage such as bruises, through broken limbs and blindness to death resulting from the injury. For each of the twenty-seven stages on the *saktinā* list, forty-two different injuries were legally recognized and the amount of compensation for each was prescribed by law. The compensation to a slave for having a limb broken unlawfully ranged between 50,000 and 70,000 cowry shells, depending on the nature of the injury, and if he were blinded the sum was set at 105,000 shells. The compensation for similar injuries to an official at 10,000 *saktinā* was, for a broken limb, a sum between 6,280,000 and 8,792,000 cowry shells, and 12,756,000 for being blinded.[43]

The *saktinā* system is of particular interest to the historian because it encompasses the whole Siamese population, and by an examination of all those who, for example, were worth 50 or less on that scale, a few glimpses of ordinary people may be obtained.[44]

A rating of 50 *rai* on the *saktinā* scale was given to scribes (*samian*) and legal counsellors (*thanāi*) attached to officers of *mū'n*, *khun*, *luang*, and *phra'* rank, provided that these officers had not yet reached the *saktinā* of 1,000. Artisans attached to a great variety of departments often had 50 *rai*, as did soldiers in charge of a small group of ordinary soldiers; for example, a *naimuat* (literally, master of a group) or a *sārawat* (assistant supervisor) would be worth 50. Also given a rating of 50 *rai* were messengers, or first-class soldiers who could fire a cannon (*chāngpū'n*), and those who could manufacture a cannon, such as the people who kept the fire going, who made the cast, and who smelted the metal. The lowest of the court Brahmans, those responsible for the maintenance of a shrine, fell in this category, as well as those guarding a herd of elephants. In a subsidiary department of the Mahātthai, the position of clown was rated at the level of 50 *rai*, as were a group of palace women described as a dwarf, a half-size person, a transvestite and an albino (probably forming an entertainment group).

A rating of 30 *rai* was allotted to the man in charge of a platoon of ten regular soldiers, but in some more specialized *kroms*, every ordinary soldier might be given this status. This was the case with the buglers and gong-carriers who formed part of all marching armies. In the Phrakhlang department, 30 *rai* was allotted to some skilled workmen who did not reach the dignity of full artisan status.

A *saktinā* level of 25 was given to a foreman, probably one supervising unskilled work. It was also the level allotted to some food distributors, cleaners, and watchmen.

A level of 20 was given to an ordinary man of the social

class of *phrai*, or freeman, who was head of a household. It was also the level of some unskilled labourers in the palace, such as water-carriers, and palanquin bearers attached to the female section of the palace.

A rating of 15 *rai* was allotted to commoners in general (*phrai rāp*), both men and women. It also was the number attached to women servants in departments other than the palace.

The base level for commoners was 10 *rai*, and none of the fixed positions in government departments descended to this level.

The lowest in the scale, 5 *rai*, was given to beggars, mendicants, slaves, and the descendants of slaves.

The list of officials and their *saktinā* positions reveals that, although women are not found among the holders of the highest offices, when they are appointed to a position they are given a *saktinā* rating commensurate with their responsibilities. Some important women at the palace rated 1,000. Among the helpers and servants, it is clear that a woman and a man doing the same work obtain the same position on the scale. This may be seen as an indication of an aspect of Siamese culture, probably related to the corvée system, which gave Siamese women considerable responsibilities at home while the men were forced to labour for the government.[45]

By examining the *saktinā* system in some detail, it has become clear that a large number of Siamese must have been classed as various categories of *phrai*, or commoners. Thus far, the categories *phrai* who supervise, *phrai* with family, and base-level *phrai* have been encountered. The term *phrai* was in use for all those who fell between the *saktinā* ranks of 10 and 350 inclusive. Below the *phrai* were the mendicants and slaves. Legally speaking, the whole population can therefore be divided into four broad classes: royalty (*čhāo*), nobility (*khunnāng*), commoners (*phrai*), and slaves (*thāt*), beggars for convenience being thrown in with the latter category.

While the *saktinā* system provides us with a fascinating glimpse of the hierarchical subdivisions within the whole population, it ought not to be forgotten that this is but one, fairly legalistic, system and that it reveals only part of the social reality. Just as in order to understand more fully a noble's position, his title, department, name, insignia, and *saktinā* number must all be taken into account, so the lower ranks need to be further distinguished before a person's position can be adequately assigned.

One method of looking at the ordinary people at the lower end of the scale is by noting their position with regard to corvée. In principle, all *phrai* had to serve the king six months each year. All commoners were therefore registered in bands (*mū*) and departments (*krom*), and in addition it was noted whether a person belonged to the right-hand part of the population, the "guards" (*thahān*), or to the left-hand part, the "civilians" (*phonlaru'an*). This information was recorded for all men and women. The children were assigned partly to the section of their mother and partly to that of their father, according to an intricate set of tables.[46] Each *mū* and *krom* had its administrative personnel, the *chaomū* and *chaokrom* being responsible for those registered under their names. There was a special government department, the *krom* Satsadī or Suratsawadī, which maintained the lists on which all men, women, and children were noted. With the help of these lists, it was possible to assess the strength of corvée groups in all districts. From time to time the government held a census (*samanokhrua*) during which fresh lists were made up to serve as a new basis for the corvée.

Corvée was supervised by government administrators appointed for this task. The *phrai* assigned to work under such an administrator called their supervisor the *nāi*, or "master". Some of the *phrai* served the king throughout the year; they were the king's personal retainers who had specific functions at the court, such as helping look after the elephants or doing guard duty or porterage. The king was responsible for their keep. Most *phrai*, however, did not fall into this category. They served the king at their own expense for six alternate months a year, one month on corvée, one month off. During the months when they worked for the king, they were assigned work by their *nāi*. Often their tasks were carrying earth for public works, making bricks, or helping provide building material by cutting and sawing wood, or providing the king with minerals by working in the mines.

There were many *phrai* who were left to their own devices for the remaining six months. If a commoner was prosperous and wished to avoid corvée service, already in late-Ayutthaya times he could buy himself an exemption. In 1688 it reputedly cost fifteen *baht* for a year's exemption.[47]

Apart from the commoners who were free to dispose of their own time during the months that they did not have to serve corvée, a large number of men were attached to particular nobles or princes. Each man of rank was allowed to maintain his own band, and the more important the person was, the larger the number of men who worked for him, who rowed his boat, who protected his property. These men would still be subject to the king's corvée and would have to divide their time between corvée for the king and tasks for the prince or noble. The ranking prince or noble would be responsible for their maintenance. Understandably, men of rank would often use their influence to protect "their" *phrai* from the onerous corvée, and thus being assigned for duties to a private individual became a way of escape from performing duties for the king.

Another, very popular, method of changing one's status was to sell one's freedom and thereby attach oneself to a master. According to the Siamese legal system, it was possible to borrow considerable amounts of money using oneself and one's dependants as collateral. So long as the borrowed sum was outstanding, the person who had furnished the sum had a right to the labour of the borrower. In other words, people worked instead of paying interest. Debt bondage was not identical with slavery, because the bonded person retained his civil rights, he could buy himself free for the original sum of money, or change master by persuading another man to furnish the amount owed. A person who had made such a contract may be called a fiduciary slave, a person held "in trust". People who had become fiduciary slaves had, in theory, to serve four months each year in government corvée, four months for their master in order to "pay interest", and were given four months in which to look after themselves.[48] If a master wished to keep a fiduciary slave during the months that they had to serve corvée, he had to pay the government a sum of money smaller than that necessary to obtain corvée exemption for an ordinary *phrai*.[49] The number of fiduciary slaves was large.[50]

Whilst fiduciary slaves retained their basic civil rights, there were several categories of people who were completely owned by their masters and who thus counted as their personal property. These were people who had borrowed upon their person more than the legal limits set for fiduciary slaves, war-captives, the offspring of slaves, and people who had been given to a monastery in perpetuity. The state could not demand corvée from these "absolute" slaves.

It is therefore clear that many men were liable to be called up every alternate month to do government service. Their families and farms were often left in charge of their wives, who were not subject to corvée. Adult married women were therefore often given considerable responsibilities, and much of the burden of keeping the farm going fell upon the women's shoulders. Of necessity, the division between "typical" men's work and "typical" women's work became rather blurred in Siam. When a man was available, he would do the most strenuous labour, such as ploughing the field, but a strong woman would not hesitate to tackle such tasks in the absence of men.

## The System in Practice

It has been necessary to consider the administrative system in ideal terms because that system provided a secure framework; it is reflected in legal documents and occasionally it guided people's actions. However, that ideal system provided norms which were often difficult to follow, and individuals tended to bend the rules to suit their private needs and ambitions. In order to obtain a more realistic historical perspective, it is therefore necessary to balance the depiction of the ideal system with a few remarks on its practical limitations.

The office of the king appears to have been potentially extremely powerful. The king officially assumed the headship of the judiciary; he was by right the commander-in-chief, and in theory he appointed and dismissed all officers of state. Once a king had been anointed, only very subtle forces prevented him from acting arbitrarily. It may have been hoped that the king's accession promise to behave in accordance with the ancient time-honoured laws would be taken seriously. His senior advisers may have indicated by silence or veiled allusions that they disagreed with one of the king's pronouncements. An unpopular king may have found it difficult to obtain reliable information upon which to act.

The power of an anointed Siamese king was so great that the whole system was weakened when an incompetent individual came to the throne. Only a quite exceptional individual could fulfil the monarch's duties in the manner intended by the law. For this very reason the succession often caused problems. Although the eldest son of the king and his queen had precedence, in actuality, more often than not it was another relative of the king who succeeded. Sometimes there were rival claimants and the assumption of power resulted in considerable bloodshed. The divine powers and status of the reigning king in themselves often prevented a peaceful succession. The king was so elevated and ritually superior that even openly to discuss his succession could be regarded as treason. Thus officially, as long as the king was in charge, only the king himself arranged for his succession, and when the king neglected to do so, dangerous rivalry could occur. Thus, paradoxically, it was the very power and exaltation of the office that caused a weakness in the system. "Despite the absolutism and divinity of kingship, the court history of Siam in the seventeenth century is filled with intrigue, coups and vicious succession disputes."[51]

The remarkable exaltation of the king's person not only often hampered a smooth succession but in addition prevented a clear and open flow of information. "He often times punishes ill Advice, or recompences good. I say good or bad according to his sense, for he alone is the Judge thereof. Thus his Ministers did much more apply themselves to divine his sentiments, than to declare him theirs, and they misunderstand him, by reason he also endeavours to conceal his Opinion from them."[52] In order to keep track of what was happening, the king therefore had to send out trusted men to find out the truth. The *krom* Mahātlek was probably the most important source of informers. This indirect and devious manner of obtaining information was not conducive to effective government. If a king ordered a major task to be done without specifying the details, his advisers would often have to improvise. If consequently the job was ill performed, the responsible officers would break the bad news by stages, trying to avoid ascribing the blame to him who first suggested the action while also making a valiant effort to shield themselves. The difficulties arising from the ineffectual system of passing on information led to a proliferation of methods for finding out the truth. Often the invisible powers would be invoked to assist the king in assessing information, or he would resort to trial by ordeal.[53] The king had to take strong measures in order to keep reasonable control over the court. It has been described above how all his officers regularly had to swear allegiance and give proof of their good intentions by swallowing sanctified water. If there was any doubt in the king's mind regarding the loyalty of any of his subjects, he could have them flogged, deprived of rank and title, or punished in whatever way he thought fit.

The state offices were all in the hands of the king, and all appointments were subject to his approval. The system did not provide for hereditary offices. Yet the government servants formed a class apart, for only they had access to an education which would lead to an administrative career. It often occurred that a son followed in his father's footsteps and rose high in the nobility. Usually this system was moderated by a lengthy period of apprenticeship at the court, during which a promising youth would be attached to the Mahātlek. The king's control over the Mahātlek gave him probably the strongest weapon in his efforts to create an effective administration. Through the corps of pages he could obtain information. From the pages he would select officers to represent his interests in the various *kroms* in the capital as well as in the provinces. Through his control over the Mahātlek the king also gained a measure of power over older, experienced civil servants who had managed to place a younger relative among the pages.

A legal weapon in the hands of the king was the fact that by tradition he had the right to hold a person's whole family responsible for the misdeeds of one of its members. A father would be held accountable for the behaviour of his son, and vice versa. This principle was extended to chains of command, a senior officer being responsible for the faults of a junior.[54] It also applied regionally, because in some cases where a culprit could not be found, the neighbours were punished.[55] This principle of law Siam shared with traditional China.

While it was therefore possible for a senior official to place his sons on the first step of the ladder leading up to a career in the administration, he had to relinquish parental control in doing so. It was the king's favour that catapulted a young man into powerful positions, and the king's ire could annihilate all ambitions at a stroke. The court was therefore a fairly dangerous place. From de la Loubère can be gleaned that it was a hotbed of intrigue:

> The Ministry there is tempestuous: not only thro the natural Inconstancy, which may appear in the Prince's [i.e., the king's] Mind; but because that the ways are open for all persons to carry complaints to the Prince against his Ministers. And though the Ministers and all the other Officers, do employ all their artifices to render these ways of complaints ineffectual, whereby one may attack them all, yet all complaints are dangerous, and sometimes it is the slightest which hurts, and which subverts the best established favour.[56]

There are accounts of the most senior ministers of state being flogged or otherwise punished at the king's command. De la Loubère adds that "these examples, which very frequently happen, do edifie the people".[57] Indeed, the king's relation to his courtiers may be seen from the ordinary people's point of view as much less threatening. Commoners did not have the honour of being admitted to the presence of the king; at the same time they did not run the risk of incurring his displeasure. Occasionally there may have been a feeling of mischievous joy at the news that a particular officer had been punished, because for the common people officers of state were often equated with forms of oppression.

Officers of the Department of Land (*krom* Nā) collected one quarter of a *baht* for each *rai* of rice land. There was a tax on boats, there was a tax on distilleries of alcohol as well as on the retail of alcoholic drinks. Half a *baht* annually was paid for possessing a durian tree, one *baht* for a betel tree, and for each areca-nut tree a number of nuts had to be delivered to customs officers.[58] Whenever a state official acted for the people, whether it was to give a voucher for the payment of land tax or that on fruit trees, he exacted a fee for administrative costs. From this fee the officer paid his scribes and legal staff as well as personal expenses. It was because of the existence of a large number of fees that the administration thrived. It is likely that in the lower echelons of the civil service, efforts were made to increase the value and number of fees. To counteract this, from time to time the king announced an official list of administrative fees.

The immense power of the king may have been seen by the commoners as a check upon the greed of the king's agents. If a case of oppression found its way to the king's ear, punishment of the offender was almost assured. An apt illustration of the system and its restraints may be drawn from the method of organizing corvée:

> In every quarter there is a mandarin who supervises the public works: he is called a *Nai*. For this post they generally choose a severe man who punishes defaulters rigorously. Often he is corrupted and bribed with gifts which they give him voluntarily or which he extorts from them, but he is always punished as an extortioner if the king becomes aware of his malpractices.[59]

One of the king's weapons against an unchecked oppression of the commoners by his officers was the fact that one *krom* could be appointed to supervise the work of another *krom*. The *krom* Mahātthai supervised the "civilian" corvée, but there was a separate *krom* that registered men, women and children on lists which formed the basis upon which the Mahātthai officers could do their work. The Mahātthai officers directed the *nāi* and their bands of workers. In principle, the various departments were to keep each other in check. In practice, however, the state officers tended to assist one another. A clear example is given from the provincial administration:

> *Oc-Pra Sassedi*[60] makes and keeps the Rolls of the People. 'Tis an Office very subject to Corruption, by reason that every particular person endeavours to get himself omitted out of the Rolls for money. The *Nai* do likewise seek to favour those of their

Bang, who make presents to them, and to oppress those with labour who have nothing to give them. The *Maha Tai*, and the *Sassedi*, would prevent this disorder, if they were not the first corrupted.[61]

The difference between the system in theory and the actual practice is especially apparent in the administration of corvée. Large numbers of people escaped the six months' service by changing their legal status and becoming fiduciary slaves. Also it was common practice to avoid registration. This malpractice must have been particularly widespread in the late seventeenth century, because it led to the proclamation of new laws regarding the upkeep of the manpower lists.[62] Even during times when the central government had a considerable grip on the populace, a number of people avoided registration by moving about or by claiming to be somebody else. The laws of 1690 probably assisted the government officers in catching many who otherwise would have escaped corvée.

An interesting aspect of corvée in the late seventeenth century is that people could be set to work in mines and forests to provide the king's warehouses with supplies. In fact, especially in the outer provinces where little public work was being conducted, the maintenance of a supply of forest products and minerals became the chief task of many commoners. In these outer regions many people made their living by extracting forest products or minerals, and the king would not force them to abandon this work for six month's corvée. Instead he allowed them to pay tax by delivering some of their produce to his agents. These people had gained a special place on the rolls and were known by names such as "salt-levy commoners" (*phrai luang suai klu'a*) or "tin-levy commoners" (*phrai luang suai dĩbuk*).

This sketch of some of the features of Siamese society as it was in the late-seventeenth and early-eighteenth century could be expanded considerably, but it would then cease to be only a "backdrop", a setting of the scene for the detailed history that follows.

# Notes

1. From the Sanskrit *dharmasāstra*, book of laws. The transcription for Thai words chosen in this volume comes close to the actual present-day pronunciation.
2. H.G.Q. Wales, *Siamese State Ceremonies, Their History and Function*, p. 67, and *Supplementary Notes on Siamese State Ceremonies*, p. 11; S. de la Loubère, *The Kingdom of Siam*, p. 101.
3. From the Sanskrit or Pali *Mahā uparāja*, "Great Viceroy" or deputy-king.
4. This frequently occurred during the Ayutthaya period, leading some commentators, such as Schouten, to take the brother's succession as the rule rather than the exception. See F. Caron and J. Schouten, *A True Description of the Mighty Kingdoms of Japan and Siam*, p. 100.
5. It is somewhat misleading to call the ceremony a "coronation", for, although a crown formed part of the regalia to be carried about in procession and presented, the actual placement of that crown on the king's head as symbol of his changed status, which has been a feature of the Siamese ritual only during the Bangkok period, is probably a result of European influence. There is no reason to suspect that the crown occupied a pre-eminent position in the ceremony during Ayutthaya times.
6. De la Loubère, *The Kingdom of Siam*, p. 81, and B.J. Terwiel, *Monks and Magic: An Analysis of Religious Ceremonies in Central Thailand*, pp. 251-52.
7. For details, see Wales, *Siamese State Ceremonies*, pp. 102-6.
8. De la Loubère, *The Kingdom of Siam*, p. 42.
9. N. Gervaise, *The Natural and Political History of the Kingdom of Siam*, p. 121. For further details see J. Kemp, *Aspects of Siamese Kingship in the Seventeenth Century*, pp. 1-19.
10. Officially the palace was called Phrarātchawangbǫwǫnsathānmongkhon. See *kromphra'* Damrong Rātchanuphāp, *Tamnānwangnā*, PP, vol. 11, p.1.
11. De la Loubère, *The Kingdom of Siam*, p. 95 and p. 100. De la Loubère states that the Uparāt carried the honorary prefix of *čhaophayā*, which caused Wales to surmise that it was not the Uparāt, but the *čhaophayā* Uparāt, a person of lower rank, mentioned in the Law of Civil Hierarchy, who was described by de la Loubère. There can be little doubt but that Wales is wrong in this identification. The person seen by de la Loubère is indeed the "deputy king", while the entry in the Law of Civil Hierarchy refers to the chief of that prince's department. Further supporting literature on this issue can be found in F.H. Giles, "Analysis of Van Vliet's Historical Account of Siam", *Journal of the Siam Society* (hereafter *JSS*) 30, pt 3 (1938): 353ff. I am grateful to Dr M. Vickery in this respect for his comments on the Law of Civil Hierarchy.
12. H.G.Q. Wales, *Ancient Siamese Government and Administration*, p. 236. The *baht* was a lump of silver weighing some 15 grams.
13. *Čhaofā* seems to be an old Tai title (i.e., one that has not been used not only among the Siamese but also among other Tai-speaking groups). It appears for the first time in Siamese history in the late sixteenth century as an honorary prefix to the titles of King Naresuan. In late-Ayutthayan times the title was bestowed only on princes and princesses as a mark of royal elevation to the highest rank. For further details on the use of the title, see M. Vickery's review of R.B. Jones's *Thai Titles and Ranks*, *JSS* 62, pt 1 (1974): 158-73.
14. Wales, *Ancient Siamese Government*, p. 236.
15. Caron and Schouten, *A True Description*, p. 98.
16. De la Loubère, *The Kingdom of Siam*, p. 101.

17. It is possible that the custom of attaching these particular terms of civilian ranking to distinguish between princely titles reflects the earlier situation when *krom* titular headships were first bestowed upon princes. At that time a fairly small department may have had as its head (*čhaokrom*) a person of *mū'n* rank, a middle-size department may have had a *khun* and a major department may have been ruled by a *luang*. In subsequent times these direct links probably were lost as the number of civilian titles grew and increasingly higher titles were given to the *čhaokroms*. The series of princely ranks thus may throw light upon an early stage of the Siamese administrative system.

18. Compare de la Loubère, *The Kingdom of Siam*, p. 100, with the Tamnaengnāphonlaru'an, in the *Kotmāi Trā Sām Duang* (hereafter *KTSD*) 1: 223. It is interesting to note that the four officers in question are divided into two "at the head of the rope", and "two at the tail of the rope". The reason why these four officials are connected with a rope remains to be elucidated.

19. De la Loubère, *The Kingdom of Siam*, p. 99.

20. J. O'Kane, trans., *The Ship of Sulaimān*, p. 96. Soldiers with tattooed arms were also found in the provinces (see de la Loubère, *The Kingdom of Siam*, p. 83). For a wider view of the history of Siamese administrative tattooing, see B.J. Terwiel, "Tattooing in Thailand's History", *Journal of the Royal Asiatic Society*, 1979, pt 2, pp. 156-66.

21. Wales, *Ancient Siamese Government*, p. 114.

22. It is possible that the ritual feature of the division of the king's audience into a right- and a left-hand side was adopted some time during the first millennium A.D. by the Tai peoples when Chinese influence was strong; see B.J. Terwiel, *The Tai of Assam, and Ancient Tai Ritual*, vol. 1, *Life-cycle Ceremonies*, pp. 10-11.

23. These numbers have been extrapolated from *An Index of Officials in Traditional Thai Governments*, by Yoneo Ishii, Osamu Akagi, and Shigeharu Tanabe, vol. 1, pt 1.

24. *Ministry Seals of Thailand*, a wall-chart prepared by the Agency for International Development, United States Operations Mission to Thailand, 1966.

25. Wales prefers to read the name as Thammātnibodī, or Minister of Justice, ignoring the Thai spelling with a long *ā* in the first syllable (*Ancient Siamese Government*, p. 92). It is most likely, however, that the Siamese title is derived from a Pali or Sanskrit word meaning "palace". I suspect that the Sanskrit *dhāman*, meaning "dwelling-place", "house", "abode", was the root of the word.

26. M. Vickery in his review of Ishii et al., *An Index*, in *JSS* 63, pt 2 (1975): 428-30.

27. This arrangement apparently was not wholly satisfactory, and one of the first measures of King Rama I was the return of many, but not all, of the southern provinces to the jurisdiction of the Kalāhom.

28. Literally "scribbling money". The word *bia* is an extremely old Tai word, originally meaning "cowry shell", going back to the time when the cowry was the chief form of currency. The shell was still legal tender in Ayutthaya times, to a value of 6,400 shells per *baht*.

29. Wales, *Ancient Siamese Government*, p. 236.

30. De la Loubère, *The Kingdom of Siam*, p. 80.

31. In the intimate circle, the Siamese usually avoid using a person's real name or his nickname. The strategy of most people is instead to substitute certain kinship terms. For example, contemporaries find out who is slightly older or higher in status and that person obtains the honorary name of *phi*, or "older relative", while those slightly less in status become *nǫng*, "younger relative".

32. Ibid., p. 81.

33. Wales, *Siamese State Ceremonies*, chap. 14, and *Supplementary Notes*, pp. 23-27.
34. De la Loubère, *The Kingdom of Siam*, p. 82.
35. The *kūp* is better known as the Siamese type of howdah used on the back of an elephant. For the boating *kūp*, see de la Loubère, *The Kingdom of Siam*, p. 41.
36. Throughout South-East Asia the preparation of a betel quid has acquired ritual significance, and in many countries it is possible to assess a person's rank by the quality of his betel-box.
37. A different version of such a system could be observed in the Shan states in the days when the Shan Sawbhas still wielded immense power. The Sawbha would allot villages to his wife and chief concubines, and these villages would provide servants and goods to the appropriate section of the palace. In return, the villages would be exempt from various other forms of taxation.
38. See the "Aiyakān Nā Tamnaeng Nā Phonlaru'an" and the "Saktinā Thahān Huamu'ang" in the *KTSD* vol. 1. I have also consulted the edition by *kromaluang* Rātchaburīdirēkru't.
39. The positions of 250 and 350 appear to have been seldom or never used. They did exist, at least as legal categories, as can be seen from the *Kotmāi Lilit*, which was gleaned from *kromaluang* Rātchaburīdirēkru't, *Kotmāi Lem 1*, pp. 728-29 and 732-33.
40. Chaianan Samutwanit, *Saktinā kap Phatanākān khong Sangkhom Thai*, as cited by A. Turton, "Thai Institution of Slavery", in *Asian and African Systems of Slavery*, ed. J.L. Watson, p. 253.
41. J. Low, "On the Laws of Mu'ung Thai or Siam", *Journal of the Indian Archipelago and Eastern Asia* 1 (1847): 351.
42. Akin Rabibhadana, *The Organization of Thai Society in the Early Bangkok period, 1782-1873*, p. 103.
43. Extrapolated from the *Kotmāi Lilit*, cf. the *Kromasak* section of *kromaluang* Rātchaburīdirēkru't, *Kotmāi Lem 1*.
44. The following paragraphs are based upon a survey of the Law of Civil Hierarchy and the Law of Military Hierarchy, *kromaluang* Rātchaburīdirēkru't, *Kotmāi Lem 1*, pp. 165-260.
45. It has often been remarked by travellers that the position of women in Siamese society is relatively high. Women are often in control of a large share of the family finances. This feature may thus possibly be traced back to Ayutthayan times. Only with regard to religious and ceremonial life are Siamese women severely disadvantaged. Some of the reasons for their exclusion from this aspect of culture are explored in B.J. Terwiel, *Monks and Magic*.
46. *KTSD* vol. 2: 13-19.
47. Gervaise, *The Natural and Political History*, p. 60.
48. R. Lingat, *L'esclavage privé dans le vieux droit siamois*, pp. 84-85; and Wales, *Ancient Siamese Government*, pp. 200-201.
49. Wira Wimoniti, *Historical Patterns of Tax Administration in Thailand*, p. 39.
50. O'Kane, *The Ship of Sulaimān*, p. 122 and p. 131.
51. Kemp, *Aspects of Siamese Kingship*, p. 41.
52. De la Loubère, *The Kingdom of Siam*, p. 103.
53. Many types of ordeals are mentioned by G.E. Gerini in "Trial by Ordeal in Siam and the Siamese Law of Ordeals", *Asiatic Quarterly Review*, April 1895, pp. 415-24, and July 1895, pp. 156-75.
54. De la Loubère, *The Kingdom of Siam*, pp. 105-6.
55. Gervaise, *The Natural and Political History*, p. 60.
56. De la Loubère, *The Kingdom of Siam*, p. 106.
57. Ibid.

58. The amounts of taxation are those valid in the 1680s and subject to change (de la Loubère, *The Kingdom of Siam*, pp. 93-94).
59. Gervaise, *The Natural and Political History*, p. 60.
60. An officer of ǭ*kphra'* rank of the *krom* Satsadi.
61. De la Loubère, *The Kingdom of Siam*, p. 84.
62. "Phra Aiyakān Bān Phanaek", *KTSD* vol. 2: 1-26.

**2**

# Siam Under Taksin: Tumult and Reform

## The Fall of Ayutthaya: the Conventional Picture

Virtually all history books that deal with the fall of Ayutthaya in 1767 present the events leading up to this debacle in the same manner. They point out that when the reign of King Bǫromakōt (1733 — 58) ended, a dispute arose about the succession.[1] Up till 1755 it had been generally accepted that Prince Thammathibēt would inherit the throne, especially since this prince had demonstrated his intelligence and great gifts as a poet.[2] However, in 1755 Thammathibēt was accused of having amorous relations with young women who had been presented to the king, and when he was found guilty he was executed in accordance with the law. This execution raised the question of the succession to the throne. There were two other sons of *čhaofā* status, namely Ekathat and his younger brother Uthumphǫn, but apparently neither of these candidates was outstanding, and Bǫromakōt hesitated about indicating his preference until just before his death. Among the king's many sons who were not of *čhaofā* rank was an ambitious and able person who had been given the distinction of a *krom* rank: *kromamū'n* Thēpphiphit, who later was to play a major role in Siamese politics.

On his deathbed, King Bǫromakōt selected Uthumphǫn to be king, and consequently in 1758 Uthumphǫn was proclaimed monarch and was officially anointed. A major crisis ensued when Ekathat refused to accept his younger brother's elevation. In the subsequent confrontation which, normally speaking, would had led to one party annihilating the other, a surprising compromise was reached between the brothers. Uthumphǫn voluntarily stepped down and disappeared from public life by becoming a Buddhist monk, and Ekathat was made king.

The two appointments, almost immediately one after the other, had serious consequences for the court and the administration. Uthumphǫn had been accepted by a group of able administrators who had heeded Bǫromakōt's advice. Ekathat, on the other hand, had successfully challenged the succession. As a result, many senior officers who had declared themselves for Uthumphǫn found themselves summarily dismissed, while a group of Ekathat's personal friends, who had backed him against his younger brother, were rewarded with the headships of ministries.

The deposed officers were dismayed at the turn of events and banded together in order to try and re-establish Uthumphǫn. Prince Thēpphiphit was conspicuous among the conspirators. When Uthumphǫn was told about the attempt to overthrow Ekathat's rule, he decided to forestall this. He personally revealed the identity of the group of dissatisfied men, on condition that they were not to be executed. *Kromamū'n* Thēpphiphit consequently was exiled, and the others imprisoned.

It was a bad time for the Siamese to be divided, because King Alaungpaya of Burma was at the height of power and the Burmese had been extending their realm by re-establishing all around Burma proper a ring of vassal states. This included the effective overlordship over the Shan States, Chiang Mai, and other northern-Tai *mū'angs* and led to efforts by the Burmese to be recognized as masters of the northernmost Lao principalities. The Burmese also tried to regain full control over Tavoy, Mergui, and Tenasserim, a region that had come to be regarded as part of the Ayutthayan sphere of influence.

In 1759 Burmese troops took the southern Mon principalities, and when the Siamese retreated, the Burmese, using their advantage, moved on deep into Siamese territory, travelling from the south upwards through Phetburi, Ratburi, and Suphanburi. The Burmese king took advantage of the apparent weakness of the Siamese defence and sent for reinforcements while he pressed on towards Ayutthaya. During the first months of 1760, Ayutthaya itself was threatened. King Ekathat found himself desperately in need of experienced men, some of whom belonged to Uthumphon's faction. He was forced to ask Uthumphon to leave the Sangha[3] and take charge of the capital's defence. The able administrators who had been arrested for plotting against Ekathat were released from prison. Just before the rainy season was expected, the besieging Burmese were suddenly struck with a major setback: King Alaungpaya was severely wounded in an accident, and this precipitated a Burmese retreat. Alaungpaya died on the way home, and he was succeeded by his son Naungdawgyi, who lacked his father's power and ambition.

For the time being Siam appeared saved, and the two factions at court resumed their struggle for influence. In 1762 Uthumphon once more retired to a Buddhist monastery, leaving his brother as the sole monarch. In the following year Naungdawgyi of Burma was succeeded by his brother Hsinbyushin, a much more effective and strong leader. In 1765 Hsinbyushin led an army into Siam proper, following the southern route explored by his father, and ordered the troops poised along Siam's northern towns to move southwards. King Ekathat sent a massive army down south, but when his troops approached the Burmese, the latter attacked so boldly that the Siamese force had to retreat in confusion. Many elephants and provisions fell into enemy hands. The Burmese were able to extend their effective control over most of western Siam, taking stronghold after stronghold and living off the local resources. Often the towns fell after little or no resistance, but occasionally the Siamese resisted the invaders and gave battle before finally submitting.[4]

Once more the Siamese mustered a huge army to meet the Burmese, but again this force was compelled to retreat. By the beginning of 1766 the enemy had reached the outskirts of the capital. A long siege began, and eventually, in April 1767, the capital fell. The victors took all they could carry in weapons and other valuables and also transported a large number of prisoners to Burmese territory, leaving only a relatively small force behind to keep the peace. King Ekathat met with his death during the fall of the city, and Uthumphọn died not long after.

## Factors Related to the Fall of Ayutthaya

The picture that emerges from most historical sources is one whereby the chief blame for the fall and destruction of Ayutthaya is placed upon King Ekathat. The story of how, through personal ambition, he weakened and undermined the strength of the court, thereby losing all to an outside enemy, has the makings of a classical literary tragedy. While having two kings and their factions must be considered a factor of importance in the fall of Ayutthaya, it is doubtful whether that aspect alone suffices to account for the long series of misfortunes that befell Siam between 1759 and 1767. Another major factor was that the Siamese military was no match for the Burmese. During the reign of Bọromakōt, there had been peace and security. The relations with the Burmese court were quite friendly. No major battles were fought by Siamese armies in any of the outer regions. When King Alaungpaya pushed the Siamese out of Tavoy in 1759, the Siamese had not been at war for a generation or more. They relied upon the latent force of their populace. If one of the *mū'angs* under Ayutthayan control became disloyal, the king could readily summon a massive army to march upon the vassal town and subdue it. For the maintenance of order in Ayutthaya itself, the king had professional soldiers who performed guard duties, but the number of troops involved was not very great. During peacetime, much of the central army was engaged in caring for a large number of elephants, which would form an essential part of the country's army in case of war.

The traditional system of warfare between Siam and

Burma seldom involved a direct large-scale confrontation. But if a Siamese army were to engage a Burmese one in battle, the traditional strategy on the part of the Siamese was to amass a sufficiently large number of men to satisfy the enemy of the seriousness of the Siamese intentions. A huge number of people could be involved, moving by land or by water towards the opposing party. They would barricade themselves behind bamboo fences and send out a front guard to fight the first battle. Both parties would continuously spy upon each other regarding the strength and condition of the troops.

Cannons had become a feature of South-East Asian warfare. They were dragged along with the armies, and they played an important role in the battle. However, they were not used in a European manner. For the Siamese, the description by de la Loubère less than a century earlier still may have applied: "*Kill not* is the order, which the King of *Siam* gives his Troops, when he sends them into the Field: which cannot signifie that they should not kill absolutely, but that they shoot not directly upon the Enemy."[5] The Persian assessment of Siamese warfare attests to the same:

> They have no intention of killing one another or inflicting any great slaughter because if a general gained a victory with a real conquest, he would be shedding his own blood, so to speak.
>
> The fixed custom is that when two factions have lined up before one another, a group from each side comes forward, beating kettledrums and playing flutes and the infantry and the horsemen on both sides begin dancing and shouting and raising all the noise they can. Every so often one army advances and the other retreats and in that way one that has some luck manages to catch the other off guard. They rush up and surround their rivals and when the victorious group like a pair of compasses draws a line around the other army the vanquished being a dot in the centre, admit defeat and place their will in the circle of obedience.[6]

A successful general managed to give the opposition the impression that he was fully confident of his success. He selected the bravest troops to fight skirmishes, ready to press forward if they perceived an advantage. The cannon blasts, the power of the decorated war elephants, the roar of war drums, and the stirring sight of colourful troops pressing forward with pennants in the air were used at the right moment to intimidate the opposition. These armies moved slowly. Not only was it impossible to go quickly with heavily laden elephants and other beasts of burden, but also the slow, co-ordinated rolling forward itself was part of the effort to cause the enemy to withdraw and avoid battle.

In 1759 the Burmese armies had been engaged in various battles. They were the attackers, driving away the Siamese from Tavoy, Mergui, and Tenasserim. They met with very little, if any, resistance. It appears that the incursion into the heart of Siam was provoked by the Siamese lack of resistance itself. Apparently the Ayutthayan court was unable to muster the forces needed to stop Alaungpaya. Siamese morale must then have suffered considerably, but it was to receive much heavier blows during the 1765 and 1766 invasion. This time the Siamese were somewhat better prepared, and they rallied a truly impressive army, reputedly some sixty thousand men, a much larger army than that of the invaders. At the first en-counter, however, the Burmese appeared undaunted by the large numbers opposing them, and they directly attacked *en masse* the main Siamese force. That first battle, not far from Suphanburi, in which the great Siamese army was put to rout may be regarded as the decisive one. The Burmese demonstrated that a new phase had emerged in mainland South-East Asian warfare: that of the direct, fast, and effi-cient attack where troops were pushed to the limit and men killed indiscriminately in order to gain a victory. The Siamese leaders had at that time neither the effective command nor the measure of control over the troops to withstand such all-out attacks, and therefore they had to take refuge in the capital.

Originally Ayutthaya had been an almost impregnable city. It was surrounded by broad waterways and strong fortifica-tions. It was bristling with weapons and lacked neither provisions nor valiant men. Yet in a year's time this city was subdued. Again, the inner divisions at the court may have played a role, but it is argued that this was but one factor con-tributing to the debacle. The fact that considerable numbers of capable men managed to slip out of the city in order to reach safer regions must also have weakened Ayutthaya. The court's rejection of Prince Thēpphiphit's offers to come to Ayutthaya's assistance was a sign that there was no unified defence. A great fire occurring during the later stage of the siege probably further underminded morale. The chief factor may well have been the fact that Ayutthaya had grown out of its protective ring and that at various places surrounding the city major monasteries had been established. These contained brick buildings, often surrounded by equally solid brick walls.[7] It is not known when the Siamese first realized that these monasteries could become fortresses from where the Burmese could bombard the city. If they did notice the danger, they did not manage to meet it, because the enemy troops took monastery after monastery until only the walled city was in Siamese hands. From these vantage points the Burmese kept an iron grip upon the capital, and they were able to erect tall towers from the tops of which they could shoot over Ayutthaya's walls into the heart of the city.

Between 1759 and 1767 the Siamese lost many battles and skirmishes. However, the Siamese were not long in taking up the challenge. Out of the devastation arose a military genius who built up an efficient, hard-hitting army, with thousands of men marching and fighting, accustomed to bloodshed. This man, usually known by the name of Taksin, occupies from about 1769 until 1782 the centre of the Siamese stage. The remainder of this chapter is devoted to a study of him and his times.

## Taksin's Background

The man who later was called Taksin, or *phrayā*[8] Tāk, was born in 1734. His father was a Chinese immigrant who, like many other immigrants from that country, was a Teochiu speaker. He must have been remarkably resourceful, for it has been recorded that he successfully bid for the gambling monopoly in Ayutthaya, which meant that he was allowed to run gambling dens in the capital district, for which he paid the government a prearranged tax. This automatically gained him a place in the official Siamese bureaucracy, and he became known formally by the rank of *khun* and the name Phat Nāi Akǫn. He married a Siamese woman, and his son, the future Taksin, grew up fully bilingual.

There is a strange legend attached to this son's early childhood.[9] Apparently, when he was only three days old he was found with a snake coiled around his body. His father took this as an omen that the child had to be killed, but his mother resisted this interpretation with the utmost vehemence. The parents' quarrel became known at the residence of the *čhaophrayā* Čhakrī, the chief of the Mahātthai Ministry, who happened to live just across the road from *khun* Phat, and this nobleman decided to settle the issue by adopting the boy. The *čhaophrayā* Čhakrī noticed that from that moment onward his financial dealings were more successful. That is why he called the boy Sin (wealth). The boy was diligent and clever; he received the best education available in the land, first at a monastery school (at Wat Kōsawat) and later at the palace, where he served several years in the Mahātlek, the corps of royal pages.

The extraordinary appearance of a snake which did not bite the baby and the fortunate intervention of the country's chief minister are typical of miraculous legends that become attached to the personal history of famous men, and they need not be taken as factual. Yet it is quite possible that *khun* Phat and his wife arranged for their promising son to be adopted into a Siamese household which was far more elevated in rank and status than their own. It has been customary in Siam for parents to present a bright child to a family in better circumstances. This practice is called *liang*. The child makes himself useful in the rich person's household, and in return he benefits from the resources of his foster-parents. If he is very intelligent, his foster-parents will not deny him a first-rate education.

Following the footsteps of most privileged young men, during the year when he became twenty, Sin became a Buddhist monk. He chose to live at Wat Kōsawat, where he had received his first formal schooling. What is remarkable, however, is that young Sin did not leave the order after having completed the prescribed period of one Lenten season. Instead he remained a full three years, studying and learning. Only men who are attracted to a disciplined and studious life tend to prolong their traditional retreat in the Sangha.

After three years in the order, Sin returned to the court, where he obtained a position as one of King Bǫromakōt's assistants in matters dealing with the Mahātthai Ministry. However, in 1758 King Bǫromakōt died, and after the first wrangle over the succession had been settled in favour of Prince Ekathat, Sin was sent on an inspection tour to some northern provincial *mū'angs*, and soon afterwards was appointed *luang* Yokrabat in the small provincial town of Tak. This *mū'ang* was not a very important one, being one of the many fourth-ranking provincial towns where the *luang* Yokrabat would automatically have a *saktinā* of 500. In 1760 Sin rose to the position of deputy-governor[10] with a *saktinā* of 600, and when the governor of Tak died he was appointed to the post of governor, or *čhaomū'ang*, with a *saktinā* of 3,000 and the rank of *phrayā*. From this period date his popular names of *phrayā* Tāk, and Taksin. As governor of the town, he was automatically its chief military commander, and when the Burmese again invaded Siam in 1764 he played a prominent role in a battle near Phetburi. Western Siam was gradually invaded by the Burmese, and Taksin spent the years between 1764 and 1766 as one of the senior officers in the Ayutthayan army.[11]

He gained a reputation as an able leader and a brave soldier, albeit rather impulsive. This latter aspect of his character brought him into serious trouble when he was engaged in Ayutthaya's defence. It was the rule that no cannon could be fired before permission had been obtained from the palace. Taksin, on duty at a monastery on the eastern side of Ayutthaya and seeing a tempting target, did not follow the prescribed cumbersome procedure and ordered a large cannon to be fired. As a result of this breach of discipline, Taksin was brought before a court and severely reprimanded for his headstrong behaviour. According to Prince Damrong, this reprimand caused Taksin to think about fleeing from the capital. Whatever Taksin's real motivation may have been — either disgust with those who did not allow him to press a military advantage and who rigorously stuck to the rules, or a growing awareness that Ayutthaya was incapable of withstanding the prolonged Burmese onslaught — what is certain is that in November 1766 he used the opportunity of his taking part in a raid outside Ayutthaya's walls to withdraw his troops from the direct command of his superiors and to occupy a strategic stronghold not far from the city. Taksin remained there several months until in January 1767 a big fire broke out in the capital. He chose that moment to retire from the battlefield altogether and, with about a thousand men, broke through the Burmese siege. There are some indications that many of Taksin's followers were Chinese.[12] The direction in which Taksin and his troops fled may have been influenced by their racial background. They could have fled north or eastwards, but went in a south-easterly direction towards the regions where Chinese settlers were numerous. Taksin and his followers were now outcasts, pursued by Burmese, and also liable to be attacked by Siamese. His escape was successful; he reached *mū'ang* Chonburi and moved further on towards Rayong.

Reputedly at this stage Taksin held a meeting, declaring that Ayutthaya's power had dissipated and that he would create an independent army in the eastern part of Siam. By acclamation he was elected the absolute leader (*čhao*) and when local village headmen came to offer their services, *čhao* Tāk appointed them to such ranks as *mū'n*, *khun*, *luang*, and *phra'*, thus assuming the legal right to do so. The leaders of the town of Rayong presented food but also secretly invited troops from Chanthaburi to come and attack *čhao* Tāk. This plot failed, and *čhao* Tāk was able to establish his power over the whole region of Rayong and Chonburi. To the east, the ruler of Chanthaburi prepared himself for a confrontation with this new forceful half-Chinese general. After several attempts to solve the issue by diplomacy, in June 1767 a full-scale battle erupted, and *čhao* Tāk conquered the town of Chanthaburi, gaining control of all of south-eastern Siam, which included a long stretch of the coast and several small harbours, as well as a number of ships.[13]

# The Country's Subjugation

It was now two months after Ayutthaya had fallen, and central Siam was under Burmese control. If the Burmese had maintained a strong military presence, they might have continued their occupation of Siam for a considerable time. However, the main armies were pulled back to Burma, leaving only a few thousand men under the command of a Mon general. This man had distinguished himself in Burmese eyes by finally taking the stockade at Bāng Račhan, where Siamese defenders had long defied Burmese attempts to dislodge them. The Siamese, deprived of the immense power, wealth, and status of Ayutthaya, had fallen back upon their provincial administrative system to regain a measure of order. The governors of towns (*čhaomū'ang*) and their staff could no longer expect directives from the king's central bureaucracy, and many were for the time being responsible to no one but themselves. However, there were *mū'angs* of various types: some were relatively large centres, traditionally supervising a number of subordinate *mū'angs*, and others occupied strategic positions. Soon it was possible to recognize, in the area that was not directly ruled by the Burmese and Burmese-appointed governors, a series of regional leaders. If Taksin had not boldly escaped from Ayutthaya, the leader of south-eastern Siam would undoubtedly have been *phrayā* Chanthaburi. Directly east of Ayutthaya, the rulers of Phimai and Nakhon Ratchasima, respectively *kromamū'n* Thēpphiphit (safely returned from exile) and *luang* Pheng, vied for control of the Khorat plateau. To the north of Ayutthaya was the important provincial town of Phitsanulok, to which many Ayutthayan officials had fled. The governor of Phitsanulok soon declared his independence, and the Burmese not having sufficient troops to deal with this problem, allowed this to happen. Even further northwards, the town of Sawangkhaburi also became an independently governed centre, under the inspired leadership of the chief Buddhist monk, Phra' Fāng, who was renowned for his supernatural powers and who took over the rule of this region, helped by many other monks. He marched south and besieged Phitsanulok, but when after six months it showed no sign of yielding, he returned to Sawangkhaburi. In the south, the acting governor of Nakhon Si Thammarat declared himself absolute ruler and governed in his own right.[14]

The Burmese had appointed governors in the regions they had conquered between 1764 and 1767, but they could no longer spare the manpower to rule even that area effectively. It was not long before the boldest of the self-appointed independent rulers, *čhao* Tāk, decided to attack Burmese-held territory. In October 1767, half a year after the fall of Ayutthaya, he went westwards with an army of some five thousand men and more than a hundred boats. He took the stronghold at Thonburi and ordered the execution of the Burmese-appointed governor. The Burmese headquarters just outside Ayutthaya were alerted, and troops were sent south to quell the disorders and re-establish Burmese control. *Čhao* Tāk did not wait for reprisals, but marched out to meet the enemy. He won the first skirmishes, put the Burmese-led troops to flight, and pushed his advantage by attacking the main Burmese camp, which he overran.[15] In one bold and decisive campaign he thus succeeded in taking the lower part of the Chao Phraya River valley, the traditional heartland of Siam, and as commander of this part of the country, *čhao* Tāk now became a chief contender for the throne of the Siamese kingdom as a whole.

*Čhao* Tāk's exultation at having delivered the old capital from the Burmese must have been tempered by his realization of the magnitude of the tasks confronting him. Sooner or later he could expect the Burmese to send a massive army to resubjugate Siam, the capital of which lay in ruins and which would have to be rebuilt. Moreover, he realized that, though he was possibly the country's most daring general, this did not automatically give him the right to rule. There were many men in the country who, less than a year before, used to be superior to him in rank and position. He knew well that he had no royal blood in his veins and that he would have to deal with immence opposition if he were to declare himself Siam's absolute ruler. Indeed, it is likely that at first he ruled simply as a military man, issuing effective orders to restore law and order, proclaiming it to be illegal to oppress farmers and the poor. From the earliest days when he had torn himself free of the besieged capital, he had set himself up as a leader of the common folk, a protector of the people, who ordered his soldiers to be just, to assist those in need, and to foster the Buddhist religion.[16]

There has been much speculation as to why *čhao* Tāk did not make Ayutthaya his base. According to legend, he had a dream in which the former kings drove him away from the old capital and he therefore had to search for new head-quarters.[17] It is impossible to ascertain whether indeed such a dream upset the leader. Many other possible motives for the abandonment of Ayutthaya have been suggested. For example, the fields in the Ayutthaya region had been left untended, making it difficult to supply the city. It would have needed an enormous effort to rebuild Ayutthaya's fortifica-tions. Not only would this have been costly; it would have had to be completed with great speed to provide effective shelter for the city's defenders.[18] Whatever the exact reasons, it remains a fact that *čhao* Tāk decided to make his head-quarters in the fortress at Thonburi, a stronghold which had traditionally guarded the approach to Ayutthaya from the sea. At Thonburi, on the west bank of the Chao Phraya River, the existing fortifications provided him with a much more manageable township, closer to the other towns already under his command, and easier to reach from the sea.[19]

Before he left the devastated city of Ayutthaya, *čhao* Tāk took some measures which are indicative of his stature as a leader. He organized the ceremonial cremation of King Ekathat's corpse and treated the few stray members of the royal family and palace staff who were still living in the city with consideration. At the same time, there could be no doubt who was lord and master, for he took as his personal consorts four ladies from the palace, one of them the daughter of *kromamū'n* Thēpphiphit. Less than two years later Thēpphiphit's daughter and one of the other high-ranking women were found guilty of consorting with other men. Taksin's punishment was merciless: the culprits were publicly raped before their arms and heads were hacked off.[20]

The Burmese soon attempted to resume their hold over

Source: L. Sternstein, "An 'Historical Atlas of Thailand' ", *JSS* 52, pt 1 (1964), map 4.

central Siam. In 1768 some two thousand soldiers from Tavoy were sent to reinforce those still stationed at Ratburi, south-west of Thonburi. *Čhao* Tāk's quick reaction to the news of the Burmese reinforcements is in line with his intrepid character. He went by sea with a large number of troops to the mouth of the river Maeklong, thus trapping the Burmese fleet which had been stationed there since early in the Burmese invasion. At the same time a land force under the command of his trusted comrade Bunmā[21] attacked the Burmese from a different direction. This bold manoeuvre succeeded in putting the enemy to flight, and *čhao* Tāk thus extended the territory over which he held sway and captured much-needed ships and weapons.

Some time early in 1768, reputedly encouraged by his chief advisers, who reported to him that everyone — officials, tradesmen, soldiers, and farmers — wanted him to be proclaimed king, *čhao* Tāk agreed to this, though there is no firm evidence of his formal anointment.[22] It was clear from the outset, however, that King Taksin would not be a traditional king, surrounded by protocol and removed from ordinary people. He was a man who often insisted on knowing even the smallest details, and he would not allow court procedure to isolate him. He was, after all, at the beginning of his reign, a king without a proper palace; indeed, he then possessed as yet only a small part of his kingdom.

Taksin realized that most of the outer regions that traditionally had been subject to Ayutthaya did not recognize him as the new overlord, and that soon this would result in armed confrontation. As usual, he preferred to take the initiative, and in 1768 he marched against Phitsanulok. The ensuing battle turned out unfavourably for Taksin, who was wounded in the leg and had to retreat. The ruler of Phitsanulok, who considered that he had decisively defeated his chief opponent, now in his turn proclaimed himself to be Siam's king.

Soon afterwards, however, he became seriously ill and died, leaving his son in charge. The latter, probably fearing that claiming a throne was rather hazardous, did not follow his father's lead and contented himself with just the title of *čhao*. Meanwhile Phra' Fāng of Sawangkhaburi again marched south and began his second siege of Phitsanulok, and after three months took and ransacked the town. The monk-ruler now held the northern part of what used to be Siam.

Taksin had not been seriously wounded at Phitsanulok and before long decided to march to the north-east, where some of the Burmese-led troops had joined *kromamŭ'n* Thēpphiphit. Fierce battles were fought on two fronts, and Taksin's troops were victorious. Thēpphiphit escaped further eastwards, but eventually was captured and brought before Taksin and soon afterwards executed. Late in 1768 yet another military venture was begun: the subjugation of the southern regions. Taksin sent two armies southwards, this time remaining himself in Thonburi. However, when these armies were defeated by the ruler of Nakhon Si Thammarat, Taksin went to their assistance with a fleet of warships and managed to subjugate the region. He stayed in the south until March 1769, as usual enforcing strict rules upon the soldiers, forbidding them to kill the farmers' cattle or to rob the populace. He kept them busy building more warships. He also provided funds for the repair of monasteries, and large amounts of rice were donated to Buddhist monks and novices. In a typical gesture he ordered a sum of money to be given to every mendicant when it was *wanphra'*.[23] In the descriptions of Taksin's rule, such episodes of "merit-making" are often encountered, usually immediately after order has been forcefully restored. It is quite likely that the two types of activities are linked. Up till the present day there are still many Siamese who feel that an act of merit is called for immediately after the performance of an act that carries demerit. Although Buddhist doctrine does not allow for it, many Siamese feel that the effects of the meritorious activity will offset the ill effects of the evil deed.[24]

F.H. Turpin's *Histoire civile et naturelle du royaume de Siam*, which was published at the beginning of Taksin's reign and which mentions events up to 1769, confirms the new king's position, his reputation as a stern warrior, and his distribution of ranks and titles among those who aided them. Two further aspects, which are relevant for an assessment of King Taksin, are brought forward by Turpin. The first concerns his measures to alleviate famine, and second is his "well-known" hatred of Buddhist monks.[25]

It is not certain whether the food shortages of 1768 and 1769 must be fully attributed to the effects of the war. Turpin also mentions drought, a perpetual hazard to the farmers in central Siam. In addition, there were plagues of rats and insects, attacking rice and vegetable crops.[26] Another source mentions a severe contagious disease, one that affected people's ability to talk, as well as their brains. Presumably this was an outbreak of typhoid fever. The severity of the outbreak is attested by the statement that "every morning the river was filled with corpses".[27] Whatever the cause of the food shortages, it is certain that when Taksin returned from the south his leadership was direly needed. Not only were many people starving, but also bands of robbers were making life uncertain.

Using treasury funds, Taksin imported large amounts of rice, which he distributed free of cost. In this respect, he took the same measures as did previous kings in similar circumstances. In addition, he ordered all government employees, regardless of rank or status, to work on fields that lay fallow. This latter decree was probably unprecedented, and it reflects the pragmatic and impulsive character of the general-king. Also it may have been inspired by Taksin's personal dislike of pomp and ceremony.

The second aspect touched upon by Turpin, Taksin's "aversion" to Buddhist monks, is more difficult to assess. Turpin is unambiguous in his report, which may be translated as follows:

> He had learned by experience that the priests, in the abuse of their power over the unlettered masses, were wont to foment sedition and stir popular feeling. He took a violent dislike to them, which he did not try to conceal, and considered that the respect they enjoyed was a slight on his authority. He therefore wished for the extermination of these idolatrous priests who, poor by profession, enjoyed the fruits of the labour of the artisans and farmers, without doing anything in return.[28]

Turpin continues with an example of how Taksin treated the "idolatrous" priests:

A *Sancrat*[29] of great renown was accused of incontinence. Phia-Thae[30] made him appear before his tribunal and condemned him to a trial by fire. The soles of his feet were burned by the glowing charcoal, and that was the proof that he was guilty. He would have been condemned to decapitation had not powerful interceders obtained his pardon, under the specious pretext that his death would cause a scandal, and that when their servants were done away with, the gods would be less respected.[31]

These two quotations need to be examined separately. The first one, in which Taksin is accused of wishing to kill all Buddhist monks because he felt the respect given them was a slight on his own authority, does not fit in with the facts known about him from other sources. Firstly, Taksin had of his own free will once stayed a considerable time in the Buddhist order. Secondly, in Rayong, in Thonburi, and again later in Nakhon Si Thammarat he had exhorted people to respect the Buddhist religion and had personally dispensed rice to the monks and novices. Taksin appears to have been not only a competent general but also a devout practising Buddhist. If there is any truth in Turpin's account, the dislike reputedly felt by Taksin might have been directed towards priests who did abuse their position, who broke the rules and who by their bad behaviour undermined the venerable Sangha. Taksin's preoccupation with the good name of the order of monks is also testified in Siamese sources.[32] It is possible that Turpin's informants had in mind the priest-general Phra' Fāng and his monks who had control over the northern part of Siam. These were Taksin's political enemies, and in addition, their involvement in warfare would have made them renegade Buddhist priests in the eyes of a devout Buddhist.[33] Turpin's remark about idolatrous priests enjoying the fruits of the labour of others without doing anything in return must be accounted for by the fact that Turpin's informants were French missionaries who held Buddhism in contempt, and the statement reflects not so much Taksin's views as the prejudices of the authors of the documents upon which Turpin based his account.

Turpin's example of the high-ranking priest being tortured, found guilty, but let free under some spurious pretext also must be read with caution. According to Siamese sources, there indeed was an inquiry into the behaviour of the patriarch, who, it was rumoured, had planned to enrich himself at the expense of various wealthy citizens. Taksin ordered the patriarch to appear before a tribunal, and when the venerable monk refused, he forced him to undergo a trial by fire. The ordeal turned out unfavourably for the patriarch, and accordingly he was sentenced to leave the order of monks.[34] This apparently was the story upon which Turpin's informant built his account. A chief priest thus did have the soles of his feet burnt, but this may not be seen as an example of Taksin's blind jealousy. The trial by fire was a well-accepted method of finding out whether or not a person was guilty. A broad ditch was filled with burning pieces of wood and after some time the accused man was forced to walk through the hot charcoal and ashes. The gods and benevolent powers were invited beforehand to protect the innocent. Since people always walked barefoot and often had strong, hardened footsoles, it was not uncommon for a man to come through the ordeal unscathed.[35]

The year 1770 again was full of martial activity. In March of that year Taksin boldly went up north, skirting Phra' Fāng's domain, towards the Burmese-dominated city of Chiang Mai. He succeeded in reaching this heavily fortified town with an army of fifteen thousand but was unable to find a weak spot in its defences. Realizing that the task was too much for his present resources, he ordered a retreat. The Burmese attacked the withdrawing army and succeeded in causing a stampede. Taksin reputedly drew his sword, forcing his troops to make a stand and give battle. Finally he reached the town of Phichai, where his boats made a rapid return to Thonburi possible. There, ships loaded with rice had just arrived, and large amounts were distributed throughout the population. Taksin can hardly have had time to recuperate from his unsuccessful excursion to Chiang Mai when he set out again for the north, but this time to eliminate a less formidable foe, the "renegade-monk" Phra' Fāng in Sawangkhaburi. It is possible that this second exploit of 1770 was prompted by intelligence gathered on the first, namely that Phra' Fāng's hold over the region was not very firm.

This time he did not leave much to chance: between May

and July three armies were sent up, the chief one numbering some twelve thousand soldiers led by Taksin himself, flanked on each side by forces of five thousand men. The armies travelled mainly by boat, the most efficient means of transportation. The defenders of Sawangkhaburi were not able to withstand the first attacks, and Taksin incorporated the northern region into his kingdom. He stayed some months in order to supervise and direct the region's submission. As usual, he ordered his troops to desist from plundering and he invited the farmers to reoccupy their farms. Taksin's attitude to religion and his talents for organization are demonstrated in his manner of dealing with the problem of the purification of the northern Buddhist church.[36] Phra' Fāng had fled, but his four chief advisers were caught, disrobed, and transported to gaol in Thonburi. All the monks in the region were assembled. Those who had killed, stolen, or consorted with women, thus having broken one or more of the four rules of the Sangha which entail expulsion, had no right to wear monks' robes and were told to immediately change over into civilian clothes. They would be employed in positions in the new state administration. Those who pleaded not guilty would have to prove their innocence by diving under water for the prescribed time.[37]

> The King pronounced a solemn invocation and adjuration. . . .
> After this adjuration the King sat down on a chair by the river-
> bank to watch the proceedings. Many of the priests succeeded in
> the Ordeal, but others who were not equal to the occasion were
> ignominiously divested of their robes and then executed. Their
> remains were thrown into a heap and burnt.[38]

The monks who safely came through the ordeal received new robes and positions in the hierarchy of the Sangha. Taksin then summoned a group of fifty learned monks from Thonburi to supervise the continued purity of the doctrine, paid homage at the important Buddhist sanctuaries of the north and donated funds to some of the monasteries.

Taksin's handling of the case of the aberrant monks must have seemed proper and just to the traditional ecclesiastical authorities. It demonstrates that he venerated the Sangha when all unworthy individuals had been removed. Further proof of Taksin's friendly attitude towards Buddhist monks is the fact that at some moment in his reign he decided to include monks who held the exalted position of member of the *rātchakhana* (the highest advisory body in the Siamese Buddhist church) and those who possessed a *parien* diploma in ecclesiastical studies among the officials who received a regular sum of money from the king's purse. The fact that he included some monks in the select group so honoured confirms Taksin's sincere admiration for scholarly monks, and it denies Turpin's picture of a man who wished the extermination of all priests.

By the end of 1770 the early years of Taksin's rule were over. In a frenzy of activity he had managed to do battle with each of the contenders for the throne and he had brought most of the region that used to be governed by the kings of Ayutthaya under his control. He had travelled with his armies in all the outer regions and had personally supervised the setting up of a unified administration.

The beginning of Taksin's rule seems to have been characterized by sternness and steadfastness, well suited to the turbulent years after the devastation of Ayutthaya. He provided a rallying point when Siam was hopelessly divided, and he repulsed the foreign occupying troops. Although information on these early years is scanty and incomplete, nevertheless it shows Taksin to have been a pragmatic and quite popular ruler. His popularity was partly based upon his military successes, which provided a measure of pride and self-esteem for the humbled nation; partly upon the efficacy of his measures to restore security, rules and regulations; and partly upon his forthrightness and his unwillingness to bend the laws for his personal gain or that of his chief advisers. Taksin was a man of the people. This is confirmed by hints in the literature that he was reluctant to assume the position of king, preferring the more modest title of "preserver of the kingdom". It can be seen in his concern for the common soldiers, including his raising their wages considerably above what had been customary.[39] His care for the ordinary folk is shown in his decree preventing people from falling into debt through immoderate gambling.[40]

## Consolidation

By 1771 Taksin could regard himself as master of a large kingdom, and this was when he took the next step in the formation of a viable state: the creation of a capital. Up to 1771 Thonburi had remained little more than a fortress surrounded by a rapidly growing population of traders, soldiers, and administrators. If Taksin had harboured thoughts of returning to Ayutthaya, a possibility that has been mooted in the literature,[41] in 1771 he must have abandoned such plans and have come to a firm decision to make Thonburi the new capital. In that year he organized a massive corvée, collecting manpower from Thonburi as well as from the provinces, comprising both those who traditionally belonged to the "military" (*thahān*) as well as the "civilians" (*phonlaru'an*). They were employed in digging out waterways and heaping up earthen walls around Thonburi. On two sides of the town, canals were constructed, both to help develop these regions as rice-growing areas and as a defence measure, because in case of emergency these regions could be flooded quickly to hinder enemy movement.[42]

During 1771 the king decided upon a military expedition to Cambodia, which had during Ayutthayan times become a Siamese vassal state but which had asserted its independence ever since the Burmese invaded Siam.[43] Just after the rainy season of 1771 had ended, two large armies moved eastwards. One of these armies, numbering some ten thousand men, was under the command of the elder brother of Taksin's old friend Bunmā, mentioned earlier.[44] King Taksin, commanding the second army of about the same size, travelled by boat. He took the Cambodian harbour town of Phutthaimāt (Ha Tien), and the Siamese armies at first met with little resistance. However, early in 1772 an army from Annam temporarily managed to expel the occupying Siamese troops. During 1772 and 1773 the Burmese attempted to invade Siam proper from their base in Chiang Mai, and Taksin had to battle repeatedly to retain the northern town of Phichai, north of Phitsanulok.

The year 1774 is noteworthy for Taksin's decree on the tattooing of the populace. Every person of *phrai* status was to have his wrist tattooed, receiving a mark indicating who was his master (*nāi*), and another mark indicating in which *mū'ang* he resided. Persons who wilfully had themselves falsely tattooed, as well as those illegally in possession of tattooing implements, would be liable to suffer the death sentence.[45] Although during Ayutthaya times the practice of tattooing certain soldiers with a distinguishing mark on the arm had already been known — originally probably as a safety measure for identifying the king's or governor's bodyguard[46] — the decree to tattoo each and every *phrai* probably constituted an innovation. The measure undoubtedly would have assisted the quick identification of ordinary subjects and must have greatly facilitated the allocation of corvée duties. There can be little doubt that this decree was obeyed; Taksin did not suffer people to ignore an official decree.

It will never be known whether at this stage Taksin could have held out against a full-scale Burmese attack. By a stroke of fortune, the Burmese were deflected from settling their score with Taksin by the outbreak of a rebellion in the predominantly Mon areas of Burma. Taksin, always quick to seize an opportunity, attacked the Burmese stronghold at Chiang Mai. Late in 1774 he moved his armies northward. When by January 1775 Taksin himself arrived before the walls of Chiang Mai, his armies had encircled the town and were ready to attack. The town fell relatively easily, and the Siamese captured a considerable number of cannons and guns. King Taksin, as was his wont after a successful campaign, paid homage in the chief temples and donated valuable presents to some monasteries. On the return to Thonburi he had to divert his army to the town of Tak, where he had once been governor, to defeat a Burmese-led attack.

When he eventually arrived back in Thonburi, in February 1775, he heard that a large-scale Burmese invasion was reported at the south-western part of the central plain. This was the long-expected confrontation. Orders were given to his not-yet-demobilized army to proceed southwards immediately, as he called up reserve troops from the north-east. In the circumstances, he forbade his troops to rest or even visit their families. When he learnt that one of his senior officers had disobeyed the order, Taksin personally beheaded him. He instructed the army to hold back the Burmese at Ratburi and arrived there himself in mid-February. When, during deliberations with the highest officers, one officer disagreed with Taksin about what tactics to follow and uttered incautious remarks, that man also was beheaded and his body exposed as a frightful example of what a breach of discipline would entail. The troops from Nakhon Ratchasima arrived rather belatedly, because some of the soldiers had insisted upon visiting their families and had even brought along women and children. Taksin had these families executed. It seems that on the verge of the long-awaited full-scale clash with the Burmese, Taksin would not allow even the slightest disobedience. At this crucial moment, he pushed himself and his soldiers with all his willpower to the utmost of their capacity. The ensuing battles between the Siamese and Burmese were convincingly won by the Siamese, and in April they returned victoriously to Thonburi.

Attempting anything that might strengthen his position, Taksin sent, with the annual fleet to China, a personal appeal to the Chinese emperor requesting cannons and sulphur. He mentioned in his request that these would be helpful in his battles with Burma, their common enemy. Apparently the Chinese were not amused by the idea of such an insignificant ally, for the answer was a carefully worded snub.[47]

In March 1776 the Burmese invaded northern Siam and captured the major town of Phitsanulok, gaining control of large tracts of the region. Fortunately for the Siamese, Hsinbyushin, the Burmese king, died, and after one unsuccessful effort to regain Burmese control of Chiang Mai, the new king called off the whole expedition. Siamese troops were sent in different directions to harass the retreating enemy. When one section of Taksin's army failed to make contact with the Burmese, Taksin called eleven senior officers before a military tribunal; he found them guilty, and they were all executed. This illustrates Taksin's passion for discipline and the ruthlessness with which this passion was pursued. This was the man who at this time was being defied by the Catholic missionaries at Thonburi.

## The King and the Missionaries

The conflict between King Taksin and the Christian community of Thonburi[48] arose in September 1775. In accordance with established practice, Taksin had arranged for the court to hold a regular ceremony of swearing the oath of allegiance, during which all senior government servants would swallow some water which had been blessed by a chapter of Buddhist monks. The Catholic bishop, Mgr Lebon, deciding that this ritual was against Christian principles, had taken aside the three members of his flock who held government positions and had administered the oath himself in the name of the evangelical saints. The bishop then blithely proceeded to make out certificates stating that these three men had formally sworn the king's allegiance. Apparently he had not fully informed himself of the Siamese law in this matter, which stated that all the king's servants, of whatever race or creed, had to undergo the ceremony and that refusal to do so would be regarded as treason, punishable by the death penalty.

The three officials, armed with their certificates, were promptly imprisoned. Three days later the bishop and his two missionaries were brought before Taksin. When the king heard that the bishop would not recommend his charges to say the appropriate oath and drink the water, he was furious and had all six culprits stripped and tied between pillars. The three officials received fifty lashes of the rattan, but the three priests were freed without a lashing, apparently in the hope that the example would make them realize that the authorities were in earnest. Later that night the six appeared before a tribunal. The three officials were solemnly commanded to make their formal oath, and the priests were invited to submit a formal apology to the king. The six adamantly refused. The following day all six appeared again before Taksin, and he displayed even more anger than before. This time the bishop and his missionaries received one hundred lashes and were sent to prison manacled, with irons around their necks and limbs. The three officials were also sent to prison under the same circumstances. After two months of confinement, the three officials indicated their willingness to comply with the rules, and they were marched off to a Buddhist monastery, where they drank the water of allegiance.

The three officials having repented, the case should have been closed. However, the priests persisted in their original attitude. The situation was further complicated by a rumour that a cloth, stained with the bishop's blood, was being smuggled to Europe in order to gain general support for the unfortunate priests. As a result, all communication between the prisoners and local Christians was forbidden until the matter had been investigated. At the same time the Burmese threat on two fronts in the north developed into a serious situation, and in January 1776 Taksin himself went there, without having resolved the awkward confrontation with the missionaries. The bishop and his two helpers remained in gaol, constantly hindered in their movements by the shackles and irons.

There they remained until August 1776. In July of that year, after intercessions by various Catholics and an English officer resident in Siam, most of their irons had been removed. In August they were again led before a tribunal, where they were presented with a document to sign. The document in question was a general statement in which the signatories promised not to act against the person of the king. However, it included a special clause allowing people to drink the water of allegiance and the priests refused to sign, at the same time informing the court that they promised to refrain from actions against the king. A day later the last chains were removed and it appeared that they were to be freed. However, this was a false hope; soon they were back into prison, shackles and all. At the beginning of September 1776, after signing a general statement only, they were finally released.

The confrontation between Taksin and the missionaries can be viewed in various ways. Pallegoix in his *Description du royaume Thai* gladly provides the details, because they show how these brave men were willing to die for their faith. The case also provides an instance where the regulations and prescriptions of the Catholics clashed with those of traditional Siam. Looking at it from Taksin's point of view, the missonaries simply incited people to act against the law. The ceremony of the oath of allegiance was an important, frequently held ritual, administered not only in the capital but also in outer regions. It was a valuable security measure. Taksin could have ordered the priests' execution, but, probably because they were foreign nationals as well as religious leaders, he did all he could to try and convince them to retract. Having failed to do so, a truce developed between the king and the Christians.

## Taksin and Buddhist Meditation

For some time the country remained poised for the next Burmese invasion, but when this did not materialize Taksin began to realize that under Hsinbyushin's successor, Singu, Burma was not likely to send a large army. For the first time since the fall of Ayutthaya, the king could give his mind to things other than warfare.

From this time probably dates his involvement with the study of Buddhist meditation. Taksin ordered a search for the most authoritative texts on the subject, and in 1777 the most senior monks of the country presented him with relevant Pali texts. He obtained similar books from foreigners.[49] He must have already had some training in Buddhist meditation and methods of concentration when as a young adult he spent three years in the Sangha. Now, at a much later stage of his life, he arranged for monks with a great reputation as teachers on this subject to advise him regularly on his exercises.

The king's widening interests at this time are also demonstrated by the fact that he sponsored the edition of a famous Siamese text on cosmology, reputedly written in the mid-fourteenth century.[50] Taksin planned a magnificent launching ceremony, to which he invited people from all nations. Unfortunately, Bishop Lebon knew the work to be full of superstitions, totally unsuitable for Christians, and forbade members of his congregation to attend. Taksin was annoyed when he saw the absence of that small but noticeable community and angrily proposed to have all the missionaries executed. Reputedly the *phrayā* Čhakri managed to appease

him, and the following day Taksin shrugged off the affair,
saying: "I am leading this nation in the right and proper direction, and if the Christians do not want to follow my lead,
worse luck for them, it is their own business [or words to that
effect]."[51]

Late in 1778 Taksin ordered an invasion of what was traditionally Laotian territory. The reasons for this campaign are
not altogether clear. Taksin had communicated with Laotian
rulers and had established what seemed to be cordial relations
with some of them. Apparently he had some reason to believe
that their friendly statements were but lip-service, and probably felt that a demonstration of Siamese might was appropriate. A minor provocation sufficed as an excuse for sending
the two brothers Thọng Duang (the future Rama I) and
Bunmā, who had become his trusted top generals, with some
thirty thousand men to the Laotian territories.[52] The invasion
of Laos was a success, at least from the Siamese point of
view, and in April 1779 the men returned home, bringing with
them large numbers of Laotians, many of whom were settled
in the district of Saraburi.

While his armies were on the warpath, Taksin remained in
the capital. He became more and more interested in meditation. In 1779 a Danish visitor, J.G. Koenig, remarked on the
king's passionate and all-consuming interest:

> He believes that according to their religious creed he will one day
> be a god. To be able to draw breath so that one does not perceive
> any movement in the pit of the stomach is considered a sign of
> his commencing divinity. Moreover there are some other sure
> signs thereof, consisting in his being able to sit perfectly rigid for
> hours like the idol Rill, with meditative features and fixed eyes,
> and lastly he believes that by reading he is going to have white
> blood, as the gods are said to have that too. With these
> capacities he believes he will finally succeed in flying.
>
> He relates all this nonsense to all who appear before him, and
> asks them whether they do not think them possible, and whether
> they do not believe that one day he will be able to fly, whereupon
> he is assured by all his courtiers, doctors and Talapoins[53] that he
> surely is right.[54]

Dr Koenig, a European scientist and a pupil of Linnaeus,
did not hesitate to label the king's ambition to fly as
"nonsense". However, the Buddhist scholars and advisers

could not dismiss it so easily. Famous Buddhist saints reputedly had achieved such powers. Taksin asked top-level advisers to check on the possibilities. The head of the Siamese Sangha personally went with him through a list of the thirty-two marks of a great man (*mahāpurusha*) and found it was possible to identify twelve on the king's body.[55] This probably encouraged Taksin into believing that he was a person destined for greater things than ordinary people.

Two monks, Phra' Wannarāt and Phra' Rattanamuni, especially stimulated and encouraged Taksin. They judged Taksin's accomplishments as proof of having reached the status of *sodāban*, the first stage towards enlightenment. According to Siamese textbooks the *sodāban*, literally "one who has entered the stream [of insight]", was a saintly person who had reached such a state of perfection that he could not have more than seven further births among men and angels before reaching the blissful stage of *niphān* (nirvana). Taksin, ambitious and enthusiastic, seems to have accepted the two monks' opinion that he was a *sodāban*. This belief was soon to lead him into direct conflict with the Buddhist church.

Meanwhile, the king's behaviour to the Christians displayed little of what they would have called saintliness. Late in July 1779, while his soldiers were being paid, when the Christian contingent which formed part of his personal bodyguard arrived to receive their money, the king suddenly shouted that the Christians would have to do without. He accused them of not appearing at the royal ceremonies and of even refusing to play music on the official festive days. He added that he was considering expelling all Christians from the country. A few days later a state procession was held and a group of Christians, alarmed at the news of a possible expulsion, acted against their bishop's advice and attended this non-Christian ritual. Bishop Lebon thereupon threatened to expel from the church all those who had attended. Of the eleven culprits, ten confessed and demanded pardon; one remained adamant.[56]

The head of the Treasury, *phrayā* Phrakhlang, a Muslim by faith, had apparently urged Taksin to carry out his threats against the Christians. Some time later, during a royal audience, Taksin addressed the Phrakhlang and warned him, using words to this effect: "The other day you caught me in a moment of anger against the Christians and you even tried to increase my rage. They are united and firm in their religion, but you are like a two-faced animal. You may rest assured that if I had acted hastily and excessively against them, you would have paid for it, you would have been the real victim."[57] As an aftermath of this public reproof, Taksin decided to allow the Christian soldiers to have their pay after all.

The above incidents may serve to convey the eccentric manner in which the king held his daily audience, or the fear even his chief advisers might sometimes have felt. At the same time it shows that Taksin had, probably somewhat begrudgingly, developed an admiration for the principled staunch defenders of the Catholic faith. Perhaps the most important conclusion that can be drawn from it is that in 1779 Taksin fully realized that he had a short temper and that he could act hastily.[58]

Late in 1779 or at the beginning of 1780, Bishop Lebon and his two helpers were again brought before a court, found guilty of having broken a law, imprisoned, and finally deported. Apparently the priests had been asked to comment upon the king's attempts to reach superhuman powers through meditation and especially upon the possibility of the king being able to fly. The Catholic leaders had told him frankly that flying was incompatible with the physical form of the human body. Naturally this advice would have been unwelcome. However, the priests also found it necessary to tell the king that polygamy was in their eyes unlawful. According to information collected more than forty years after these events, the bishop and his clergy each received a hundred cuts of the bamboo and were banished from the kingdom.[59]

There exists yet another account of Taksin's preoccupation with the acquisition of supernatural powers which probably belongs to this period. Reputedly he demanded from the courtiers who had assembled at a regular audience to know who could go up to heaven. There was an awkward silence, which finally was broken by a reply from the governor of

Patthalung, who boldly declared that this was something beyond human experience, at least as long as the human was still alive. The story goes that Taksin answered: "That is right! These are boldly spoken words which are right!" This is given as one of the possible reasons why the governor of Patthalung gained himself the nickname of *khānglēk* or "he who speaks courageously".[60] If this episode really did take place, it would demonstrate that the Thonburi courtiers had become very reluctant to enter into a debate with the king, uncertain what his reaction would be. It also may be taken as an indication that Taksin appreciated a simple, brave, and direct answer.

## The Final Years

Early in 1780, King Taksin heard that a Siamese boat had been intercepted off Ha Tien. The crew had been massacred and the cargo taken. Taksin immediately requested an inquiry, but the Vietnamese rulers were tardy in their reply. Aggravating matters further, a secret communication from the Tay-son brothers, who had recently conquered most of the region now called Vietnam, to Ha Tien proposing a joint surprise attack upon Thonburi was discovered just at the time when a large Vietnamese fleet was manoeuvring off the Cambodian coast. The more important Vietnamese residents in Thonburi were interrogated, and during November 1780 more than fifty of them were executed. Other Vietnamese were deported to the frontier areas.[61]

This was also the time that Taksin had to quell a secessionist uprising which was led by an Ayutthayan Buddhist monk named Phra' Mahā Dā.[62] The scanty information on the Mahā Dā movement indicates that it had millenarian overtones. Phra' Mahā Dā went among the people sprinkling holy water, and he appointed assistants to whom he gave traditional titles up to the rank of *phrayā*, a prerogative reserved for independent rulers. Taksin was able to suppress the movement, and he had Mahā Dā arrested, brought to Thonburi, and executed.[63]

During 1781 and 1782 the irascible king became involved in

two conflicts with sections of his people which must have seriously damaged his prestige. The first conflict was with a large number of Buddhist monks. It may be seen as the outcome of Taksin's strenuous efforts to master various types of meditation practices. He questioned the Sangha on whether a layman who had reached the state of *sodāban* would be higher, ritually speaking, than an ordinary Buddhist monk who had none of the accomplishments of a *sodāban*. If the answer were that a genuine lay *sodāban* was more worthy than an ordinary unaccomplished monk, and if it were accepted that the king was such a *sodāban*, ordinary monks would have to pay homage to the king.

The supreme patriarch and some of the country's highest monks pondered over this question and advised the king in no uncertain words: "Although a layman can be a *sodāban*, he is still in a defective, inferior guise. A monk, even though he may come from the common classes, is in a complete, superior guise because he wears the yellow robe. Monks who observe the four percepts of purity should not pay homage to a layman who is a *sodaban*."[64] This statement is fully in accordance with ecclesiastical jurisprudence in Siam, and Buddhist monks have never been obliged to prostrate themselves, bow down, or even raise their hands in a polite "thank-you" gesture before a layman even if he were king.

Taksin, however, apparently feeling that the rare combination king-*sodāban* was such a special case that the simple, often ignorant Buddhist monk ought to show respect, took this answer as a personal affront. He was so certain of his higher status that he decided to force the issue, calling monks before him and testing whether or not they would pay homage and prostrate before their King. The patriarch found himself in a very similar situation to Bishop Lebon six years earlier; this was a matter of principle. To his credit, it has been recorded that he and many other monks would not bow down. Taksin punished all of them. The supreme patriarch was demoted, as were many other high-ranking Buddhist monks, some even being given fifty or a hundred lashes. More than five hundred monks were sentenced to cart dung, a defiling and rather abhorrent task. Naturally, there were many monks who, when confronted with the fierce and angry monarch-*cum-sodāban*, did bow down, if not out of reverence, then out of fear.

This conflict between Taksin and a large section of the Sangha has often been misreported and misunderstood. Taksin did not try to be worshipped as a god, he never claimed to be a Buddha, he had not accepted the idea that he was a Bodhisattva: he simply objected to the idea that a recently ordained, simple young Buddhist monk should be higher in status and ritual rank than a king who had proved to his own satisfaction that he had advanced far along the path towards enlightenment. Taksin was unwise to take the advice of his most knowledgeable informants as a personal insult and to rush into a confrontation. He must have lost considerable good will by literally forcing monks to bow to his will. Although nobody would have dared to tell him so face-to-face, virtually all principled, traditionally minded Siamese would have sided with the monks who had ruled against the king's wish.

The second serious problem that arose between Taksin and a section of the populace developed from his hasty attempts to suppress illegal trade and corruption. Apparently there had been a flourishing illegal trade in rice, salt, rhinoceros horn, ivory, and valuable wood. People who engaged in this trade, avoiding paying tax and customs duty, had made many thousands of *baht* profit. These illegal practices were first brought to light by a denunciation. When he heard about the corrupt practices, Taksin apparently wanted to find out speedily who had been involved. He encouraged people to inform him on these matters and acted rapidly on every report, taking the sworn evidence of an informer as sufficient proof of a person's guilt; he had people flogged if they denied the accusations. Some of the informers were rewarded with government positions.[65]

The harsh methods of punishing those who had made illegal profits and a general dissatisfaction with his rule appear to have been the chief factors leading to the undoing of King Taksin. Again there were troubles in Ayutthaya, where a group of rebels had killed the governor. In March 1782 the king sent a contingent of troops under *phrayā* San to restore order. However, the rebels marched towards Thonburi, with a close relative of *phrayā* San reputedly among them. If *phrayā* San did not join the rebels, at least he did not prevent them from entering the capital. Taksin's palace was beleaguered one night, but his Christian bodyguard managed to hold his opponents back. Aware of his vulnerable position, Taksin negotiated his abdication, using the newly appointed supreme patriarch and his two meditation teachers Phra' Wannarāt and Phra' Rattanamuni as go-betweens. Taksin succeeded in obtaining permission to withdraw from the scene, and during the evening of the day of his abdication he became a Buddhist monk and took up residence at Wat Chaeng.

The main army was at that time in Cambodia, together with many prominent and powerful figures such as the head of the Mahātthai Ministry, Thǫng Duang, who now carried the title *čhaophrayā* Mahākasatsu'k, his brother Bunmā, now known as *čhaophrayā* Surasī, and Taksin's son *kromakhun* Intharaphitak. In the capital, *phrayā* San's troops at first looted the Treasury, but soon some form of government was established. *Phrayā* San, the senior administrators such as *čhaophrayā* Mahāsēnā and *phrayā* Rāmanwong, and the most senior relative of Taksin's available, *kromakhun* Anuraksongkhrām, all joined to restore order and form a government. Although Siamese sources do not state this explicitly, it appears that *kromakhun* Anuraksongkhrām was accepted as the new head of state.

This interpretation is somewhat unorthodox. It is based upon two facts. Firstly *kromakhun* Anuraksongkhrām, who had been arrested and imprisoned by *phrayā* San, suddenly emerged not only a free man but also as leader of Thonburi's defence. Secondly, Rama I is invested in Chinese records with Taksin's family name, a name that would have been appropriate to *kromakhun* Anuraksongkhrām. The yearly Chinese trade fleet may have been sent early because of the troubled situation with a letter stating that Taksin had abdicated in favour of his younger relative. The Chinese court appears to have had no official account of the events of early April when Rama I took power.[67]

Meanwhile, *čhaophrayā* Mahākasatsu'k had heard about Taksin's abdication, and he acted promptly in order to put himself forward as Taksin's successor. He asked his brother Bunmā to keep *kromakhun* Intharaphitak isolated and sent an urgent message to his nephew *phrayā* Suriyā Aphai, who was governor of Nakhon Ratchasima, asking him to march post-haste to Thonburi and seize control. *Phrayā* Suriyā Aphai raised more than a thousand Siamese and Laotian troops and marched upon Thonburi less than a fortnight after Taksin's abdication. *Kromakhun* Anuraksongkhrām marched up to give battle, lost the fight, and was taken prisoner. *Phrayā* Suriyā Aphai took possession of Thonburi, and when *čhaophrayā* Mahākasatsu'k arrived with a large force he found the capital waiting for him and nobody challenged his claim to be Siam's new king.

The man who had risen to become Taksin's most trusted general was a strict disciplinarian and a veteran of many campaigns. Ironically, this general now became the instrument of Taksin's destruction. As soon as the new leader had taken control of Thonburi, he ordered a ruthless purge. Among those who died were more than forty members of *kromakhun* Anuraksongkhrām's clique, including the prince himself, also *phrayā* San and his supporters, and many people who had been personally attached to Taksin. Taksin's son Intharaphitak and six followers were brought to Thonburi as prisoners and killed.

Taksin himself, now in the "superior guise" of the yellow robe, was taken from his monastery and put to a court martial, where he had to listen to charges pertaining to the later years of his rule. He was accused of having ill-treated the former supreme patriarch and of having sentenced people without giving them an opportunity to defend themselves before a tribunal. Taksin was found guilty, and the new ruler ordered him to be beheaded in the fortress Wichaiprasit.[68] The execution took place on 7 April 1782. When he died, Taksin was forty-seven years old.[69]

## A Controversial Man

Most of the historical works that mention King Taksin state that during the later years of his reign he lost his ability to rule. It has been suggested that Taksin suffered from delusions of grandeur, or that he developed "a kind of Caesar complex".[70] The information that has been collected above indicates, however, that Taksin's unorthodox behaviour was consistent throughout his reign. It has been shown that his treatment of law-breaking Catholic missionaries, of offending Buddhist monks, and of illegal traders during the later years of his rule was quite similar to his treatment of deserters, of officers who did not promptly follow orders, of those who contradicted him, and of those who hampered him in achieving full control over the country during the earlier years.

Taksin may have been physically smaller than many,[71] but he consistently set himself high goals. Even before Ayutthaya fell, it was clear that he could not abide a setback to his career, being unable to accept the fact that he was court-martialled for disobeying an order. From that moment onwards, throughout his fifteen years of rule, Taksin drove himself mercilessly, and the high standards he set himself were applied to those he selected as his aides.

In this book, the idea that during the later years of his rule Taksin began to suffer from a mental disease is rejected. Possibly such an idea was put forward as one of the legitimizing measures by those who succeeded him. Taksin was a remarkable person, quick off the mark and volatile. At the same time he remained absolutely sincere, determined and uncompromising. These characteristics helped him become Siam's supreme military leader, one of the most remarkable generals of his time. These same characteristics hampered him when the campaigns were over and when, during the last five years of his reign, he could lay down his sword and take up the sceptre. The qualities that were virtues in a general who had to win battles became liabilities to a sedentary ruler. As an army commander he could give short shrift to officers who lacked courage or to men he disliked for being sycophants or hypocrites, but not so as a peacetime king. While Taksin was a highly successful general, he cannot be regarded as an altogether successful king.

Taksin seems to have had a clear idea of what his behaviour as monarch ought to have been: a king should be just, he ought to protect the population, lift the nation's moral standards, and lead when leadership is called for. Taksin fulfilled these kingly duties in many instances, such as when he ordered his soldiers to respect farmers' property, when he cleansed the Buddhist order in Sawangkhaburi, and when he proudly sponsored the copying of an ancient document on cosmology. However, when the period of rapid and hurried establishment of order, of improvization and extemporization, was over and the king remained in Thonburi for lengthy periods of time, a good measure of caution and statecraft was needed. An absolute king surrounded by a court during a period of relative peace must be able to act slowly; he must be able to win friends in whom he can confide and who are willing to act for him. Taksin must have realized that during the last years of his rule he had disappointed many people, and that he should have refrained from trying to change people's convictions by sheer force and from combating corruption by a frenzy of punishments. He must have sometimes felt that his personality did not suit Siam's highest office. During the last years of his reign he appears to have been unhappy and irascible. He abdicated readily as if he were glad to be rid of that office and welcomed the opportunity to withdraw from the secular world. If his successor had taken the risk of letting Taksin live, Siam would probably have been one exemplary Buddhist monk the richer.

# Notes

1. W.A.R. Wood, *A History of Siam, from the Earliest Times to the Year A.D. 1781*, pp. 243-50; R.B. Smith, *Siam or the History of the Thais, from 1569 A.D. to 1824 A.D.*, pp. 90-99; M.L. Manich Jumsai, *Popular History of Thailand*, pp. 250-301; Abha Bhamorabutr, *A Short History of Thailand*, pp. 60-68; Rong Syamananda, *A History of Thailand*, pp. 89-92; G. Coedès, *The Making of South East Asia*, pp. 161-62.
2. For details on Thammathibēt, see *Čhaofā Thammathibēt, Phraprawat lae Phraniphon bot Rǭykrǭng*.
3. The Sangha is another word for the Buddhist order of monks and novices.
4. The most stubborn resistance was put up at the stockade of Bāng Račhan, in the province of Singburi, where the Burmese had to resort to drastic measures, including a cannonade from high positions built for that purpose. The heroes of Bāng Račhan are still remembered in Thailand, the stockade having been reconstructed and a huge monument having been erected. For details, see

Khana Kammakān Fū'nfū Būrana Khāi Bāng Račhan, *Wirachon Khāi Bāng Račhan* (published at the royal opening of the Bāng Račhan monument).

5. S. de la Loubère, *The Kingdom of Siam*, p. 90.

6. J. O'Kane, trans., *The Ship of Sulaimān*, p. 90. An eyewitness account of warfare in the early seventeenth century is given by C. van Nyenrode, published in F.H. Giles, "*A Critical Analysis of Van Vliet's Historical Account of Siam in the 17th Century*", p. 181.

7. For details, see F.H. Turpin, *Histoire civile et naturelle du royaume de Siam*, pp. 293-319.

8. In Ayutthaya times this title is more often than not known as *phayā*, and this has been its rendering in chapter 1. However, gradually the spelling *phrayā* came to be fashionable, and eventually it supplanted that of *phayā*. For simplicity's sake henceforth in this book both *phayā* and *čhaophayā* are given in their later spellings of *phrayā* and *čhaophrayā*.

9. Various versions of this legend can be found, in G.E. Gerini, "Shan and Siam", *Imperial and Asiatic Quarterly Review*, 1898, pp. 158-59; K.P. Landon, *The Chinese in Thailand*, pp. 6-7; J. Stransky, *Die Wiedervereinigung Thailands unter Taksin, 1767-1782*, pp. 50-51; M.J. Smith, "Taksin the Savior of Siam", *Sawaddi*, March–April 1968, pp. 18-19; and Pradit Kraiwong, *Tāksin Mahārāt*.

10. Gerini, "Shan and Siam", p. 159.

11. It is often reported that he was appointed governor of Kamphaeng Phet, a *mū'ang* of the second rank, and thus a major promotion. However, in the troubled times just before the fall of Ayutthaya, this promotion was probably never put into effect. The remark by King Mongkut that *phrayā* Tāk bribed the *čhaophaya* Čhakrī in order to obtain this promotion must be viewed as an unsupported opinion. It is unlikely that Taksin would have been so keen to gain the governorship of a town which was then in Burmese hands. See "Brief Sketches of Siamese History", *Siamese Repository*, 1869, p. 258.

12. *Kromphra'* Damrong Rātchanuphāp, *Phongsāwadān Ru'ang Thai Rop Phamā*, *PP*, pt 6, vol. 6, p. 131.

13. Stranski, *Die Wiedervereinigung Thailands*, p. 55.

14. For details, see Damrong Rātchanuphāp, *Phongsāwadān Ru'ung Thai Rop Phamā*, pp. 143-53; Stranski, *Die Wiedervereinigung Thailands*, pp. 43-48; and Chaloem Yuwiengchai, "Prawatisāt Nakhǫn Sī Thammarāt samai Krung Thonburī", in Rāingānkānsamanāprawatisāt Nakhǫn Sī Thammarāt, Nakhǫn Sī Thammarāt Withayalaikhrū, *Prawatisāt Nakhǫn Sī Thammarāt*, pp. 218-19. Several other contenders for power sought refuge in Cambodia and Cochin-China. See Chingho A. Chen, "Mac Thien Tu and Phrayataksin: A Survey on Their Political Stand, Conflicts and Background", *Proceedings, Seventh IAHA Conference 22-26 August 1977, Bangkok*, pp. 1545-48.

15. According to Wood (*A History of Siam*, p. 252), the Siamese contingent under Burmese command began to desert and ran over to Taksin.

16. Stranski, *Die Wiedervereinigung Thailands*, p. 61.

17. This has given rise to some romantic poetry; see, for example, Montri Umavijani, *A Poetic Journey Through Thai History*, pp. 10-15.

18. Some of the arguments surrounding *čhao* Tāk's decision not to revive Ayutthaya can be found in L. Sternstein, "From Ayutthaya to Bangkok", *Hemisphere* 17, no. 11 (November 1973): 14-21.

19. Whichever argument the reader may prefer, it should be avoided to look at this decision with the benefit of hindsight. *Čhao* Tāk did not know he would succeed in becoming the ruler of Siam; it was by no means certain that he would be able to withstand the Burmese, nor could it be taken for granted that

he would be able to hold a throne against a throng of men with better claims to the throne. King Bǫromakōt had 123 children, many of whom were still alive. Moreover, the choice was not simply between Ayutthaya and Thonburi; according to the *Phrarātchaphongsāwadān Krung Thonburi*, Taksin did at first not rule out the possibility of making Chanthaburi his permanent headquarters.

20. Stranski, *Die Wiedervereinigung Thailands*, pp. 73-74.
21. At this stage in his career, Bunmā carried the title *phra*'Mahāmontrī. This man was the younger brother of the man who would take the throne after Taksin had abdicated, and he became Siam's Uparāt, playing a key role in the country's affairs.
22. Turpin (*Histoire civile*, p. 336) states: "Il fut appelé au commandement par la voix unanime des grands & du peuple. Il ne prit d'abord que le titre modeste de défenseur de la nation; & couvrant ses desseins ambitieux du voile de la moderation, il ne voulut paraoitre que citoyen, pour être véritablement Roi."
23. *Wanphra'* is the Buddhist regular "sacred" day held four times each lunar month.
24. Thus the Thai executioner declared in an interview that he was not worried about the fact that he killed people, because after each execution he bought food for the monks. See the *Far Eastern Economic Review*, 23 July 1976, pp. 24-25.
25. Turpin, *Histoire civile*, pp. 334-40.
26. Ibid., p. 338.
27. A. Pallegoix, *Description du royaume Thai ou Siam*, vol. 2, p. 259.
28. Turpin, *Histoire civile*, p. 337. B.O. Cartwright's English translation of Turpin, which was published in 1908 in Bangkok at the American Presbyterian Mission Press under the title *History of the Kingdom of Siam*, is not wholly accurate, and these passages have therefore been rendered into English with the original at hand.
29. *Sangkharāt*, or leader of the Buddhist church in the country.
30. Turpin, working from missionaries' reports, consistently spells Taksin's name in this manner, probably a misreading from a manuscript where the name might have been spelt Phaia-Thac.
31. Turpin, *Histoire civile*, pp. 337-38.
32. *Phrarātchaphongsāwadān Phrarātchalēkhā*, vol. 2, pt 1, pp. 4-6.
33. According to the ancient rules of the Pāṭimokkha, a priest is not allowed to involve himself with military affairs. He is not even allowed to look and enjoy the sight of a military parade. See Nānamoli Thera, trans., *The Pāṭimokkha, 227 Fundamental Rules of a Bhikkhu*, pp. 58-59. If a Buddhist priest engages in war and intentionally kills a human being, he is automatically expelled from the order and forfeits all respect.
34. Stranski, *Die Wiedervereinigung Thailands*, p. 78.
35. For details, see G.E. Gerini, "Trial by Ordeal in Siam and the Siamese Law of Ordeals", and de la Loubère, *The Kingdom of Siam*, p. 86.
36. The following account is based upon Gerini, "Trial by Ordeal", pp. 123-24; Stranski, *Die Wiedervereinigung Thailands*, pp. 90-91; and C.J. Reynolds, "The Buddhist Monkhood in Nineteenth Century Thailand", pp. 30-31.
37. The Siamese sources state that the prescribed time was three *klan*, or three "exertions". Since we do not know how long one "exertion" lasted, it is impossible to determine the severity of the trial.
38. Gerini, "Trial by Ordeal", pp. 423-24.
39. Pallegoix, *Description du royaume Thai*, vol. 2, p. 97 and p. 262.
40. Before this decree came into effect, many people had been thrown into gaol and were forced to part with their belongings and often with their freedom and

that of their wives and children because they attempted to recoup gambling losses by betting more than they possessed. Taksin therefore issued a decree absolutely forbidding the lending of money to the players. Gamblers henceforth could only play with what they brought along. Since it was now forbidden for them to exceed staking that amount, it was no longer possible for the managers of such establishments to enforce extra payment. This has been extrapolated from the preamble of "Phrarātchakamnot Mai", no. 26, *KTSD* 5: 290-91.

41. Sternstein, "From Ayutthaya to Bangkok", pp. 19-20.
42. Stranski, *Die Wiedervereinigung Thailands*, p. 74.
43. A detailed description of the events leading to this invasion can be found in Chen, "Mac Thien Tu and Phrayataksin", pp. 1544-50.
44. It is quite likely that the future Rama I was, at this time, not yet promoted to the *phrayā* Čhakrī position, and that the official Thai sources often depict his career wrongly. This has been noted by Stranski in *Die Wiedervereinigung Thailands*, p. 129.
45. "Phrarātchakamnot Kao", no. 34, *KTSD* 5: 95.
46. See de la Loubère's remarks on the "painted arms" soldiers in *The Kingdom of Siam*, p. 83 and pp. 96-97.
47. For details, see G.W. Skinner, *Chinese Society in Thailand: An Analytical History*, pp. 22-23. The Ch'ing court was apparently strongly influenced against Taksin by information received from Cochin-China. See Chen, "Mac Thien Tu and Phrayataksin", p. 1549. This was not the first time that Taksin had contact with outside powers regarding military supplies. Already in 1770 the Dutch had sent cannons from Batavia. See W. Blankwaardt, "Notes upon the Relations between Holland and Siam", *JSS* 20, pt 3 (1927): 257.
48. Since Taksin's behaviour towards the Catholic missionaries is often brought forward as proof of the king's "madness", the events are here given in some detail. Further particulars can be found in Pallegoix, *Description du royaume Thai*, vol. 2, pp. 263-70.
49. Reynolds, "The Buddhist Monkhood", p. 32.
50. This edition became well known; it has been published many times under the title *Traiphūmiphraruang*, and it has been translated into French by G. Coedès and C. Archaimbault as *Les trois mondes (Traibhūmi Brah Ryaṅ)*. Regarding the date of compilation of this work, the critical remarks of Vickery ought to be taken into account. See M. Vickery, "A Note on the Date of the Traibhūmikathā", *JSS* 62, pt 2 (1974): 275-84.
51. Pallegoix, *Description du royaume Thai*, vol. 2, p. 271.
52. Further details can be found in D.K. Wyatt, "Siam and Laos, 1767-1827", *Journal of Southeast Asian History* 4, no. 2 (September 1963): 13-32.
53. The word *Talapoin* is used in the older literature in European languages to indicate a Buddhist monk. It has often been stated that this word is derived from the Siamese word *tālapat* or *tālipat*, a fan made out of the *tān* leaf, which monks and wise people often carry. However, Gerini has pointed out that the origin is more likely to be found with the Mon words for "Our Lord" or "Lord of Piety" (see G.E. Gerini, "Historical Retrospect of Junkceylon Island", *JSS* 2, pt 2 [1905]: 175-76 and especially p. 259).
54. J.G. Koenig, "Journal of a Voyage from India to Siam and Malacca in 1779", *Journal of the Straits Branch of the Royal Asiatic Society*, no. 26 (January 1894), pp. 164-65.
55. Reynolds, "The Buddhist Monkhood", pp. 32-33.
56. Pallegoix, *Description du royaume Thai*, vol. 2, p. 272.
57. Ibid., p. 273.

58. See also Koenig, "Journal", p. 165. Sir John Bowring mentions that if a king in anger calls for his sword, the sword-bearer cannot give it, on penalty of death. He is not to be the instrument of the king's anger, but at any risk must refuse to place the means of gratifying the king's passions within his reach. See Bowring, *The Kingdom and People of Siam*, vol. 1, p. 435.

59  J. Crawfurd, *Journal of an Embassy to the Courts of Siam and Cochin-China*, p. 182.

60. Luang Sĭwọrawat, *Phongsāwadān Mŭ'ang Phathalung, PP* vol. 12, pt 15, p. 35.

61. Chen, "Mac Thien Tu and Phrayataksin", pp. 1562-63.

62. The title Mahā was used in connection with the name of a Buddhist monk to indicate a high degree of learning.

63. Stranski, *Die Wiedervereinigung Thailands*, p. 138.

64. Translated by Reynolds in *The Buddhist Monkhood*, p. 33.

65. Stranski, *Die Wiedervereinigung Thailands*, p. 139.

66. Pallegoix, *Description du royaume Thai*, vol. 2, p. 275; Prince Chula Chakrabongse, *Lords of Life: A History of the Kings of Thailand*, pp. 77-78.

67. Skinner raises the problem of Rama I's Chinese name and gives several possible explanations for this. However, he does not consider the possibility that indeed Taksin's relative may have sent the tribute mission of 1782. See Skinner, *Chinese Society in Thailand*, p. 24.

68. Stranski, *Die Wiedervereinigung Thailands*, p. 158.

69. In southern Thailand, particularly in Nakhon Si Thammarat, it is often said that Taksin was saved and sent in exile to the south. People point to the remnants of a building at Lan Sakā, which is called "Taksin's palace", where reputedly the abdicated monarch lived for many years enjoying a peaceful old age. (I thank Dr A. Diller of the Australian National University for calling my attention to the existence of this palace and its reputation.) However, it is most unlikely that Taksin was indeed allowed to live. If Rama I had been willing to let that happen, he would undoubtedly have preferred to keep Taksin under close observation. Probably the legend is to be interpreted as a reflection of the important role Taksin played in the south, not only during the time he resided there, in late 1768 and early 1769, but also when he reinstated the old ruler of Nakhon Si Thammarat and elevated him to a special honorary rank of *čhao* Prathētsarāt, a title that was disallowed by Rama I. Morever, when Taksin was executed, one of his consorts, the daughter of this governor, was sent back to Nakhon Si Thammarat, where she gave birth to a male child. This son of Taksin became governor of the city. See J. Low, "On the Government of Siam", *Asiatic Researches* 20, pt 2 (1836): 268.

70. K. Wenk, *The Restoration of Thailand Under Rama I, 1782-1809*, p. 7.

71. Koenig, "Journal", p. 164.

# 3

# *The First Reign of the Čhakrī Dynasty: Innovation in the Guise of Orthodoxy*

## Background

The man who was later to become the founder of the Čhakrī dynasty was born on 20 March 1737[1] as the fourth child of a ranking government official and his Chinese wife. The boy's given name was Thọng Duang. As was appropriate for the son of an established officer in the government administration, Thọng Duang was sent to the court at Ayutthaya, and at the age of eight he became page to Prince Uthumphọn. In 1757 he served the customary Lenten season as a Buddhist monk and afterwards returned to the court, where he resumed his position as one of Uthumphọn's men. He must have been directly affected when King Bọromakōt died and a succession struggle developed between Uthumphọn and Ekathat. Not long before the large-scale Burmese invasion of 1764 began, he had been appointed *luang* Yokrabat to the governor of the provincial town of Ratburi. There Thọng Duang married, and when the Burmese took Ratburi he went to live with his wife's family not far from the coastal town of

Samut Songkhram. During the siege of Ayutthaya, Thǫng Duang seems to have been cut off from his family. After the fall of Ayutthaya, when communications improved, it was clear that his family was divided between two camps: his younger brother Bunmā had joined Taksin in south-eastern Siam, but his father and the other members of his family were living in Phitsanulok, where the governor asserted his independence. Thǫng Duang's father became Phitsanulok's *čhaophrayā* Čhakrī, and it is likely that, as the governor's chief adviser, he played a role in the battle against Taksin.

Bunmā had become one of Taksin's favourites, and it was he who persuaded his elder brother to join their army. During the fifteen years of Taksin's reign, the two brothers steadily rose to become Taksin's most trusted military commanders. Apparently they never came into conflict with the short-tempered king. Between 1767 and 1782 Thǫng Duang took part in eleven military campaigns. During the first battle, he had been given the title of *phra'* Rātcharin, two years later he held the important position of *phrayā* Yomarāt, and by 1770 had already gained the rank of *phrayā* Čhakrī. During the later years of Taksin's reign, the *phrayā* Čhakrī was entrusted with the command of several campaigns in Laos and Cambodia, and in late 1781 he marched eastwards to assert Siamese domination over Cambodia once again. When at the beginning of 1782 Taksin was suddenly forced to abdicate, *phrayā* Čhakrī (who by then had been elevated even further and possessed the personal title of *čhaophrayā* Mahākasatsu'k) was speedily informed of the crisis through a middle-ranking officer, *luang* Sorawichit.

As noted in the previous chapter, *čhaophrayā* Mahākasatsu'k promptly broke off his campaign and sent his nephew *phrayā* Suriyā Aphai, whose troops were closer to Thonburi, to march at full speed upon the capital and hold it until the main army could arrive. When *čhaophrayā* Mahākasatsu'k finally arrived at Thonburi, he claimed full command of the country.

There can be no doubt that the man who was accepted as the new king was usurping the throne. It has been argued that *kromakhun* Anuraksongkhrām, Taksin's nephew, had already been chosen to be the successor. The battle between

*phrayā* Suriyā Aphai and *kromakhun* Anuraksongkhrām
may therefore be seen as the decisive move in a coup d'état.
*Čhaophrayā* Mahākasatsu'k may have been contemplating
such a move for some time and Taksin's sudden abdication
only hastened events. Several facts support this interpretation
of events, such as the hurried message sent by *luang*
Sorawichit, and the sending of *phrayā* Suriyā Aphai with
orders to establish control over Thonburi. The latter incident
is often presented as a routine measure to quell disorders in
the capital, but the civil disturbances seem to have ceased
before *phrayā* Suriyā Aphai could have possibly arrived
there, and his forces had to fight a reasonably organized, if
small, army from Thonburi. Moreover, the large number of
executions that took place during the first days after the chief
general entered Thonburi appear excessive for a "quelling of
disorder" and more in line with the aftermath of a coup
d'état.

Probably the details will never be known, because the coup
was successful and thereupon an elaborate process of
legitimization was set into motion. Whether or not the new
king had previously contemplated this move, it is certain that
he had been for some time in disagreement with several of
Taksin's decisions, because he did not wait long before rever-
sing them. Also, it may be safely assumed that the king who
later became known as Rama I, and also as Phra'
Phuthayǫtfā Čhulalōk,[2] had not been in agreement with
Taksin's idiosyncrasies and his personal style of ruling. From
the very first day after he was accepted as Siam's new ruler,
on 6 April 1782, Rama I took measures which seem to be
related specifically to a wish to restore a dignity to the highest
office, which had suffered during Taksin's years.

## A New Capital

Fifteen days after taking full command, the king-elect
attended a ceremony to establish a "city pillar" on the land
just opposite Thonburi, across the river Chao Phraya.[3] This
can be seen as a firm commitment to move the country's
capital to the other side of the river. The speed with which

such a major policy decision was reached indicates that for some time the Thonburi site had been considered unsatisfactory. As Thonburi had grown in size and importance, Taksin's palace, hemmed in by two monasteries, became much too small. Moreover, the Thonburi bank of the river was the concave side, subject to constant erosion. In addition, the eastern bank, even though it was low and swampy, would be easier to defend against a massive Burmese attack, because the wide loop of the Chao Phraya would provide a natural defence. The strategic argument may have weighed heaviest in this case, because news must have filtered through that a month before Rama I took command a new ruler had emerged in Burma. An additional thought might have been that an immediate move would demonstrate that there was a clean break with all that Taksin stood for. The fact that Rama I did not wait until a proper palace was built but rapidly moved to a building which had been provided with a temporary stockade supports this interpretation of the move to the east bank.

The construction of Rama I's palace, which involved driving a large number of piles into the marshy ground, must have proceeded at a feverish pace, because it had to be completed before July, when the new ruler's ceremonial elevation to the throne would take place.[4] In July the new residence of the Uparāt, the Wang Nā, was also officially opened. It was decided to build a city of considerable size and to create a grid of canals similar to that of the old capital of Ayutthaya. As well, the layout of Rama I's palace followed that of the Ayutthayan royal palace.

The decision to create a replica of Ayutthaya cannot be seen simply as a falling into line with an old pattern, or Ayutthaya being the best paradigm that could be remembered. Instead, the recreation of a city along Ayutthayan lines was, like many of Rama I's decisions, replete with symbolic meaning. By ordering his craftsmen and surveyors to build a new Ayutthaya, he underlined his intention to rule in the manner of an Ayutthayan king. At the same time he affirmed that Siam was again a country in its own right, with a splendid capital to demonstrate this. During the years of frantic construction that followed, many shiploads of bricks were taken from Ayutthaya and Thonburi, where derelict buildings were completely demolished to furnish the basic materials from which new palaces, fortifications, and monasteries were created. Invariably the removal of Ayutthayan bricks has been seen as an economic means of supplying the architects and craftsmen with building material. However, it could be argued that cheap manufacture of bricks from the many local deposits of river clay would have been equally possible, and that Rama I could have left the old capital in its half-ruined state. Again, the decision to take bricks from Ayutthaya may have had ritual value: by using parts of the old buildings of the legendary capital, some of its glamour and greatness was transferred to the new city site, known of old as Bangkok.[5]

The ceremonial assumption of the throne took place according to the old traditions, with senior monks chanting for three days over the container of water which would be used to transform the general into a king. At an auspicious moment, the new ruler crossed from Thonburi to Bangkok in a formal procession and he was carried solemnly by palanquin to his new palace, anointed, and presented with a suitable array of royal names.

## Appointments

After his formal elevation to kingship, the founder of a new dynasty can be expected to announce the elevation of his relatives and the presentation of their new titles and names. Rama I raised as many as nineteen relatives to the highest princely rank of *čhaofā*.[6] In these appointments the new king especially honoured his two elder sisters. He not only made them and all their offspring *čhaofā* but also gave them the personal rank of *kromphra*; and an official of the rank of *phrayā* was assigned to be the head of the elder one's personal staff.

Bunmā, the king's younger brother, who had served Taksin since the early days and who had proved himself a brilliant tactician and army leader, was elevated to the office of Mahā Uparāt, Ruler of the Front Palace. Six of the other *čhaofā* princes obtained *kromaluang* rank (including the king's eldest son), and two reached *kromakhun* status. The king's generosity towards his own family is clear from the fact that the more common princely honour of *kromamū'n* rank was not given to the immediate relatives but only to the husband of the king's half-sister. The princely appointments in general seem to differ from traditional norms in that so many obtained the rare title of *kromaluang*. It is quite possible that Rama I deliberately did this because Taksin had not given such high titles to members of his own family. It can be seen as yet another sign of reaction against the previous rule.

The nominations of the civilian state ministers included few surprises. The *kroms* Mahātthai, Kalāhom, Mū'ang, and Nā were all headed by close companions of Rama I whom he had learnt to trust during military campaigns. The remaining two senior executive posts, that of the headship of the *krom* Wang and the *krom* Phrakhlang, were filled by men who had already served with distinction under Taksin. The names and ranks of more than fifty other senior appointments were announced.

Those who had played an active role in the coup d'état that had put Rama I in power were amply rewarded. *Phrayā* Suriyā Aphai, the king's nephew, not only obtained the rank and title of *čhaofā* and *kromaluang*, and the honourable name of Anurakthēwēt, but also was awarded the right to be seen under a three-tiered umbrella with an inlaid mother-of-pearl handle, and he received two special ceremonial boats. A certain *nāi* Saeng, who had helped by sending a secret note,[7] rose to become *phrayā* Thipphakosa. *Nāi* Bunnāk, who had first planned the suppression of disorders in Thonburi, became governor of Ayutthaya with a rank of *čhaophrayā*. *Luang* Chana and *luang* Sura, who had assisted *nāi* Bunnāk, became officials with *phrayā* rank. *Luang* Sorawichit, who had first brought the news of the disturbances in Thonburi, also was raised to be *phrayā*.

Thus, for the second time in fifteen years, Siam's bureaucracy was dramatically changed. The promotion of large numbers of executive officers from the lower ranks, whose members would in normal times not have been able to penetrate the higher levels of administration, accounts to a certain extent for the continuous spirit of innovation which characterizes the reign of Rama I. Although the country was no longer ruled by a king who seemed to relish unorthodoxy, even under Rama I's apparent policy of narrowly applying the rules as of old there was ample scope for fundamental reform. A sign of the king's willingness to adopt judicious reform measures was the reorganization of the provincial administration. The *krom* Kalāhom, which had during late Ayutthayan times been deprived of the administration of the southern provinces, was given the jurisdiction over twenty *mū'angs*; the *krom* Thā, or Harbour Department (traditionally a part of the *krom* Phrakhlang) was assigned the responsibility for nine central and eastern *mū'angs*, and the remaining northern provinces[8] were given to the *krom* Mahātthai.

Also in 1782, the new king regulated some affairs of the Sangha. He reinstated to the highest ecclesiastical council three monks who had been stripped of their rank because they had refused to prostrate themselves before Taksin. These three monks were given special honours because they had proved steadfast, and on matters regarding the interpretation of Buddhist scriptures they were given ultimate authority. The two monks who had led Taksin to believe in his special status of *sodāban* were ordered to leave the Sangha altogether, for they were given to disingenuous flattery and their influence had caused grave dissension among the Buddhist monks. Rama I demoted monks who had been elevated by Taksin, he reversed Taksin's rule that certain monks receive money stipends, and he changed some of the monks' titles he considered unorthodox. One government official who had been accused of having stolen while he was a Buddhist monk, and who had been forcibly defrocked under Taksin's rule — presumably a victim of his drive to fight corruption — had his case re-examined and was officially declared free of guilt and invited to rejoin the Sangha.

The Uparāt apparently once had been wronged by one of the two monks who had influenced Taksin, and he therefore demanded that the man be tortured and executed. However, the king decided that his life should be spared, and then appointed him to a post in the *krom* Mahātthai. It seems therefore that the king went out of his way to demonstrate his power *vis-à-vis* his brother. Thus already at the beginning of the reign there are signs of hostility between the king and his younger brother, which later in the reign would result in serious confrontations. In 1783 there was an unsuccessful attempt upon the Uparāt's life, in which a personal friend of the king was implicated, and this possibly further cooled relations between the two brothers.[9] In the subsequent investigations, it transpired that two monks claiming supernatural powers had been among the instigators. They were reputed to be able to make themselves invisible and had thus gained access to the Front Palace. Probably the sight of Buddhist monks was so familiar that the conspirators had used this guise to gain easy access. Not long afterwards, the king issued a proclamation requiring every monk to obtain a certificate of identification bearing his name, his monastery of residence, the name of his perceptor, and the seal of the highest ecclesiastical official in his place of residence.[10]

## Administrative Measures

Just as in 1771, when people from the capital and the provinces came and built Thonburi's fortifications, so in 1783 and 1784 large numbers of workers descended upon Bangkok to dismantle the constructions at Thonburi and create a new city. An order to tattoo all members of the *phrai* class throughout the provinces may be seen as connected with this massive work. The amount of labour thus raised was still insufficient, and ten thousand Cambodians were brought in to dig a wide canal, almost three and a half kilometres in length, which would serve as a moat for the region where the Chao Phraya River did not provide protection. These Cambodians also dug another canal right through the city, which would, it was hoped by the king, become the place where people would enjoy going boating and would hold spontaneous singing contests during the wet season, just as had been the custom in Ayutthaya. When the Cambodians had finished digging the canals, thousands of Laotians were pressed into helping with the construction of walls and parapets all around the city. In 1783, the definitive buildings of the royal palace and of the

Uparāt were begun, together with many of the chief officials' residences. The new city was built speedily, so that the kingdom would have a safe and unassailable centre from which the country could be ruled even if foreign armies invaded. The organization of such large numbers of workers for such a protracted period must be regarded as a feat of historic dimensions. It illustrates the effectiveness of Rama I's administration, and the measure of control it exerted over the population. The strict military discipline which had been enforced during Taksin's reign and in which Rama I also firmly believed made it possible to bring together tens of thousands of people and to assign and supervise the completion of a great variety of tasks.

By 1784, Bangkok began to look like a capital city. An audience hall, a temple, a library, and various other buildings had been erected within the palace compound. The king developed a fixed routine in his palace. At daybreak he would present food to a group of Buddhist monks. Then he often took time to deal with the court finances before mounting the throne and ordering the royal bodyguard to let in members of his family and the Mahātlek pages. After they had had a chance to discuss matters, the audience was opened to include non-royal senior members of the administration. In the middle of the day and during the afternoon, the king relaxed. After an early evening meal he listened to a sermon in the audience hall, before giving his attention to the evening audience.[11] A steady stream of information from various government departments and the provinces thus found its way to the king and his senior advisers. Out of the discussions would arise further business, instructions might have to be written and sent to provincial officials. Matters of general importance often arose from the daily business, and from time to time the king would order the Department of Registration (*krom* Satsadi) to disseminate a royal edict.

These edicts serve as an indication of the range of matters brought to the king's notice. At the same time they show what type of information may have stirred the king into action and what image he wished to present to the wider public. Thus from 1782, the year of his succession, dates an edict prohibiting all civil servants from indulging in gambling. Any administrator caught at it could lose all his prerogatives, and both the gambler and the person responsible for organizing the game would receive thirty cudgel strokes.[12] Sometimes the preamble to an edict, which indicates what caused the king to proclaim a new ruling, is quite revealing, not only of the king's intentions but also of the state of the country. Thus it was declared in March 1784:

> Nowadays there are but few amongst the populace who are truthful and who make a living in a law-abiding manner. There are many people who are dishonest, who fear neither past, present nor future, who only think about accumulating wealth and spend it on their own families and wives. They intrigue with rogues in order to set up [slave-selling] rackets. They take children, wives, siblings, grandchildren and servants and, having sold them at one place, they take them to be sold at one or two other places. . . . Such shameless and fearless rogues are more numerous now than in the past, and they need to be punished.[13]

The king declared such rackets illegal and decreed that if a legal suit against a breach of the rule were proved,[14] all guilty would be flogged three times and for three days be publicly exposed. The slave was to be restored to the master to whom he originally belonged. The seller and guarantor would be forced to repay those they had cheated and also to perform hard labour for the government, attending elephants if they were males, and helping grind rice at the government storage units if they were female.

Sometimes matters were brought before the king which caused him to remind litigants of the proper procedures for solving disputes. The question of interpretation of the Buddhist texts, for example, which had led to a quarrel among senior monks, caused the king to proclaim: "Henceforth it is forbidden . . . to bring a case concerning monks quarreling over the Vinaya . . . before the king, asking for his generous consideration. This darkens things for Siamese monks. Let [cases] be presented to the Supreme Patriarch, the Phra Rachakhana, and the abbots."[15]

Not all administrative matters mentioned for 1784 were dominated by procedural considerations. Six years earlier, in 1778, when Rama I was Taksin's chief army commander and had invaded Laos, he had brought back to Thonburi the miraculous Buddha image known as Phra' Phuthapatimakon Kaewmorakot, or the Emerald Buddha.[16] When a beautiful temple had been constructed in the new royal palace, the king ordered the ceremonial transport of the Emerald Buddha to this new abode. This temple also became the place where members of the Mahātlek would assemble twice a year in order to drink the water of allegiance.

By 1784 Rama I's administration was proving effective, and it was in this year that the king made the somewhat surprising decision to exhume Taksin's remains and to provide the previous ruler with a proper cremation. Both the king and his Uparāt attended the final rites. It is not clear whether this was a sign of respect for Rama I's former chief, or whether it can to be seen merely as the outcome of growing confidence. Those who are inclined to ascribe less laudatory motives to the monarch might even suggest that it could have been intended to prevent the development of a cult at the monastery of Bangyiru'atai, where Taksin had been buried.

An equally surprising measure was the king's announcement that he intended to hold a formal second anointment. While it was not altogether unknown for a king who had been installed somewhat hurriedly to hold a proper ceremony some time later, this could hardly apply to Rama I, whose anointment had been prepared for several months and had lasted several days. Moreover, considerable time had passed and the king had no reason to feel seriously challenged.

It appears that the king identified his rule with the creation of a new capital and that he wished to underline the intimate relationship between his ascent to power and the creation of a new city by deciding to undergo a second formal anointment as part of the elaborate celebration of the completion of the transfer from Thonburi to Bangkok. With much pomp and ceremony, the king was bathed, dressed, anointed, and presented with regalia and the kingdom.[17] Not long afterwards, the new capital city was formally opened. Poor people received free meals at many points around the city, and along the new city wall "wish trees" were set up for three days from where daily eighty *baht* worth of coins were scattered around. The people were entertained with spectacular theatrical performances and other forms of amusement. A focus of the celebration was the Temple of the Emerald Buddha.

The Dynastic Chronicles place the official opening of the capital, together with the second anointment of the king, in the year 1147 Chula Era, the year of the snake, the seventh year of the decade, which corresponds with 1785–86 in the international calendar, and historians have hitherto accepted this date. However, these events are reported as having taken place before the large-scale Burmese invasion, and a senior government adviser who was demoted early in 1785 is reported to have played a role during the anointment.[18] Therefore it has been decided here to correct the year and place these events some time during 1784.

Having been reaffirmed in his position of king, and having celebrated the official opening of the new capital, Rama I was in a position to give his full attention to the crisis that developed in late 1784.

## The Great Invasions

At that time some disastrous flooding had occurred and much of the year's rice crop had been destroyed. The price of rice rose to eighty *baht* for a cartload, and many people suffered because of the scarcity of food. In accordance with time-honoured custom, the king ordered large amounts of rice from the royal granaries to be distributed to the people. At that time, King Bodawpaya of Burma was completing his annexation of Arakan and, encouraged by the wave of military successes which had gained him overlordship over Burma, he decided to launch a massive attack upon Siam. The Burmese opened up five different fronts simultaneously: one army was sent down to the far southern provinces; one moved southwards and then up toward Phetburi and Ratburi; the main army took the Three Pagoda Pass and headed straight for the capital; another army crossed the mountain ridges further north and entered Siam near the town of Tak, and a large number of troops were also deployed in the Chiang Mai region.

Upon the news of a general invasion, the Siamese troops

were divided into three forces: a southern flank led by the heads of the *krom* Mū'ang and the *krom* Wang, the main army under the Uparāt's command, aided by a supporting army under the chief of the *krom* Mahātthai, and a northern flank led by two of the king's nephews, assisted by the heads of the *krom* Kalāhom and the *krom* Phrakhlang.

Bodawpaya's army and that of Siam's Uparāt made contact just north of the town of Kanchanaburi. The first skirmishes between the advance units showed the Burmese in good fighting spirit, and the Siamese were at first worsted. Morale was low. When the Uparāt sent small forces into the jungle areas to harass the Burmese supply line, he learnt that his commanders did not carry out orders. Almost a decade of respite from Burmese invasions had resulted in a much slacker discipline, so the Uparāt arrested those commanders who were at fault and had them beheaded. From then on the Burmese supply routes were effectively attacked, and soon the Burmese camp suffered from lack of food.

Rama I anxiously awaited news from the front, and when no good news was forthcoming, he decided to rally the whole reserve army and went with his fleet up-river to Kanchanaburi. With great pomp and ceremony, trumpet-blasts, drum-beating, and victory flags unfurled, he entered his brother's encampment. The Uparāt was, however, extremely annoyed at receiving unsolicited aid. By that time the Burmese were starving, and the Uparāt felt he could soon risk a decisive battle. He urged the king to return to the capital and to be ready to render assistance where it was really needed. The king agreed to this and left the same evening.

Meanwhile, smallpox broke out among the beleaguered Burmese, and in due course the Uparāt attacked and captured the Burmese camp. Bodawpaya decided to pull back his army and was harassed all the way to Burmese territory. The victorious Siamese troops were immediately diverted southwards, and the troops of the northern flank under the chiefs of the Kalāhom and Phrakhlang departments suddenly ran into a major Burmese camp near Ratburi, an encampment that had escaped the notice of the southern Siamese army under the ministers of Mū'ang and Wang. The ensuing battle was a close contest, but finally the Siamese gained the upper hand and pursued the fleeing Burmese to the border.

When the Uparāt arrived by boat in Ratburi and heard that his troops had given battle while the original southern army had failed to make contact, he sent a message to Bangkok asking permission to execute the ministers of Mū'ang and Wang. These two were close friends of Rama I, and the request was refused; the king told his brother that he could punish them but that their lives had to be spared. The guilty generals were then stripped of titles and rank, and their heads were partly shaved before they were marched around the camp. Subordinate officers of that army were all flogged.

The Uparāt tnen returned to Bangkok to confer with his brother. It was decided that the king would march northwards, where troops were badly needed; the Uparāt took a fleet to the southernmost provinces, where the Burmese seemed to have wrought havoc. Most of the northern region had readily fallen to the Burmese troops. The area was only sparsely populated, and Chiang Mai city still lay in ruins as a result of the fighting in 1776. Only the city of Lampang, under the inspired leadership of *phrayā* Kawila, offered resistance and was under siege. The Siamese troops under the command of Rama I's nephews had stalled and prevaricated, and it was the imminent arrival of the king, who threatened to behead all the commanders who had failed to fight, that spurred them on. One Burmese encampment was taken, and upon reaching a second fortified position it was found that the enemy had begun a general retreat northwards. The Siamese then broke the siege of Lampang. Though Burmese troops still remained further north at the town of Chiang Saen, it was decided to recall the troops to Bangkok. Possibly the precarious food situation had a bearing upon this decision. Officers who had fought bravely were rewarded. The two army generals who had been punished by the Uparāt and stripped of their ranks and titles were accepted back in government service, the former *čhaophrayā* Thanmathikon receiving the rank of *phrayā* Sithanmathirāt and the former Yomarāt becoming *phrayā* Mahāthirāt.

Meanwhile the Uparāt had sailed to Chumphon and begun marching overland in the direction of the southernmost

Burmese army. When contact was made with the Burmese vanguard, the Siamese immediately engaged in a full-scale battle and were able to rout them, causing the withdrawal of all remaining enemy troops. The Uparāt restored peace and order, punished some government officials, and rewarded others. Having settled these affairs, the Uparāt decided of his own accord to extend Siamese influence. Rather than return to Bangkok, he sent messages to various independent sultans in the Malay Peninsula asking them to accept Siamese overlordship. The sultan of Pattani and various other Malay rulers resisted and were duly subjugated. When the king was informed of his brother's exploits, he expressed his pleasure but also ordered him to return. The Uparāt returned victoriously, taking weapons and prisoners as well as much rice from the south, because the food scarcity was not yet over. The king accepted the newly conquered provinces and incorporated them into the Bangkok administration, raising the fourth-class Siamese provincial town of Songkhla to a third-class one and relegating the Malay states to Songkhla rule.

After the war, the king reconsidered the corvée duties and issued a proclamation by which commoners belonging to the category of *phrai luang*, who had been obliged to work in the king's service six months each year, were now forced to work only four months in a year.[19] This relinquishing of the State's claim upon a large proportion of the population's time may be related to the rice shortage of the previous season. The king's advisers may have felt that the heavy demand upon people's time had aggravated a situation which developed into a serious lack of food. In addition, however, it is likely that the king was aware of the fact that people tried to attach themselves to powerful individuals and become *phrai som* in order to escape the onerous state duties;[20] therefore the lessening of the corvée burden was also an attempt to gain better control over the general populace.

At the beginning of 1786 a massive Burmese army crossed the mountains again, this time making certain that ample stacks of food were available along the route. The Siamese king and the Uparāt moved up with troops to meet the invaders, leaving *phrayā* Phonlathēp, head of the *krom* Nā, in command of Bangkok. The advance units of the Burmese and Siamese met and fought fiercely but inconclusively for three days, after which the Siamese suddenly poured in heavy reinforcements and broke through the Burmese lines. When the Burmese supreme commander found out that his vanguard had been beaten, he hastily withdrew, leaving many weapons behind.

It was this battle which finally convinced the Burmese of Siam's status as a truly independent country, a status temporarily lost through the fall of Ayutthaya. Siam pressed its temporary advantage to regain control in the Tavoy area, as well as pushing its influence further north to encompass the whole Chiang Mai area, which had long been under Burmese overlordship. Although the Burmese continued to be regarded as a traditional enemy who was only waiting for a moment of Siamese weakness to take advantage and invade the country, from 1786 onward the skirmishes between the two countries were largely the result of Siamese initiatives.

The position of Siam as an international power was affirmed in 1786 when the Chinese emperor officially acknowledged Rama I as the new king of Siam. Interestingly, the imperial edict, quoted by G.W. Skinner in his *Chinese Society in Thailand*, referred to Taksin as Rama I's father: "We see that the present head of their state has succeeded to his father's estates and aspirations. He has sent envoys to pay tribute and his sincerity is commendable."[21] Skinner surmises that the mention of Taksin is either the result of some translator substituting the term "son" for "son-in-law", or that Rama I deliberately sent a misleading allusion to a "proper succession". However, if *kromakhun* Anuraksongkhrām had been chosen to succeed Taksin, as has been suggested above, it could well have been during his short period of power that a tribute mission was sent, together with a letter indicating that the new king was a close relative of Taksin. The Chinese imperial court may have assumed the ruler who sent a mission in 1784 to be the same as the one of 1782. The remark that Rama I may have inherited his "father's" aspirations may have been sarcastically intended, for Rama I had boldly requested a thousand copper shields for his troops, apparently disregarding the fact that the export of copper was expressly banned by Chinese law.[22]

In November 1786 a Portuguese boat arrived at Bangkok with a message for the king, seemingly following on contacts which had been made at the beginning of his reign. Some extracts of Rama I's reply to the queen of Portugal reveal his preoccupation with the Burmese:

> Recently in a great battle I defeated six Burmese armies which had penetrated into my country and thereby gained a great deal of booty, weapons, horses and elephants. . . . With regard to Your offer of help, I have difficulties in the transportation of the troops and ammunition which I need. I am deeply gratefully for Your Majesty's offer . . . and would feel very much obliged to receive 3,000 muskets which, in accordance with my wishes, the governor of Goa could send to me during this year. I will make payment upon receiving Your Majesty's instructions about this.
>
> I am delighted with Your request to establish a factory in my country for the convenience of Your Majesty's Christian subjects. Your representative may search for a suitable location for it, and also for a church; moreover, priests may be sent.[23]

Rama I was quite amicably disposed towards Christians, at least sufficiently so to support the idea of establishing a church. This concession can be seen more as an indication of his awareness of the European eagerness to build churches than of his religious tolerance. He considered the Buddhist faith the best for his subjects, and when some years after the letter had been sent, one of his officials wanted to join the Catholic church, Rama I forced him to become a Buddhist monk and imprisoned his family.[24]

In the Chiang Mai region, some of the northern Tai leaders revolted against the Burmese in 1787 and captured the Burmese governor of Chiang Saen. Knowing that they needed powerful allies in order to survive such an open challenge, they handed the prisoner over to *phrayā* Kawila, the governor of Lampang, famed for his stubborn resistance against the massive Burmese army a few years before. *Phrayā* Kawila in his turn sent the prisoner to Bangkok. There the Burmese governor revealed his country's intent of re-establishing Chiang Mai as a fortified city. Upon hearing that the Burmese were invading again, the Uparāt quickly marched north,[25] where the presence of Siamese troops was sufficient to establish Kawila as the vassal ruler of the region with the task of rebuilding Chiang Mai. This was probably the time when the Siamese Uparāt married Kawila's younger sister, the beginning of an alliance between the two generals which would last until the Uparāt's death in 1803.

During the time that the Uparāt was in the north, Rama I decided to lead an army to Tavoy and invade Mon territory, which had long been under Burmese rule. He managed to reach the city, which had largely been abandoned by the defending troops, but fearing a ruse he decided to return without giving battle.

## A Strong Siam

A feeling of relative peace and security prevailed in the years between 1787 and 1793. The building of Bangkok continued, and fortifications were steadily improved. This was the time of the curious incident mentioned in the Dynastic Chronicles arising from the visit of a French ship to the capital city. The captain's younger brother was apparently a pugilist of some renown, and he sent a challenge to the Siamese by way of the *krom* Phrakhlang. The Uparāt took it upon himself to find a first-rate boxer. Prize money was set at fifty *chang*, or four thousand *baht*. The Siamese champion was prepared according to tradition and, in order to increase the man's chances, magical herbs were added to the oil with which he was rubbed.[26] In the fight, the Frenchman apparently tried to close in on the Siamese boxer, but the latter, in accordance with Siamese rules, kept out of his reach, occasionally darting forward to deliver a blow and jumping back whenever the Frenchman moved forwards. The Europeans were not familiar with this light-footed technique, and impatiently the captain leapt into the ring and seized the Siamese in order to force him to "give battle".[27] The Uparāt, outraged by this breach of the rules, jumped into the ring and with a well-placed kick brought the captain down. General pandemonium broke out; the two brothers were beaten up and had to be carried back to their ship. Probably realizing that the French brothers had been rather severely punished for their provocation, the king sent some medical practitioners to their ship to offer treatment. Once the brothers had sufficiently recovered, they left Bangkok.

The king's decision to organize the revision of the Siamese version of the Buddhist Tripitaka may also be seen as a sign of Siam's state of security. Considerable funds had already been channelled into the copying of the sacred texts on strips of palm leaves. Men were employed to transliterate Laotian and Mon versions into the characters traditionally reserved for sacred writing in Siam,[28] and these rewritten texts were kept in the library building of the main palace. However, when it was brought to the king's notice that the old texts contained many mistakes, he decided to organize a council of learned men to sift through all extant versions and write an authoritative set. In this Rama I was guided by examples of former great kings who had sponsored Buddhist councils. Two hundred and fifty men of learning worked for five months at the revision of the texts. When the work was completed in 1789, a great festival was organized to commemorate the new Tripitaka. However, during the fireworks the roof of the royal library caught fire and the new edition had to be carried out in order to escape the flames. The king decided that this was a sign that the existing library had not been suitable and ordered a more imposing edifice to be built.

The second Siamese attempt to establish control over the Mon regions was triggered off in 1792 by the decision of the Burmese authorities to replace their governor at Tavoy. This governor rose in rebellion and asked the Siamese to assist him, offering Rama I the overlordship of the whole Mon country, stretching from Mergui and Tenasserim up to Martaban and Rangoon. After ripe consideration, Rama I decided to send troops under the chief of the *krom* Mu'ang, *phrayā* Yomarāt, and later the Uparāt moved with another contingent to the border region in order to be able to render assistance if necessary. The Siamese troops were not warmly received, however, and the *phrayā* Yomarāt advised the destruction of the Tavoy fortifications, the taking of much of the population as slaves, and a withdrawal. The Uparāt agreed to this and ordered his soldiers to begin executing this plan. However, Rama I overruled his brother and ordered the uprooted people to be repatriated. Rama I personally took command and ordered troops from Cambodia and Laos to be moved up. He sent his brother southwards to cross the Isthmus of Kra and to send up a fleet so as to increase the Siamese mobility.

Burmese troops arrived before the Siamese had consolidated their position, however. The first skirmishes outside Tavoy early in 1793 turned out unfavourably for the Mon and Siamese, and when many Mon troops crossed over to the Burmese side, Rama I decided to beat a hasty retreat. During this retreat, the Siamese armies suffered heavy losses, which for the time being put an end to their ambitious plans.

## Legal Measures

The king again devoted his attention to internal matters of state. From 1794 dates the law regarding the management of gambling houses. This law[29] not only provides an example of the type of decisions Rama I made, and the detailed manner with which the legal provisions are set out, but also gives some insight into the social system and the values prevailing at that time.

In the preamble it is told how Taksin had forbidden gamblers to borrow any money. Rama I had at first let this innovative measure stand, for it was perceived that it was in the common interest of the people, preventing them from falling into debt. However, as a result fewer people were attracted to gambling houses, the holders of the royal patents were bidding less for the right of keeping these institutions, and the State revenue therefore diminished. Moreover, some licensed patent-holders, who had illegally furnished players with stakes, could not recoup from gamblers hiding behind Taksin's law.

In order to solve these problems, in 1784 the king decided to abolish Taksin's regulation and to allow gamblers to borrow again. However, in order to ensure that players would gamble within their means, licence-holders were given orders to lend up to a certain amount only, depending on the wealth of an individual. A list of examples was attached. If a gambler of *phrai*, or commoner, status had a family of two or three persons, possessed one or two pairs of buffaloes, four or five cartloads of rice, and twenty or thirty *rai* of rice-fields, up to two *chang*, or 160 *baht*, could be lent. If the commoner had no family and could not demonstrate that he had any possessions, he would be allowed to borrow 20 *baht*. In the case of women gamblers, the licence-holder was advised to scrutinize them carefully before allowing them to borrow. If a woman had rings on both hands, was well dressed, and was accompanied by three or four slaves who carried valuable betel-chewing equipment, one *chang* or 80 *baht* would be the maximum allowed. In general, the king allowed women to borrow half the amount permitted to men. Thus an unaccompanied single woman, not a slave (for slaves were strictly prohibited from gambling) and with no apparent wealth, could be lent a maximum of 10 *baht*.

The years 1794 and 1795 saw several other royal proclamations which provide some insight into the social fabric of the time. For example, it was brought to the king's attention that the law books gave no guidance on the problem of whether someone who had borrowed money upon the security of his person and had neglected to pay for more than ten years would have to pay the whole interest due to the money-lender. The king ruled in the affirmitive.[30] Another problem concerned the laws of inheritance. In a former proclamation, apparently in an attempt to prevent much litigation, it had been ruled that after fifteen days' duration, no suits could be entered.[31] The king amended this to read that cases dealing with criminal charges and impeachment could be entered at any time and that the fifteen days' limit ought only to be applied in cases of quarrels, insults, and fights connected with an inheritance.[32] In another instance the king proclaimed that he had had numerous cases of people who had borrowed money upon their own person although they were still bound to a previous money-lender, and that henceforth the judges who supervised the drawing up of such contracts ought to examine carefully the financial history of the persons involved.[33]

## The Two Brothers

Although Rama I appears to have been a capable administrator who managed his team of government civil
servants skilfully, he did not succeed in maintaining a cordial
relationship with his brother the Uparāt. The Uparāt was
strong, brave, quick of action, and a capable military leader.
In contrast, the king was much more cautious, intent upon
knowing exactly where his path led before he would step.
During the excursions to Mon territory, the king's overruling
of his senior officers' advice cost the Siamese dearly. The
Uparāt, on the other hand, could look back upon an
unblemished military record. As a result of his successful
campaigns, Siam had expanded its influence both southwards
and northwards. In this situation, feelings of rivalry between
Rama I's palace and that of the Uparāt could flourish. In
1796, during the preparations for a boat race where the king's
crew would vie with that of his brother, the latter secretly had
a team of rowers trained, in the hope that the king's crew
would be tricked in believing they would easily win. When the
ruse became known, the king cancelled the boat race. For two
months the Uparāt did not appear at the daily royal audience,
and when he finally did he asked for an increase of his annual
allowance, which had been one thousand *chang*, or eighty-
thousand *baht*.[34] The king answered that the provisions for
*biawat* were already a heavy burden, and suggested that his
brother trade in order to supplement his income. This caused
a break in the relations between the king and the heir-
apparent. The Front Palace armed itself, and preparations
for a battle were made. It was only through the intercession
of the two elder sisters that bloodshed was prevented and
peaceful relations restored.

The Uparāt may have shone as an inspiring military commander, but during the 1780s and 1790s Rama I left his own
mark upon the court as a patron of the arts, particularly in
the revival of a literary tradition. The chief creative artist on
the literary scene was not the king but one of his advisers, the
same *luang* Sorawichit who had warned the king about
Taksin's abdication and who had been promoted to *phrayā*
Phiphatkosa. Some time later he became *čhaophrayā*

Phrakhlang. The literary revival took the form of re-creating the "great classics' which had featured in earlier days. Examples of these works are *Unarut*, based on a story from the Mahābharata, and *Dalang* and *Inao*, which were derived from the Javanese Pantji cycle. *Čhaophrayā* Phrakhlang translated a history of the Mon struggle against the Burmese, an apt topic considering the campaigns between 1791 and 1793, and also *Sām Kok*, a Chinese historical novel. Another Chinese historical novel, *Sai Han*, is attributed to the king's newphew, *čhaofā* Anurakthēwēt, who had by then been promoted to *kromphra'* rank. Yet another courtier, *phrayā* Thammapurohit, translated the Sinhalese chronicle *Mahāvangsa*. Probably the best-known work of foreign derivation in Siamese literature is the *Rāmāyana*. The wide range of sources translated should be seen as an inheritance of the broad interests of the Ayutthayan court rather than as a reflection of Bangkok's international contacts. Rama I intended not only to build a new Ayutthaya, inspired in architecture and layout by the old city, but also to stimulate a similar cultural scene. At the same time, the literary works were not mere faithful imitations; there was scope for personal poetic styles which are recognizably late eighteenth century.[35]

Not all the literature of the early Bangkok times was so international in taste. Some of it was typically Siamese, such as a poem in the *nirāt* style, attributed to Rama I himself, and dated 1786, just after the massive Burmese invasion had been repelled. Another typical Siamese genre was the royal chronicle, of which an Ayutthayan version was brought up to date by one of the court officials. This work was completed in 1796.

Meanwhile, the Burmese tried several times to bring Chiang Mai under their control, but each time Bangkok's Uparāt came to the rescue. *Phrayā* Kawila, safe under Siamese protection, even began conquering traditional Shan towns and moving the population towards regions more firmly under his control. These incursions provoked the Burmese ruler Bodawpaya into a large-scale attack upon Chiang Mai in 1802. Again the Uparāt moved up north with both his personal troops and some from the king's force. The fact that the king's own troops did not fight as bravely as those under the Uparāt's own command may have rekindled the dormant feelings of rivalry between the two brothers. During the campaign of 1802 the Uparāt became ill, but it has been recorded that already before his illness[36] he had been considering a palace revolution, encouraging his sons Lamduan and Inthapat secretly to prepare themselves for taking over the government. It is quite possible that he had also taken Kawila into his confidence.[37]

The Uparāt did not recover from his disease; gradually he became more and more ill, and the realization that his powers were waning and that his early demise would weaken the chances of his party taking power seemed to drive him to despair. At one moment he threatened to take his own life, and Lamduan had to wrest a sword from his father's hands. The Uparāt lamented that he personally had won the treasures which surrounded him and that upon his death these would revert to the descendants of his brother, rather than to his own offspring. This incited them to seize power. The Uparāt's chief adviser, a certain Thong-In, joined the conspirators. The preparation for the coup d'état included the testing of some magical means by which the plotters reputedly could become invulnerable. Unfortunately for the Uparāt's party, the test failed, several members died, and these had to be secretly buried in Lamduang's compound. Rumours reached the king's palace around the time when the Uparāt died, and Rama I sent some agents to infiltrate the ranks of the intriguers. Before long the whole plot was known to the king, the group was arrested and the guilty were executed.

With the death of the king's brother at the age of sixty, the last period of Rama I's long reign begins. Two features of this period deserve special attention, namely the codification of Siamese law and the proliferation of state ritual.

## The Legal Code

With respect to legal matters, Rama I had always shown a keen interest in the meticulous drawing up of decrees. He appears to have taken his judiciary function quite seriously. His legal advisers based themselves upon Ayutthayan laws, which were quite inadequately documented, and this often led to difficulties. The first effort to bring a variety of legal sources together and establish a "pure" set of rules concerned the laws of appeal. These were studied by a court official, *luang* Thammasāt, who in 1801 produced a summary in verse, the so-called *Kotmāi Lilit*.[38] In 1804, however, when the king's legal advisers brought a certain inconsistency in other texts to his notice, Rama I ordered a complete overhaul of all Siamese laws. A committee of eleven went through all the court documents on legal matters, arranged them in sections, and discussed various versions. Rama I himself checked and revised the purged set of laws and ordered copies to be made. The new body of laws received the seals of the *krom* Mahātthai, *krom* Kalāhom and *krom* Phrakhlang, and have therefore became known as the *Kotmāi Trā Sām Duang,* or Laws of the Three Seals.[39] It is quite possible that the old documents upon which the Laws of the Three Seals were based were then deliberately discarded so as to underline the authority of the new body of laws.[40]

## State Ritual

The second feature of Rama I's later years is the great stress laid on ceremonial. Every royal celebration was the occasion for a massive display of pomp and ceremony. Between 1802 and 1809 there were no less than twenty-seven royal tonsure ceremonies. In addition, this is the period during which a large number of the king's trusted relatives and advisers died, including *kromaluang* Thēpharirak, and the king's half-brother *kromaluang* Čhakčhētsadā. These deaths in the royal family led to elaborate cremation rituals. When one of the king's daughters miraculously escaped from drowning, she was raised in rank and title and for three days the court held a festival in her honour. In 1806, three years after the death of the previous Uparāt,[41] the king's eldest son, who was then thirty-two years old, was formally anointed and became the new chief of the Front Palace. The celebrations lasted many days. Rama I once organized a great elephant procession, in which the senior members of court marched along carrying imitation weaponry.[42] Members of the court were encouraged to have ceremonial boats constructed, and they were allowed to use their imagination regarding the boat's ornamentation, taking care not to outshine the king's barge. Buddhist ceremonies were good occasions for a display of the courtly splendour, and both the elaborate Kathin ceremony and the great Mahāchāt preachings were held during the first reign.[43]

The proliferation of court ritual continued unabatedly throughout the first reign. This feature cannot be seen simply as Rama I's reaction against King Taksin's lack of formality, because during the later years of Rama I's life there was no longer any reason to fear a comparison between his rule and that of his predecessor. Neither is this preoccupation with ceremonial just a matter of legitimation of a new rule; the only direct threat to the throne now came from within the ruling family.

Three further considerations seem necessary to appreciate this proliferation of ritual. In the first place it must be realized that Rama I had created a "new Ayutthaya", resplendent with palaces and temples. By organizing a multitude of court ceremonies, the king may have been motivated by the wish to make the new city come to life. Secondly, the king was a devout Buddhist of mature age, and for that reason it is likely that he was interested in playing a key role in a variety of rituals which would increase his personal store of good *karma*, the merit of which would ensure him a fortunate rebirth. When, for example, in 1809 the king invited two thousand monks to come and chant for three days at the Temple of the Emerald Buddha, half of these monks were fed from money provided by the king, and the responsibility of the other half was divided among the rest of the court. The resources poured into the building, upkeep, and improvement of the temples brought immense merit to the king. Most Siamese would have heartily agreed with the king's spending on the Sangha, because the merit channelled from state funds would increase the chances of a happy, prosperous Siam, whose enemies would remain powerless. The third consideration regarding the manifold state rituals concerns Rama I's personality. Although there are only few accounts that allow a judgement on this matter to be made, those there are agree that throughout his rule Rama I never relaxed protocol. For example, when he was more than seventy years old, as the vassal-king of Cambodia went to take his leave and entered the audience hall without the customary formal announcement, the Siamese king took offence, and "King Phra Uthairacha was greatly humiliated in front of the officials".[44]

King Rama I died in 1809, just over twenty-seven years after he had seized the throne. It had been a remarkable period in which the Siamese had successfully withstood a large-scale invasion. The country's prestige had risen considerably, and its sphere of influence had greatly expanded. The great project of building a new capital city had progressed throughout the reign, and this had given a stimulus to artists and craftsmen. New initiatives found scope, and as the city took shape it began to diverge from the capital as Rama I had known it during his youth. The new times and novel circumstances made for considerable reform. The corvée duties had been lessened, and the legal position of various social classes had been greatly simplified. There was also greater internal security. For most people, life in Siam under Rama I was fundamentally different from life as it must have been in Ayutthaya.

## Notes

1. Prince Dhani Nivat, "The Age of King Rama I of the Chakri Dynasty", *JSS* 46, pt 1 (1958): 51.
2. The name Phra' Phuthayọtfā Čhulalōk is the name of the king's statue in the royal pantheon, and this name has been used posthumously to refer to the king. The designation Rama I, which is widely used in later Western sources, was invented by King Wachirāwut, 1910–25. During Rama I's lifetime, he was simply known as "the king", and referred to by one of his many titles.
3. For details on the Siamese "city pillar", see B.J. Terwiel, "The Origin and Meaning of the Thai 'City Pillar' ", *JSS* 66, pt 2 (1978): 159-71.
4. Most historical sources place the assumption of the throne in June, but the Thiphākọrawong chronicle leaves little doubt about the real date. Possibly the first person to transpose the Siamese date into the Western Calendar overlooked the fact that 1782 was a year with two eighth lunar months, and that the coronation took place in the repeated lunar month.

5. Apparently the old name of a village, Bān Kǫk.
6. One of Rama I's daughters had been accepted in Taksin's court and had given birth to a son. This daughter had died before Rama I's accession, but the grandchild, Taksin's son, was recognized as *čhaofā* Supantuwong (see Chula Chakrabongse, *Lords of Life*, p. 82).
7. Thadeus and Chadin Flood, ed., *The Dynastic Chronicles Bangkok Era, the First Reign*, Čhaophrayā Thiphākǫrawong edition, vol. 1 (hereafter *DC First R*), p. 10. This could be taken as another indication supporting the hypothesis that the coup was not altogether improvised.
8. Including one central province, that of Chachoengsao.
9. Of the senior conspirator, *phrayā* Aphaironnarit, it is said in a different context that he had served the present king in many military campaigns, that he had fought gallantly, and that he was an honest man. *DC First R*, p. 10.
10. C.J. Reynolds, "The Buddhist Monkhood in Nineteenth Century Thailand," pp. 42-43.
11. *DC First R*, pp. 305-7.
12. K. Wenk, *The Restoration of Thailand under Rama I, 1782-1809*, p. 32.
13. "Phrarātchakamnot Mai", no. 39, *KTSD* 5: 350-52.
14. The careful statement that guilt had to be proved might have been inspired by a wish to show the difference from Taksin, who had not shown much regard for legal niceties.
15. Reynolds, *The Buddhist Monkhood*, pp. 45-46.
16. For the history of the Emerald Buddha, see C. Notton, trans., *The Chronicle of the Emerald Buddha*.
17. For details, see *DC First R*, pp. 74-84.
18. This was *čhaophrayā* Thanmathikon, the head of the *krom* Wang, who was punished for neglect of duty during the Burmese invasion.
19. See "Phrarātchakamnot Mai", no. 12, *KTSD* 5: 239.
20. This is quite clear in "Phrarātchakamnot Mai", no. 7, dated 1789. The king also tried to increase the number of *phrai luang* by offering a reward to people who caught unmarked commoners and brought them to be tattooed. A person convicted of maliciously plotting to subvert the law on this point could be sentenced to death (see "Phrarātchakamnot Mai", no. 17, dated 1787).
21. G.W. Skinner, *Chinese Society in Thailand*, p. 24.
22. Ibid.
23. Wenk, *The Restoration*, p. 120.
24. A Pallegoix, *Description du royaume Thai ou Siam*, vol. 2, pp. 278-79.
25. Wenk, following the Phongsāwadān Yōnok, mentions a Burmese invasion in some particulars not unlike that which has been described as part of the massive attacks of 1784-85 (see *The Restoration*, pp. 66-68).
26. The rubbing of oil is standard practice in Thai boxing; see H. Stockmann, *Muay-Thai: The Art of Siamese Un-armed Combat*, p. 32.
27. I disagree with Wenk's rendering of this story, in which he describes the slipperiness of the oil being the cause of the European's irritation. The account in *DC First R* does not warrant that interpretation.
28. During the Ayutthaya period, there was a strong Cambodian influence, and formal documents were often written in Cambodian characters, to which Siamese tone-markers could be added. The Cambodian script was again adopted as the most formal manner of writing in the time of Rama I, and the Tripitaka was rendered completely in Cambodian characters.
29. "Phrarātchakamnot Mai", no. 26, *KTSD* 5: 284-92.
30. "Phrarātchakamnot Mai", no. 28, *KTSD* 5: 295-97.
31. The simplicity and directness of the former proclamation has the flavour of

Taksin's ruling, but there is no indication in the law which guides us in the establishment of the age of the former rule.

32. "Phrarātchakamnot Mai", no. 28, *KTSD* 5: 297-99.
33. "Phrarātchakamnot Mai", no. 30, *KTSD* 5: 303-5.
34. This is double the amount the Uparāt received in late Ayutthayan times.
35. Much of the information in this paragraph is based upon Prince Dhani Nivat's article "The Reconstruction of Rama I of the Chakri Dynasty", *JSS* 43, pt 1 (1955): 21-48.
36. *DC First R*, p. 266.
37. This is a conjecture, based mainly upon the cordial relations existing between the two men and Kawila's sudden wish to break off relations with Siam when he heard of the Uparāt's death and the execution of members of his family.
38. I have used the version as published by *kromaluang* Rātchaburīdirēkru't, *Kotmāi Lem 1*, pp. 681-705. It is interesting to note the conversion of *bia*, or cowry shells, into silver. During Ayutthayan times, 6,400 *bia* had been equivalent to one *baht*. However, after the fall of Ayutthaya the shells had been rare and their value increased relative to the *baht*. Foreign merchants were quick to exploit this situation and brought in many shells, so many that the value dropped even below that of Ayutthayan times. In the *Kotmāi Lilit*, it appears to have been as low as 8,000 *bia* to one *baht*.
39. There have been various editions; for this study, two versions have been consulted: the Khurusapha edition of 1963 and the version in *Kotmāi Lem 1*, mentioned in note 38.
40. Dhani Nivat "The Reconstruction of Rama I", p. 28.
41. I follow Wenk, *The Restoration*, p. 15, in accepting this year as the one of the appointment of a new Uparāt.
42. *DC First R*, p. 302.
43. For details, see G.E. Gerini, *A Retrospective View and Account of the Origin of the Thet Mahā Ch'at Ceremony*.
44. *DC First R*, p. 307.

# 4

# *The Second Reign:*
# *Peace and Trade*

After Rama I's death, the senior court officials and princes decided to recognize the Uparāt as the person to be anointed king. This decision was not unanimously supported, however, and a few days later a plot against the succession was discovered. The other candidate, the son of Taksin and Rama I's daughter, had proved himself to be a very able prince.[1] He had plotted with the minister of the *krom* Nā, *čhaophrayā* Phonlathēp, and others to take power, but this was revealed in an anonymous letter and all the conspirators were executed, more than forty persons in all, including the prince's male offspring.[2] The prince's wealth, palace, servants and rice were given to the eldest son of the new king-elect.

The day after the execution, the shortened version oi royal anointment began, and when the complex ceremonies had been performed, the customary swearing-in of members of the court and government officers took place. There was no immediate announcement of a list of royal appointments comparable to that after Rama I took office, because the same family remained in power and most experienced officials retained their positions. The Front Palace was given to the new king's only full brother, *kromaluang* Sēnānurak,[3] who now became Uparāt. The few senior administrative appointments represented minor changes, mainly a shifting around of men who already held positions of great responsibility. Thus the head of the *krom* Phrakhlang became head of the *krom* Mahātthai, a post that had been vacant, and a personal attendant of the previous king of *phrayā* rank took the position as head of the *krom* Phrakhlang. The chief of the *krom* Mu'ang was moved to become *čhaophrayā* and head of the Kalāhom, and the *phrayā* who had discovered the planned coup d'état was rewarded with the *krom* Mū'ang.⁴

The first decree of the new king was an order to grant an amnesty to certain types of prisoners and to clear the courts of pending litigation matters. The court costs for both defendants and accusing parties were borne by the Crown.

Another early decision was the ordering of a complete census of manpower, which involved checking the numbers of people for whom each *nāi* was responsible, the tattooing of appropriate symbols on the wrists of subjects who had not yet been tattooed or who had changed status, and the making of a new written record. In the decree, the king decided on the following measures:⁵

1.  The settling of all disputes regarding people's registered status, during the general registration drive.

2.  The general announcement to reach all the run-away *phrai*, prisoners-of-war, and debt-slaves who were in hiding, to return to their old patrons. If they gave themselves up they would not be punished. If the *phrai luang* and redeemable slaves felt unable to return to their old patrons, on this one occasion they could choose themselves a new patron. However, once they had chosen, they could not use this right again. Moreover, this right was only given to *phrai* in Bangkok and its immediate surroundings; provincial people had to remain in their provinces.⁶

3.  The forceful arrest and imprisonment of those run-away people who did not give themselves up voluntarily.

4.  The tattooing of all people according to their patrons, and the punishment of all those who connived to circumvent the registration.

5. The lowering of the period of corvée for *phrai luang* in the provinces to one month of service in every four months, releasing them to work for themselves the other three months.

The offer to run-away, unregistered people to select their own patron was without precedent. It indicates the existence of a serious problem regarding the registration of *phrai*. So many people had been able to escape the rules and regulations that a massive drive was warranted, and in order to prevent the overfilling of prisons and the courts from having to deal with too many cases, the king offered this novel incentive. It is not known, however, how successful the 1810 decree was in establishing a better record of the population.

The king did not grant the right to choose a new patron to provincial *phrai*, because he wanted to prevent further population movement from the provinces to the city. For the same reason, the corvée burden in the provinces was lowered. The shortage of people in the provinces was most striking in the northern regions, which had been severely affected by the wars with Burma. Though the custom of taking a census of the work force may be regarded as customary at the beginning of a reign, the specific instructions refer to the circumstances of that time; they indicate problems of administration pertaining to the whole country.

Following the census of the work force in 1810, during the next year the king ordered a survey of the arable land. The instructions to the provincial governors have been preserved, and these provide further interesting information regarding the administration of Siam at the beginning of the Second Reign. In the document,[7] the governors were told that the main aim of this impending land survey was to decide which land was pledged to the Buddhist church and which belonged to the people. All lands were to be measured and changes in land use or ownership had to be reported to the Yokrabat and the Sēnā,[8] and applications had to be made at the *krom* Nā for certificates of ownership.

Already during Ayutthaya times there must have been surveys of the agricultural regions in order to facilitate the enforcement of the tax on certain trees and the collection of a proportion of the rice crop for transportation to the king's warehouses.[9] Undoubtedly it was the *krom* Nā, the Department of Lands, under the guidance of the *phrayā* Phonlathēp, which supervised the collection of rice tax, the opening up of new lands, and the mediation in boundary disputes. Taksin and Rama I must have perpetuated the system, because the court consumed large amounts of rice, and the *krom* Nā must have maintained its departmental activities. Yet the document of 1811 is the earliest that reveals the details of one such survey. Since no documentation regarding the land and tree surveys before this date have been found, it is impossible to determine with certainty in which aspects the proclamation of Rama II differs from previous ones.

The region surveyed in 1811 covered the whole central plains area and some of its immediate surroundings. The size of the area covered was surprisingly large. It reflected, at least from the *krom* Nā's point of view, the region that could be administered directly from Bangkok. Towards the south, this direct administration included Phetburi; further south were regions that were administered through the Kalāhom. Towards the east, the territories of Chanthaburi and Trat were not included: these came under the jurisdiction of the *krom* Thā (part of the *krom* Phrakhlang).[10] If the *krom* Nā's responsibilities reflect central control, eastern territories directly controlled by the capital compared with the situation fifty years earlier. It is to the north that the greatest changes seem to have taken place. During the 1810 survey the whole area of Sukhothai and Sawangkhaburi was included, as far north as the borders of the states of Phrae and Lampang. During late-Ayutthayan times, the *mū'angs* of Kamphaeng Phet, Phitsanulok, Phichai, and Phetchabun were governed through appointed governors and a few representatives of the central power, and it is unlikely that they would have been included in a direct survey from the capital. The inclusion of the northern region probably reflects Siam's expansion to the north. Since the reign of Rama I, the area covered by the *mū'angs* of Phrae, Nan, Lampang, Lamphun, Chiang Mai, and Chiang Rai had become the kingdom's northern protective belt. A second reason for the inclusion of such a large northern area in the survey could be the fact that the region had been severely depopulated and was thus relatively easy to cover.

King Rama II appointed eight committees to supervise the land survey, two of them headed by a man of *phrayā* rank, with the remaining six groups under less exalted officials. Each of the committees contained representatives from the departments of Mahātthai, Kalāhom, Nā, and Mahātlek and an officer of the Wang Nā. This could have been a standard procedure followed to minimize risks of collusion and bribery. After all, each committee was empowered to issue title deeds, so that its officials were likely to be approached by parties wishing to influence their decisions.

After the list of the committee members' names, a series of specific instructions follow. These are quite varied, ranging from matters concerning methods of measuring to describing the rate of taxation. Since the document has hitherto received little publicity, and since it is quite revealing regarding domestic situations in Siam at the beginning of the nineteenth century, the medley of clauses will be here summarily translated and annotated.

> *a.* When a title deed is issued, the document must contain the name of the owner, his place of domicile, and a description of the type and size of the fields. The leader of the measuring party and the representative of the *krom* Nā must press their seals on the document in each other's presence, and each page must be marked on the back.

*Comment:* Officials of more than one department had to be involved in order to increase the chance of creating an accurate and truthful picture of land holding. After all, such documents form the basis of one of the chief sources of revenue.

> *b.* If landowners wish to possess only a small area of land and they feel that the officers of the committee have issued too much in their name, they have three days in which they can rectify this.

*Comment*: This clause is indicative of a situation of a good supply of arable land and a relative scarcity of people to work it. It confirms the picture obtained from the general census instructions regarding the provinces.

*c.* Before measuring takes place, the customary ceremonies ought to occur, including an offering to the spirits of the field and the measuring rope ritual. The prices for ritual objects and administration costs are determined: one *baht* for pulling the ritual rope, three-quarters of a *baht* for white cloth, one quarter for an umbrella, half a *baht* for a water container, one-eighth for a mat, one-eighth for blessing the water, and one-and-a-half *baht* as the cost for obtaining the fully sealed title deed for land [up to] one hundred *rai*. The oath-taking ceremony by the group of officials involved in the measuring must be done every Buddhist prayer day, four times each lunar month in the precinct of a monastery. Persons who become tired while pulling and wish to hand over their place at the rope to somebody else ought to finish their oath before handing over.

*Comment*: The king's instructions regarding religious ceremonies were basically intended to increase the chance of obtaining honest and trustworthy records. The various ceremonies appear to be of a kind related to judiciary rituals, such as the ordeals by fire and water and the regular oath of allegiance to the king. Thus far I have not come across a more detailed description of this rope-pulling ritual.

*d.* The type of tax called *khāwčhatsū'* ought not to be levied upon upland farms which are mentioned in title deeds.

*Comment*: The tax *khāwčhatsū'* was, as will be shown in the following paragraphs, usually two buckets (40 litres) of rice per *rai*, and was not levied in all places.

*e.* If there are people with valid title deeds on certain lands and other people take that land [against the owner's wishes], let the committee and the *Sēnā* drive the squatters away.

*f.* In the regions of Bangkok, Ayutthaya, Angthong, Suphanburi, Nakhon Chaisi, Samlok, Nonthaburi, and Sakhon-buri, the tax is forty litres of rice per *rai* as tax *khāwkhā*, and another forty litres as tax *khāwčhatsū'*, to be brought to the Bangkok granaries. In the region of Chainat, Uthai Thani, *mū'ang* San, *mū'ang* Sing, *mū'ang* In, *mū'ang* Phrom, Manoram and Lopburi, the tax is forty litres per *rai*, tax *khāwkhā*, also to be taken to the Bangkok granaries. In the regions of Prachin-buri, Nakhon Nayok, Chachoengsao, and Chonburi, the tax is forty litres *khāwkhā* and forty litres *khāwčhatsū'*, to be put in the granary of Prachinburi. At Saraburi, Phetburi, and Samut Prakan, the same taxation is imposed and the grain is to be put in the municipal granaries. At Nakhon Sawan there had been a shortage of rice in the granary, so during the year 1810/11, the tax *khāwkhā* is set at forty litres per *rai*. Ratburi, Kanchanaburi and Kamphaeng Phet farmers are charged forty litres *khāwkhā* per *rai* for the town granaries. In Phetchabun, Tharong, Buacham, Chaibadan, Khamphran, Sukhothai, Phichai, Sawankhalok, Phichit, and Phitsanulok, the tax is one-fourth of a *baht* per *rai*, and the amounts, together with details of land holdings, have to be forwarded to Bangkok.

*Comment*: This is probably the earliest detailed record of land taxation in Siamese history. Though there must have been similar types of instructions before Rama II's time, these have not been preserved. It shows the areas that delivered rice directly to Bangkok — Nakhon Sawan this particular year being exempted — and where subsidiary government storage centres were kept. These subsidiary centres probably were kept as a defence measure so that armies could draw upon them. There was one such secondary storage place in the east, at Prachinburi, one near Bangkok, at Samut Prakan, and five in the west. This reflects the fact that the main external threat to the country was still felt to be Burma. The actual taxation amounts varied; close to the capital they were highest, and further away they were lower. This was in accordance with the king's policy to make the outer regions attractive for farmers. The northern belt, which was particularly affected by the wars and depopulation, was taxed not in rice but in silver. Since the king was following a policy of attracting farmers to the region, the taxation of these northern provinces must have been equal to that of other outer provinces, such as Kamphaeng Phet and Ratburi, or even less. Therefore we may draw the conclusion that in 1811 a coin of one-fourth of one *baht* would buy not more than forty litres of unhusked rice, or possibly a little less. This is confirmed in the calculations made eleven years later, when the value of that amount of rice is almost equal to one-fourth of a *baht*.[11]

    *g.* If the measuring rope is lying on the field during measuring, and someone accidently steps over it, let that person perform a *tham khwan* ceremony with balls of puffed rice and sugar, flowers, and candle for the measuring rope. The government officer is strictly forbidden to ask for restitution in money.

*Comment*: Siamese are taught from a very early age not to step over worthy objects, and the measuring rope must be considered important. When such a rope is accidently stepped over, its *khwan*, or "invisible vital element", may escape; hence the appropriateness of holding a *tham khwan* ceremony.[12] The king's instruction seems to be a reaction upon hearing that such practices may have been provoked in the past and his wish to put a stop to this manner of raising money from the general populace.

> *h*. The fields of Laotian, Cambodian, Burmese, Manipurian,[13] and Mon war slaves who have been assigned lands of government officials, mainly in the districts of Bangkok, Nonburi, Samkhok, Ayutthaya, and Saraburi, and who have been assigned buffaloes and oxen need to be measured and title deeds must be issued. Even when people rent or borrow fields, both *khāwkhā* and *khāwčhatsū'* tax need to be paid.

*Comment*: This ordinance appears intended to close a possible tax loophole. The fact that a piece of land was worked upon by a war slave or by someone who borrowed the land did not constitute a case for exemption from the two types of tax. Incidentally, the distribution of war captives seems to be limited to the heartlands of the kingdom, probably the result of a deliberate policy which would make it difficult for such slaves to escape and flee back to their country of origin.

> *i*. If there are disputes regarding such (borrowed) fields, the leader of the government measuring party should decide according to the laws, but he is not allowed to accept payment for this adjudication.
> *j*. If people have large stretches of land upon their title deeds, but it is found that these are not cultivated, they must be given to the *krom* Nā official and the capital city be notified.
> *k*. If one works upon the fields on an official ceremonial day, the *krom* Nā official should hand the fields over to others.
> *l*. Hoarding land and letting it lie fallow is absolutely forbidden.

*Comment*: At first sight, the latter three regulations may throw some doubt upon the question whether there was private ownership of lands in Siam. Nominally all the kingdom belonged to the king. However, there can be little doubt about the general acceptance of the principle of private ownership. Land could be owned, sold, donated, and inherited. Only on the death of an official who had a *saktinā* of more than 400 would the king receive one-fourth of the estate. People of lower status passed all their possessions on to their relatives. The three stipulations mentioned here were intended to encourage land to be worked upon and to discourage any circumstance that would lead to arable land lying fallow.

In the document's concluding paragraph officials are told to submit their census data to the capital, and warned that conniving to provide false information was reprehensible and would be punished under the law.

Both the decree on the population census and the one on the land survey reveal at least partially the complex system of administration that existed in the early nineteenth century. In addition, they show the direction of the new king's thought. He apparently had been convinced of the need to make regulations that would encourage the repopulation of some provinces and the resumption of lands. At the same time, he saw that the ordinary people had to be protected against rapacious civil servants.

A series of royal appointments elevating the new king's close relatives to higher ranks was announced only in early 1814, after Rama II had been a considerable time in office.[14] We cannot be sure what the King's motivation was in waiting so long before creating a number of new princes of *kromamū'n* rank, but it is quite possible that the discovery and subsequent execution of a contender for the throne within the family may have delayed such appointments. Rama I's queen, now the mother of a king, was given the title of *kromsomdet* Amarintharāmāt. Seven of the king's half-brothers, four of his sons, and two nephews were all given *kromamū'n* ranks and new names, but other relatives were also among those promoted. Altogether twenty-two persons were elevated to *krom* rank. Hitherto Rama II had apparently given little attention to honouring his own family. A notable exception was the ceremonial bathing ritual of the eldest son of his most senior wife, held in 1812 with proper pomp and ceremony.[15] This son had been born before Rama II's accession to the throne, in 1804, and had received the name *čhaofā* Mongkut. The ritual bath can be seen as a token of the king's acceptance of the young prince as a promising youngster of the highest rank. In 1816 this was further underlined by the very elaborate manner in which the cutting of Mongkut's topknot took place.[16]

In 1813 the king ordered a large party of Laotians to come and construct a sluice at the lower end of the Bāngkaew Canal, because the water had been running off too fast and the canal had fallen dry, an intolerable situation in a country where rivers and canals form the chief communication channels.[17] The next year the king ordered a new fortification to be built along the stretch of river between the capital and the sea.[18]

The years 1815, 1816, and 1817 were probably long remembered in Siam as the years during which some shocking incidents occurred in the court. First *phra'* Inthra Aphai, one of Taksin's sons, was discovered to have been engaged in a love affair in which three of the king's women were compromised. According to the law, all four were executed. Then the Uparāt, the king's full brother, became ill and died, aged thirty-seven. Not long afterwards the Sangha was shaken by a scandal. The Buddhist monk who had been chosen to become patriarch of the Siamese Buddhist church was accused of homosexual activities. A committee of three princes of *kromamū'n* rank investigated the matter, found the man guilty, and sent him to gaol. Unfortunately this did not conclude the matter, for *kromamū'n* Sīsurēn, one of the king's half-brothers and a friend of the imprisoned man, wrote anonymously a poem on the case in which the king himself was slandered. Another committee of inquiry investigated the poem, and on grounds of style it was decided that prince Sīsurēn must have been the author. During interrogation the prince died. However, the case was further investigated by the king's eldest son, *kromamū'n* Čhētsadābodin, and eleven courtiers who had been involved in the production and distribution of the poem were condemned to death.[19]

The year 1817 also saw the beginning of a new state festival, namely the commemoration of the Buddha's birthday, enlightment and passing into nirvana, coinciding with the full moon of the Siamese sixth lunar month. This festival was presided over by the new patriarch.[20] The Dynastic Chronicles, Second Reign, also report a case of self-immolation for religious reasons. A certain *nāi* Nok, having done many good deeds during his life, wished to proceed to the state of nirvana, and thus, after having prepared himself, he set fire to himself under the sacred fig-tree in front of the old temple of Wat Chaeng. Many people came to pay respect to the corpse.[21]

The first half of Rama II's reign was relatively quiet. Though the king had to be on guard against Burmese hostilities, though all was not quiet in the Laotian principalities, though there were signs of Vietnamese expansion into areas that had come under Siamese control during the First Reign, and though in the far south the Siamese overlordship of Kedah was being undermined, none of these troubles developed into the type of provocation that caused the king to order firm measures to be taken.

During the early part of Rama II's reign also, Siam's relationships with the outside world caused little concern. China was still regarded as the greatest power on earth, and the trade with China dominated foreign relations. As often as possible the king would send a tribute mission to the Chinese court, and consequently obtained lucrative trade concessions. Also he sent an ecclesiastical mission to Sri Lanka, in the hope of fostering closer relations which would benefit Theravāda Buddhism. The mission returned and reported favourably on their adventures.[22] Siam attracted the attention of traders of various nations. A few American ships came, one bringing a letter from the American president, and were received very much in the same manner as a Siamese tribute mission was received in China: they were allowed to trade and departed loaded with sugar. The Portuguese, also well acquainted with Siamese customs, came with a letter from their king, and eventually a Portuguese consul was permitted to settle in Bangkok, receiving the customary title at the Siamese court of *luang* Aphaiphānit.

## The Later Years

In 1818 the king was inspired by a report from members of the tributary mission returning from China that the emperor had created a large pleasure ground with rare plants and animals. This gave rise to the Siamese version of such grounds, and before long many corvée workers were engaged in the creation of the courtly garden, complete with artificial lakes, islands, and pavilions. This new project constituted a break with Rama I's plans for the new capital. Rama II definitely had abandoned the idea of being guided and being restrained by emulating the old capital. The pleasure gardens became the place where the king's passion for poetry and dance could be given free rein. Much of the literary heritage, so carefully reconstituted along traditional lines during the reign of Rama I, was rewritten in a new and modern style. The king gathered a considerable circle of artistic people, chosen from his own relatives, from the nobility, and from the commoners. Among the latter, the poet Sunthǭn Phū was outstanding. In 1818 this gifted man was just in his early thirties. His abilities were greatly appreciated by the king, who honoured him with the rank of *khun* and later with that of *phra'*.[23]

The later years of the Second Reign also did not bring any serious external threats to the kingdom, which allowed the king to proceed with his development of Siam's defence and with the further building of Bangkok. An example of the first interest is the development of the town of Samut Prakan, at the mouth of the river Chao Phraya, where a "city pillar" was set up.[24] The great *prāng* at Wat Chaeng, which was begun during the Second Reign, is a good example of the second type of pursuit.[25] However, these years were replete with minor problems of statecraft, and from time to time disturbing situations developed.

In 1819 there was a big prison revolt. Burmese prisoners of war killed their warders and took to the streets, where they were overpowered.[26] A much greater crisis occurred when a particularly virulent strain of cholera reached Siam. An epidemic had begun in India in 1817 and had arrived at Sri Lanka during the following year. From there it spread in various directions, by way of trading vessels. In 1819 it reached Penang; by April 1820 it had reached Bangkok. The death toll in Bangkok was great. The monasteries could not keep up with the cremations; many corpses were thrown in the river.

During the emergency the king issued a decree to his people explaining how the sickness had come from abroad and how ordinary medicine had no effect. Therefore a special royal ceremony for the expulsion of evil was held: sacred stanzas were chanted, all around the city large guns were fired, and a procession was held with the nation's most sacred objects. The king temporarily relieved all people of their duties and exhorted all to make merit, chant sacred mantras, and practice munificence. Even those on palace duty were requested to remain home and look after their families. All through the province of Bangkok, the king advised people to let the animals roam around freely in the markets, and prisoners (with the exception of Burmese war prisoners) were freed. The populace was asked not to kill any living being, thus avoiding harmful acts. Soon the epidemic abated. At that time there was a rumour that the disease was the result of the recent building activities in the palace. In order to build a mound in the palace pleasure grounds, large rocks had been taken from the sea, and it was thought that this could have caused the guardian spirits to be angry and that these could have sent the cholera as a punishment.[27]

Not long afterwards news arrived that in Vietnam a similar epidemic was raging. To ward off this danger the king ordered the court's most famous magical specialists to memorize the strongest and most difficult spells. Day and night there were chanting sessions, and yet another warding-off ceremony was held during which bells were beaten and guns were fired.[28]

This was also the time when news reached the capital that the Burmese were again planning to invade Siam. A large army was raised and moved towards the central-western side of the kingdom. *Kromamū'n* Čhētsadābodin, the king's eldest son, was given charge of the main force. During 1821, when it became clear that the Burmese were not invading after all, the armies were pulled back. Many conscripts were rescheduled to continue the work on making a large mound in the palace, and instead of fighting the Burmese they cut trees, made rafts, and fetched large rocks for the king's pleasure garden. The troops that had been sent as a precaution to the south-western region of Phetchaburi under the command of *kromamū'n* Sakdiphonlasēp had been accused of having oppressed the populace. The Phrakhlang, *čhaophrayā* Senāthibēt, sent strict orders that the army could not requisition boats and food from the people without offering a compensation: "If a farmer has only one wagon-load of rice, you ought to buy only half that amount. If the price of six pots of sugar is one-and-a-quarter *baht*, offer one *baht* for seven pots as a government price. Good relations between the army and the populace are in the interest of the country and must be fostered."[29] The mild, coaxing letter is indicative of the style of government under Rama II.

Meanwhile, the resident councillor of Singapore, aware that friendly relations had been established between the government of Siam on the one hand and those of Portugal and the United States on the other, had taken it upon himself to send a British trader, John Morgan, with a letter for the Siamese king, informing him of the British presence in Singapore and the hope that commercial links between the countries would be strengthened. A gift of a double-barrelled gun and two mirrors accompanied the letter. Morgan arrived in May 1821 and was duly interviewed by the Phrakhlang and subsequently by *kromamū'n* Čhētsadābodin. They questioned him mainly on the relations between Britain and Burma, since this was foremost in Siamese thought at that moment. Morgan presented his gifts and letter to Rama II and received permission to trade. He met, however, with many obstacles in the disposal of his cargo. The difficulties Morgan encountered must be interpreted as a snub, probably delivered on the highest orders. The reason for this somewhat ungracious Siamese behaviour is not difficult to ascertain: Morgan had brought a quantity of opium, a product that had been expressly declared contraband by the king, and thus the semi-official contact between the Siamese and the British was marred.[30]

A year later, probably unaware of the unfortunate impression Morgan had made upon the Siamese, the British sent an official envoy, John Crawfurd, to Bangkok. Crawfurd arrived at an awkward moment, because the Siamese king had recently sent a trading vessel to Bengal, which returned during Crawfurd's stay having incurred a great trade loss.[31]

Moreover, official envoys were expected to be the bearers of a missive from the hands of the highest authority. When Crawfurd could produce no letter from King George IV, but only a document signed by the king's representative in India, his prestige must have suffered considerably.

At that time, when a British vessel arrived in Bangkok, the king's officers not only would charge duty on the merchandise and a harbour tax, dependent upon the ship's tonnage, but also would insist upon having the first choice of buying, paying less than the market price. Only after the court's agents were satisfied that they had bought all that was of interest to them did they allow the trader to have free access to the public.[32] While the Europeans were thus unable to exploit an open market, and therefore it was difficult for them to be certain of large profits, there were possibilities for those who adapted to the Siamese system. Up to August 1821, the cargoes of twelve American ships had been sold, and sugar had been taken on the return journeys.[33]

Although Crawfurd was unable to ameliorate the trading possibilities of British merchants, he accumulated knowledge about Siam's commercial position in the international trade network of eastern Asia. Trade with China dominated the whole pattern. Probably this had been the case from the end of the seventeenth century onwards, when King Phraphetrāchā decided to cut most links with European powers. After the fall of Ayutthaya, Taksin had hastened to dispatch trade missions to China. In a general statement about the reign of Rama I, the pre-eminent position of China in matters regarding trade is clear:

> The greatest revenues in that era came from the Chinese junk trade. There were Chinese junks built like the Chinese style *tuakang* (tiller steerage) ships, with a *rahu* demon head at the bow. Some of these demon heads were painted green, some red. The junks measured each from five to seven *wa*[34] across the beam. There were a large number of them. Some belonged to the Crown, some to members of the royal family, some to government officials, and some to merchants.
> These ships were either built in Bangkok or in provincial areas outside the capital. They were loaded with merchandise to be sold in China every year. Some ships sold only their cargoes of merchandise, some ships sold both their cargoes of merchandise

and the ships themselves as well. The profits of this junk trade were tremendous.[35]

What was true for the First Reign also applied to the time of Rama II. When Crawfurd arrived in Bangkok in early 1822 the annual fleet from China had already arrived. This fleet comprised approximately 140 boats. Products carried from China to Bangkok included massive amounts of crockery, such as cups, dishes and bowls,[36] tea, brassware, copperware, silk, sugar candy, playing cards, dice, paper, and dried vegetables. Apart from these goods, the vessels would often carry large numbers of people. Crawfurd mentions in his *Journal of an Embassy to the Courts of Siam and Cochin China* how one junk had been known to bring twelve hundred passengers to Bangkok, and he was told that the annual immigration of Chinese to Bangkok was a least seven thousand.[37]

For the return journey, the fleet would carry rice, black pepper, sugar, cotton, tin, cardamom, hides, feathers, ivory, various woods for furniture making, sapan wood, mangrove bark,[38] stic-lac,[39] esculent swallows' nests, and *bêche-de-mer*. The goods exported to China were much more valuable than those brought from China to Bangkok, and the Chinese had to make up the difference in money. Boat-building also continued steadily, and every year between six or eight junks of the largest size were manufactured in Bangkok.[41]

Apart from the annual Chinese fleet, there was an extensive coastal trade with ports controlled by Cambodia, with the region later known as Cochin-China, especially with the harbour of Saigon, and with places far to the south, including Patani, Kelantan, Trengganu, Pahang, Singapore, Malacca, Penang, Batavia, Semarang, Cheribon, Palembang, and Pontianak. This trade around the Gulf of Siam and further south into the Indonesian archipelago was conducted with vessels smaller than those used in the trade to China. From the Siamese point of view, most of the coastal trade and that into the archipelago was a corollary of the trade with China: some of the goods obtained from the annual fleet were exported to these smaller ports, and goods China wanted were brought back to Bangkok. Through this secondary trade network Siam also became linked up with other markets and obtained goods from India and Europe. A large number of the coastal trade junks belonged to the king.[41] Crawfurd reports that the Siamese trade with many parts of the Malayan archipelago had greatly increased, Siam exporting mainly rice, sugar, salt, and oil, and importing products for the Chinese market as well as European goods. Singapore was rapidly gaining importance for this trade,[42] not only because of its strategic position, but also because just then the relations between the Siamese and the Dutch were not very cordial.[43]

Crawfurd also provides an account of the government, the corvée system, and taxation, which complements the information that can be obtained from other sources.

Regarding the general appreciation of the king's rule, Crawfurd states that the country had prospered under his administration and that the monarch was generally regarded as one of the mildest sovereigns who had ruled Siam for at least a century and a half.[44] The person of the king is described as short, of ordinary features, and somewhat corpulent.[45] With respect to the court, Crawfurd had the impression that there were two factions, one led by the prince Čhētsadābodin and the head of the *krom* Phrakhlang, *phrayā* Suriyawongkosā, the other by "the prince Caw-fa" and his maternal uncles.[46] Crawfurd was not familiar with the Siamese system of princely titles and did not realize that *čhaofā* was a title, not a name. This title had been bestowed upon many of Rama I's younger relatives, as well as on Rama II's sons Mongkut and Čhuthāmanī. From the context, and from the allusion to the *čhaofā*'s uncles, it may be deduced that prince Mongkut is meant as a central figure of one of the two "parties". As to the nature of these "factions", it may be assumed that this refers to the question of who was most worthy in the king's eyes to occupy the vacant position of Uparāt. Prince Čhētsadābodin was already in his mid-thirties and had served his father well on many occasions. According to the Dynastic Chronicles, Čhētsadābodin had been assigned the task of receiving people's petitions, and often late at night the king would consult with this son regarding the day's legal affairs.[47] On the other hand, in 1822 Prince Mongkut was in his eighteenth year, young and untried, but senior to his elder half-brother in rank because Mongkut was the eldest son of the queen, a status which had been underlined by the splendour of the ceremonies that had marked his leaving childhood.

Crawfurd provides also a summary account of the corvée system. He states that all adult males were compelled to serve the state four months a year. This confirms the general idea mentioned above, that Rama II did not lower the corvée period for the general populace to three months a year, as is often mentioned in history books: only certain groups in the provinces had been given an alleviation of the corvée burden. Exemption from corvée was granted to members of the Sangha, to the Chinese, to slaves, to government civil servants, to men who had three sons already serving, to those who could provide another person to serve instead, and to those who had been able to purchase a certificate of exemption from the government. In certain parts of the country, a commutation of corvée was given to people because they provided the capital with certain goods, such as sapan wood, saltpetre, ivory, or animal hides.[48] This information complements that of Siamese sources. The Chinese did not serve corvée, but paid a head tax of two *baht* and one-and-a-half *fu'ang*[49] per annum, of which two *baht* went to the government and the remainder was the tax collector's fee. This head tax was much lower than the amount needed for a Siamese to buy himself an exemption from corvée. In 1822 there appear to have been some 31,500 people paying this head tax in the capital district. Crawfurd estimated that there were another seventy thousand Chinese adult males spread over the rest of the country. Unlike the *phrai*, the Chinese were not tattooed but had to wear on the wrist a badge, bearing the seal of the taxation officer.

Crawfurd's mention of slaves among the people who were exempt from corvée also agrees with the picture that can be obtained from Siamese sources. Already during Rama I's reign it had been recorded that a registered slave did not have to perform corvée,[50] his master being charged with a slave's head tax.[51] Crawfurd mentions that all ordinary *phrai* could pay the government a sum of six to eight *baht* for an exemption of one month's work. This sum must have been absolutely out of reach for most common people. Only wealthy *phrai* would have been able to make use of this right. The alternative of sending a substitute for oneself must have been a much more practicable solution for a fairly prosperous *phrai*.

The category of people who supplied goods instead of serving corvée was known in Siamese laws as *phrai luang suai*. By freely amassing specific products, they were an indispensable link in the trade with China. The Dynastic Chronicles of the Second Reign mention the quest for *suai* products from a quite different perspective. In his general assessment of the whole reign, *čhaophrayā* Thiphākǫrawong mentions government servants negotiating the supply of *suai* products with bands of runaway *phrai* and slaves.[52] This indicates the king's dependence upon *suai* products as well as the propensity for compromise which pervades the whole period. Rather than meet the problem of run-away slaves with force, the king's agents traded with them for mutual benefit.[53] With regard to the land tax, Crawfurd mentions a fixed tax on all corn lands, according to their extent, without regard to their quality, and a tax on orchards, according to the number and type of trees. All lands cultivated with rice were taxed 2½ *thang* per twenty Siamese fathoms square, or *rai*. This is half a *thang* higher than that announced at the beginning of the reign. Crawfurd sheds no light upon the distinction between *khāwkhā* and *khāwčhatsū'*. Since the former was the most widespray, and since Crawfurd did not travel inland, it may be surmised that Crawfurd's information relates to *khāwkhā* tax and that this had been raised by half a *thang* between 1811 and 1822.

Apart from these items of general information, Crawfurd provides a lengthy statement about Siam's revenue. Many of the estimates regarding the various taxes provide a measure with which to gauge trade, the number of people involved, and the relative importance of certain occupations. The state's income from the monopoly of pepper, together with the rate of taxation, for example, could lead to an estimate of plantation size. However, the tax figures published in Crawfurd's *Journal* are extremely suspect.

It appears that Crawfurd, probably in order to aggrandize his mission's importance and to stimulate British interest in the kingdom, deliberately changed many of the figures he had collected, boosting the Siamese revenue, at least on paper. A clear indication of this process can be obtained from a com-

**Table 1.**   Estimated Siamese revenue in 1822, two Crawfurd accounts (in *baht*)

|  | Crawfurd Papers | Crawfurd's Journal |
|---|---|---|
| Land tax | 258,000 | 2,295,338 |
| Spirit tax | 264,000 | 460,000 |
| Gambling monopoly | 260,000 | 460,000 |
| Shop tax | 165,000 | 121,880 |
| Fishing tax | 64,000 | 64,000 |
| Chinese poll tax | 200,000 | 201,250 |
| Monopoly edible nests | 100,000 | 100,000 |
| Monopoly tin | 60,000 | 54,000 |
| Monopoly pepper | 320,000 | 400,000 |
| Other monopolies | 335,000 | 109,000 |
| Custom duties | 200,000 | 264,000 |
| Corvée | 7,344,000 | 20,000,000 |
| Fruit trees | — | 520,000 |
| Sugar | — | 105,000 |
| Turtle eggs | — | 5,000 |
| Total revenue | 9,650,000 | 25,159,468 |

parison of the figures in *The Crawfurd Papers* and those published in the *Journal* (see table 1).

Crawfurd's original estimate of Siam's revenue of less than ten million *baht* is boosted by more than fifteen million *baht* in his official report. The discrepancies in the two accounts can occasionally be explained by the fact that Crawfurd uses a different method of calculating totals, as in the case of the land tax and the value of corvée. In other instances, however, it is impossible to divine the methods used to reach the figures.

One of Crawfurd's companions, George Finlayson, provides a list of the spirit tax in fourteen towns, and Crawfurd also provides such a list in his *Journal*.[54] Again, the two lists show great discrepancies (see table 2).

There can be little doubt that Finlayson and Crawfurd based their report upon the same list of figures, for in all cases where Crawfurd differs from Finlayson, he has given exactly double the amount. Only in the cases where Finlayson mentions piculs does Crawfurd differ; where catties are mentioned he gives the same figure. Therefore it appears that Crawfurd drew up his list from figures that mentioned piculs and catties, and that he took a picul of spirit to be worth

**Table 2.** Two accounts of spirit tax for fourteen towns in Siam (in *baht*)

| Town or region* | Amount in Weight | | Finlayson Value | Crawfurd Value |
|---|---|---|---|---|
| Bangkok | 18 | piculs | 72,000 | 144,000 |
| Ayutthaya | 6 | piculs | 24,000 | 48,000 |
| Sukhothai | 1 | picul | 4,000 | 8,000 |
| Prachinburi | 1 | picul | 4,000 | 8,000 |
| Rayong | 1 | picul | 4,000 | 8,000 |
| Kamphaeng Phet | 1 | picul | 4,000 | 8,000 |
| Chainat | 20 | catties | 1,600 | 1,600 |
| Nakhon Ratchasima | 2 | piculs | 8,000 | 16,000 |
| Vientiane | 3 | piculs | 12,000 | 24,000 |
| Kanchanaburi | 20 | catties | 1,600 | 1,600 |
| Chumphon | 30 | catties | 2,400 | 2,400 |
| Pathiu | 20 | catties | 1,600 | 1,600 |
| Chaiya | 8 | catties | 640 | 640 |
| Patthalung | 30 | catties | 2,400 | 2,400 |

*The spelling of names in Finlayson and Crawfurd is inconsistent, and in some cases the identification in this list is tentative. Pathiu was a town just north of Chumphon, and Chaiya is not far south of that town.

twice as much as did Finlayson. Finlayson's total comes to less than 150,000 *baht*, while Crawfurd's figures add up to almost 275,000 *baht*. From table 1 it can be seen that neither figure bears resemblance to Crawfurd's two other estimates of the spirit tax.

As to the question of whether Crawfurd or Finlayson is right with regard to the value of a picul, there can be little doubt that Finlayson calculated from the accurate unit of measurement. A picul (*hāp*) was equal to fifty catties (*chang*), and this was already so established in Ayutthayan times.[55] Crawfurd, however, took the picul to be twice as heavy, apparently assuming the Siamese *chang* to be equivalent to the "standard catty", of which there were one hundred to the picul. The *chang* was worth eighty *baht*, whereas the "standard catty" was worth only half that.[56] Finlayson's list in table 2 can be taken as the more accurate one. The list of towns seems to cover a considerable area, with each town at some distance from the other. It is tempting to surmise that the Siamese had, for the purposes of tax on alcohol, divided the country up in fourteen districts and that the list represents thus a complete picture. However, until further evidence is found, this must remain but speculation.

## The Court

The news that worried the administrators throughout 1822 and 1823 was the growing confrontation between Burma and England. The Siamese were by no means certain how to interpret these events, and many feared that the Burmese would emerge the stronger of the two parties. It was decided to keep troops alert near the border.

Internally, the court was amused by a strange incident between the two chief ministers. One evening, after these two had attended the cremation rites of the king's younger sister, both approached the same exit from the palace grounds. The litter of the head from the *krom* Kalāhom, in which also one of his minor wives was sitting, reached the exit first. They had not yet passed through the gate when they were jostled by the bearers of the litter of the head from the *krom* Mahātthai, who felt that they had precedence. In the scuffles that broke out, the Kalāhom's men managed to snatch away the official sword of state belonging to the chief of the Mahātthai, who thereupon alarmed a section of the Palace Guard (a section commanded by the minister's younger relative). These followed the Kalāhom's party and forcefully recaptured the sword. The next morning the Kalāhom lodged an official complaint against his colleague. A tribunal, headed by *kromamū'n* Čhētsadābodin, was appointed to investigate the matter. The Kalāhom's case was dismissed on a technicality, related to fact that he had been accompanied by one of his minor wives.[57]

The incident itself is trivial, yet it is indicative of some jealousy and hostility among the chief executives. The minister of the Kalāhom, *čhaophrayā* Mahāsēnā, had only recently been appointed to the post, and etiquette would probably have demanded that he make way for the minister of the Mahātthai, *čhaophrayā* Aphaiphuthon. The fact that he allowed his men to carry away his colleague's sword of state also indicates a distressing lack of statemanship. Bearing these aspects in mind, it becomes clear why the tribunal was pleased to be able to brush aside the minister's complaint. It also explains why *kromamū'n* Čhētsadābodin dismissed *čhaophrayā* Mahāsēnā the following year when he succeeded his father.

More disturbing was the death of two white elephants.[58] While the finding of such an elephant was generally regarded as an auspicious omen, as a sign that the gods looked favourably upon the reign, the death of such a "heavenly sign", let alone the death of two of them, was an indication that some great evil was about to happen to the reign.

By this time, *čhaofā* Mongkut had reached his twentieth year and, following established custom, he entered the order of monks. After his Lenten season he could have expected to be given his first duties, and his father would then have had the opportunity to decide whether the eldest *čhaofā* prince would be worthy of the status of Uparāt, which would have made him a strong candidate for the succession. However, Mongkut had been but a few weeks in the monastery when his father became ill and, on 21 July 1824, died.


## Overview

The Second Reign lasted almost fifteen years. At his death, the king was only fifty-six (sixteen years younger than Rama I had been when he died). Compared with the reigns of Taksin and Rama I, that of Rama II is noteworthy as a period of relative peace and calm. This was partly due to the fact that Rama II's predecessors had already given battle so often: by 1809 Siam was firmly established among the independent nations of mainland South-East Asia. The relative peacefulness of the period 1809–24 also reflects a lack of belligerence directed against Siam by the neighbouring countries. Between 1812 and 1819 Bodawpaya of Burma was occupied with troubles at the western and north-western sides of his kingdom, disturbances that led to increased hostilities between the Burmese and the British. In the south, British power became firmly established in Penang, Singapore, and Malacca, while the Siamese felt that they had the traditional overlordship in Kedah, Perak, Kelantan, and Trengganu. They were not so certain about their rights in Pahang, and Selangor, Negri Sembilan, and Johore were free of Siamese intrusion. Siam's intervention in the affairs of Kedah and Perak between 1818 and 1821 caused anxiety in Penang over Siamese territorial rights. The Europeans had, in contrast to the Siamese, an "all-or-nothing" approach to the rights of influential countries over their vassals. The Siamese, however, still used their traditional system of letting their vassal states organize their own affairs as long as they sent tribute and allowed Bangkok to confirm the position of the local ruler. Only when the unwritten rules of vassalage were broken would Bangkok send a punitive force. One of Crawfurd's duties while visiting Bangkok was to assess Siam's actual military might and its ability to back up territorial claims in the south in the event of a clash between Britain and Siam. Crawfurd's conclusions and attitudes are worth noting:

> Should the arrogance of the Siamese embarrass us in the manner I have pointed out as probable, it appears to me that it will unquestionably be the best policy to meet the difficulty at once. The military preparations for this purpose may be made on the most moderate and economical scale. A simultaneous attack by a few companies of sepoys from Penang and the blockade of the Menam [Chao Phraya] by 2 or 3 cruziers of the smallest class, it appears to me, will be adequate to every object. . . . The blockade of the Menam will be the easiest, safest and most effectual measure that can well be contemplated.[59]

To the east, Siam's relations with Cambodia saw a reversal of the situation under the First Reign. The Cambodian ruler, who had been closely watched by Rama I, asserted his independence soon after Rama II gained the throne by ignoring a Siamese request for troops. The Cambodian court was divided among pro-Siamese and pro-Vietnamese factions, and the Cambodian king chose to place himself under Vietnamese protection, at the same time continuing to send tributary missions to Bangkok. Rama II allowed the vassal state to fall more and more under Vietnamese control, accepting the yearly tribute as a sign that Siam was still master. The Siamese king's personal character seems to have played a role in this unusual complacency.

After the first spate of administrative measures, the king seems to have settled into a life of courtly splendour, preferring to compose poetry and supervise the building of the large pleasure garden to keeping a personal watch upon the affairs of state. These were largely delegated to the senior ministers and a few princes.

The Second Reign was a time when the court was often short of money. Probably this was a result of a slackening of the rules which allowed tax evasion to become so widespread as to seriously affect the State's income. It has been recorded that some years the king could pay the full *biawat* to his senior administrators, but in other years he paid them three-quarters or only half the amount.[60] All the king's efforts to raise more money seemed to be directed towards increasing the trade with China. By sending with the yearly fleet an ever-increasing number of royal ships, the king managed, in good years, to pay his court, or even give a bonus.

The internal revenue, where it was raised, seems to have been dissipated before it reached the Treasury. The laxity prevalent at the time is apparent from a statement in the Dynastic Chronicles, Second Reign, which can be translated as follows "In this reign princes and nobles sent out people to go to the secret meeting places of people who live in the forest regions in order to obtain forest products, and thus obtain *suai*. Runaway freemen and slaves secretly lived there and could not be arrested, because their leaders had great power."[61] Little wonder that Crawfurd could report that the monarch was one of the mildest sovereigns that had ruled Siam for at least a century and a half. It appears that the government of Siam was slipping from Rama II's control, and this probably influenced the question of the succession which arose in July 1824.

## Notes

1. At Rama I's rise to power, the boy was raised to be *čhaofā* Suphantawong, and later to *čhaofā* Aphaithibēt. Subsequently Rama I changed this name to Thammathibēt. On the occasion of the anointment of Prince Itsarasunthǫn (the future Rama II) to Uparāt, Prince Thammathibēt was among the few to receive further honours, and he was appointed to *kromakhun* rank and changed his name to Kasatrānuchit.
2. See *čhaophrayā* Thiphākǫrawong, *Phrarātchaphongsāwadān Krungratanakōsin, Ratchakān thī Sǭng* (hereafter *PKRt Sǭng*), pp. 2-3. The attempted coup is confirmed in the records of the court astrologers, in

*Čhotmāihēthōn, chabap Phrayā Mūnlathonrak*, p. 29.

3.  For details on Prince Sēnānurak's career, see *mǫmrātchawong* Saengsom Kasēmsī and Wimon Phongphiphan, comps., *Prawatisāt Thai Samai Ratanakōsin Ratchakān thī Nu'ng thu'ng Ratchakān thī Sǫng*, pp. 20-21.
4.  Further details, also regarding the senior appointments during the reign itself can be found in *PKRt Sǫng* pp. 6-9.
5.  The full text of the edict was printed in *Prawatkitčhakānthahān Samai Krungratanakōsin*, pp. 16-20. A rough translation can be found in H.G.Q. Wales, *Ancient Siamese Government and Administration*, pp. 131-34.
6.  The provincial men are called *lēk huamu'ang*, rather than *phrai* of one category or another. This has led L.M. Gesick to assume that there existed a fundamental difference between *phrai luang* and *lēk huamu'ang* (see L.M. Gesick, "Kingship and Political Integration in Traditional Siam, 1767-1824", pp. 174-75). I rather doubt this interpretation and suspect that the words *lēk huamu'ang* are used in order to indicate that the king was making certain laws only for the benefit of people in the provinces. Rama II was concerned to stimulate the repopulation of the countryside.
7.  "Rāngthǫngtrā th'ung Huamu'ang ru'ang Khāluangrangwatnā ǫktrāčhǫngthidin", in *Čhotmāihēt Ratchakān thī Sǫng, C.S. 1173*, pp. 37-42.
8.  The Sēnā is an officer of the *krom* Nā, responsible for the collection of tax on rice lands (Wales, *Ancient Siamese Government*, p. 89).
9.  De la Loubère mentions one-quarter of a *baht* per *rai* land tax as well as tax on various fruit trees (*The Kingdom of Siam*, p. 93).
10.  *DC First R*, p. 13.
11.  J. Crawfurd, *Journal of an Embassy to the Courts of Siam and Cochin-China*, p. 385.
12.  The *tham khwan* ceremony belongs to the ancient Tai tradition. For references and further details, see B.J. Terwiel, "The Tais and Their Belief in Khwans", *South East Asian Review* 3, no. 1 (1978): 1-16.
13.  Probably Burmese war slaves, captured during the wars with Burma.
14.  *Čhotmāihēthōn*, pp. 31-32.
15.  *PKRt Sǫng*, pp. 43-48.
16.  Ibid., pp. 82-85.
17.  Ibid., pp. 51-52.
18.  Ibid., pp. 61-62. See also Shigeharu Tanabe, "Historical Geography of the Canal System in the Chao Phraya River Delta", *JSS* 65, pt 2 (1977): 42.
19.  *PKRt Sǫng*, pp. 80-82, and *Čhotmāihēthōn*, p. 35.
20.  This festival has been regularly held ever since that time. It is called Wisākhabuchā. Further details can be found in *Kromphra'* Damrong Rātchanuphāp, *Phrarātchaphongsāwadān Krungratanakōsin Ratchakān thī Sǫng*, vol. 2, pp. 4-10.
21.  *PKRt Sǫng*, pp. 87-88. For further details, see R. Lingat, "Les suicides réligieux au Siam", *Felicitation Volumes of Southeast-Asian Studies Presented to His Highness Prince Dhaninivat Kromamun Bidyalabh Bridhyakorn*, vol. 1, pp. 71-75.
22.  *PKRt Sǫng*, pp. 94-97.
23.  Sunthǫn Phū's works are still being reprinted and read. They often provide glimpses of social life and rules of behaviour which must have been valid during Rama II's time. Some of his works have been thoroughly studied, notably his *Suphāsit Sǫn Ying*, translated and annotated by K. Wenk ("Ein Lehrgedicht fur junge Frauen—Suphāsit sǫn ying—des Sunthǫn Phū", *Oriens Extremus* 12, pt 1 [1965]: 65-106), and Wenk's book *Phali Lehrt die*

*Jüngeren—Phāli sǫn nǫng*. For Sunthǫn Phū's biography, see C. Notton, trans., *La vie du poète Sounthone-Bhou*.

24. *PKRt Sǫng*, pp. 154-55.
25. Further details can be found in Prungsī Wanliphōdom, "Phraprāng Wat Arunrātchawārām", in *Chaloem Phrakiet Phrabātsomdet Phraphuthaloetlā*, pp. 41-51.
26. *Chotmāihēthōn*, p. 36.
27. *PKRt Sǫng*, pp. 115-16; *Chotmāihēthōn*, p. 37; and Crawfurd, *Journal*, p. 455. The latter reports that the Phrakhlang estimated that one-fifth of the populace had died from the cholera epidemic. Although Crawfurd takes this to mean one-fifth of the whole population of the country, it may be surmised that the losses in Bangkok were relatively higher than in provincial towns.
28. *PKRt Sǫng*, pp. 128-29.
29. Ibid., pp. 136-37.
30. O. Frankfurter, "The Unofficial Mission of John Morgan, Merchant, to Siam in 1821", *JSS* 11 (1914–15): 1-8.
31. Crawfurd, *Journal*, p. 141.
32. Ibid., pp. 144-45; G. Finlayson, *The Mission to Siam and Hue the Capital of Cochin-China, in the years 1821-2*, pp. 168-77.
33. Frankfurter, "Unofficial Mission of John Morgan", p. 6.
34. The *wā* is equal to two metres.
35. *DC First R*, vol. 1, pp. 304-5.
36. When some crockery was damaged in transit, it could be used to decorate monastery edifices simply by chipping off pieces and using them in mosaics. Most of the decorations of the gigantic *prāng* at Wat Chaeng (now Wat Arun) were thus obtained.
37. Crawfurd, *Journal*, p. 412; however, his figures often appear rather inflated, as is discussed below.
38. Both sapan wood and mangrove bark were used in the Chinese tanning and dye industry.
39. Excretion from the lac beetle, used as sealing wax.
40. Elsewhere Crawfurd states that from eight to ten were manufactured (*Crawfurd Papers*, p. 117).
41. Crawfurd, *Journal*, p. 413.
42. Ibid., p. 414, Frankfurter, "Unofficial Mission of John Morgan", p. 8.
43. There had been remonstrations against the Siamese because of alleged kidnapping of Javanese subjects. (Frankfurter, "Unofficial Mission of John Morgan", p. 7). That there was reason for the Javanese protests is borne out by Crawfurd's account of kidnapped slaves from Semarang (*Journal*, p. 148).
44. Crawfurd, *Journal*, pp. 136-37.
45. Ibid., p. 94.
46. Ibid., p. 105.
47. *PKRt Sǫng*, p. 203.
48. Crawfurd, *Journal*, pp. 374-75.
49. A *fu'ang* is one-eighth of a *baht*.
50. "Phrarātchakamnot Mai", no. 17, *KTSD* 5: 257.
51. A figure mentioned by Wales (*Ancient Siamese Government*, pp. 200-201) is that of an annual sum of five *baht*. It is not certain, however, that this sum would have remained unchanged over a long period, nor is it certain that this sum was charged for all classes of slaves.
52. *PKRt Sǫng*, p. 205.
53. *Crawfurd Papers*, p. 133, describes how the king naturally pays a sum considerably less than those goods would be worth in Bangkok.

54. Finlayson, *Mission to Siam*, p. 248; Crawfurd, *Journal*, p. 379.
55. De la Loubère, *The Kingdom of Siam*, p. 164. The standard Thai-Thai dictionary also gives one *hāp* the value of fifty *chang* (*Photčhanānukrom Chabap Rātchabanthitsathān*, p. 963.)
56. A succinct statement of the ancient Siamese system of weights can be found in G.B. McFarland's *Thai-English Dictionary*, p. 59, where the difference between a *chang* and a "standard catty" is shown. The "standard catty" was probably introduced into the Siamese system as a result of the intensive trade with China, for the measure was used in China.
57. *PKRt Sǫng*, pp. 198-99.
58. *Čhotmāihēthǒn*, pp. 37-38.
59. *Crawfurd Papers*, p. 151.
60. *PKRt Sǫng*, p. 204.
61. Ibid., p. 205.

# 5

# The Third Reign:
# Efficiency and Centralization

The succession in 1824 was by far the smoothest thus far recorded in this book. *Kromamū'n* Čhētsadābodin, the previous king's eldest son, to whom much of the burden of government had been delegated during the preceding years, was unchallenged when *kromamū'n* Sakdiphonlasēp, one of Rama II's half-brothers, proposed his name.

Gossip among foreigners would have it that the accession had not been a smooth affair and that the legitimate heir had been deprived of the throne. Thus the American Edmund Roberts blithely relates the following account of the accession: "The present king, the illegitimate son of the late monarch, by the sudden death of his father, aided by bribes, placed himself on the throne, to the exclusion of the eldest legitimate son, who, on the death of his father, fled the palace, and became a Talapoy to save his life."[1] This view, which was widely held among foreigners, was probably confirmed whenever visitors from other countries met with *čhaofā* Čhuthāmanī, who would be eager to let them know that he and his brother were really of a higher rank than their elder half-brother. Indeed, according to the letter of the law, the eldest son of *čhaofā* rank would be the first to be considered as successor to the throne. However, Mongkut's greatest supporter, his uncle *Somdet čhaofā kromaluang* Phithakmontrī, had died two years before Rama II. It is quite possible that Mongkut was being groomed for the position of Uparat, but when his father died he was only nineteen years old.[2] Čhētsadābodin, on the other hand, was by no means illegitimate; he was the king's eldest son by a wife who was not queen. Čhētsadābodin had been a prince of *krom* rank for ten years and had gradually become one of the most powerful men of Siam. Since the Siamese had never felt bound to the rule of letting the eldest *čhaofā* prince ascend the throne, the choice of Čhētsadābodin was the natural and expected one. In the Chronicles it is stated unequivocally that it was Čhētsadābodin's past record, his proved wisdom, intelligence, and experience, which decided the issue, and all available information fits in with this presentation of the facts.[3]

The gossip regarding Mongkut's fleeing to a monastery in order to save his life is simply untrue. In accordance with established practice, Mongkut had been ordained a Buddhist monk just before his father became ill.[4] He had no cause to fear for his life on account of his elder half-brother becoming the king; on the contrary, Rama III was well disposed towards *čhaofā* Mongkut and occasionally helped to further his career.[5]

That the accession of Rama III was uncontested is strongly supported by the fact that all senior civilian appointments were carried over from the reign of Rama II to that of Rama III. Had there been dissent among some of the *krom* heads, a change in senior portfolios would have occurred. Rama III chose his uncle *kromamū'n* Sakdiphonlasēp as Uparāt. In addition, the Chronicles mention a general amnesty and orders to clear the courts of litigation cases, just as had been done at the king's father's accession in 1809.[6] Another measure, which would prove to be the first of many of its type, was the proclamation of a new tax, one on salt.[7] A further decree which appears indicative of the new king's style of government was the digging of a new canal, together with the construction of a bridge at the edge of the capital city.[8]

The new king's anointment, which took place in April

1825, necessitated an adjustment in the ranks of royalty, and before Rama III had been one year on the throne he issued a list of royal appointments, in which eight relatives were elevated to *kromamū'n* rank.

Meanwhile, the news from Burma was disconcerting. The incursions of Burmese troops into Assam, Manipur, and Cachar had caused the British to declare some of the small states Burma regarded as its vassal regions to be under British protection. Hostilities broke out. In March 1824 the British formally declared war against the Burmese, and the Siamese were anxious about the outcome. If Burma defeated England, Siam would have a strong and quarrelsome neighbour on her western borders. Already during the last months of Rama II's reign, the Siamese had been encouraged by the British to harass and threaten the Burmese. Siam had eagerly responded to the British strategy, and the new king continued to regard himself as Britain's ally in the conflict with Burma.[9] Rama III considered Burma likely to be the loser and hoped that Britain would accept Siamese help in return for Siamese control over all of Martaban and Tavoy.[10] However, after due consideration the British did not feel the need of a firm alliance and apparently did not wish to strengthen the position of a country that controlled some of the Malay states in which the British were becoming interested.

In December 1825 another British envoy arrived in Bangkok, again armed with a letter from the governor-general of Bengal. This was Captain Henry Burney, who spent almost eight months trying to persuade the Siamese to grant the British more favourable trading conditions. His mission was made difficult by the fact that he could offer no concessions to the Siamese other than the prospect of more trade if tariffs were lowered. The situation was further complicated when in February 1826 the envoy sent his ship southwards. This led to the rumour that it was fetching a large British fleet, which would attack Bangkok. The fact that the British had gained a resounding victory over the Burmese had made the Siamese courtiers wary and distrustful of them. When the formation of a British fleet of sixty ships was reported, Bangkok mobilized. As Burney reported:

"Troops were called into the capital from the interior, the forts at Paklaat and Paknam were manned and additional defences commenced. All was war and bustle. The situation of the Mission was now by no means comfortable. Not a word uttered by any of us received credit. The boatmen allotted to us were removed and we were evidently viewed with indignation as well as distrust."[11] This situation lasted for more than a month. Finally, at the end of July 1826 Burney left Bangkok with a not wholly satisfactory draft treaty.

The Siamese had not believed Burney's protestations regarding Britain's friendly attitude, and they proceeded to improve their defences so as to be able to withstand an attack from those who had just defeated the Burmese with alarming ease. Three warships continuously cruised near the mouth of the river Chao Phraya, and large sheds were erected in Bangkok to house the war boats. In the largest of these sheds were 136 boats, each one capable of carrying about thirty men, and a second shed contained another one hundred of such boats. Other similar, smaller sheds had been constructed further along the banks of the river. As a further deterrent, the king ordered the casting of a truly massive brass cannon, weighing almost 2,500 kilograms. Almost two thousand men were occupied for two months with this work.[12]

D.E. Malloch, who had acquired considerable knowledge of life in Bangkok during three years' residence in Siam, provides further information about the court which neatly complements Siamese sources. In contrast to his father, Rama III did not wish to be personally involved with trading, leaving much of this in the hands of the Phrakhlang and the deputy Phrakhlang, *phrayā* Sïphiphat. Apparently Rama III intended to reduce the number of public holidays so that more time could be given to more useful employment.[13] This information, meagre and incomplete by itself, gains importance when it is seen in connection with the many other initiatives taken during the Third Reign.

Meanwhile, the rumour of an imminent British attack on Bangkok was seized by *čhao* Anuwong, the ruler of Vientiane, as the best opportunity for a revolt against Bangkok. He apparently had been contacting the rulers of other Laotian vassal states with the aim of throwing off Siam's overlordship. *Čhao* Anuwong had planned a raid deep into Siamese territory to the province of Saraburi, where some ten thousand Laotians, people who had been deported from Vientiane more than four decades earlier, were living. In a cleverly devised strategy, *čhao* Anuwong sent a message to Rama III explaining that he was sending a large number of troops in order to fortify Bangkok against the imminent attack of the English. Apparently he hoped that thereby he would be able to move freely across Siamese territory without raising the alarm and collect the Lao families who had been forcefully moved into Siamese territory. Unfortunately for *čhao* Anuwong, the ruler of Luang Prabang, instead of assisting him, actually warned the Siamese king of *čhao* Anuwong's intentions, and in late February 1827 the Siamese were able to move their troops up to Saraburi. They expelled Anuwong's troops and marched on to take Vientiane. The town was looted and all its fortifications destroyed. Large numbers of farmers were moved westwards, to settle in what is now north-east Thailand.[14] *Čhao* Anuwong eventually was captured and died ignominiously in captivity.

The *Records of the Astrologers* note that in the year 1829 the Huai Kǭ Khǭ lottery was begun.[15] This grew rapidly to be a very popular State-sponsored gambling organization.[16] The introduction of a State lottery can be regarded as typical of the Third Reign. While Rama II often had insufficient cash to pay the traditional *biawat* in full, Rama III appears to have been more successful in raising funds. During 1829 he also ordered a nationwide survey of all taxable fruit trees, undoubtedly another measure intended to boost the State revenue.

Rama III's success in increasing revenue enabled the execution of several expensive projects. For example, a new fortress was built at the mouth of the river Tha Chin, some thirty kilometres south-west of Bangkok, and the Chinese bricklayers were paid just over 3,800 *baht*.[17] This fortification was an extension to the defences of Bangkok, because the mouth of the Tha Chin was directly linked with the capital by the old Mahachai Canal. Having fortified that strategic position, the king ordered a number of Mons, under the leadership of *čhaophrayā* Mahāyothā, to live there. At the same time, a large number of Chinese workers were hired to excavate approximately another thirty kilometres of canal to the mouth of the river Maeklong, at a cost of more than 8,100 *baht*.[18] When these canals had been made, it was possible to travel by boat from Bangkok to Ratburi without having to cross stretches of open sea. Thus the south-western parts of the central lowlands were now firmly linked with the capital, and troops could be rapidly moved at all seasons via the canals and rivers. The recent fear of a British invasion could well have been the catalyst in making the decision to dig this canal.[19]

Rama III did not order corvée labourers to do the work, as had been customary during the reigns of Taksin and Rama I. Already in the days of Thonburi and the first building of Bangkok, massive tasks such as digging new canals had not been done by the regular corvée labour, which always was available to the central authorities, but by manpower from vassal states. This suggests that even in those early days people liable for regular corvée were usually otherwise employed. Many of them would have made up the regular standing armies. Again, during the Third Reign there was a continuing need for a considerable number of reliable troops, not only because there had been an uprising in Vientiane, but also because the Siamese were still uneasy about the Burmese and distrustful of the English. The situation in the south also needed constant attention, and Cambodia was a seat of potential trouble. Therefore many ordinary *phrai luang* may have served corvée performing military duties. The length of time that people served varied according to military needs. Around the main palaces there were always many bands of permanent soldiers who received a small salary. Other less essential but still fairly important platoons consisted of men who served half a month and were free to earn their living the other half. Most *phrai luang* in and around the capital served one month and were free for two months to earn their living. Those who served part-time did not receive food or money during corvée. However, when there was a campaign, all who were under marching orders would receive their victuals and also a small amount of money. If the army was not on campaign, the king could allot it other tasks, and it has been noted that many soldiers were employed in cutting timber and collecting sapan wood for the royal warehouses.[20]

This explains at least partly why Rama III decided to hire Chinese labour for the building of a new fortress and the digging of a long canal. Not only did he not want to tie down his standing army to one small area of the kingdom, but also the labour of his troops provided him with valuable trading goods. In addition, there was a large supply of Chinese labour. Siam was still regularly receiving Chinese immigrants eager to work. The annual intake of Chinese in the late 1820s has been estimated at more than two thousand people.[21]

During the early years of the Third Reign, the position of the Phrakhlang was undoubtedly the most important one in Siam next to that of the king. He had been closely allied to the king when the latter was still *kromamū'n* Chētsadābodin, and during the first decade of the Third Reign he appears to have been the king's chief adviser and executive officer. It was he who was in charge of the digging of a canal to the Maeklong River. He had already been offered the post of head of the *krom* Kalāhom once, but had declined it, probably because the *krom* Phrakhlang, though not as high in status as that of the Kalāhom, gave the opportunity for many lucrative deals.[22] Later, in 1830, the offer was repeated, and this time the *čhaophrayā* Phrakhlang was able to add the acting headship of the *krom* Kalāhom to his existing position, a combination of offices unprecedented in Siamese history.[23] The Phrakhlang handled all matters regarding foreigners, and to his attention came the matter of two enthusiastic Protestant missionaries, Jacob Tomlin and Karl Gutzlaff, who had arrived in late August 1828 to preach Christianity in a manner different from that of the long-established Roman Catholics.

Gutzlaff relates how the British conquest of lower Burma had greatly impressed the populace and how the fact that Christian soldiers had defeated Buddhist ones could be interpreted as a sign of the triumph of the Christian philosophy. He freely distributed literature regarding the imminent eclipse of false doctrines such as Buddhism.[24] This resulted in the *čhaophrayā* Phrakhlang's request to the British agent, Robert

Hunter, to assist with the expulsion of the two missionaries. Hunter protested that neither had broken any law and that their presence was allowed under the treaties of 1822 and 1826. The Siamese let the date on the expulsion order lapse and created a new law prohibiting the distribution of Christian booklets.[25] Near the end of 1829 Gutzlaff left Bangkok for a visit to Singapore, where the first printing press using Siamese characters was established, so that he could have some of his biblical translations printed in Siamese. Meanwhile, he and Tomlin had sent a letter to America to ask for the speedy sending of more Protestant missionaries. Not long afterwards the first American missionaries began to arrive.[26]

In 1830 *phrayā* Rāchasuphāwadī, an official who had shown considerable leadership qualities during the Laotian campaign, was rewarded with the headship of the *krom* Mahātthai and received the new name of *čhaophrayā* Bǫdindechā. Until his death in 1849, this man was to play an extremely important role throughout most of Rama III's reign.

In 1831 the rice harvest was largely lost because of disastrous floods, and the price of rice rose to 400 *baht* for a cartload of paddy.[27] Edmund Roberts, who arrived two years later in Bangkok, reported that as a result of the food shortage the number of Buddhist monks had "doubled".[28] That year the *čhaophrayā* Phrakhlang led an army to the south. Several governors of *mū'angs* in the southern region had been feuding, and if Bangkok had not asserted itself, it was felt, there could have been danger of further British involvement. *The Records of the Astrologers* mention also that in this year taxes on bamboo and teak logs were introduced.[29]

In 1832 the Uparāt died. Speculation was rife about who would be chosen to fill the post and thus automatically be dubbed heir-apparent. However, then, as later, the king saw nobody of sufficiently outstanding qualities among his close relatives to groom as his successor. Therefore he decided to leave the post open for the time being, but at the same time he promoted eight relatives to higher *krom* ranks. Three became *kromaluang,* and four *kromakhun,* so that, together with the remaining *kromamū'n* princes, a distinct hierarchy was created. One of the princes elevated was *čhaofā* Čhuthāmanī, who became *čhaofā kromakhun* Itsarēt. Among the princes singled out for promotion were several who hoped to be elevated even further to head the Front Palace.[30]

In 1833 Bangkok was honoured by the visit of another envoy from a Western trading country, the American Edmund Roberts, who came to see whether, as the English had done, he could ensure more equitable trade terms. He received quite a warm welcome, since his country was at that stage not contemplating territorial conquest in Asia, and previous contacts had been quite amiable. Roberts collected information on the various important people in Siam. He described the continuation of a lively ship-building industry in Bangkok and estimated the number of war boats to be no less than five hundred, and that there were fifty or sixty sailing boats, the largest of which did not exceed a hundred tons.[31]

Probably the most important document produced by Roberts was his appendix on the annual Siamese revenue from farms and duties, as well as some items of the king's expenditure. Since Roberts appeared eager to attract American trade, he was unlikely to have underestimated the annual quantity of produce, or the Siamese government's revenue. Yet in many instances the figures given for both are only a fraction of Crawfurd's lowest estimate. Birds' nests, for example, are shown by Crawfurd to have given the Siamese government 100,000 *baht* in tax in 1822. Roberts makes this 30,000 *baht*. Tin in 1822 reputedly earned 60,000 *baht* (in another report, 54,000 *baht*), whereas Roberts estimates it to have been only 18,200 *baht*. Even greater discrepancies can be found in the case of pepper, which appears to have dropped almost ninefold in revenue. It is tempting to account for these differences by rejecting Crawfurd's figures as deliberate fabrications, because he has been shown in many instances to have inflated his figures. However, part of the discrepancy may also have been the result of a comparative slackening of trade between 1822 and 1833. Rama II had invested heavily in the trade with China, hoping to amass sufficient revenue thereby to pay for the court's expenses. Crawfurd estimates the size of the annual fleet to have been about 140 ships and is unlikely to have greatly inflated this number, because this could be readily verified. Rama III, on the other hand, had withdrawn the king's large trade interests,[32] and possibly this partly accounts for a much lower estimate of the size of the fleet in the early 1830s. Gutzlaff, well acquainted with the Chinese junk trade, says the fleet that left for China every year between May and August comprised approximately eighty junks,[33] and this was confirmed in 1835, when the annual fleet was said to have from sixty to eighty seagoing vessels.[34]

Roberts's figures on the Siamese revenue are probably the first fairly reliable ones to indicate the state and size of the Siamese economy. With the help of these figures it is possible to make an estimate of the area of arable land, the number of fruit trees, and the relative size of the country's largest marketplaces. The details of the tax on alcoholic beverages, the manufacture of which apparently was almost completely in the hands of the Chinese, may be compared with Finlayson's list,[35] and from this it would seem that consumption increased in Bangkok but decreased in various provincial towns. The increased figure for Bangkok is easily explained by the steady increase in the Chinese population. The provincial figures are more difficult to understand. The decrease possibly reflects a relative lack of opportunity in the provinces, but the possibility of a high rate of Chinese assimilation must not be excluded. The list of "farms and duties" provides the first estimate of the number of teak logs cut; a massive 127,000 trees were felled and processed in Siam. Another interesting aspect of the list is the fact that so many new taxes seem to have been added after the reign of Rama II.[36]

Roberts also provides an estimate of the revenue derived from the outer provinces. The northern provinces contributed 32,000 *baht* annually, the southern ones under the *krom* Kalāhom 24,000 *baht*, and the coastal central provinces 12,000 *baht*. In addition, he gives estimates of the revenue of the *čhaophrayā* Yomarāt (4,800 *baht*) and of the (king's?) tribunal (8,000 *baht*). As for the state gold revenue, *phrai suai* delivered approximately 3,600 grams, and the Malay gold mines paid a tax of just over 3,200 grams. Finally, there is a statement of the annual amount paid by the king to his officers. Out of a total of 618,800 *baht*, princes with or without *krom* rank received 47,400 *baht*, and the Front Palace 29,000 *baht*.[37] These figures suggest that the rate of *biawat* was approximately half that reputedly paid in late Ayutthayan times.[38]

In 1833 the Siamese were drawn into a conflict with Vietnam. In July of that year rebels in Cochin-China sent a request for military assistance to Bangkok. A weakening of Annamese power would automatically increase Siamese influence in Cambodia, and therefore Rama III boldly decided to extend the Siamese umbrella over Cochin-China. In late 1833 a main force of some forty thousand men under *čhaophrayā* Bǫdindechā left Bangkok. At the same time a conscripted Laotian force was ordered to descend the Mekong River and invade Cambodia from the north, and the *čhaophrayā* Phrakhlang went with a fleet along the coast to take the harbour of Ha Tien and then move inland. The Siamese forces overran Cambodia without encountering much resistance. However, in January 1834, moving further eastwards in the direction of Saigon, the Annamite forces brought the advance to a halt. The Siamese planned a simultaneous attack by the forces of Bǫdindechā and the Phrakhlang, but the Phrakhlang's troops were late in arriving at the scene of the battle and, according to Bǫdindechā, this forced the Siamese to retreat, suffering heavy losses. The Phrakhlang would not agree to the immediate execution of his chief officers, demanded by Bǫdindechā, nor could the two military leaders come to an understanding about a renewed attack. The invasion was therefore called off, and all troops hurried back to Siamese territory. The plan had failed, and Annam was able not only to strengthen its dominance of Cochin-China but also to occupy Cambodia and rule it for a period of seven years. Then a popular revolt against the Annamese gave the Siamese another opportunity to add Cambodia to its vassal territories.[39] The military debacle of 1833 and 1834 must have had a sobering effect upon the court. It was realized that there was no longer a buffer state protecting the eastern borders, and the coastal town of Chanthaburi was immediately fortified.[40] The finding of a white elephant, always a welcome sign of a good rule, in the Khorat region, must have been especially valued at this time.[41]

One of the American missionaries, D.B. Bradley, arrived in 1835 armed with the Siamese printing press from Singapore mentioned above. Bradley was to become intimately involved with Siam during the course of his long life. He provides probably the liveliest and most informative picture avai! ible of the annual fleet to China:

> Junks in the China trade would then as now make but one voyage in a year, taking advantage of the favouring SW monsoon in June to sail from Bangkok, and of the NE monsoon to return the latter part of January and first part of February. From February to June there were annually from 60 to 80 of these *monsters of the deep* moored in the river, forming two lines, all heading down the stream, always ready as to position, to start on another voyage. These two long lines of junks were practically a great Bazaar for a period of two months or more from the time of their arrival. Each junk was freighted with the goods of several parties, each of whom occupied a part of the deck for the display of his wares until they were all sold out. The goods they brought from China were chiefly teas, silks, crapes, cotton fabrics, paper, crockery, Chinese cutlery, Chinese trunks, chests, betel boxes, Japan wooden ware, mirrors and a thousand other similar articles of Chinese manufacture.[42]

Bradley reported on 8 September 1835 a peculiar incident between Siamese and Europeans. On that day the British merchant Robert Hunter, who was regarded as the general agent of the British and the unofficial consul, and who had been given by the Siamese the rank of *luang* and an honorary name,[43] had as his guest Captain Wellar of the bark *Pyramus*, which he had chartered. In the cool of the evening, Hunter and Wellar had strolled out into the fields with their guns, intending to shoot crows and pigeons. Hunter had fallen into conversation with Bradley, whom they had met, while Wellar strolled on. Wellar soon found himself within the precincts of a Buddhist monastery, where evening prayers were going on, and shot two pigeons. The Buddhist monks, alarmed at the unfamiliar sound of firearms in a monastery, rushed out to find Wellar collecting his dead birds. Wellar apparently had no idea of the enormity of his act, and when the Buddhist monks tried to wrest the birds from his hands and to take his gun, a scuffle ensued. This ended when someone dealt Wellar a heavy blow on his head, stunning him.

Hunter ran to the captain's aid and found him badly wounded. Bradley described the ensuing scene as follows:

> Mr Hunter sent forthwith for the Port Captain and demanded that the case should without delay be brought before the government, threatening that if this were refused, he would take the *Pyramus* in front of the Royal palace and let the King hear from the mouth of her guns. The Port Captain appeared not a little alarmed and went post haste to the acting P'ra K'lang to lay the matter before him.[44]

The affair caused great commotion, and Hunter made heavy demands, threatening that if these were not granted he would send for foreign troops and "establish British rule in Siam".[45]

Soon Wellar recovered, however, and the king let Hunter know that the monks had their own ecclesiastical judiciary in which he could not meddle. It was quite clear to the Siamese that the monks had been provoked, and eventually they were punished fairly lightly.

The incident indicates Hunter's extraordinary position at the court. Apparently he was quite friendly with the Phrakhlang, with whom he often conducted business and traded jointly. At the same time the threat of a possible British invasion, which had seemed imminent less than a decade earlier, still carried weight. Hunter's high-handed attitude is also related to the fact that at that time he held the monopoly of square-rigged vessels of which the Siamese could make use. The days of this monopoly were coming to an end, however, because two European-type ships were being built under the Phrakhlang's supervision. Late in 1835 they were presented to the King, who, after a few trial runs, ordered more such boats to be built.

In 1835 the renovation of Wat Phra Chetuphon, popularly called Wat Pho, was begun. Rama III had already decided that the monastery, which had been built upon the ruins of an older one by his grandfather Rama I, needed considerable repair. In 1832 there had been some rebuilding of the monks' quarters. However, in 1835 it was decided to renovate the whole complex. Siamese monarchs as well as other members of the royal family and rich nobles were frequently involved with the building and restoring of monasteries. Wat Pho, however, was of particular interest. Rama I had housed various famous Buddhist images and relics in the monastery, and artists of that time had made many paper illustrations which hung from the walls.[46] Since then, many of the decorations had deteriorated, and during the Third Reign it was therefore decided to make a more permanent record by supplying many of the images and mural paintings with inscriptions. Apart from the many inscriptions on religious topics, some, such as those found in the cloisters surrounding the central area of the monastery, provide secular, contemporary records. There are allusions to literary works of the period, and a list of *mū'angs* of the kingdom, together with the titles of their governors. Unfortunately, many of the stone slabs have been lost and the record is now incomplete.[47] In addition, there are many maxims and exhortations conducive to proper moral conduct. Other inscriptions relate to the Jatakas (stories of the Buddha's previous births), to contemporary moralist poetry, and to practical formulae to ward off evil. A fascinating series of statues and inscriptions composed by the court physician *phrayā* Bamroe Rāchaphaethaya[48] deals with medical matters.

During the decade or more that it took to restore and rebuild the monastery, it gradually acquired the status of an encyclopaedia, where the best moral literature was displayed, where court artists depicted the best-known Buddhist stories, and where an extensive "medical library" was permanently exhibited at this "university in stone".[49]

## The Two Čhaofā Princes

In 1836 Rama III arranged the appointment of his half-brother, *čhaofā* Mongkut, to the position of abbot of Wat Bowoniwēt,[50] a new monastery in the heart of Bangkok. During the years preceding this appointment, Prince Mongkut had resided many years in Wat Samorai, a monastery on the outskirts of the city. Mongkut had at that time become somewhat notorious in the Buddhist church for his unorthodox opinions. During an earlier stage of his career in the

Sangha, he had come under the influence of a learned Burmese monk who had informed him of the great debate on a pure ordination which had rocked the Burmese Sangha. As a result, Mongkut had become convinced that the Siamese order of monks had unwittingly lost the proper way of ordaining. In the quiet atmosphere of Wat Samorai he had arranged a new, meticulously organized ordination. Moreover, not far from the Wat Samorai was one of the Catholic churches, where Mgr Pallegoix had resided since 1830. Pallegoix was an intelligent, knowledgeable, and observant man who enjoyed frequent contact with the young prince-priest. Mongkut, like many other progressive young men of his days, was fascinated by glimpses of European culture, and he arranged regular meetings with the bishop, during which he learnt a smattering of Latin and frequently engaged in debates on the respective merits of Buddhism and Christianity. The bishop had little but contempt for the Buddhist faith, and Mongkut appears often to have been forced to admit that some of the beliefs and practices of the average Buddhist were incompatible with the new scientific facts brought from the West. As a result, Mongkut became intent upon sifting out a mass of accretions and superstitions from what he sincerely believed to be the deep true core of Buddhism. Admirable as this may appear to his twentieth-century admirers, especially to those steeped in Western education, to most leading Siamese of the 1830s Mongkut's acceptance of a Burmese point of view regarding ordination and his translation of this into a re-enactment of the ritual were extremely contentious and dangerous issues, implying doubt about the validity of the ordination of all other monks in Siam. At the same time, Mongkut's contact with Europeans had led him to reject as fables several of the most highly revered Siamese classics, such as the *Traiphūmikhāthā*. Rama III might have been sympathetic to a serious attempt to eradicate some lax practices which may have crept into the Siamese Sangha, but on no account could he view with equanimity the Burmese-inspired reordination.

Rama III's motivation in arranging Mongkut's appointment as abbot of Wat Bowoniwēt should not therefore be regarded as a sign of royal support for the reform movement.[51] It is more likely that the king had become somewhat worried about Mongkut's activities and that he placed him in Wat Bowoniwēt in order to draw him more into traditional Siamese life, away from the relative isolation of Wat Samorai, where he depended too much on the intellectual stimulus of Pallegoix. Probably he hoped that the responsibility of being abbot and the daily business of supervising a major monastery would also help Mongkut to settle down. Mongkut was to remain just over fourteen years as abbot of Wat Bowoniwēt, where he was able to bring into practice many of the ideas he had developed earlier. There was a stricter adherence to the rules in Wat Bowoniwēt and a great deal of intellectual inquiry, which set Prince Mongkut and his followers apart. Rama III may have been successful in that Mongkut did not develop his new approach into a direct confrontation with the rest of the Sangha. Only after Mongkut's death did this movement formally split off from the orthodox order and form a separately administered body, the *Thammayutikanikāya*.

Prince Mongkut's activities may thus occasionally have been frowned upon by the king; the same can be said about those of his younger brother, *čhaofā kromakhun* Itsarēt, who had developed an even keener appetite for matters European. At the beginning of the decade, Gutzlaff had described him as follows:

> Chow-fa-nooi, the younger brother of the late king and the rightful heir of the crown,[52] is a youth of about 23, possessing some abilities, which are however swallowed up in childishness. He speaks the English language; can write a little, imitate works of European artisans; and is a decided friend of European sciences and of Christianity. He courts the friendship of every European; holds free conversation with him, and is anxious to learn whatever he can. He is beloved by the whole nation, which is wearied out by heavy taxes; but his elder brother, Chow-fa-yay, who is just now a priest, is still more beloved.[53]

In December 1835 it was rumoured that Prince Itsarēt was considered as a husband for Rama III's favourite daughter and that his appointment as Uparāt was imminent. Bradley noted that the prince was treading lightly so as not to incur the king's displeasure. Other missionaries appear to have received the same impression.⁵⁴ It is not known whether It-sarēt had been encouraged in this belief by some action of his elder half-brother, or whether this was the *čhaofā's* way of giving a hint, in the hope it might be followed up. At any rate, after some twelve months the rumour died out and It-sarēt remained in his old position at the court.

## Opium Suppression

In each of the years 1837, 1838, and 1839 the Siamese govern-ment was active in the suppression of robber bands. The first big concerted drive was in 1837, when many weapons and much opium were handed in to government officials in return for a free pardon.⁵⁵ The following year the Phrakhlang's men heard about a ship transporting opium, and soldiers were able to catch one Chinese smuggler red-handed. Through him, an intricate network of opium traders was discovered. In 1839 a last free pardon was offered to those who surrender-ed opium, and the penalty for being caught and convicted was increased from the traditional fine — of ten times the worth of the contraband articles found — to the death penalty. Four committees of senior officers were set up to clear up the evil of opium in specific regions. The clearing of the Bangkok district was given to the three most powerful Siamese of the day: *kromaluang* Rakronarēt, the king's uncle and the highest-ranking prince in the country, *čhaophrayā* Bọdin-dechā, and *čhaophrayā* Phrakhlang.⁵⁶ This drive was not without success. The *Records of the Astrologers* mention laconically that opium was found in the city and beyond.⁵⁷

The American missionaries' printing press was used to print ten thousand copies of the royal edict against the sale and use of opium. Relations between the relatively newly arrived Protestant missionaries and the court had become very cordial. Apart from printing the royal decree, Bradley had been paid 240 *baht* for inoculating some ten thousand Siamese against smallpox between January and April 1839, "principally in the palace and in the families of the nobles".⁵⁸ The missionary account of the drive against opium traffick-ing is as follows:

For nearly two months, the king's officers have been scouring the country, and numbers have been thrown into prison for endeavouring to secrete the drug. The king seems determined to free the country of this drug, at all hazards. We pity the poor creatures who have been accustomed to use it, but cannot but rejoice at the prospect of the removal of so great an evil. His majesty, however, has permitted a very small quantity to be restored to those who cannot break off the use of it immediately, but gives them to understand, that when it is gone they are to have no more for ever. Two or three ships from Singapore, etc. happening to come up at the time having, as was said, opium were obliged to secrete it and take it back. The opium business is not yet completed; new discoveries are daily made, and for a number of days past, it is said the burning of the precious drug has gone on at a great rate.[59]

The spate of robber-band and opium-trade suppression in the late 1830s can probably best be understood by taking the wider trade practices into account. Opium had been imported into Siam for a considerable time. Originally it had been almost exclusively consumed by Chinese, and the great number of Chinese immigrants probably caused an increased demand for the product. Already at the end of Rama I's reign, opium-trading and consumption was felt to be a problem, hence Rama II's edict against the sale and use of the drug. In this the Siamese king followed the Chinese emperor's example of 1796.[60] Opium was being produced in various areas of British India and loaded onto British trading vessels at Calcutta. Traders sent the chests of opium to local dealers, mainly in China, but also directly or indirectly to those in Siam. By 1832, when the matter of Indian revenue was discussed in the British Parliament, mercenary interests outweighed considerations of morality and justice, and the opium trade thus gained the semi-official approval of the British government. This was one of the factors involved in the rapid increase of opium production in India. While in 1820 just over 4,000 chests of opium were sold in Calcutta, by 1830 this had increased to more than 8,700 chests, by 1835 to almost 13,000 chests, and by 1837 to circa 16,000 chests, and almost all of this opium was destined for the Chinese market.[61]

In China, as in Siam, the number of addicts rose, and the central government issued harsher warnings and increased the fines and punishment. One result of the severe legislation coupled with increased supply and demand, was that in both countries the trade was forced "underground": secret networks were set up to carry on this lucrative business. The big Siamese drive against the opium traffic in the late 1830s may be seen as the central government's realization that the illegal trade had reached dangerous proportions and that the use of opium had to be regarded as an endemic social evil. It is no coincidence that the Chinese emperor also decided in late 1839 to send one of his ablest and most trusted mandarins as special commissioner to Canton to suppress the opium trade.[62] However, while the Siamese were able to conclude their drive with limited success, the Chinese became involved in a series of confrontations with British merchants which led to the Opium War.

The Siamese opium problem was by no means resolved by the raids following the decree of 1839. By 1844 opium was being imported again, with the tacit agreement of state officers. In addition, a large number of people had switched to using cannabis (*kanchā*), which could be grown locally. The government's stance in protecting the people from the ill-effects of opium was weakened by its lenient attitude to alcoholic intoxication, for the Treasury gained a large sum every year through tax-farming liquor licences throughout the country. Finlayson had reported that the licence for the Bangkok district brought the government a sum of 72,000 *baht* in 1822; this had risen by 1832 to 104,900 *baht*, [63] and the trade in ardent spirits had become one of the largest sources of income.[64]

## Renewed Expeditions to the Kingdom's Outer Regions

The southern dependencies were fairly restful after the expedition of the *čhaophrayā* Phrakhlang in 1832. Six years later, however, trouble began again in Kedah, which was attacked by supporters of the deposed sultan. The revolt spread into an anti-Siamese movement, and even the Siamese stronghold of Songkhla was at one stage threatened. The governors of Nakhon Si Thammarat and Songkhla assembled all their forces and, urgently asking for reinforcements from Bangkok, gave battle. Just before the advance troops from the capital arrived, the Malay insurgents suffered defeat and the large army that arrived in April 1839 was too late to assist in the suppression of the revolt. However, the situation in the south remained tense, and it was not until 1842 that the Bangkok forces could be withdrawn.[65]

Late in 1840 the Siamese were again drawn into a conflict on their eastern borders, where Cambodia had been a Vietnamese buffer state since 1834. In 1840 there was a general popular revolt there against the Vietnamese rule, and Cambodian representatives came to Bangkok to ask not only for the return of a scion of the Cambodian royal family residing in Siam to become the new king but also for assistance in throwing off the Vietnamese yoke. Various armies from Siam, mainly consisting of people of Cambodian descent,[66] rallied to liberate their country. After a few skirmishes, the Siamese advance came to a halt, and for several years Cambodia was partly under Vietnamese control and partly under that of the Siamese, each side sponsoring their own candidate for the Cambodian throne. Gradually, the Siamese-backed candidate gained the upper hand, and in the late 1840s the Siamese could once more count Cambodia as their eastern buffer state.[67]

## Expulsion of Hunter

It may be recalled that the *čhaophrayā* Phrakhlang had decided in 1835 to build square-rigged vessels, which proved seaworthy and further ships were commissioned.[68] Thus the *Singapore Free Press* on 27 July 1837 noticed the arrival of

> his Siamese majesty's frigate "Conqueror", a vessel of 600 tons, just launched from the docks at Chantibun [Chanthaburi]. She is armed with forty guns, of what calibre it is not said; but, notwithstanding her warlike equipment and name, she is at present to be employed only as a peaceful carrier of the goods of his golden-footed majesty's subjects. Another vessel of 1,000 tons has been laid down, and is to be similarly equipped and employed.[69]

Rama III planned to create a royal fleet of Western-style ships which would be able to augment the king's income by trading and which at the same time would be heavily armed, by local standards, so as to increase Siamese might. Gradually new ships were added to this incipient merchant navy, and, according to reports, by 1847 the king had eleven to thirteen European-type ships, with his nobles owning another six.[70]

It was not long before the king gained confidence in the new venture, and by 1840 he was a serious competitor for Robert Hunter, who until then had had a virtual monopoly of space in European vessels, which he rented out to Siamese traders. In 1841 a shipment of teak in the hands of the firm of Hunter and Hayes was seized and confiscated. Until then, the product had been allowed to be shipped openly. The next year, the king suddenly declared a new levy on sugar leaving the country, and by seizing part of the cargo being handled by Hunter's firm, managed to extract a considerable sum.[71] Hunter's remonstrations were to no avail, even though the Siamese had been deeply shocked to hear that the British had attacked China and were waging a war in which the Chinese suffered defeat after defeat. Hunter's firm provided Siam with chain cables which were drawn over the mouth of the river Chao Phraya, where the forts were also repaired and partly rebuilt. At the same time Hunter, who had been supplying the king with arms, ordered 250 guns of small calibre from England, in anticipation of hostilities between England and Siam. In addition, Hunter was asked to supply Siam with a steamer to defend the country from the expected attack by the English when they returned victorious from China. However, when the British troops returned to India without stopping at Bangkok, the king, possibly feeling that Hunter had misled him about the situation, no longer wanted the arms or the vessel.[72]

The merchants' growing hostility is demonstrated in a series of remonstrations and memoranda sent to the British authorities. Hunter and Hayes report a case of mishandling of a British subject by the Siamese authorities[73] and repeatedly accuse the Siamese of acting contrary to the treaty of 1826. They would have welcomed a show of power from a few British warships, and at least one influential senior officer sympathized with them and stated that "such a measure would tend to do good throughout the Malayan Archipelago, where the Petty Chiefs have assumed a tone quite inconsistent with their insignificance".[74]

Relations between Hunter and the Siamese government deteriorated further. It became known that Hunter had sold opium[75] and had thus knowingly broken Siamese laws. Early in 1844 two Chinese traders were given the right to collect the new sugar levy, for a prearranged fee, which made the new tax a more permanent feature of the state revenue. It seems that at this time the steamship ordered, a vessel called the *Express*, arrived, and Hunter learned that Rama III was no longer interested in buying it. Apparently Hunter declared that if the agreed price for the ship were not paid, he would sell it to the Vietnamese.[76] Thereupon he was ordered out of the country and left on the *Express* for Calcutta. Hunter tried hard to convince the British authorities of the need to send a punitive expedition against the "ignorant and haughty despot", but the British authorities found that there was no flagrant breach of the existing treaties and also that Hunter had brought much of his trouble upon himself, and no action was taken. It was noted, however, that there were grounds for a revision of the international trade agreements between the two countries.[77] In July 1844 Hunter made a voyage to Bangkok, where he was coolly received but obtained permission to remove his personal possessions. In December 1844 he finally left the country, ending a relationship which had lasted just over twenty years.

The events leading up to Hunter's expulsion from Siam demonstrate the deep impression China's defeat had made upon the court. Up until 1840 the emperor of China had been regarded as the world's most powerful person. From the Siamese point of view, the Chinese nation was on a different scale from "ordinary" countries such as Annam, Burma, and also until 1840, countries such as the United States of America, France, and England. Britain's conquest of lower Burma in the 1820s had shaken this view, but the relative might of the European weaponry and European command of a new technology was definitely established in the eyes of the Siamese court during the Opium War. It appears that the

British merchants probably wishing to pay back for the un-expected seizure of teak and for the sugar levy, had gladly helped spread the rumour that British troops would make a foray into Siam. The cashing in on Siamese ignorance regard-ing British intentions did not succeed when the king realized the merchants' duplicity. Hunter's loyalty was not to the British, as was shown by his supplying weaponry, but neither was it to the Siamese, as was proved by his threat to sell the steamer to Siam's greatest foe at that time: the Vietnamese.

Rama III's decision to turn Hunter out appears therefore not unjustified. At the same time Hunter and Hayes were not physically molested, they were never called before a tribunal, and their possessions were not confiscated, though Siamese law, which at that time applied also to British residents in Siam, would have called for severe punishment for some of Hunter's actions. At any time he could have been arrested for dealing in opium or threatening the safety of the kingdom. The king acted with caution and restraint, no doubt aware of the fact that Hunter would attempt to call in an expeditionary force. However, Hunter seems to have brandished that weapon so often that his ability to call in troops must have been doubted. The Siamese action shows that in 1840 Siamese confidence was fairly strong and that they, no longer depend-ing upon Hunter's skills, now preferred to act without him.

Meanwhile Hunter's case was soon overshadowed by local problems. In 1844 yet another opium-smuggling ring was discovered, and it was clear that Chinese secret societies were deeply involved in the continuing opium trade. In this and the following year a series of raids was made by government forces to break up some of these secret societies.[78] This was also a year with a considerable rice shortage: the price of a cartload of unhusked rice rose to 18 *chang*, or 1,440 *baht*, and there was widespread famine.

Hunter's hurried departure marks for the time being the end of the merchants' position of power and influence at the court. A cloud of suspicion now hung over all Westerners. Only the staunchest believers in European technology con-tinued for a while to flirt with the West. Prince Mongkut had been very friendly with the American missionaries who had helped him medically.[79] During the years when Europeans were favoured, he had learnt something of the English language and of printing techniques, and he continued his English lessons in 1845 and 1846 with Jesse Caswell, one of the American Protestant missionaries. However, upon a strong hint from the king that he disliked his subjects learning English, the classes stopped.[80] Late in 1845 Siam's first periodical, the fortnightly *Bangkok Recorder*, was discontinued after having been printed for just over a year. The main reason for its lack of success was apparently the fact that the news-sheet was too blatantly a vehicle for missionary propaganda.[81] *Čhaofā* Itsarēt was probably the last high-ranking Siamese to demonstrate publicly pro-European leanings in the 1840s. With the help of his European friends, Itsarēt had obtained a small steam-engine and had it fitted in a ship in which he travelled up and down the Chao Phraya River. Eventually, however, even Itsarēt sensed the mood at the court and in 1847 he abandoned his pro-Western display.

## The Chinese Revolts

Early in 1848 riots broke out among the Chinese in the region between Nakhon Chaisi and Sakhonbusi, west of Bangkok. A police force was sent to establish order, but it met with violence. Consequently, the *čhaophrayā* Phrakhlang took a large number of troops and suppressed the revolt, killing some three to four hundred Chinese and taking a few hundred prisoners. This was followed by the news of an even larger uprising east of Bangkok in the provincial town of Chachoengsao, where the Chinese rebels were reported to have taken the local fortress. This time the nation's two most senior generals, *čhaophrayā* Bọdindechā and *čhaophrayā* Phrakhlang, took several thousand soldiers to Chachoengsao. Meanwhile, the folly of open revolt had been seen by a faction of the Chinese, and these aided the Siamese in retaking the fort. In the aftermath of this rebellion thousands of Chinese were reputedly killed. A great number of sugar plantations were also destroyed during the hostilities.

Both uprisings seem to have been caused by a rapidly

worsening economic situation in the sugar plantations, probably the result of the imposition of a series of new taxes on sugar refineries and on the finished product. It might be argued that Rama III's policy of increasing the tax burden in order to raise state revenue had been pushed much too far with respect to sugar.[82]

## Prince Rakronarēt Executed

For many years Rama III's uncle Prince Rakronarēt, who had been promoted from *kromamu'n* rank to that of *kromaluang* in 1832, had been the most senior relative of the king. He had been given considerable responsibilities, especially in the judiciary. In this respect his position resembled that of Rama III when he was still Prince Čhētsadābodin during the latter part of the reign of Rama II. Prince Rakronarēt was disappointed in his hope to become Uparāt in 1832 when Prince Sakdiphonlasēp had died. Apparently Rakronarēt had indulged in abuse of power. Many princes were reported to have arrested members of the populace and judged legal cases to their own advantage. Thus, princes such as Rakronarēt would take attractive girls to be their concubines without obtaining the permission of parents or guardians.[83] Since the highest princes were involved in such cases, people dared not protest. However, in November 1848 the king received a formal complaint and an inquiry was made into the legality of princes' actions. Prince Rakronarēt's personal life was investigated, and it became clear that he had often acted dishonourably. In addition, his ambition to become Uparāt was revealed, together with the opinion that he would stand a good chance to be Rama III's successor. Rakronarēt was found guilty and Rama III ordered his execution.

## Rama III and the Representatives of Western Culture, 1849–50

In June 1849 Bangkok was again ravaged by a serious cholera epidemic, reminiscent of the days of 1819 and 1822. In a few weeks an estimated thirty to thirty-five thousand people died. One of the victims was *čhaophrayā* Bǫdindechā, the head of the *krom* Mahātthai.[84] Rama III emulated the measures his father had taken to combat the disease, admonishing people to generate good *karma*. One of the traditional methods of doing so was by freeing all captive animals. However, the Christian missionaries at first refused to condone what they considered heathen ceremonies. A situation reminiscent of Taksin's confrontation with European priests developed — a Siamese king, already distrustful of Westerners, found that his measures intended for the good of the country were being opposed. In this case, however, the missionaries, both Protestant and Catholic, decided to ease their consciences by considering the release of animals to be a civil state ceremony rather than an act pertaining to a false religion, and co-operated with the king. However, as a result Rama III investigated the activities of foreign missionaries and had four Protestant converts arrested on charges that the missionaries had printed documents pertaining to Siamese laws without having obtained the necessary permission, that the Siamese translation of the Bible contained sacred expressions borrowed from Buddhism, and that the foreign missionaries persisted in depicting Siamese Buddhism as a false creed.[85]

This action of Rama III has been depicted as a reflection of the king's increasing distrust of foreigners as well as of his worsening health.[86] This view is not wholly supported by evidence. Rama III distrusted foreigners, but this was already apparent at the beginning of his reign. His wariness abated a little in the 1830s, but it returned when the most prominent Westerner, Hunter, who had been granted many favours at court, proved to be a grasping and selfish man with no loyalty to the country where he was making his fortune. The Western priests' refusal to help "make merit" in order to combat an outbreak of cholera must have looked like further proof that Europeans had no concern for Siam's welfare.

At the same time, Rama III's reaction, understandable as it was, was not precipitate or hasty. When he discovered that the Protestant printers were acting in contravention of Siamese regulations, he did not force the missionaries to go to court and listen to charges. Instead he vented his anger upon a few Siamese subjects who were close to the missionaries. From Rama III's point of view, the missionaries were offensive. He was a king intensely proud of the best achievements of Siamese culture, as exemplified by the display at Wat Chetuphon.[87]

The failure of two Western trade missions in 1850 has been depicted as a further sign of Rama III's choleric, stubborn anti-Western policy. Again, the circumstances in which the missions failed are not wholly in accordance with the view that the king and the "conservatives" at the court obstructed more friendly relations between Siam and foreign powers.

The first mission to arrive was that of Joseph Balastier, the American consul at Singapore, who was sent to attempt to secure better trade conditions and obtain permission to establish an American consulate in Bangkok. Balastier came armed with a letter from the American president, but he arrived at the court bringing only a Chinese servant and a local missionary as his retinue. The Siamese had looked forward to receiving the delegation with all honours, but became suspicious of Balastier's credentials when he arrived so unceremoniously.

To make matters worse, Balastier's initial interview with *phrayā* Sīphiphat, the *čhaophrayā* Phrakhlang's younger relative and deputy, went very badly. Balastier cut straight through the traditional preliminary questions and answers and demanded an audience with the king. He and *phrayā* Sīphiphat could not come to an agreement regarding matters of protocol, and the interview ended in an atmosphere of hostility. When the *čhaophrayā* Phrakhlang, who had been in Chumphon supervising a tattooing drive, returned to Bangkok, attempts were made to reopen meaningful contact, but no progress was made and Balastier left Bangkok without having met any other high officials. His whole attempt had lasted less than a month.[88] The failure of the mission was clearly the result of Balastier's inability to adapt to Siamese protocol. The American envoy displayed such a lack of dignity and, to Siamese feelings, such a rude directness, that all Siamese who were involved were united in their efforts to shield the king from such an unpredictable and strange individual. The king never set eyes upon Balastier, and he can hardly have been sorry to have missed an audience with the American.

The second envoy to reach Bangkok in 1850 was Sir James Brooke, sent by Lord Palmerston to attempt to improve commercial relations between Siam and Britain. He arrived in August at the mouth of the Chao Phraya, and, ominously, the larger of the two steamers on which the mission travelled became stuck in the mud and Brooke had to transfer to the smaller boat to proceed further. His preliminary meeting with the *čhaophrayā* Phrakhlang went smoothly, and by the end of August he had good hopes of securing a favourable result. However, suddenly at the end of August 1850 there occurred a marked change in the conduct of the Siamese towards the mission: everybody became distrustful and cold. Brooke valiantly wrote several proposals for a new treaty, but received nothing but evasive replies. He too left Bangkok without having seen the king, feeling insulted.[89]

In Brooke's case the *čhaophrayā* Phrakhlang had advised the king to agree to a new treaty. The king, however, had had Brooke's credentials examined and found them wanting, and even before Brooke had his meeting with the *čhaophrayā* Phrakhlang the king had already issued an order not to proceed with positive discussions. Probably it will never be known what decided the king to act against the *čhaophrayā* Phrakhlang's advice. He certainly was not alone in his view, because several other senior ministers also disagreed with the *čhaophrayā* Phrakhlang on this matter.[90]

When it was clear that his mission was not going to succeed, Brooke did not attempt to hide his ill feelings. To Lord Palmerston he wrote to advise a British take-over: "The time for conciliation with this people never was; reasonable remonstrance will no longer be attended to, a blockade would aggravate and not cure — and intimidation will fail unless followed up to its legitimate consequences."[91]

Brooke had been aware that there were people at the Siamese court who would favour a new treaty with England. When he was still preparing for his voyage to Bangkok and residing for a while in Singapore, he was told of the existence of two princes at the court who were generally favourably inclined towards Europeans. Rather prophetically he had written about *čhaofā* Mongkut and his younger brother *čhaofā kromakhun* Itsarēt as "worthy instruments" to bring about better relations between the two countries.[92] From this letter it is also clear that in Singapore the myth of Rama III usurping the throne and the *čhaofā* princes being the legitimate heirs to the throne was generally believed.

In Bangkok, however, the problem of the succession looked quite different. In principle there was nothing to prevent Rama III from elevating his chief wife to be the queen and nominating a series of relatives to *čhaofā* rank. However, he refrained from doing so, just as he deliberately omitted to fill the position of Uparāt when it became vacant, possibly because he was himself full of vigour and because he did not find any of his relatives outstanding enough to merit an elevation to the Front Palace. However, speculation remained rife at the court, and as the king became older it seemed that the two *čhaofā* princes had the best chances of succession to the throne, not least because of their friendship with members of the *čhaophrayā* Phrakhlang's family.

## The End of the Reign

The king became ill in September 1850. At first the illness was treated as a temporary lapse of health. However, when his condition worsened, he was forced to discuss his succession. At first the king asked a committee to select a successor, a highly irregular procedure. The committee could not come to a conclusion and reported back that it was inappropriate to discuss such matters when the king was ill and that they hoped he would soon recover. Realizing that there was no one who would please all parties, Rama III reputedly discussed some of the candidates frankly with *phrayā* Sīsuriyawong, then *čhāngwāng* of the Mahātlek:

> I cannot see any prince who can lead the country. For example, *kromakhun* Dēt [Dētadisōn] is a gullible person, whatever people tell him, he will readily believe it, he cannot be the leader. As to *kromakhun* Phiphit [Phiphitphubēn] he does not know how to work, he has not got an enquiring mind, he only thinks of his pleasure, he has not got the character to look after the

country. That leaves us only the two *čhaofā* princes about whom I have reservations, namely that the elder [prince Mongkut] holds Mon [Buddhist] beliefs, and if he became king he might order the Sangha to dress like the Mons throughout this country; whilst the younger *čhaofā* prince does have knowledge about various matters concerning warfare, this is not sufficient to lead a government, he only loves pleasure and therefore he has not got my approval.[93]

If this account is a faithful record of what was said, it is clear that the Siamese king dispassionately went through a list of possible candidates. It is interesting to note that the *čhaofā* princes were not mentioned first and succession by them was not seen as the only right course, a view often expressed in later literature. Of the four candidates, the king is enthusiastic about none, but of all the objections, the ones against Mongkut seem the least devastating. The statement demonstrates that Rama III was not wholly in agreement with Mongkut's reformist movement. The fact that Mongkut and his followers wore the Buddhist robes in a manner that differed from that of the rest of the Siamese Sangha evidently preyed on the king's mind, because in late February, after having donated large sums of money to many monks, Rama III ordered all monks to dress in an orthodox fashion, and the "reformists" were quite mortified to lose such a distinguishing feature.[94]

When the king's health further deteriorated, full executive responsibility fell upon the *čhaophrayā* Phrakhlang as the most senior and experienced administrator.[95] On 15 March, when it seemed that the king would not survive the night, the *čhaophrayā* Phrakhlang made the crucial decision regarding the succession. He formally invited Prince Mongkut to become heir to the throne and, when the latter accepted, ordered troops to guard the future king at his monastery. Not long afterwards, on 2 April 1851, Rama III died, aged sixty-three, having been in command for just over twenty-five years.

The Third Reign is often depicted as reactionary and conservative, probably as a result of the failure of Western powers to secure a firm trading base in Siam. However, it has been argued that the Siamese were not unwilling to renegotiate the existing treaties and that more diplomatic and sensitive envoys could have secured much of what was being sought. At the beginning of Rama III's reign, the Burmese had suffered a humiliating defeat by the British, and fourteen years later the Chinese had a similar experience. Throughout the reign, Europeans appeared everywhere to be increasing their domination. The Dutch strengthened their hold upon the Indonesian archipelago, and the French felt obliged to stage several naval demonstrations against the Vietnamese. In these circumstances Rama III appears fully justified in his noncommittal and circumspect dealings. While keeping foreigners at a distance, he did not close off his country altogether. With laudatory prudence, Rama III usually avoided direct clashes with foreigners, and when forced to react, as in the case of Hunter, he did so without provocative harshness. In so far as the policies of Siamese kings helped the country escape becoming a colony, Rama III certainly deserves to be recognized as a shrewd leader who managed to sail the ship of state through turbulent waters.

# Notes

1. E. Roberts, *Embassy to the Eastern Courts of Cochin-China, Siam and Muscat during the Years 1832-3-4*, pp. 247-48, and an even more garbled version on p. 300.
2. For the date of birth of Mongkut I have relied upon Prince Damrong, *Phrarātchaphongsāwadān Krungratanakōsin Ratchakān thī Sǭng*, vol. 2, pp. 222-23.
3. This is confirmed in *The Burney Papers*, vol. 2, pt 4, pp 112-13.
4. *PKRt Sǭng*, pp. 201-3.
5. R. Lingat, "La vie réligieuse du roi Mongkut", *The Siam Society Fiftieth Anniversary Commemorative Publication*, vol. 1, pp. 24-28.
6. Čhaophrayā Thiphākǫrawong, *Phrarātchaphongsāwadān Krungratanakōsin, Ratchakān thī Sām* (hereafter *PKRt Sām*), p.11.
7. *Čhotmāihēthōn*, p. 39.
8. Ibid., p. 39.
9. See the letter of the *čhaophrayā* Phrakhlang to John Crawfurd, dated 21 August 1825, reproduced in *Burney Papers*, vol. 1, pt 1, pp. 6-7.
10. See the letter of Henry Burney to the governor of the Prince of Wales Island, dated 22 December 1825, *Burney Papers*, vol. 1, pt 1, p. 22.
11. From a report by Burney dated 2 December 1826, published in *Burney Papers*, vol. 2, pt 4, p. 41. Apparently these rumours had already been rife several months before, because they are mentioned in a letter dated 2 September 1825 by J. Gillies to J. Crawfurd (*Burney Papers*, vol. 1, pt 2, pp. 3-4), and serious distrust of British intentions must have undermined all negotiations at that time.

12. D.E. Malloch, excerpts from his private journal, published in *Burney Papers*, vol. 2, pt 4, pp. 227-31.
13. Ibid., p. 226.
14. For details, see W.F. Vella, *Siam Under Rama III*, p. 80 ff., and D.K. Wyatt, "Siam and Laos, 1767-1827".
15. *Čhotmāihēthōn*, p. 44.
16. For details on the lottery, see B.O. Cartwright, "The Huey Lottery", *JSS* 18, pt 3 (1924): 221-39. Cartwright gives a different date for the first organization of the lottery, namely 1835.
17. *PKRt Sǭng*, p. 92.
18. Ibid., p. 93.
19. For details, see Shigeharu Tanabe, "Historical Geography of the Canal System in the Chao Phraya River Delta", pp. 43-44 and fig. 4.
20. From Captain Burney's notes, published in *Burney Papers*, vol. 1, pt 1, p. 180.
21. Malloch's journal, *Burney Papers*, vol. 2, pt 4, p. 223.
22. The fact that the position of head of the *krom* Kalāhom had been offered to the *čhaophrayā* Phrakhlang before 1830 is mentioned in Captain Burney's diary, which was dispatched in February 1826 (see *Burney Papers*, vol. 1, pt 1, p. 65).
23. *PKRt Sǭng*, pp. 107-8; Vella, *Siam Under Rama III*, pp. 7-8.
24. K. Gutzlaff, *Verslag van een Driejarig Verblijf in Siam, en van eene Reize langs de Kust van China naar Mantchou-Tartarije*, p. 2.
25. K.E. Wells, *History of Protestant Work in Thailand, 1828–1958*, p. 12.
26. Udom Poshakrishna, "Geschichte der Chirurgie in Thailand, *1828-1922*", *JSS* 51, pt 1 (1963): 60.
27. A cartload (*kwian*) of paddy was reckoned to be equal to 16 *hāp*, each *hāp* weighing sixty kilograms.
28. Roberts, *Embassy to the Eastern Courts*, p. 259.
29. *Čhotmāihēthōn*, p. 46.
30. Six years later, this led to considerable trouble at the court, see later in this chapter.
31. Roberts, *Embassy to the Eastern Courts*, p. 311.
32. Malloch's journal, *Burney Papers*, vol. 2, pt 4, p. 223.
33. Gutzlaff, *Verslag*, p. 30.
34. Extract from D.B. Bradley's journal, published in the *Bangkok Calendar*, 1870, p. 90.
35. G. Finlayson, *The Mission to Siam and Hue, the Capital of Cochin-China, in the Years 1821-2*, p. 248.
36. Many more still were to be added; for details, see *PKRt Sām*, pp. 361-62.
37. Roberts, *Embassy to the Eastern Courts*, p. 427.
38. H.G.Q. Wales, *Ancient Siamese Government and Administration*, p. 236.
39. Further details can be found in Vella, *Siam Under Rama III*, pp. 96-99, and D.P. Chandler, "Cambodia's Relations with Siam in the Early Bangkok Period: The Politics of a Tributary State", *JSS* 60, pt 1 (1972): 162.
40. Bradley's journal, *Bangkok Calendar*, 1870, p. 96.
41. *Čhotmāihēthōn*, p. 49.
42. *Bangkok Calendar*, 1870, p. 90.
43. According to *PKRt Sām*, p. 279, he had in 1831 been given the title of *luang* Awutwisēt. Hunter had gained considerable power at the court, having by 1835 four vessels working for him (Vella, *Siam Under Rama III*, p. 126).
44. *Bangkok Calendar*, 1870, p. 97.
45. Ibid., entry for 9 September 1835.

46. For a description of the monastery before its restoration, see J. Crawfurd, *Journal of an Embassy to the Courts of Siam and Cochin-China*, pp. 163-67.

47. The available evidence is enumerated by Prince Dhani Nivat in "The Inscriptions of Wat Phra Jetubon", in *Collected Articles by H.H. Prince Dhani Nivat Kromamun Bidayalabh Brdihyakorn*, pp. 13-16.

48. For details, see A.B. Griswold, "The Rishis of Wat Pho", in *Felicitation Volumes of Southeast-Asian Studies Presented to His Highness Prince Dhaninivat Kromamun Bidyalabh Bridhyakorn*, vol. 2, pp. 319-28.

49. Prince Dhani Nivat, "Inscriptions of Wat Phra Jetubon", p. 19.

50. Lingat, "La vie réligieuse", p. 33.

51. If the king had been an enthusiastic supporter of Mongkut's ideas, he could have arranged much greater honours than an abbotship in Bangkok. It has recently been suggested, however, that Mongkut's behaviour was not altogether exemplary and that he had repeatedly left the order for amorous reasons, only to be reordained again (see Ki Thanit, *Prawat Khana Song Thai kap Thammayutprakān*, pp. 96-106).

52. Gutzlaff is wrong in two particulars: Itsarēt was not the brother of Rama II, but his son, and he was not the rightful heir to the crown. However, it is quite possible that the prince liked to give the impression to foreigners that he was the legitimate and rightful heir.

53. Gutzlaff, "Journal of a Residence in Siam", *Chinese Repository* 1 (1832): 19.

54. W.L. Cowan, "The Role of Prince Chuthamani in the Modernizing of Siam and His Court Position During the Reigns of Rama III and Rama IV", *JSS* 55, pt 1 (1967): 49-50.

55. *Čhotmāihēthōn*, p. 52. This is the event alluded to in Rama III's proclamation of 1839, which appeared in the *Singapore Free Press*, 13 June 1839. It was reprinted in the July 1839 edition of *The Chinese Repository* (vol. 5, pp. 125-32) and again Bowring, *The Kingdom and People of Siam*, vol. 2, pp. 368-77. The translation is a remarkable piece of work in that it is practically unintelligible to those unfamiliar with the Siamese language; it is a literal translation by someone apparently unfamiliar with Siamese court language and legal terms.

56. *Chinese Repository* 5: 131.

57. *Čhotmāihēthōn*, p. 53.

58. *Chinese Repository* 8 (November 1839): 384. The king's interest in European technology caused *čhaofā* Itsarēt to indulge openly in European pastimes, impressing fellow-Siamese with daily sessions of "watch-repairing" where he would sit with a pair of huge goggles protruding from his eyes, fixing some clock. Itsarēt still liked to impress his European friends with the romantic fantasy that he was in fact a "prisoner", someone jealously watched and guarded. At the same time this did not prevent him from organizing, at great expense, a noisy Christmas party in December 1840, where British sailors were encouraged to drink to excess, dance, play leap-frog, and demonstrate a boxing match. For details see F.A. Neale, *Narrative of a Residence in Siam*, pp. 87-94.

59. *Chinese Repository* 8 (November 1839): 384.

60. There are many sources dealing with the opium trade between India and China. The figures mentioned here are mainly drawn from E.W. Stoughton, "The Opium Trade — England and China", *Hunt's Merchants' Magazine* 2 (1840): 394-413.

61. Apparently the Calcutta market was not the only source for opium, because the total number of chests brought in by the clippers is reported in a contemporary source to have been 34,000 (see "The Opium Trade with China", *Christian Examiner* 24, no. 48 [1838]: 114-15).

62. See A. Waley, *The Opium War through Chinese Eyes*.
63. E. Roberts, *Embassy to the Eastern Courts of Cochin-China, Siam and Muscat*, p. 426. A missionary mentions a much larger sum for 1832, namely forty-five piculs of silver, or 180,000 baht (*Chinese Repository* 13 [April 1844]: 202).
64. *Chinese Repository* 13: 215-17.
65. Further details in Vella, *Siam Under Rama III*, pp. 71-73.
66. Possibly a reaction to the hostile reception of Siamese troops in 1834.
67. Further details can be found in *PKRt Sām*, pp. 208-14; Vella, *Siam Under Rama III*, pp. 101-5; and Chandler, "Cambodia's Relations," pp. 165-69.
68. It is unlikely that anyone would still have remembered the unfortunate experiences with the very first European-type shipbuilding in Siam, the building of a galleon in 1725, a joint venture of the Spanish of the Philippines and the Siamese king. That ship was apparently very badly built, made a few short runs, requiring extensive repairs after each journey, and was finally pronounced unseaworthy and condemned at a great loss to the owners. For details, see *Chinese Repository* 8 (1839–40): 258-59. During the reign of Rama II, several square-rigged trading vessels had been built, and these were used especially as the king's vessels during the missions to China, but also for general trading purposes (see R. Adey Moore, "An Early British Merchant in Bangkok", *JSS* 11, pt 2 [1914–15]: 25).
69. "Journal of Occurrences", *Chinese Repository* 6: 256.
70. Vella, *Siam Under Rama III*, p. 128, citing the *Bangkok Calendar* 1847, 1850.
71. Letter from J. Hayes to the governor of Prince of Wales Island, Singapore, and Malacca, dated 1 November 1843, *Burney Papers*, 4, pt 2, pp. 92-94.
72. Letter from W.B. Butterworth, governor of Prince of Wales Island, Singapore, and Malacca to the Government of India, dated 8 November 1843, *Burney Papers*, 4, pt 2, pp. 88-89; see also p. 162.
73. In January 1844 the British authorities received a detailed statement from the *krom* Phrakhlang regarding their handling of cases of smuggling. This statement was detailed and convincing. The British authorities accepted that Hunter and Hayes had not informed them properly in this matter, and this was noted in the subsequent confrontation.
74. *Burney Papers*, 4, pt 2, p. 91.
75. Letter from the Phrakhlang to the governor of Prince of Wales Island, Singapore, and Malacca, *Burney Papers*, 4, pt 2, p. 102. See also Vella, *Siam Under Rama III*, p. 129; C.M. Wilson, "State and Society in the Reign of Mongkut, 1851–1868: Thailand on the Eve of Modernization", p. 180 and p. 187; and Adey Moore, "An Early British Merchant", pp. 29-30.
76. Letter from W.J. Butterworth, governor of Prince of Wales Island, Singapore, and Malacca to the government of India, dated 13 February 1845, *Burney Papers*, 4, pt 2, p. 163 and p. 165.
77. Ibid., p. 162.
78. *Čhotmāihēthōn*, pp. 60-61.
79. D.B. Bradley's journal entry for 23 April 1836. An interesting account of the early days of Bradley's medical practice can be found in *Chinese Repository* 5 (1837): 445-56. Prince Mongkut was treated for paralysis of a facial nerve, a condition affecting his physiognomy throughout his life.
80. W.L. Bradley, "Prince Mongkut and Jesse Caldwell", *JSS* 54, 1 (1966): 31-32.
81. See D.B. Bradley's remarks in his private journal on 12 May 1867, when the new publication the *Siam Weekly Monitor* is being discussed. Details regarding the *Bangkok Recorder* can be found in *Periodicals and Newspapers Printed in Thailand between 1844–1934, a Bibliography*, p. 3. The *Bangkok Recorder* was revived in 1865.

82. Vella, *Siam Under Rama III*, p. 18; G.W. Skinner, *Chinese Society in Thailand*, pp. 143-44.
83. *PKRt Sām*, p. 361.
84. Letter by the American missionary S.R. House, reported in *Chinese Repository* 18 (September 1849): 503-4. See also Wells, *Protestant Work in Thailand*, p. 1.
85. *PKRt Sām*, pp. 330-31; Vella, *Siam Under Rama III*, pp. 36-37.
86. Ibid., p. 37.
87. The "University in Stone" was officially opened in 1848 (*Čhotmāihēthōn*, p. 61).
88. A detailed account of Balastier's dealings with members of the court is given in "Čhotmāihēt ru'ang Ballestier Thūt Amērikan khaomā nai Ratchakān thī Sām mu'a pī čhǭ Ph.S.2393", *PP*, vol. 35 (1969), pp. 3-71.
89. For details, see N. Tarling, "Siam and Sir James Brooke", *JSS* 48, pt 2 (1960): 43-72.
90. Vella, *Siam Under Rama III*, p. 135.
91. Dispatch from Singapore, 5 October 1850, as cited by Wilson, "State and Society", pp. 190-91.
92. Tarling, "Siam and Sir James Brooke", p. 49.
93. *PKRt Sām*, p. 365.
94. D.B. Bradley, journal, 1 March 1851.
95. After the death of *čhaophrayā* Bǫdindechā in 1849, the *čhaophrayā* Phrakhlang, who still held simultaneously the position of Kalāhom, was by far the most powerful man in the kingdom next to the king.

**6**

# The Fourth Reign:
# Westernization from Above

## The Succession

Prince Mongkut's succession to the throne was decided just
before Rama III's demise. The best account of the events was
written on 28 March, when Rama III was still alive.

> All parties concerned in the question of the succession were
> preparing themselves with arms and troops for self defence and
> resistance. There is no doubt that had it been determined that
> the King's sons should have the throne there would have been a
> fearful civil war here before now. It now appears that on the
> night of the 15th inst. when the King was very low, when the
> affairs of the Royal palace seemed to be on the very eve of a
> terrible outbreak, there was convened at the King's Palace, or at
> a place within its walls, a meeting of all the Princes, nobles, and
> chief rulers of the land to confer together on the all engrossing
> question who shall become the successor of the present king. Up
> to this time it would seem that no one of the three political
> parties had ventured to take any very positive steps to carry out
> its intentions. Each party maintained great reserve towards the
> others, and consequently they became suspicious of each other's
> intentions, and were ready at a word to come into fearful colli-
> sion.
>     As His Excellency the Phraklang, the prime minister of the
> foreign department, was one of the most powerful rulers of the

land, he was vehemently pressed to declare his purposes touching the question before them. He had borne a conspicuous part in placing the present king on the throne, and he had ever been a highly favourite ruler under him. This minister, it is said, had the boldness to declare firmly that he saw no man in the kingdom, who had equal claims with his Royal Highness T.Y. Chaufat Mongkut with his brother Chaufat Krommakhun Izaret as his colleague to become successor to the Throne.[1]

The presentation of Mongkut and his brother as a pair, to succeed their elder half-brother, is unusual. It would have been more in accordance with Siamese custom if Mongkut had been chosen king, and after his enthronement had formally announced who would be made Uparāt. The proclamation of the headship of the Front Palace at such an early stage in the proceedings was probably the result of a difficult compromise. The choice of Mongkut as the new king must have been a great disappointment to Itsarēt, who had long regarded himself as the leader of the "modernists". He had many more connections with Westerners than did Mongkut and was known as a leading innovator with a passion for technical reform.[2] In October 1848 the *Singapore Free Press* had published a glowing account of his first steamboat, with its two-horsepower engine. "This little phenomenon has made several trips up and down the river, his Royal Highness the Prince generally acting steersman himself, in full view of thousands of astonished and admiring spectators, who crowded the banks of the river on each occasion."[3] Itsarēt had a much more intimate knowledge of the workings of the administration than Mongkut. While Mongkut did not even hold *krom* rank, Itsarēt had risen from *kromamū'n* rank to *kromakhun*.

It is quite likely, therefore, that Itsarēt had wished to become king himself, and that Mongkut and the *čhaophrayā* Phrakhlang, aware of this ambition, attempted to overcome Itsarēt's objections to being delegated to second place by giving an extraordinary amount of honour and attention to that office. This explains why both brothers were formally invited to succeed Rama III, and why both received the oaths of allegiance.[4] Only a week after Rama III's death, D.B. Bradley, prompted by the king-elect Mongkut, wrote to the *Straits Times* about Prince Itsarēt: "[He] is to have titles equally honourable though the part he will take in the government must necessarily be a little lower than that of his elder brother."⁵

The honours bestowed upon Mongkut's younger brother were quite unprecedented. His regular income from the Treasury was doubled to 160,000 *baht*. After his formal investiture, he was given a royal tour of the city, and in his offical name could be found the royal epithet *čhao yū hua*, "the Lord in Charge". How much the "Second King" valued the epithet is shown by the fact that he often used it as part of his signature. Mongkut called himself Somedetch Phra Paramendr Maha Mongkut (or S.P.P.M. Mongkut), but his brother signed letters "S. Pin Klaw chau yu hua, Second King of Siam". The words "Pin Klaw" refer to names devised by Mongkut not long after ascending the throne. In common parlance, people had often called the reign of Rama I *phaendin ton*, or "the first reign", and that of Rama II *phaendin klāng*, or "the middle reign". Already during Rama III's time these reigns had been officially named Phraphuthayōtfāčhulālōk and Phraphuthaloetlāsulālai respectively, probably in order to avoid the implication that the Third Reign would be called "the last". Mongkut changed the appellation of his father slightly to Phraphuthaloetlānaphālai, and not long afterwards issued a decree in which he announced a name for the third ruler: Phra Nangklāo. While it was traditional to give a king a name posthumously, Mongkut broke with tradition by himself devising specific appellations for himself and his younger brother: King Phra' Čhōmklāo and King Phra' Pinklāo respectively.

All these unprecedented honours bestowed upon the king's younger brother may have blinded some observers to the Second King's actual position in court. He was seldom involved in matters of state, he did not have the ear of the king or the king's chief advisers. The Second King was engrossed in enlarging his collection of European goods, which in 1855 was described as a "museum of models, nautical and philosophical instruments, and a variety of scientific and other curiosities".⁶ He used his position as Second King to try to impress his English friends in particular, but in the Siamese court he increasingly became an isolated, somewhat ridiculous figure.[7]

## The New Administration

The general populace appeared genuinely glad to celebrate Mongkut's accession. The military parade and royal procession after the formal anointment were such cheerful events that the new king abruptly decided to extend the festivities another day and to add a boat procession to the programme. Palace attendants must have worked long hours to prepare the more than ten thousand wooden presents, in the shape of legendary fruit painted red and green, in which money was hidden. From the royal state barge, these gifts were dropped in the water as gifts to the well-wishing populace. During the following week yet another procession took place, this time with Phra' Pinklāo as the centre of attraction, who at great personal expense also gave away money and gold and silver flowers to Siamese and foreign spectators.[8]

The long list of promotions in the royal family of 1851 can best be understood by considering Mongkut's personal position genealogically. The new king came to the throne at the ripe age of forty-seven, and although the royal family was quite extensive, there were not many alive who were older than Mongkut himself. Eight of these elderly relatives were given high ranks, often skipping several steps in the princely ladder of *krom* ranks, three being created *kromaluang*, three *kromphra'*, and two *kromsomdetphra'*. The two selected for the highest honours were Mongkut's uncle, the Buddhist monk who became *kromsomdetphra'* Paramānuchitchinōrot, and Prince Dēchādisǫn. Two of Mongkut's younger half-brothers were promoted to *kromaluang*, one being Prince Wongsāthirāt, who was to become one of King Mongkut's closest advisers. One of Mongkut's older relatives became *kromakhun*, and so did two of his younger half-brothers. Twenty-one younger relatives received the lowest *krom* rank of *kromamū'n*. These were five younger half-brothers, ten of Rama III's children, and six sons of the long-deceased Uparāt of the Second Reign, Prince Sēnānurak.[9]

An interesting feature of the long list of promotions is the honour done to offspring of former Uparāts. It is possible that Mongkut decided to include them to boost further the dignity of the office of Uparāt and thus soothe his brother's injured pride. Mongkut's bestowal of posthumous titles on previous Uparāts may also be seen in this light. By the Fourth Reign the *krom* titles had lost their former direct link with state duties. They had become primarily an honour, a sign of the king's approval.

There were many changes in the civilian ranks of the administration. By 1851 the chief state executives were the brothers Bunnāk, who held the top position in the Treasury and the acting headship of the Kalāhom, and *phrayā* Rāchasuphawadi, acting head of the Mahātthai ministry. Almost all senior posts, as well as many lower positions, had become vacant during the later years of the Third Reign. Mongkut had therefore ample scope to select a vigorous team. First and foremost came the Phrakhlang (Dit Bunnāk) who had been a minister of state since 1822 and whose word had decided the succession. Since he already occupied the top of the civil honours scale, Mongkut, for the first time since the development of the *saktinā* system, broke the rule that a commoner could not hold more than 10,000 *rai*. He awarded the Phrakhlang honours appropriate to that of a royal prince with *krom* rank, his *saktinā* was raised to 30,000 *rai*, his title was raised to the new rank of *somdet čhaophrayā*, he was given a new name engraved on a golden nameplate, a special umbrella, palanquin, a new sword of state and a new seal, and his personal attendants were raised in rank. The Phrakhlang became Siam's "senior statesman", with executive authority throughout the kingdom. Similar honours were given to the Phrakhlang's brother, *phrayā* Sīphiphat. The two brothers became known as the Elder *somdet* (*somdet ǫng yai*) and the Younger *somdet* (*somdet ǫng noi*). It has been recorded that, during the auspicious occasion of the Younger *somdet*'s receiving a new name in September 1851, King Mongkut prostrated himself before the two *somdet čhaophrayā* officials.[10] Such a humble act would have been quite unthinkable in any Siamese king other than Mongkut, who during the first two or three years of his reign occasionally shocked the courtiers by breaking all protocol. Even taking Mongkut's unorthodox character into account, the king's public prostration may be seen as the strongest evidence for the view that the Bunnāk brothers were "king-makers", and that Mongkut felt he ought to express his gratitude.

The Elder *somdet*'s son (Chuang Bunnāk) was given the rank of *chaophrayā*, and retained his name of Sīsuriyawong. He was placed in charge of the *krom* Kalāhom and had such a prominent place in the administration that Europeans and Americans refer to him from early 1852 onwards as the "Prime Minister".[11] The king offered him princely insignia, which he apparently did not accept. Yet another member of the Bunnāk family, one of Dit Bunnāk's sons, Kham, was soon raised to *čhaophrayā* rank, with duties in the Harbour Department, a subsidiary of the Treasury.[12]

At no stage of Siamese history had one family been able to gain so many prominent positions in the administration. In the junior appointments, the key posts also went to members of the Bunnāk family. *Čhaophrayā* Sīsuriyawong's son was given his father's old place in the Mahātlek, and one of the positions of *čhāngwāng* of the royal pages went to Yaem Bunnāk, *phrayā* Sīphiphat's son, whilst another of Sīphiphat's sons gained a place in his father's section at the Treasury.[13]

While various members of the Bunnāk family occupied the most influential and lucrative posts, and some of them gained honours beyond what could traditionally be expected, only one other official was singled out for exceptional honour. This was *phrayā* Rāchasuphāwadī, the last member of the triumvirate who controlled Siam's administration at the end of the Third Reign. He was promoted to *čhaophrayā* Nikorabadin and also received his full new name on a golden nameplate.[14] All other appointments and insignia of rank were in accordance with the system in use during the previous reigns. The *krom* Nā was given to *chamū'n* Sīsǫrarak, who thus became *čhaophrayā* Phonlathēp.[15] *Phrayā* Phētphichai became *čhaophrayā* Thammāthikǫn, head of the *krom* Wang.[16] A *phrayā* Surasēnā became *čhaophrayā* Yomarāt, leading the *krom* Mū'ang.

In 1851 the new administration was entrusted with its first major task: the enlargement of Bangkok's city area by the digging of a new canal parallel with the existing outer moat, but further out from the centre. The new canal, more than five kilometres in length, was dug, just as in previous reigns, with the help of Chinese labour. The whole project was placed in the hands of *čhaophrayā* Sīsuriyawong, and his son *čhamū'n* Waiwǫranāt (Won Bunnāk), who completed the whole work in ten months at a cost of more than 31,000 *baht*.[17] The expense was of little consequence to the king, because Rama III had left considerable funds in the Treasury, reputedly 3,200,000 *baht* in silver and 8,000 *baht* in gold.[18] The work also involved the building of forts approximately a kilometre and a half apart along the canal, as well as the construction of forts on the Chao Phraya River, just where the actual city began. These forts were built not only to give the people of Bangkok a sense of security but also to impress foreign visitors. In addition, a small stronghold was constructed solely for the purpose of firing salutes, which can be seen as a clear indication of the new Siamese administration's wish to accommodate itself to European customs. A European man-of-war visiting a foreign nation had to greet that nation's flag with twenty-one gun shots while hoisting the flag on the forward mast. A fortress or ship of the nation visited was expected to return the honour with an equal number of shots. This alien custom had caused anxiety and misunderstanding among many Asian states, where the firing of guns had invariably been interpreted as the crudest and most blatant token of aggression.

There were other signs of the new government's pro-Western stance. At the beginning of his reign, Mongkut ordered that all attending the king's audience must wear an upper garment to complement the formal dress, a ruling intended to make the court "more civilized" in the eyes of the world.[19]

During the first three years of Mongkut's reign the European and American trading and missionary community was especially favoured. In July 1851 customs duty was almost halved, and during the first year of the reign restrictions on rice export were lifted and a state opium monopoly was established, to obtain some measure of control over its use.[20] In August a group of missionary women were admitted to the inner palace to set up a class, mainly to teach the English language.[21] On the king's birthday on 18 October, all Westerners were entertained in European style. During the cremation rituals for the late king, which were attended by many foreigners, King Mongkut espied Bradley and suddenly clambered down from his platform to shake the American's hand.

> This mark of respect was regarded as being a great departure from the customs of all former kings of Siam. The Officers of Government of the highest rank skulked away from His Majesty in order to get as low before him as they could. One of them remarked after the king returned: "Where has Siam ever heard of a king who was pleased to show so much respect to Foreigners". Another said: "He would not do this to sailors. He will do it only to foreigners of respectability like the Doctors".[22]

In July 1853 the king presented a plot of land to the Protestant missions to use as a cemetery, and in January of the following year he decided to have his family vaccinated against smallpox.[23] However, all was not well in the kingdom, and the great, sometimes unreasonable, expectations cherished by many Europeans at the time of Mongkut's accession were not fulfilled.[24] The first frustrations arose during the campaign in Burmese-controlled territory.

## The Battle of Chiangtung

In 1851, not long after Mongkut had been elevated to the throne, a serious confrontation arose between Britain and Burma. Three British warships were dispatched to Rangoon in order to force the Burmese king to cease anti-British action. The Burmese met the challenge of a blockade with troops and a few cannon shots. The British commander destroyed every Burmese war boat within reach and returned to Calcutta to report. During most of 1852 there was war between Britain and Burma. The British seized some coastal towns, and when the Burmese king did not negotiate for peace, the invading army continued its progress, gradually occupying most of lower Burma. Eventually, early in 1853, a palace revolution brought to the throne Mindon, who immediately sued for peace. To his consternation he discovered that the British had resolved to annex lower Burma, which cut off Amarapura from the sea.

The Burmese involvement in a full-scale war and the subsequent loss of Burmese territory were major factors in Siam's decision to send an army to Chiangtung, one of the Shan towns traditionally under Burmese overlordship. The Burmese hold over towns such as Chiangtung and Chiangrung was only indirect, the local Shan *sawbhas*[25] managing their own affairs. However, Siam's attack upon Chiangtung was not merely an opportunistic gesture resulting from Burma's weakness. It was also provoked by a succession struggle in the town of Chiangrung, in which one of the contending parties had requested Siamese recognition. Rama III had decided to throw his support behind this faction and had ordered his vassal states of Chiang Mai, Lamphun, and Lampang to assemble an army and attack Chiangtung, so as to free the whole of the Tai-Lue area from Burmese control. This army had been duly dispatched and reached Chiangtung in February 1850. However, the various generals quarrelled among themselves and supplies ran out, so that the troops had been withdrawn in July 1850.[26]

The chief ministers advised Mongkut to again assist Chiangrung, and since Chiangrung was subject to Chiangtung, it was necessary to make another effort to subdue the latter town. The campaign would bring honour to the king and the country, and both officers and men would gain skill in warfare. This time, the battle would be under direct Bangkok control. Mongkut's younger brother, *kromaluang* Wongsāthirāt, was given general command, with the *čhaophrayā* Yomarāt as second-in-command. The latter left Bangkok in October, 1852, with authority to recruit troops from Chiang Mai, Lampang, and Lamphun, and in the following month *kromaluang* Wongsāthirāt went to do likewise in Nan, Phrae, and Lomsak. In March 1853 the Siamese-led armies arrived before Chiangtung, where leaders had long been forewarned, however, and had prepared their defence. The attackers soon suffered a lack of fresh water for the elephants and horses, and they ran into gunfire from un-suspected fortified positions in the hills. Moreover, the Siamese generals found to their alarm that their troops were not in the least motivated to give battle to the Chiangtung defenders. When Wongsāthirāt reported to Bangkok that there was fraternization among his troops and the local populace,[27] Mongkut recalled his half-brother for consulta-tion. However, Wongsāthirāt did not heed this command, replying that he wanted additional troops and was preparing to attack again after the rainy season was over.

The king was displeased with Wongsāthirāt and in June 1853 asked him once more to return to Bangkok, an order again disobeyed.[28] At the same time Mongkut tried to per-suade the rulers of Chiang Mai, Lampang, and Lamphun to take up arms with more enthusiasm; he elevated all three of them from *phrayā* rank to that of *čhao* and gave them insignia and regalia commensurate with their position as semi-independent rulers of vassal states.[29] Mongkut finally seems to have agreed to let Wongsāthirāt attack Chiangtung for a second time. In late October that year, *čhaophrayā* Sīsuriyawong went up north to meet Wongsāthirāt and *čhaophrayā* Yomarāt in order to give instructions and hand over weapons and some troops.[30] By November the weather permitted large-scale troop movements, and a new expedition was formed. The recruiting of troops had not been as success-ful as expected, and morale again was low, even though this time the army was better supplied than the year before. However, when Wongsāthirāt arrived before Chiangtung he found that he had to give battle to Burmese troops, because by this time the Anglo-Burmese war had come to an end and King Mindon had been able to send some reinforcements. Moreover, the ruler of Chiangtung had been able to enlist large numbers of local troops. During the ensuing skirmishes the Siamese ran low in ammunition and food. To make matters worse, the army under leadership of the *čhaophrayā* Yomarāt, which had taken a different route to Chiangtung, ran into severe problems and failed to arrive. Disease broke out among the beleaguerers, and when the rainy season of 1854 began, the siege was broken off and the Siamese returned to Chiang Mai. When the news of the failed expedition reached Bangkok, Mongkut decided to call off the whole campaign.[31]

This expedition must have had a sobering effect upon Siam's leaders. In 1852 they believed that a large number of troops combined with some rather sophisticated weaponry would be sufficient to give them an easy victory. However, the modern guns were heavy, and the troops not trained in the use and positioning of artillery. There were many other factors leading to the ignominious retreat; they included problems of supply, disease among men, elephants, and horses, and the spirited defence by Chiangtung's leaders. Possibly the most important factors, however, were the lack of military discipline and morale among the Siamese-led soldiers.

## Relations with the West, 1854–56

In most standard history books dealing with this period, the treaty between England and Siam dominates the scene, and the fact that it may be called a successful treaty which had a great impact upon the development of the country makes it eminently suitable as a feather in King Mongkut's cap. In biographical accounts we find statements such as: "When Sir John Bowring arrived at the head of a British mission, he [King Mongkut] received him with open arms and the two became firm friends. Within a relatively short time, they agreed upon a diplomatic and commercial treaty that was mutually advantageous to both countries."[32] In reality, Mongkut's role in the drawing up of the treaty was not as prominent as such statements would lead us to believe.

In mid-1854 a rumour regarding the imminent arrival of an American punitive mission headed by the redoubtable Commodore M.C. Perry alarmed Bangkok; the forts at Paknam and Paklat were put in fighting order, and the chain cable purchased during the previous reign was prepared for positioning across the river to prevent the Americans from entering.[33] It is not clear what caused such a panic in the capital. Possibly it was the outcome of a confrontation between the king and a certain "Captain" Trail, which had resulted in

Trail's imprisonment. Trail was released and reinstated in his old command, but he had to atone for having displeased the king by undergoing a formal bathing ceremony in Ayutthaya.[34] These events were reported in the *Straits Times*, together with an account of the disastrous expedition to Chiangtung, and a note of disappointment that Mongkut's reign had not been able to improve matters for foreigners or for the Siamese people. Foreigners were greatly inconvenienced by Siamese customs officials, while the Siamese were oppressed by taxes. People were fined for not obeying the king's commands regarding the use of proper language.[35] Mongkut was accused of treating his officers more like dogs than human beings, of not consulting with his ministers, and of spending his time with his wives instead of looking after the country's welfare. This very critical report, apparently written by some irate Westerner, caused great consternation at court.

All European and American residents were summoned to the residency of *čhaophrayā* Sĭsuriyawong, where they were asked to give a written testimony that the statements in the article were untrue. However, while there were some statements that might have been considered false, there were many "which had much the appearance of being true".[36] The Westerners decided to declare instead that they were "in many respects more pleasantly situated under the reign of His Majesty Somdet Phra Chom Klao",[37] an answer that could hardly have satisfied the king.

In subsequent inquiries it was found that one of the American missionaries had had not long before a small altercation with Siamese customs officials.[38] Since rapacious customs men feature large in the article, the king decided for himself that this missionary was the author, or that at least he had furnished the author with details. To make matters worse, two months later, on 5 December 1854, while the king was travelling along the new canal around much of the city as part of the festive celebration surrounding its completion,[39] he noticed a new Western-style house being constructed much nearer the edge of the canal than the regulations allowed. Upon inquiring, he learnt that it was being built for the same missionary suspected of authorship of the critical letter. The king had not even given permission for that plot of land to be used by foreigners. Greatly enraged, he had the Siamese parties involved with the land-transaction thrown into prison, and forbade Protestant missionaries to travel down-river. If they resisted the king's officers in the execution of their duties, they could be shot without warning. If the missionaries could find a ship in which to leave the country, he would be glad to have them go.[40] The Protestant missionaries who had harboured such high hopes at the beginning of the reign now found their projects suspended, their Siamese teachers arrested, their building programme halted, their pupils remaining home, and most of their servants absconding.

Subsequent inquiries showed that *čhaophrayā* Sĭsuriyawong himself had given permission for the house site on the canal to be rented to the foreigners, and the people arrested were soon released. The interdiction against Protestant missionaries' going down-river remained in force until April of the following year, when Sir John Bowring, the governor of Hong Kong, interceded on their behalf.

*Čhaophrayā* Sĭsuriyawong was embarrassed by the affair, since his seal had been attached to the documents. When Bradley visited the Bunnāks to prescribe medicine, he met Sĭsuriyawong, who declared frankly that he considered the whole case to be nothing but foolishness and that he was quite dissatisfied with this manner of conducting matters of state. During Rama III's time there had been a government, but at present there was no government.[41] Three months later he again criticized the state of affairs in Siam.[42]

Early in 1855 Sir John Bowring arrived in Bangkok to negotiate a new treaty between Britain and Siam. The failure of the Brooke mission in 1850 had been felt by Mongkut and Sĭsuriyawong to be an unfortunate development, and as early as May 1851, on the day after his enthronement, Mongkut had written to the British authorities about resuming negotiations.[43] Britain undoubtedly had now supplanted China in Siamese eyes as the most powerful nation in the world. Although Mongkut had sent "tribute-bearing" missions to China in 1851 and 1852, this time-honoured custom lapsed after that.[44] Great efforts were made to receive the first foreign envoy in a proper manner. Robert Hunter's old residence was refurbished to house the mission. Lengthy and intricate deliberations took place between Bowring, his son John, and H.S. Parkes, the consul at Amoy, on the one hand, and the four most powerful Bunnāks (the Elder *somdet*, the Younger *somdet*, the Kalāhom, and his brother Kham, who was acting Phrakhlang) and Prince Wongsāthirāt on the other hand. Published and unpublished sources bear out the general conclusion of Bowring's personal journal, that Sīsuriyawong played a greater role in the treaty than King Mongkut himself.[45] The four Bunnāks controlled much of the country's internal and extenal trade, and by agreeing to lower many specific taxes they appear to have been the first affected.

King Mongkut's contribution seems to have been largely ceremonial, and during the private audience with Bowring the details of the proposed treaty were not discussed. The king appeared mainly concerned with the exchange of presents between Queen Victoria and himself. Subsequent events show that Mongkut was personally opposed to some articles in the treaty and moved to prevent their application. *Kromaluang* Wongsāthirāt had already warned Parkes and Bowring's son that the treaty was almost wholly Sīsuriyawong's responsibility and that they could not always count upon the king's support, adding that the situation might abruptly change through the king's sudden displeasure and hoping that should disagreement occur the British government would view the matter with indulgent considera-tion.[46]

However, in 1855 the Bowring treaty was still in draft form, and soon after the envoy's departure the court became preoccupied with local events. Three days after Bowring had left Bangkok, on 26 April 1855, the Elder *somdet* (Dit Bunnāk) died,[47] leaving his brother the Younger *somdet* and his son Sīsuriyawong as the most senior administrators in the country. In May the king wrote to Bradley offering a hospital site, and this proposal, which earlier had won the support of Prince Wongsāthirāt, was received with some enthusiasm by the Younger *somdet* who offered to supply all the wood needed for such a building. Bradley let this moment pass, however, and it was not until the next reign that Bangkok's first hospital was erected. A white elephant which had been brought to Bangkok with great pomp and ceremony earlier in the year — and with which King Mongkut especially identified, since it had been established that the animal had been born approximately at the beginning of his reign — died in September.

The year had also its more encouraging signs for Mongkut. In November the king's first steamboat was launched, a vessel of about forty tons with a twelve-horsepower engine, built by Sisuriyawong, with the assistance of J.H. Chandler, one of the American missionaries. The monarch astonished his people by suddenly boarding the vessel for a pleasure ride. The ship took pride of place in the royal procession to Ayutthaya, where the king toured until the end of the year. Immediately, enterprising families in Bangkok ordered steam engines for a timber mill, a rice mill, and further ships.[48]

During the year 1856 the relations between Siam and Western nations determined to a considerable extent the widening rift between the king and the most senior members of the administration. The first foreign envoy to arrive in 1856 was Parkes, returning from England where he had spent much time explaining the background and significance of the various treaty articles. Apart from ratification of the treaty, Parkes also carried letters from Queen Victoria and many presents. However, when the presents were transferred onto another ship in bad weather in Singapore, a great number of them were accidentally saturated with sea water.[49] The letters were undamaged, however, and they provided Parkes with the means of getting into direct contact with King Mongkut and drawing him into the further negotiations necessary to make the treaty more effective in the eyes of the British authorities.

Parkes was well aware of the tension between Sisuriyawong and the king. Mongkut had heard about some much less concessive arrangements between Japan and the Americans.[50] Sisuriyawong complained to Parkes that his counsel was no longer sought or listened to by the king, who received more favourably those advisers who advocated a strong stance against British-imposed changes.[51] Mongkut was not, however, prepared to insult the British envoy and received him graciously, readily agreeing to ratify the treaty and promising to do his utmost to correct any misunderstanding that might arise from ignorance or lack of knowledge regarding the articles of the treaty. Mongkut's warning that his "half-civilized" and "half-barbarous" people might misunderstand the treaty provide a clue to his tactics. There is, namely, good reason to believe that he intended secretly to obstruct the treaty, while openly professing his greatest satisfaction with the new relationship between the two countries.[52] The king's real intentions are revealed in his handbill, distributed when Parkes arrived, forbidding any Siamese to sell land to foreigners. When Parkes demanded an explanation, it was denied that the king had anything to do with it.[53] When proclamations explaining the treaty had to be printed, the king obstructed the work upon a flimsy pretext.[54] Bradley, who noticed the duplicity, remarked that he was very glad that "the king has such a man as Parkes to deal with. He will henceforth find it much more difficult to carry out his craftiness than he has done!"[55]

While Parkes was applying his dexterity to gain further concessions, on 13 April 1856 the American envoy Townsend Harris arrived at the mouth of the Chao Phraya River carrying a letter from President Franklin Pierce and a good number of valuable presents. The Siamese were hoping to rapidly conclude their post-treaty negotiations with Parkes, but the British envoy insisted on settling many detailed questions, and it was not until 15 May that Parkes finally left the country. By this time the impatient Harris was fuming, so the Siamese acted with uncommon speed appointing a committee and negotiating at such a rate that the treaty was agreed upon, copied, translated and ready for signing before the end of the month.[56] Harris left on 31 May, despite earnest efforts by the king to delay him further so as to give Mongkut time to write a personal answer to the American president.[57]

In July and August the French envoy, Ch. de Montigny, negotiated basically the same agreement that Bowring, Parkes, and Harris had wrested from the Siamese; and in the following years similar exercises were repeated with the

Danish, the Hanseatic Republic, the Portuguese, the Dutch, and the Prussians. Meanwhile, however, probably under the influence of the rather conservative Younger *somdet*, the king proceeded to block European and American land purchases. Mattoon, the new American consul, found it impossible to effect a transaction. In July 1856 Bradley wrote: "It is to be feared that the king is endeavouring to play two parts directly opposed to each other. That he is secretly infusing fear of selling into the minds of the land holders — and at the same time pretending to the foreigners that he will not only give them perfect freedom to sell but also strongly urge them to do so."[58]

During that same month the king wrote to the newly appointed British consul, C.B. Hillier, that the land the British Consulate wished to purchase belonged in part to a servant of Phra' Pinklāo, and that he had not the right to compel the owner to sell.[59] Matters came to a head in late September of that year when the king found out that a Siamese employed by the British consul as secretary had placed his name as witness on an agreement to lease a plot of land to a European. The secretary, Seng by name, was arrested and given ninety-nine lashes in King Mongkut's presence. Since Seng had acted upon the consul's orders, and since the transaction was legal under the new treaty, this punishment had the makings of an international incident. The British expressed their indignation to Prince Wongsāthirāt, who had the unfortunate Seng moved to his palace, where an opium plaster was applied to his back. Apparently too much opium passed through the wound into Seng's body, because he fell into a stertorous sleep from which he did not awaken. The British consul drew up a protest demanding Seng's body and the release of the other persons unlawfully imprisoned. Bradley, who had been called to assist Prince Wongsāthirāt when Seng's condition showed cause for alarm, noted:

It would appear that the leading rulers in the land, we call them king's cabinet, are much displeased with the late shameful conduct of His Majesty and disposed to show their disapprobation of it by unmistakable signs, even to demand of him a promise that he will henceforth take council with them on all matters concerning their relations with the English. It is quite evident that the king fears their power to depose him and has humbled himself before them.[60]

Three days later he added:

The king of Siam has humbled himself much in view of the late outrage against the foreign community which he commited a few days since. He said to Mr Mattoon today that he was willing to make an expiation of his offence by purchasing with his own personal funds ground for the British Consulate in the city and then place there a perpetual monument stating his offence and that he had given the plot of ground for the Consulate as lasting memorial of his crime. . . . He fears the displeasure of Queen Victoria.[61]

A real crisis had developed, and the king's position was, for the moment, vulnerable. Throughout the year there had been an estrangement between the king and his "Prime Minister". *Čhaophrayā* Sīsuriyawong had felt himself unpopular with the king and also with an important faction at the court, including his uncle the Younger *somdet*. He had darkly hinted to the American envoy that there was often a change during the fourth generation of princes of a dynasty,[62] so the thought of a coup d'état may have crossed Sīsuriyawong's mind. However, since Sīsuriyawong did not have the backing of all those who were critical of the king,[63] such a move would have been quite risky and possibly accompanied by considerable bloodshed. Sīsuriyawong was a clever and cautious man, and he appears to have decided that he would strengthen his position relative to that of the king, rather than risk all in open conflict.

If these were his considered tactics, they were quite successful. The anti-treaty party became silent, especially when the awkward situation was exacerbated by Hillier's death from natural causes on 18 October, only three weeks after the provocative incident. Henceforth there was no high-level obstruction against the treaties, the various foreign groups acquired the right to trade under more favourable conditions than before, and the consuls gained considerable power to protect the interests of those who wanted to take advantage of Siam's "opening up".[64]

## First Effects of the Treaties

The treaties had a dramatic impact upon life in Bangkok. Early in 1857 it was noted that there was a remarkable influx of traders. In January Bradley counted thirty-three square-rigged vessels in port and about as many at the mouth of the Chao Phraya River.[65] By 1860 the river offered a picture of lively activity, with "many boats, sailing vessels, steamships, etc. plying thereon, at all times, from sunrise to sunset".[66] This is borne out by the available statistics: in 1856 there were 141 vessels, other than junks, trading with Bangkok, in 1857 there were 204, and in the following years this number gradually rose to some three to four hundred vessels.[67] The Siamese themselves were getting their share of the increased trade, for by 1860 the Siamese already had a fleet of fifteen steamships, and the local dockyards were busy building more.[68] Mercantile houses vied with each other for good sites, and from the outset large profits were made. A sign of the rapid changes taking place was the sudden shortage of minted *baht*:

> The Royal Mint cannot nearly supply ticals for the merchants who bring in dollars to exchange. It turns out only enough to exchange $20,000 a week. Merchants and other foreigners under consular jurisdiction are allowed to go and exchange their dollars every Monday. As there are not ticals enough to exchange all the dollars presented, there has been a law made which gives each man the privilege of exchanging his proportion of the whole amount of dollars brought in that day. He may bring in $20,000 himself alone — and if there was no other person at the exchange but himself he would have the whole of the $20,000 exchanged. But as there are some 8 or 10 others with each 10 or 20 thousand he can get only his proportion among them. As I only had $196, my proportion was $12 for which I got 20 ticals. The whole amount presented that day was about $335,000.[69]

Since the government could not possibly produce sufficient "bullet-shaped" silver *bahts*, it decided to accept the Mexican dollar as legal tender at the rate of three Mexican dollars to one *baht*. At the same time new machinery for minting Siamese currency was obtained from England, and in 1860 Siam's first flat silver coins were put into circulation.[70]

The sudden influx of large numbers of traders and sailors also brought an unprecedented number of disturbances. There was sporadic fighting among ships' crews, for example. The most serious incident in the first years after the treaties were signed, however, was that of late November 1857, when a party of British and Germans was assaulted and seriously hurt by a group of Buddhist monks who attempted to stop them hunting in the monastery grounds. It was an incident very similar to that of September 1835 involving Wellar. As in the Wellar case, the Europeans' representative, the consul Gingell, protested and asked that justice be done. This time, however, there was no need for threats and heated words. A fortnight later the matter was settled, the abbot of the monastery concerned having been fined 240 *baht* and a special law having been enacted forbidding the use of firearms in temple grounds.[71]

In the years immediately following Hillier's death, King Mongkut's position in relation to his "cabinet" stabilized into a situation in which many policy matters were left largely to the senior ministers, who would confer with each other, come to a decision, and transmit this decision to the king for approval.[72] This manner of working constituted a fundamental change in court procedure. Mongkut's predecessors obtained advice on policy matters in public and private audiences and then decided themselves whose advice, if anyone's, to follow.

The king appears to have been obliged to delegate considerable power in respect of both foreign policy and internal matters. Thus, when in 1857 he was worried about the state of the corvée system, instead of ordering the various departments to prepare for a major registration, he wrote a letter to the senior administrators complaining that the lists were out of date, explaining that he had not sufficient money to hire labourers for large-scale works, and asking them whether or not it was time for a new general registration.[73] Apparently the administrators agreed that it was, and major tattooing drives were held during the following years.[74]

Although the king's influence on government had thus decreased, it would be wrong to depict him as a mere figurehead. His ceremonial role appears to have been left unaffected by the crisis, and he developed this aspect of kingship. He continued to make his annual round of monasteries during the month following the Lenten season to present robes to Buddhist monks. Every year he presided at a lavish dinner party for Europeans and Americans in honour of his birthday, which fell on 18 October. He made efforts to improve his image with the population at large, taking an interest in the occasional law suit and finding opportunities of winning the people's gratitude for his beneficence. Thus, in the middle years of the reign he sometimes called together all old and disabled persons in a district and distributed food and money to them.

In 1858 he made a lengthy tour of the eastern provinces, accompanied by many members of the court, and the year after he visited many southern towns. Certain places, especially Ayutthaya, Nakhom Pathom, and Phetburi were regularly included in his itinerary. In Ayutthaya he would occasionally ceremonially receive a white elephant or accompany visitors to see the ruins or attend a rounding-up of wild elephants. In Nakhon Pathom he instigated a gigantic project, the building of a monumental *čhēdī* on the ruins of what presumably was the oldest Buddhist shrine in the country. At Phetburi he began building an impressive palace high up on a mountain. All these travels and activities gave him opportunities to see and meet many people who under a more orthodox king would never have had a chance to catch a glimpse of the country's highest dignitary.

Another feature of ceremonial life developed by Mongkut in the years after the crisis was correspondence with other heads of state. Not only did the letter-bearing missions involve an exchange of presents, which brought a large number of prestigious and valuable objects to fill the king's palaces, but also the fact that King Mongkut had received letters from Napoleon III, from the president of the United States, and especially from Queen Victoria strengthened his position at court. A friendly letter from Her Britannic Majesty showed the Siamese that the world's strongest power approved of King Mongkut as ruler of Siam. It is in this respect that Mongkut's unfulfilled request for a British decoration must be seen. It appears that the king needed all the support he could muster, because he had lost a number of allies and associates since the beginning of his reign. His uncle *kromsomdetphra'* Paramānuchitchinōrot had died in 1853, and his uncles *kromaluang* Phisētsīsawat and *kromphra'* Rāmitsarēt not long after. In 1856 the king's elder half-brothers *kromphra'* Phiphitphubēn and *kromaluang* Phūwanēt had died, and in 1858 the Younger *somdet*. The death of the latter left quite a vacuum at court, for the Younger *somdet* had controlled vast resources and had had great influence. He had become more and more conservative and anti-Western in his later years and did not attempt to hide his antipathy. With his death, the staunchest defender of "Old Siam" passed away. In 1859 the king's elder half-brother *kromsomdetphra'* Dēchādisōn died.[75] This prince, undoubtedly the most experienced administrator in the royal family, had held high positions in the time of Rama III, and after the death of Paramānuchitchinōrot, became probably Mongkut's closest confidant.[76]

With Phra' Pinklāo left rather isolated, playing with his European toys and gadgets and never holding a position of real responsibility, the Siamese political scene in the middle of the reign seems dominated by four clever men who had learnt to work as a team. First there was Mongkut, who displayed a certain flair for public relations, occasionally marred by a fit of temper, but who was sincerely revered by much of the populace. Secondly there was Sīsuriyawong, the undisputed leader of the administrators, wealthy and progressive.[77] The third was Mongkut's half-brother Wongsāthirāt, who, even after his stroke in August 1861, held the confidence of both the king and Sīsuriyawong. *Kromaluang* Wongsāthirāt was a member of all the committees negotiating treaties with foreigners and represented the king in many other capacities. The fourth was Sīsuriyawong's brother, Kham Bunnāk, who by the middle of the reign held the title of *čhaophrayā* Rawiwong and had been appointed Phrakhlang.[78] He appears to have been a thoughtful, trustworthy man, enjoying the respect of the other three.

These four men headed an extremely intricate administration and held effective daily control over the central delta area. At the end of the 1850s and the beginning of the 1860s they supervised the internal tax collection system, but much of their time and energy was taken up by matters arising from the extraordinary influx of Europeans and Americans — for example, the creation of the post of harbour-master, the drawing up of new laws, the determination of a satisfactory exchange rate, the taxation of foreign residents, and the creation of new roads to accommodate the newcomers.

These four were in their fifties, an ageing and vulnerable group. It was remarkable that in that time no effort seems to have been made to fill positions of power left vacant by the death of members of the royal family. Bradley remarked upon the situation as one of despondency in face of the recent changes.

> . . . the usual thought among the Siamese rulers is that Siam is destined to pass into the hands of the English. They seem almost instinctively to think so and so to express themselves. And it is a remarkable fact that they are training no one for the Throne as if they really expect he will be called to it after the present incumbents shall have left it. My mind cannot light upon a single individual whom God seems in any way to be preparing for a future Sovereign in Siam. If I could see either of the present kings taking measures to educate some of their sons for the Throne as they themselves have been educated, I should by that providence be inclined to expect that the present Dynasty would be prolonged much beyond the days of the present sovereign. But they are doing no such thing. They seem to me to be wonderfully careless in educating their sons.[79]

This comment, by a man who had lived more than twenty years in Siam and who had regular access to the palaces, cannot be taken lightly. The surrounding world seemed to be rapidly changing into one dominated by colonial powers, and the chances of escaping the fate of all other traditional Asian nations must have appeared slight.[80] At the time Bradley wrote the above, the eldest *čhaofā* prince, Čhulālongkǫn, was only just five years old, too young to be groomed for future kingship.

Siam's leaders may have been pessimistic about the country's long-term prospects of independence, but this did not prevent them from appreciating the marvels of modern technology. Late in 1858 the machinery for milling rice with the aid of steam power, and a steam sawmill, arrived in Bangkok from the United States. At that time King Mongkut already owned four or five steamboats, and the engines of two or three much larger ones had just arrived. *Kromaluang* Wongsāthirāt had his steamboat, Phra' Pinklāo had one or two and the engines for two or three more, and Sīsuriyawong had a most elegant propeller-driven steamship and engines for several more. One enterprising missionary had imported several further steamship engines to sell to the Siamese.[81]

All this new enterprise had visible effects upon the educated youth of Bangkok. In the early 1860s the *Bangkok Calendar* reported that the number of highly educated Buddhist monks had fallen dramatically since King Mongkut had come to the throne, allegedly because:

> His present Majesty invites and allures out into secular life many of the smartest men in the Priesthood, and . . . in the present reign there are many extraordinary openings for such men to enter into business, and seek pleasure and honour in the way of wealth and state preferments. The treaties of friendship and commerce which have, in this reign, been made with many western nations, thus opening Siam widely to western enterprise, and developing unlooked for native resources, have had great power to this end. This is doubtless one grand cause for the great diminution in the number in the Priesthood, which is thought to be about one-half since the beginning of the present reign.[82]

One of the bright young men who left the shelter of monastic life, attracted by the new prospects in trade, was Thien, a novice at Wat Bowoniwēt, who later became well-known as the innovative and controversial Siamese author, Thienwan. Young Thien was, according to himself, the first Siamese to adopt Western customs; he abandoned the short hair-style common in Bangkok, grew a moustache, refused to chew betel-nut, and began to wear shoes and socks.[83]

## The French, Cambodia, and the Succession

Britain dominated the political scene, and the British consul therefore automatically became the senior diplomat in Bangkok. Immediately after the Bowring treaty was signed, the Siamese sent an embassy to London. The French also were rapidly establishing themselves as a formidable power, and the king suggested that the French send a ship to carry a mission to Paris. The embassy arrived at its destination in June 1861; it was cordially received by Napoleon III and enabled to visit major industrial complexes and dockyards.

These friendly gestures served little to disguise the fact that the French, who had conquered Cochin-China in 1850, were casting their eyes towards Cambodia, a country to which the Siamese believed themselves to have firm claims. In 1861 a struggle for the succession led to serious disturbances in Cambodia, and Siam asserted its dominance by once more sending troops to quell the disorders. The French protested against this incursion, initially taking the attitude that Cambodia was traditionally ruled by Siam and Vietnam concurrently, and that as the successors to Cochin-China's rights, they had acquired part-jurisdiction over Cambodia.[84] Soon afterwards the government in Paris instructed their army commander in the region not to recognize Siam's claims over Cambodia.[85] The Siamese, by then fully aware of French expansionist policies, launched a campaign to prevent further French incursions.[86] However, in July 1863 the French persuaded the Cambodian ruler to sign a treaty accepting Napoleon III's protection. The Siamese attempted to counter this action by drawing up a treaty of their own with Cambodia, which left no doubt as to Cambodia's status.[87] The full text of this treaty appeared in the *Bangkok Press* and was reprinted by the Singapore *Straits Times* in August 1864.

Since the Siamese–Cambodian treaty denied many of the French ambitions, the French consul, Aubaret, was instructed to negotiate a new treaty between France and Siam which would allow French influence in Cambodia. During the first half of 1865 Aubaret made strong demands, threatening that France would take punitive action against the Siamese if they did not agree to joint supervision over Cambodia. Aubaret's condescending and hostile attitude became widely known in Siamese circles[88] and may have played a role in pushing the Siamese more towards the British. It appears that when the British consul was secretly contacted in June 1865, he advised the Siamese to give no further concessions, intimating that the French consul was acting somewhat beyond his instructions from Paris. The British consul appears in fact to have drafted the Siamese "final reply" maintaining Cambodia's subordinate status.[89] Aubaret accepted this. However, when he presented the new treaty for ratification, the French government sent him back to extract further concessions.

The renegotiations took place in late 1866, and they resulted in little-disguised hostility between the two parties. Sīsuriyawong told Aubaret outright that he was not prepared to concede any further points. The French consul thereupon demanded that Sīsuriyawong be taken off the negotiating committee. Aubaret insisted that King Mongkut himself should take over in order to prevent a direct clash between France and Siam. Some ugly scenes allegedly took place between the two men, Mongkut threatening to write to Napoleon III personally about the consul's conduct, and Aubaret telling the king that such a letter would have no effect, that the consul was acting with the full backing of the French government.

It was during these protracted and difficult negotiations that Mongkut wrote confidentially to the British consul, suggesting that he would welcome a British take-over. In this letter of 18 December 1866, Mongkut says his opinion is a personal one made without the Siamese government's knowledge; "if the British protectorate is necessary, he [Mongkut] and his family would accept it."[90]

The negotiations between Aubaret and Mongkut finally broke down, and the king decided to send a new embassy to Paris in order to settle the matter. In his instructions to the Siamese envoy, Mongkut expressed the view that the British were inclining towards extending their territory over Siam. Then he authorized his envoy, apparently overruling Sīsuriyawong in this matter, to make as many concessions as were needed to come to an agreement with the French. Finally, he told the envoy to press for Aubaret's replacement:

> If, however, they refuse to remove Aubaret from Bangkok but insist on keeping him here with full power, then the matter would be beyond my endurance. If you fail to get Aubaret removed, then you may cross over to Britain and ask for whatever assistance that you may think fit from the responsible ministers, from the English lords both in and out of office and

from Sir John Bowring. I have my own reasons for this decision.[91]

The letter to the British consul and the one to the Siamese envoy reinforce each other. Mongkut had undoubtedly reconciled himself to Siam's becoming part of the British Empire. These remarks should not be regarded as a sudden whim or irresponsible action arising from a moment of uncontrollable anger against the French consul, for the two letters are spaced more than two months apart. If one views these communications in the light of Bradley's earlier statement and of the acceptance by many Siamese leaders of the idea that the country sooner or later would end up subject to a European power, Mongkut's two letters amount to no more than a declaration of his preference for Britain over France in the event of Siam becoming a Europen protectorate. As it was, the envoys did not feel it necessary to contact the British on this matter, for they were quite honourably received, and were able to negotiate the new treaty, and not long after their return home Aubaret was replaced.

The first letter, which had been immediately passed on to London, does not appear to have caused much excitement. It was clear that the suggestion was only the king's personal opinion, and probably also because an implementation of the king's suggestion would have fuelled anti-imperialist agitation, no action was taken. Thus this episode had few international repercussions. What Mongkut's handling of the case does demonstrate is that his position *vis-à-vis* Sīsuriyawong had changed since the late 1850s, when the king appears to have been forced to accept whatever Sīsuriyawong and his advisers decided. In the years between 1861 and 1867 the political scene seems to have become more and more dominated by Sīsuriyawong and Mongkut, the other chief actors either leaving the scene or being relegated to the background. Phra' Pinklāo, for example, after a long period of ill health, died in January 1866 without having played a prominent role in the country. Prince Wongsāthirāt still nominally held great power, but he was ill and virtually confined to his bed. Sīsuriyawong's half-brother *čhaophrayā* Rawiwong, elevated to *čhaophrayā* Thiphākǫrawong in 1865, held the senior position of Phrakhlang, but he suffered from cataracts and his progressive blindness caused him to resign his post at the beginning of 1867.

The personal relationship between Mongkut and Sīsuriyawong, at first rather cool and hostile, improved as they apparently found ways of co-operating and as the king's confidence returned. During the early 1860s the two seemed quite amicably disposed towards each other. By 1866 the king was asserting himself more and more, and he now boldly took ultimate responsibility in matters concerning Siam's relations with other countries as well as in domestic affairs.[92]

The king's new confidence was visible not only in his letter to the British consul and in the freedom he gave his envoys in settling a treaty which Sīsuriyawong had opposed, but also in several other measures. Thus, when *čhaophrayā* Thiphākǫrawong resigned his post as Phrakhlang, everybody expected one of the Bunnāk family to replace him, for a Bunnāk had been the head of the Phrakhlang since 1822. However, Mongkut made one of his younger half-brothers, *kromakhun* Wǫrasak, the new Phrakhlang.

Another matter about which Sīsuriyawong and Mongkut disagreed, and where the king's opinion prevailed, was the appointment of someone to take the late Phra' Pinklāo's place. In July 1867, to Mongkut's great sorrow, his eldest son, *kromamū'n* Mahēsuan, died, and since he had been a possible candidate for the position of Uparāt,[93] it was probably not long after his death that Sīsuriyawong suggested that *kromamū'n* Wichaichān, Phra' Pinklāo's eldest son, who was twenty-nine, should succeed his father.[94] Sīsuriyawong apparently considered Prince Wichaichān the ablest member of the next generation of the royal family. The appointment of an Uparāt when the king himself was already sixty-two was significant because, as the highest-ranking prince after the king, the Uparāt would automatically be a serious candidate for the throne. By this time, King Mongkut had begun to pin his hopes upon his first son of *čhaofā* rank, Prince Čhulālongkǫn, who had become his favourite. In January 1866, when the prince was twelve, his official tonsure ceremonies had lasted seven days and were of unprecedented elaboration. Napoleon III, who had heard through his consul that Mongkut had a favourite son, had presented the young prince with a sword at the time he gave one to Mongkut.[95] In 1867 Čhulālongkǫn was much too young to be seriously considered for the position of Uparāt, so the king, who was in excellent health,[96] decided to leave the position open for the time being.

## Mongkut and Anna Leonowens

During the early years of Mongkut's reign he had requested the American missionaries to teach in the inner palace.[97] Mrs Bradley, Mrs Mattoon, and Mrs Jones took turns teaching a morning class of more than twenty palace ladies. However, as enthusiasm waned, only a few of the king's concubines remained. These were able to learn a certain amount of English, but they were also exposed to a regular diet of Christian tracts. The missionaries' wives undoubtedly expressed their deep-felt disapproval of the custom of polygamy. There are indications that this criticism caused some commotion, and it is quite possible that this eventually led to such revolutionary measures by the king as increasing the facility with which concubines could resign from the inner palace and take up a life outside the court.[98] It is quite likely that the Christian content of the course was the reason for the king's decision to put a sudden halt to the teaching. Mongkut's increasing distrust of Europeans and Americans during the middle and late 1850s explains why the subject of an English education within the palace was not broached again until the early 1860s, when the numerous offspring born to Mongkut since his enthronement began to grow up. By then Bangkok was undergoing rapid and fundamental change as a result of the ever-growing number of Europeans and Americans trading and seeking residence in Siam. The king himself had acquired a fair knowledge of English and was quite fascinated with the steady stream of innovations and inventions coming from abroad.[99] A progressive and forward-looking king such as Mongkut could no longer neglect to give his children an opportunity to learn the most important European language.

When the king made inquiries about a good woman teacher, Anna Leonowens, who ran a small school in

Singapore, was recommended to him. In his instructions, the king expressly forbade her to preach Christianity in the palace: "We hope that in doing your education on us and on our children . . . you will do your best endeavour for knowledge of English language, science and literature, and not for conversion to Christianity."[100] Anna arrived on 15 March 1862, accompanied by her small son, Louis. She was to stay a little over five years as governess at the Siamese court, leaving Siam on 5 July 1867.[101] As a result of her experiences, Anna wrote several books, two of which were widely distributed[102] and which later formed the basis for a controversial film, *The King and I*. Anna's books provided a highly romantic, sometimes deliberately distorted, and occasionally totally false picture of daily life at the Siamese court. Most scholars have therefore discredited or summarily discarded her works. Recently, it has been established that Anna took liberties with the truth even before she went to Siam and that her claims to a genteel background and her being the widow of "an officer and a gentleman" were false.[103] Just as Bradley's religious beliefs colour his own perception, but should not prevent the historian from learning valuable facts about Siam, so Anna's account provides information that cannot be obtained elsewhere or that confirms events recorded elsewhere. Anna's graphic description of her arrival at Sisuriyawong's palace and her first interview with King Mongkut is amusing, and the reactions of both these men to Anna's petulant and haughty behaviour may well reflect what actually happened.

> Suddenly his Majesty, having cogitated sufficiently in his peculiar manner, with one long stride halted in front of us, and, pointed straight at me with his forefinger, asked, "How old shall you be?"
>
> Scarcely able to repress a smile at a proceeding so absurd, and with my sex's distaste for so serious a question, I demurely replied, "One hundred and fifty years old."
>
> Had I made myself much younger, he might have ridiculed or assailed me; but now he stood surprised and embarrassed for a few moments, then resumed his queer march; and at last, beginning to perceive the jest, coughed and laughed, coughed again, and in a high, sharp key asked, "In what year were you borned?"
>
> Instantly I struck a mental balance, and answered as gravely as I could, "In 1788."

At this point the expression on his Majesty's face was indescribably comical.[104]

During this first interview with his new employee, Mongkut, probably unaware of British feminine coyness about age, possibly did not perceive the jest and may even have doubted the woman's sanity.

In another passage, Anna reveals the little scraps of knowledge remaining from American missionaries' wives' teaching: a bit of a Sunday-school hymn and various English sentences which had lost their meaning.[105] Probably the most valuable information that can be extracted from her works concerns the description of the personal habits of the Siamese leaders. Sisuriyawong's bright intelligence, remarked upon by many contemporary authors, is confirmed, but at the same time, some personal details are added which others have failed to see or mention. A careful reading of *The English Governess* reveals not only Mongkut's short temper but also the king as a scholar and as a father doting on many of his children.

## Astronomy and the Death of the King

The king had long been convinced that the Copernican perspective of the solar system explained many natural phenomena more satisfactorily than the traditional view placing the earth at the central point of the universe. Even before his accession to the throne, Mongkut had accepted that the old Buddhist *Traiphūmikhāthā* cosmogony depicting Mount Meru as the centre of the universe could no longer be regarded as an adequate guide to heavenly bodies and their movements. Rejection of the fabulous aspects of the *Traiphūmikhāthā* was one of the features of the reform movement in which Mongkut had been so active during his years in the Buddhist order.

This movement did not totally reject all things magical and miraculous, however. The subtle debate on the adjustments in Buddhism in the light of the new scientific information can be gleaned from *Kitchānukit*, the first book written by *čhaophrayā* Thiphākǫrawong, which appeared in print in 1867.[106] Thiphākǫrawong's views are not necessarily the same as Mongkut's, but they arise from the same intellectual questions, and they appear in general to be quite in accordance with the views of other "modernists" of that time. Thiphākǫrawong rejects the *Traiphūmikhāthā's* explanation of the passing of the seasons, the origin of wind and rain, the cause of epidemics, and the movement of tides. He maintains that the Buddha never intended to make statements on these natural phenomena. While adhering to the latest scientific explanations regarding these matters, Thiphākǫrawong, and probably many others with him, accepted many other miraculous stories, however, especially those connected with the immense powers of the Buddha, and occasionally he is able to suggest a reconciliation between the scientific world-view and the old legends. Thus it is said that the Buddha spent one rainy season away from the world, preaching in the Tāvatimsa heaven, in order to honour his mother. Thiphākǫrawong suggested that this heaven was probably one of the far-away planets which the Buddha, with his exceptional powers, managed to visit.[107]

The arguments for and against a European view of the cosmos found an excellent test case in the description of eclipses. Traditionally, every eclipse was seen as an act of Rāhu, a black and ominous sky dragon who from time to time suddenly attempted to devour the sun or the moon. When the evil Rāhu opened his mouth and began consuming the heavenly body, it was the duty of all who perceived the danger to discourage the monster, and customarily the Siamese did so by making a tremendous din. Gongs were beaten, pots and pans were clashed together, and the government would order big guns to be fired, so that sooner or later Rāhu would desist. The modern scientific explanation was not in itself noteworthy; it was the fact that astronomers could actually predict, with the aid of their theories, the exact timing of all lunar and solar eclipses and the degree and precise direction of the shadow cover that carried such great conviction.

King Mongkut had long been aware of the force of this aspect of modern astronomy. He had come across the computations of eclipses for 1850 and used these to predict their occurrence,[108] and when they happened as foretold his reputation grew. Even the royal court astrologers could not say exactly when Rāhu would bite. In the following years Mongkut kept an interest in the fruits of various branches of science and technology, ordering impressive instruments from Singapore and letting it be widely known to foreign envoys that the latest gadgets relating to the fields of physics and chemistry and works on physiology, natural history, and technical innovation would be greatly appreciated if there was an exchange of gifts between Siam and a European power. He also ordered the construction of a small observatory in his palace grounds at Phetburi.

Mongkut was quite well informed, and his inquisitive mind ranged widely, yet it would be false to depict him as a competent linguist, historian, archaeologist, or astronomer; he had a superficial acquaintance with these and other fields. Occasionally he wrote short essays on some aspect of them, enough to furnish him with snippets of information useful as conversational opening gambits when meeting Europeans. A statement such as: "You have two terms, — one, the vulgar — leap-year, and another, the classical — bissextile."[109] appears to have been uttered with no other intention than to draw admiring comment from his audience.

It may safely be assumed that the king's wish to help organize an expedition to the southern part of Siam to observe a total eclipse of the sun in August 1868 was not inspired by a genuine scientific curiosity. Mongkut could follow the calculations determining that the event would take place and that the path of the total eclipse would cross a certain region of southern Siam, but that was as far as his astronomical abilities went. His interest in the event was firstly to publicize the event widely and prove the "modernists" right in rejecting certain aspects of legendary explanations of natural phenomena and secondly to foster his image as an enlightened monarch both in Siam and abroad. He invited a French astronomer, British diplomats, court astrologers, and a large number of members of the royal family as well as nobles to travel south to Hua Wan, where the total eclipse could be viewed. His trust in the accuracy and methods of

Western science was vindicated when the eclipse duly occurred.

At the same time, it may be doubted whether the expedition succeeded in convincing many Siamese of the fact that the old Siamese perception of the demonical Rāhu was false, because it so happened that many members of the royal family who had attended the event, including Prince Čhulālongkǫn, eight of the ten French scientists, and also many of the nobles became ill. To the consternation of all, Mongkut himself also fell seriously ill. By late September 1868 eight people who had attended the scientific expedition had died; the king himself expired on the evening of 1 October 1868, aged almost sixty-four after having reigned for more than seventeen years.

## The Fourth Reign in Perspective

### Trade

The Fourth Reign was a period during which many changes were instigated that eventually affected the country fundamentally. The most spectacular was Siam's abrupt lowering of the trade barriers which had prevented most Europeans and Americans from working in Bangkok. With the signing of the Bowring treaty, and with Siam's adherence to its provisions under the supervision of *čhaophrayā* Sīsuriyawong, a European quarter developed in the south of the city where a long row of wharves marked the Western presence. Consulates, churches, shipyards, warehouses, a sawmill, and a customs house soon changed Bangkok in European eyes into a city that had finally rushed into the race for "civilization".[110] The greatly increased Western presence acted as a catalyst in bringing about further changes: new harbour laws had to be written, a new and efficient system of coining money had to be set up, some government proclamations were printed in large numbers and distributed over the country. Steam-engines were imported for ships, rice mills, saw mills, and sugar mills. The Fourth Reign saw the printing of books in both Siamese and English, as well as an impressive number of periodicals.[111]

In the light of all these innovations, the signing of the Bowring treaty is often regarded as a turning point in Siamese history, before which traditional Siam prevailed, while afterwards progressive forces held sway. While it cannot be denied that the Western presence added a new and stimulating dimension to Bangkok, its immediate effect upon the country as a whole has probably been overestimated.

One misconception of the "watershed" view is that before 1855 Siam was an economic backwater, its economy was hardly developed, and its farmers existed mainly at subsistence level, self-sufficient except for occasional bartering. In fact, there are contemporary accounts that point to quite the contrary. Near the end of the Third Reign, the central plain and the south-eastern provinces appear to have become the scene of some spectacular economic development. The south-western part of the central plain became a major source of palm sugar, and the eastern provinces saw the further development of large pepper and sugar-cane plantations.

The case of sugar production illustrates the vigour and strength of the pre-Bowring economy as well as the consistently effective administration in the 1830s and 1840s. Edmund Roberts tells us that in 1832 the Siamese exported some 96,000 piculs of sugar, to a value of approximately 760,000 *baht*.[112] By 1850, the value of the sugar export is estimated to be 708,000 *baht* in the most reliable source available for that time,[113] a decrease possibly reflecting the effects of new and higher taxes.[114] It is therefore somewhat deceptive to write about people predicting that after the Bowring treaty sugar would *become* one of the major exports.[115] In 1850 sugar was already the most valuable item in the list of exports, and it had been so for some time. While the Bowring treaty may have sparked off an initial added interest in sugar manufacture, there was no sign of a "sugar boom". It is even more deceptive to state that between 1849 and 1859 the sugar export rose from just over 100,000 piculs to almost double that amount.[116] The year-by-year accounts show that 1859 was an exceptional year for sugar, and that sugar exports actually began to decline rapidly from 1860 onwards, in 1863 dropping below the 100,000-picul mark and in 1866 to almost 60,000 piculs, only to rise again in 1867, which generally was a good year in the Siamese economy.[117]

Western technological innovations such as steam-powered sugar mills and later even a steam plough do not appear to have had any positive effect during the reign. The first steam sugar mill was set up in 1862, but capital-intensive experiments such as these often proved less flexible than the traditional methods and became liabilities.[118]

The decline in the sugar industry appears to have begun in 1860 and continued during the Fifth Reign until sugar virtually disappeared from the export market in the 1880s. One contributing factor was undoubtedly the gradual drop in the price of sugar on the world market. Another may be found in the Siamese taxation system. Under the Bowring treaty, sugar was made exempt from export duty and inland transit duties were fixed at one and two *salu'ng* per picul for brown and white sugar respectively.[119] However, there were no provisions restricting taxation of sugar in the earlier stages of manufacture and, probably to make up for the loss of export revenue, fairly heavy taxes were levied on the land on which sugar-cane was grown, on the cane, on mills, on boilers, and on the boats used for transport.[120] Many of these taxes were fixed, regardless of the actual yield and the state of the market, which increased the cost of manufacture and the economic risk involved.

These observations on the sugar production are relevant also to the production of cotton. In 1821 Crawfurd mentioned Siam's export of cotton;[121] in 1833 Roberts estimated the exports to be between 30,000 and 40,000 piculs,[122] and D.E. Malloch's figures, which generally are held to refer to 1850, give the value of the cotton export as 450,000 *baht*, and another 211,500 *baht* worth of cotton-filled pillows and mattresses were exported that year. It is likely that not all that was called cotton by European travellers was cotton, strictly speaking, and that pillows and mattresses were then, as now, filled with kapok. Nevertheless, the quantity and value of the yearly export demonstrate that Siam possessed an intricate network of trade and industry which ensured that products from home industry and small-scale industrial complexes would find a market.

If the total value of import and export is taken as an indication of Siam's "openness" to international trade, the figures show a remarkable pre-Bowring activity. Siam's exports in 1832 were estimated at a value of not less than 7,500,000 *baht*, though only about five million *baht* worth appears to have been sent through the official channels.[123] Malloch reports for 1850 an export of just over 5,500,000 *baht*, and imports worth some 4,331,000 *baht*. By 1867, just over a decade after the Bowring treaty, and after an exceptionally profitable year of trading, the *Bangkok Summary* reported the total volume of export to be some 7,660,000 *baht* and the imports about 6,350,000 *baht*.[124]

Before the Bowring treaty, Siam's trade with China, Singapore, and Java was lively and lucrative,[125] and the changes after it appear to have led not so much to a sudden opening up of new markets and new sources of wealth as to an abrupt alteration in direction and a series of developments in the local taxation system. Europeans gained an increasing share of the international trade, and European ships largely supplanted the former trading junks. The limitations on Siamese export tax and the inland transit duties were intended to make international trade more profitable. In practice, although many taxes were levied at fixed amounts and a few abolished, the treaties did not provide a comprehensive taxation model; the Siamese government was able to increase other taxes and levy many new ones to make up for the concessions.

## Taxation

While import and export figures may provide an indication of Siam's economic role in the region, they reflect only an aspect of the Siamese economy as a whole. State revenue data from from various sources reflect much more the size, scope, and character of the Siamese economy. The scanty information available on taxation during the Third and Fourth Reigns shows an increasingly complex system. Roberts enumerated more than seventy separate taxes on floating houses, paddy, orchards, gambling, vegetables, alcohol, and a vast array of other products.[126] Some time during the Third Reign, taxes were added on the transport of some goods, on iron pans, on cotton-growing lands, on tobacco, jute, and indigo, on sugar-boiling establishments, on timber used for the boat-building industry, on stearin candles, on cakes, on lime, on bullock carts, on hire boats, and on towing boats.[127]

During the first five years of the Fourth Reign, a few taxes were lowered for the specific purpose of attracting overseas trade. However, this relaxation applied only to foreign traders; the general populace was taxed as heavily as before if not more so. While the income from various farms and duties amounted in 1833 to some 890,000 *baht*, by 1851 this had risen to some 1,294,000 *baht*, a figure that slowly rose in the following years to 1,318,000 (in 1855) and 1,334,000 (in 1856).[128] The Bowring treaty established a fixed scale of export duties for fifty-one articles, stipulating that these be free of all other production, inland, or transit duties, and provided a further list of twelve articles on which transit duties were allowed but which would become free of all export duty.[129] The Siamese team of negotiators themselves controlled large sections of the taxation system, and it is unlikely that they would have agreed to a great cut in their personal income simply to accommodate European traders. As a matter of fact, it seems that the Bowring treaty had little or no immediate effect upon the revenues derived from all government farms; during the years between 1853 and 1868, the amount of Siamese revenue increased by an average of some 39,000 *baht* annually.

The system of taxation had become almost wholly dominated by tax-farming, with persons handing over a prearranged sum considered appropriate for a tax to a particular government *krom*. For example, the tax on carts pulled by buffaloes was set at 2 *baht*; on those pulled by oxen, 1½ *baht*. During the first ten years of the Fourth Reign, the Siamese government could expect to receive 2,000 *baht* yearly from these particular taxes.[130] The tax-farmers would set up their own organization in order to collect the moneys, and in normal circumstances they expected to receive much more than the 2,000 *baht* which had to be handed over. If the tax-farmer had difficulties meeting his obligations, he could propose to pay the government a lower sum; if the tax-farmer was making too large a profit, the government could demand a higher tax for the following season or force the price up by inviting tenders.[131]

There never had been a centrally organized treasury; the original chief government departments had always had their own sources of income, the *krom* Kalāhom from the south, the *krom* Thā from certain coastal towns, the *krom* Nā from land tax, and the *krom* Mū'ang from tribunals. With the proliferation of new taxes in the Third and Fourth Reigns, the system of passing tax moneys on to the many separate treasuries of government departments became increasingly complex.[132] The two most important treasuries were the Phrakhlang Mahāsombat (the Great Treasury, which during the Fourth Reign seems to have been controlled by *čhaophrayā* Sīsuriyawong in his capacity as head of the *krom* Kalāhom), and the Phrakhlang Sinkhā Phra Borom Mahārātchawang (the Royal Warehouse, supervised by Sīsuriyawong's brother *čhaophrayā* Rawiwong).[133]

The system of tax-farming worked so conveniently for the Siamese administration, who handed over all the problems of tax evasion, bribery, and corruption to the tax-farmers, that it was adopted by the *krom* Nā to collect rice-land tax in the central provinces. For an annual sum of 160,000 *baht* the state gave the full powers of collection to the head of the *krom* Nā, making the whole *krom* into a tax-farm and legalizing the profits made by its officials. Tax on rice land was still levied directly in some of the "outer provinces". Thus the *krom* Kalāhom was responsible for this tax in many of the southern provinces in a region that began at Ratburi and ended in Songkhla, and the Mahātthai officially had the right to levy the rice-land tax on the belt of northern provinces such as Phitsanulok, Angthong, Saraburi, and Nakhon Nayok.[134]

Apart from tax-farms and direct taxation, which formed the bulk of the government's income, throughout the Fourth Reign the State still had various other sources of wealth. One of these was the poll tax on Chinese, another the goods and services which could be commanded by State officials under the old corvée system. The latter source was mainly used during major state ceremonies, when large amounts of wood, bamboo, and workers were needed to create temporary pavilions and ceremonial objects; and also during some of the great building programmes instigated by the king and the senior nobles. At the same time, some of the outer provinces paid their taxes largely in kind by sending shipments of *suai* for the royal warehouses. Finally, some of the vassal states would regularly send tribute, but the value of the tribute varied from time to time and from vassal state to vassal state.[135]

The general picture appears to be one of increasing state control over various sources of revenue and over sections of the populace, especially in the central plains area. Large numbers of households paid a yearly tax on firewood and often one-tenth of the value of the goods they sold in the market, and their home-industries were taxed. While some of these taxes dated from a previous reign, it may safely be assumed that their collection was more efficient during the Fourth Reign. For some there were opportunities to make a deal with a tax collector or even avoid paying any tax at all. Not far from Phetburi there were, for example, many woodcutters who

> cut timber free of duty as the forests have no owner but the king and He does not know where they are, they sell their wood to the Laos[136] and others who come with carts for it and pay them for it in rice and other merchandise at the rate of about 1 tical a picul. The cartsmen take it, a journey of two days, to Ratboree about 3 piculs to a load, and sell it for 2 ticals per picul and these [the buyers] carry it to Bangkok in boats and sell it for 2½ to 3 ticals per picul.[137]

Not everyone lived as carefree and unfettered an existence as the illegal woodcutters. For this same region there are glimpses of various other conditions under which sections of the populace laboured. There is a report of farmers who had to pay 2½ *baht* yearly for the right to burn firewood in their houses, and it is also mentioned that in 1859 the people lost in tax one-fifth of the value of all the produce they took to market. In order to raise the cash for these taxes, the people mainly worked cutting wood.[138] In the Phetburi region there were also many people employed in the palm-sugar industry and in potteries. They also appear to have been heavily taxed: "I had no idea that the manufacture of palm sugar is attended with so much labor and that so little profit is made by the manufacturer. They get but a very lean subsistence and pay heavy taxes on the palmyra trees and on their places for boiling."[139]

Phetburi was also exceptionally busy with the building of a palace on a mountain not far from the town, on which large numbers of corvée workers were engaged. Some, apparently from the north, worked one month and then were free for three months to follow their own pursuits. Their corvée was quite heavy. Bradley talked with a few from a party of some five hundred of them:

> These 8 or 10 whom I conversed with are employed in drawing brick in ox carts 1¼ miles, that is from the river up to the foot of the mount and their daily task is 10 loads, as much as 2 men can draw and one push by the outlay of nearly all their strength. This is equal to 12½ miles which they have to draw their loads daily and add to this the return trips each 1¼ miles, making 25 miles which they are obliged thus daily to travel or get a severe flogging for failing to do so.[140]

Not all groups of workers had such hard tasks, for Bradley had remarked when he visited that same site a few years earlier that there were several hundreds of corvée workers who mostly worked by the hour and who did not seem to expend much energy in their work. Moreover, they could always hire a substitute at prices ranging from six to eight *baht* per month.[141]

Many local inhabitants could not be drafted for corvée. Thus all those who laboured full-time in the king's rice-fields near Phetburi gained exemption from corvée; they were allowed to use an area of 4¾ *rai* of rice-field for their own support, and also obtained a yearly sum of six *baht*. Some 260 families were thus employed in the king's fields.[142]

From these and a few other glimpses of life outside Bangkok it would appear that during the Fourth Reign there was a considerable measure of control over the various social groups of ordinary people. However, the region around Phetburi may not be representative of the rest of the central plains. It was an area of the specialized palm-sugar industry, and in addition the town was the focus of much attention because the king had selected it as a holiday retreat. In areas further away from the gaze of the king and senior members of the court, life may well have been easier.

# Notes

1.  Letter by D.B. Bradley, dated 28 March 1851, to the Singapore *Straits Times*, as published in W.L. Bradley, "The Accession of King Mongkut", *JSS* 57, pt 1 (1969): 156.
2.  Details can be found in Somathat Thēwēt, *Čhaofā Čhuthāmanī*.
3.  A.L. Moffat, *Mongkut, the King of Siam*, pp. 49-50. A photograph of this eight-metre steamer can be found in Somathat, *Čhaofā Čhuthāmanī*, p. 123.
4.  *Čhaophrayā* Thiphākǫrawong, *The Dynastic Chronicles Bangkok Era, The Fourth Reign*, trans. Chadin Flood [hereafter *DC Fourth R*], vol. 1, p. 4.
5.  Bradley, "Accession of King Mongkut", p. 160.
6.  Sir John Bowring, *The Kingdom and People of Siam*, vol. 2, p. 449.
7.  Mongkut's sarcastic remarks in a letter to his envoys in London bear witness to this. See Moffat, *Mongkut*, pp. 56-58, citing Seni and Kukrit Pramoj, "The King of Siam Speaks", pp. 222-27. This letter was written in 1858. See also D.B. Bradley's journal entry for 19 October 1851.
8.  For details, see *DC Fourth R*, vol. 1, pp. 6-49.
9.  Ibid., pp. 49-57. The king's own two eldest sons and Phra' Pinklāo's eldest son, who are mentioned by Thiphākǫrawong in this list, were probably promoted to *kromamū'n* rank at some later date during the Fourth Reign.
10. There can be little doubt as to the accuracy of this information, which derives from D.B. Bradley's personal journal (the entry for 9 September 1851), for Bradley was sitting quite close to the two men.
11. D.B. Bradley journal entry for 7 February 1852.
12. In this case, rank is not commensurate with position in the administration. It must be regarded as one of the ways of honouring the Bunnāk family.
13. C.M. Wilson, "State and Society in the Reign of Mongkut, 1851-1868", p. 325.
14. *DC Fourth R*, vol. 1, p. 65.
15. He died soon afterwards (*DC Fourth R*, vol. 1, p. 48).
16. This official died in August 1861, aged seventy-five (*DC Fourth R*, vol. 1, p. 243).
17. *DC Fourth R*, vol. 1, p. 90.
18. Wilson, "State and Society", p. 609.
19. *DC Fourth R*, vol. 1, pp. 5-6.
20. O. Frankfurter, "The Mission of Sir James Brooke to Siam", *JSS* 8, pt 3 (1911): 31.
21. This class was set up on 14 August 1851, upon the repeated request of King Mongkut (see D.B. Bradley's journal entries for 13, 14, 16 and 30 August 1851.
22. Bradley's journal entry for 6 May 1852. The cremation rituals were held between 25 April and 9 May of that year.
23. Bradley's journal entry for 21 January 1854.

24.    D.B. Bradley, moved by sentiments not unlike those of the French missionaries in the mid-1680s, believed a massive conversion possible, and he used his greatly increased status as one of the court's regular physicians and husband of one of the teachers in the palace to go and preach all around town, in public places as well as in Buddhist temples. He was in these years so sure of himself that he did not bend to local customs. Witness his personal diary for 31 August 1851:

> In the morning preached to a company of Siamese on a bridge over a canal out far from my house. The bridge had over it a cool cover and upon it comfortable seats. While preaching boatloads of priests came along in the canal and wished me to move off from the bridge so that they might pass under without contracting sin. It is one of the teachings of Boodhism that it is wicked to live or pass under any person, particularly if the person or persons are female. I kept my seat and told them that I did not believe in such foolishness – they replied, Then we cannot pass – Well, said I, be it so. I shall not humour such a notion as that. Presently they put their paddles in the water with unusual force and spray [and moved] through with all their might.

25.    The Shan people of Burma speak Tai languages, and this title is related to the Siamese *čhaofā*, or "celestial prince".
26.    *PKRt Sām*, pp. 339-40; see also *DC Fourth R*, vol. 3, pp. 69-70; W.F. Vella, *Siam Under Rama III*, pp. 92-93; and Wilson, "State and Society", pp. 522-23
27.    Letter dated 15 May 1853, cited in Wilson, "State and Society", pp. 527-28.
28.    Wilson, "State and Society", p. 529.
29.    *DC Fourth R*, pp. 59-60.
30.    *Čhaophrayā* Sisuriyawong and a detachment of soldiers left Bangkok on 28 October 1853 (see Bradley's journal, 2 November 1853).
31.    Short accounts of the expedition can be found in *DC Fourth R*, vol. 1, p. 93-95, 109-10, and 118-19; King Mongkut's account has been published in Bowring, *Kingdom and People of Siam*, vol. 2, pp. 364-67; see also Wilson "State and Society", pp. 525-33.
32.    J. Blofeld, *King Maha Mongkut of Siam*, p. 79. Similar remarks can be found in D.R. SarDesai, *British Trade and Expansion in Southeast Asia, 1830–1914*, pp. 89-90.
33.    Anonymous letter, dated Bangkok 12 July 1854, which appeared in the *Straits Times* on 12 September 1854.
34.    Ibid. No other information could be found on Trail.
35.    King Mongkut apparently was very interested in the Siamese language, and he occasionally made a declaration on the use of words. In Proclamation 68, for example, he forbids the classifier *tua* to be used in connection with elephants. The author of the letter states that the word "*cup'per*" was forbidden by the king, who decreed that "ca-cone" should be used instead. Apparently the king wished to ban the Burmese-derived word *kapi*, and advocated the use of the Siamese word *khoei*.
36.    Bradley, journal, 28 September 1854.
37.    Ibid.
38.    Apparently it was Samuel J. Smith, calling for the luggage of J.H. Chandler and Robert Telford, representatives of the American Baptist Missionary Union (see Bowring, *Kingdom and People of Siam*, vol. 1, p. 388).
39.    *DC Fourth R*, vol. 1, p. 123.
40.    Bradley, journal, entries for 18, 24, and 27 December 1854.
41.    Ibid., 4 January 1855.

42. N. Tarling, "The Mission of Sir John Bowring to Siam", *JSS* 50, pt 2 (1962): 96; the tension between Mongkut and Sīsuriyawong was visible even during an official audience, where Sīsuriyawong knitted his brows and "pished" several times at the king's words (see Tarling, "The Bowring Mission: The Mellersh Narrative", *JSS* 63, pt 1 [1975]: 118).

43. Letter to the governor of Prince of Wales Island, Malacca, and Singapore, dated 22 May 1851, in "English Correspondence of King Mongkut", ed. G. Coedès, *JSS* 21, pt 1 (1927): 8-9.

44. G.W. Skinner, *Chinese Society in Thailand*, p. 47; *DC Fourth R*, vol. 1, pp. 47-48 and 86-90.

45. Tarling, "Mission of Sir John Bowring", p. 93.

46. Ibid., p. 110.

47. Thiphākǫrawong (*DC Fourth R*, vol. 1, p. 129) places the death one day earlier. I have relied here upon Bradley's journal entry for 26 April 1855.

48. Bradley's journal entries for 9, 10, 12 November and 25 December 1855. The vessel was named "The Royal Seat of the Siamese Forces" (an example of Mongkut's habit of translating Siamese idiomatic expressions into their literal English equivalent).

49. A list of the presents and the state in which they were received can be found in King Mongkut's letter to Queen Victoria, published in "English Correspondence of King Mongkut", *JSS* 21, pt 1 (1927): 18-20.

50. Apparently the king had not seen the actual treaty, which had been concluded at the end of March 1854, and soon after the American envoy Townsend Harris arrived, the Phrakhlang asked him for a copy. Harris replied that he would send one later. See M.E. Cosenza, ed., *The Complete Journal of Townsend Harris*, p. 104.

51. These revealing comments have been published in N. Tarling, "Harry Parkes' Negotiations in Bangkok in 1856", *JSS* 53, pt 2 (1965): 168.

52. For the exact words, see Tarling, "Harry Parkes' Negotiations", p. 171. Tarling does not seem to read any duplicity into the statement, possibly because he was unaware of Mongkut's actions to obstruct the treaty.

53. Bradley, journal, 20 March 1856.

54. The king put his printers in irons because they did not work to his satisfaction (see Tarling, "Harry Parkes' Negotiations", p. 174).

55. Bradley, journal, 10 April 1856.

56. Harris's growing impatience is responsible for many of his caustic comments on Siam and its king. They are admirably summarized in Moffat, *Mongkut*, pp. 76-87. Harris the private person thought Mongkut "quite as weak-minded as pedantic", while Harris the diplomat praised his "great acquirements in many difficult languages and in the higher branches of science" (J. Wook Moon, "United States Relations with Thailand: The mission of Townsend Harris", *Asian Profile* 1, no. 2 [1973]: 369).

57. Mongkut complained in no uncertain terms about Harris's hurried departure (see his letter to Franklin Pierce, published in "English Correspondence of King Mongkut", *JSS* 21, pt 1 (1927): 31.

58. Bradley, journal, 8 July 1856.

59. "English Correspondence of King Mongkut", *JSS* 21, pt 2 (1927): 127-28.

60. Bradley, journal, 3 October 1856.

61. Ibid., 6 October 1856. See also the letter of Charles Bell, the acting British consul, dated 4 December 1856, referring to a proclamation "stating that the land has been given as an atonement for the insult offered by the seizure and putting to death of a servant of the British Consul" (cited in Wilson, "State and Society", p. 372).

62. The full quotation runs as follows: "On being asked if there were often changes in the dynasty, he uttered the real republican sentiment that kings who claim their title by right of birth, often forget they originated from the people, consider themselves as superior beings and don't lend an ear to the sufferings of their subjects, — so there was often a change at the fourth generation of princes of the same dynasty" (Cosenza, *Journal of Townsend Harris*, p. 115). See also Neon Snidvongs, "Siam's Relations with Britain and France in the Reign of King Mongkut, 1851–1868", pp. 297-98.

63. Sīsuriyawong had to reckon with the active opposition of Phra' Pinklāo, who may have been against his brother but certainly would not have liked to see a Bunnāk on the throne. Wilson ("State and Society", p. 373) mentions hostilities between soldiers under the command of these two. Moreover, the Younger *somdet*, though a Bunnāk, was quite unhappy at the prospect of foreigners having such free access to Siam, and it is likely that he would have used all his influence to forestall any possible bid by Sīsuriyawong for the throne.

64. On the Siamese perspective of the treaty, probably the best source is the commentary on the chronicles by Chadin Flood (see *DC Fourth R*, vol. 3, pp. 96-97).

65. Bradley, journal, 3 January 1857.

66. U. Guehler, "A Letter by Sir Robert H. Schomburgk H.B.M.'s Consul in Bangkok in 1860", *JSS* 37, pt 2 (1949): 151-52.

67. For details, see Wilson, "State and Society", p. 984. Only in 1865 did the number of ships drop dramatically, but this was undoubtedly the result of the temporary rice export ban imposed because of a bad crop in 1864/65.

68. "Letter by Sir Robert H. Schomburgk", p. 152.

69. Bradley, journal, 28 February 1858.

70. For details, see Chaloem Yongbunkoet, *Thonabat Thai*, pp. 8-20; see also "English Correspondence of King Mongkut", *JSS* 21, pt 2 (1927): 150-51 and 173.

71. Bradley, journal, 14 December 1857.

72. For example, *DC Fourth R*, vol. 1, p. 179; this may be a reason for the frequency of the word *pru'ksā* (to consult, ask advice) in the description of Mongkut's relationship with his administrators, which has also been noted by Wilson, "State and Society", p. 710.

73. Chatthip Nartsupha and Suthy Prasartset, *Socio-economic Institutions and Cultural Change in Siam, 1851–1910, Documentary Survey*, pp. 10-11.

74. Ibid., pp. 17-24.

75. Bradley, journal 15 September 1857 and 8 February 1858. There can be no doubt that the Younger *somdet* died in 1858, and not in 1855 as D.K. Wyatt has asserted ("Family Politics in Nineteenth Century Thailand", *Journal of Southeast Asian History* 9, no. 2 [1968]: 221), and Wilson is wrong in the dates for both the Elder and the Younger *somdet* ("State and Society", p. 715.)

76. Wilson, "State and Society", p. 712.

77. For a description of Sīsuriyawong's European lifestyle and palace in 1861, see Philipp zu Eulenburg-Hertfeld, ed., *Ost-Asien 1860–1862 in Briefen des Grafen Fritz zu Eulenburg*, p. 350.

78. This man was later to be appointed *čhaophrayā* Thiphākǫrawong, the compiler of many of the chronicles cited in this book.

79. Bradley, journal, 7 November 1858.

80. It has become commonplace to endow Mongkut with extraordinary powers of foresight and depict many of his actions as part of a battle of wits to save

his country from colonial domination. Evidence disproving this view is brought forward later in this chapter.

81. Bradley, journal, 29 October 1858; see also the entry for 15 July of that year.

82. *Bangkok Calendar*, 1863, pp. 84-85. The editor (D.B. Bradley) adds that another reason may be the diminishing faith in Buddhism, but this coming from a man who devoted many years to discrediting the worship of idols and "false doctrines" may safely be attributed to wishful thinking.

83. K. Rosenberg, *Nation und Fortschritt: Der Publizist Thien Wan und die Modernisierung Thailands unter König Culălongkǫn (r. 1868–1910)*, p. 34.

84. See, for example, the reports in the *Straits Times* for 12 October, 23 November, and especially 14 December 1861.

85. Pensri (Suvanij) Duke, *Les relations entre la France et la Thailande (Siam) au XIXe siècle d'après les archives etrangères*, pp. 26-27.

86. Some of the letters to the *Straits Times* were apparently inspired to put the Siamese government's point of view to the English-speaking world. King Mongkut was quite active in this respect, and this article to the popular *Quarterly Review* in London was inspired by a wish to make Siam's position widely known (see *Quarterly Review* 116 [1864]: 303).

87. Wilson, "State and Society", pp. 549-51.

88. Aubaret's hostility towards some of the Siamese is commented upon in the *Siamese Recorder* of May 1865. When the consul's request to have M. Lamache appointed representative for the Portugese was denied, Aubaret reputedly had the senior government servant who came to tell him this violently expelled from his house. See Bradley, journal, 31 August 1865 and 2 September 1865; see also the reference in Pensri Duke, *Les relations*, p. 43.

89. Confidential correspondence was published in the *Siam Daily Advertiser* of 21 June 1870 and reprinted in the *Straits Times* of 16 July 1870. There can be little doubt about the authenticity of the documents. The confrontation with France drove the Siamese to seek British help, as can be seen from the letters sent by Mongkut in 1866 mentioned below.

90. The letter is cited in Pensri Duke, *Les relations,* pp. 54-55.

91. This letter was translated by Seni and Kukrit Pramoj, in "The King of Siam Speaks", a typewritten manuscript, cited extensively in Moffat, *Mongkut*. This quotation is on page 124 of Moffat's work.

92. Like Mongkut, Sīsuriyawong also travelled, including a little-known visit to Singapore from 17 July to 30 August 1861, the main reason for which was apparently an official call upon the authorities in Kedah (see the *Straits Times*, 3 August and 14 September 1861).

93. Wilson, "State and Society", p. 713.

94. This prince was originally named George Washington after the first president of the United States. The name "George" was pronounced "Yǫt" by most Siamese, and the prince was often referred to as "*phra'ǫngčhao* Yǫt".

95. *DC Fourth R*, vol. 2, pp. 380-81.

96. In July 1867 King Mongkut jested with Bradley about his strength (Bradley, journal, 18 July 1867).

97. Ibid., 13 and 14 August 1851.

98. Moffat, *Mongkut*, pp. 164-65; Bradley, journal, 25 January 1856.

99. For example, photography was introduced with the visit of "Mr Alfred's Exhibition of Dissolving Views" (Bradley, journal, 12 and 16 April 1859).

100. Letter to King Mongkut to Anna Leonowens, in W.S. Bristowe, *Louis and the King of Siam*, p. 22, citing H. Longhurst, *The Borneo Story, The First Hundred Years of the Borneo Company Limited*. See also Moffat, *Mongkut*, pp. 167-68.

101.    Bristowe, *Louis and the King*, p. 23, states that Anna held the position until 22 July 1967. Actually she left Bangkok for Singapore on July 5 of that year, never to return.

102.    First published as *The English Governess at the Siamese Court: Being Recollections of Six Years in the Royal Palace at Bangkok* and *The Romance of the Harem*.

103.    Bristowe, *Louis and the King*, pp. 23-31. Anna's shortcomings as a historian and her occasional flagrant plagiarism have been exposed by A.B. Griswold, "King Mongkut in Perspective", *JSS* 45, pt 1 (1957): 1-41.

104.    Leonowens, *The English Governess*, pp. 57-58.

105.    Ibid., pp. 62-63.

106.    An abbreviated English translation was made by Henri Alabaster and forms a large part of his book *The Wheel of the Law*.

107.    Ibid., p. 17.

108.    Bowring, *Kingdom and People of Siam,* vol. 1, p. 44.

109.    M.L. Manich Jumsai, *King Mongkut and Sir John Bowring*, p. 197.

110.    This is illustrated in an article that appeared in 31 August 1861 in the *Straits Times* under the heading "Progress of the Eastern World". Siam was assessed as follows: "Siam, though comparatively small in territory, and but new in the race of civilization, has yet advanced in some respects beyond the larger kingdoms of Asia, and is unequalled in having a sovereign who is accessible to all and who is a lover and promoter of literature, science and the fine arts."

111.    Apart from Bradley's *Bangkok Calendar* and *Bangkok Recorder*, there appeared at some time during the reign issues of the *Siam Times*, the *Bangkok Press*, the *Bangkok Summary*, and the *Siam Weekly Monitor*. The latter appeared in 1867 and 1868 and was edited by E. d'Encourt and not by Bradley, as the official bibliography states (*Periodicals and Newspapers Printed in Thailand*, p. 4).

112.    E. Roberts, *Embassy to the Eastern Courts of Cochin-China, Siam and Muscat*, pp. 316-17.

113.    J. Homan van der Heide, "The Economical Development of Siam During the Last Half Century", *JSS* 3, pt 2 (1906): 81, citing D.E. Malloch.

114.    *PKRt Sām*, p. 361.

115.    J.C. Ingram, *Economic Change in Thailand 1850-1970*, p. 123.

116.    Ibid.

117.    Wilson, "State and Society", p. 985.

118.    In February 1869 the new steam-powered sugar mill at Nakhon Chaisi was in great financial difficulties. For details, see Bradley, journal, 5 February 1869.

119.    Manich Jumsai, *King Mongkut and Sir John Bowring*, p. 137.

120.    Each palm-tree was taxed, and a tax of one *baht* was placed on each hundred pots. Every boiling establishment of two kettles had to pay six *salu'ng* per year (see Bradley, journal, 28 March 1861; and Wilson, "State and Society", p. 993).

121.    J. Crawfurd, *Journal of an Embassy to the Courts of Siam and Cochin China*, p. 383.

122.    Roberts, *Embassy to the Eastern Courts*, p. 317.

123.    Ibid., p. 318.

124.    As copied in the *Straits Times*, 27 March 1869.

125.    A short description of the types of vessels that controlled the trade can be found in Sarasin Viraphol, *Tribute and Profit: Sino-Siamese Trade, 1652-1853*, pp. 227-31. For a picture of the continued share of Siam in regional trade, the figures in G.F. de Bruijn Kops, *Statistiek van den Handel en de Scheepvaart op Java en Madura sedert 1825*, give an impression of

Siam's vigorous economy (see vol. 1, p. 394 and p. 461, and vol. 2, p. 228 and p. 543).

126. Roberts, *Embassy to the Eastern Courts*, pp. 426-27.

127. *PKRt Sām*, p. 361.

128. Roberts, *Embassy to the Eastern Courts*, pp. 426-27, and Wilson, "State and Society", p. 999. Roberts's assessment of the tax on rice land and orchards appears to be quite unrealistic, and these have been left out of the calculation.

129. See Manich Jumsai, *King Mongkut and Sir John Bowring*, pp. 136-37.

130. Wilson, "State and Society", p. 989 and pp. 995-96. She enumerates more than eighteen treasuries.

131. Wira Wimoniti, *Historical Patterns of Tax Administration in Thailand*, pp. 94-95.

132. Wilson, "State and Society", p. 1003.

133. Ibid., p. 1001-43, and Wira Wimoniti, *Historical Patterns*, p. 93.

134. Wilson, "State and Society", pp. 1056-57.

135. For details, see Wilson, "State and Society", pp. 533-55 and pp. 875-97.

136. The term *Laos* was used for all people from the north and north-east, and it was not limited to those living in the region at present known as Laos.

137. Bradley, journal, 15 March 1865.

138. Ibid., 4 February 1859. Apparently the heavy market tax was replaced that year by one on boats, buildings, and rafts (Wilson, "State and Society", p. 991).

139. Bradley, journal, 10 February 1859.

140. Ibid., 1 September 1862.

141. Ibid., 3 November 1859. Bradley states that this group worked every alternate month and it is possible that they represented a special sub-category in the Siamese system of bondage, such as the offspring of prisoners of war.

142. Ibid.

# 7

# The Fifth Reign, Part I (1868–83): The Regent and New Siam

## The Succession

In matters concerning the Siamese succession, it is not possible to reconstruct exactly how the various individuals involved interacted and what was decided in informal meetings. It is possible, however, to make at least a plausible reconstruction of the sequence which led to Prince Čhulālongkǭn's elevation to the throne.

On his return from his expedition to observe the solar eclipse, King Mongkut contracted a serious illness which lasted throughout the month of September 1868. All who visited and treated him agree on the fact that he was mentally unaffected by the illness. Therefore it would appear that, when he realized that death was imminent, the king was quite able to discuss his succession with members of his family and senior nobles. At that time *chaofā* Čhulālongkǭn was just fifteen,[1] and he had apparently impressed various parties other than the king, for the prince had a good bearing and displayed a strong measure of charm and intelligence.

Moreover, it had become quite clear to the Siamese that the idea of the succession moving to a minor constituted no obstacle in the eyes of the Europeans.

Apparently Sĭsuriyawong was able to accept Mongkut's reasoning, and before the king died he had agreed to support Čhulālongkǫn; in return for his support he was offered the regency. It has been suggested that Sĭsuriyawong's support was only half-hearted and that he only agreed because the boy was at that time seriously ill and he expected him to die.[2] However, by the time Mongkut knew he himself was dying, the young prince had already passed through his fever and was no longer regarded as dangerously ill.[3] It is not justified to surmise hostility between Sĭsuriyawong and Čhulālongkǫn at this period or even to surmise disagreements at such an early stage in their relations.

At the time of King Mongkut's illness, there was no single Siamese who could rival Sĭsuriyawong in power. Sĭsuriyawong commanded most of Siam's army; he supervised much of the government's income and expenditure; he and members of his family occupied many key positions in the administration. His situation was remarkably like that of his father's at the end of the Third Reign in that the decision with regard to the succession could not be made without his consent. The question why Sĭsuriyawong did not use the opportunity of Mongkut's death to proclaim himself king is quite relevant. This reputedly was asked of him by a younger relative years later, and at that time the elder statesman answered guardedly: "Why should I bother? I have everything a man could desire."[4] In the light of Sĭsuriyawong's earlier statements made during the period when there was considerable tension between him and Mongkut,[5] it is likely that the thought of becoming monarch crossed his mind. Sĭsuriyawong had only weak candidates opposing him, and he must have realized that he could relatively easily have staged a coup, and that after an initial period of adjustment the international world would probably have accepted such a move. It is impossible to decide what held him back; perhaps it was the embarrassment of becoming an usurper, or the difficulties inherent in an extensive royal family, or some other consideration. Only three weeks after King Mongkut's death, Sĭsuriyawong affords us a little glimpse of what had been on his mind when he suddenly asked Bradley in a playful manner "if it would not be practicable to elect a president over this people and have a republican government".[6] Bradley replied that he thought the Siamese people were as yet far too ignorant and ill-informed for such a form of government. Since this remark was made more than a month before Čhulālongkǫn's official inauguration, the remark came at a most crucial time, and it would not be too far-fetched to deduce that Sĭsuriyawong was pondering over the question of taking formal power, but at the same time he may have found the office of king, with all its pomp and ceremony, not really attractive.

Whatever Sĭsuriyawong's private thoughts may have been, it is a fact that a few hours after King Mongkut's death, on 1 October 1868, Siam's Great Council assembled and the most senior member of the royal family, *kromaluang* Thēwēt-wacharin, proposed to offer the throne to *čhaofā* Čhulālongkǫn. All agreed to this choice. Immediately thereafter, Sĭsuriyawong was elected regent. It was quite unorthodox to have someone who was not a member of the royal family appointed regent. A member of the *khunnāng* ought not to command princes. In order to deal with this situation, *kromakhun* Bamrāp (also known as *čhaofā* Mahāmālā), brother of the late king, was chosen be be "regent of palace affairs". During the same meeting, Sĭsuriyawong proposed to appoint Prince Wichaichān as head of the Front Palace. *Kromakhun* Wǫrasak, a senior prince who had considerable administrative experience and who outranked Wichaichān, criticized this proposal, and suggested that the choice of the head of the Front Palace be left to the new king. Before Wǫrasak could elaborate on the legal aspects of the case, Sĭsuriyawong demonstrated his power and openly accused Wǫrasak of angling for that position himself. The meeting decided to accept Sĭsuriyawong's proposal and Wichaichān was elected to the position once held by his father, Phra' Pinklāo.[7]

## The First Measures

During the Fourth Reign, the introduction of new copper and tin coins had met with great difficulties, for the public was reluctant to accept the idea that the government could guarantee a price on bits of base metal which apparently had little intrinsic value. Probably it was the thought that new coins would be issued at the beginning of the reign which caused a renewal of the coin panic. Buying and selling virtually stopped in the Bangkok markets. The government decided to exchange the copper coins for their full face value during a period of fifteen days only. After that, they would be exchanged at a reduced rate. In other words, the tin and copper coins of the Fourth Reign ended up being drastically devalued. The coin panic, and the resulting rush to have copper and tin coins exchanged for silver, lasted from some time during October 1868 until at least the beginning of December of that year. It forced the government to revert to a system whereby the appearance and weight of the metal would correspond more closely to the token value.[8]

The appointments of 1869 at the beginning of the Fifth Reign were headed by Sīsuriyawong, who gained authority over policy-making throughout the country and who was elevated to a *saktinā* of 30,000 *rai*, equal to that which his father had been given upon Mongkut's accession. His retired brother, *čhaophrayā* Thiphākǫrawong, was formally honoured as "senior statesman" and his *saktinā* was increased from 10,000 to 20,000 *rai*.[9] The post of Kalāhom, which became vacant with Sīsuriyawong's elevation to regent, was given to the regent's son Won Bunnāk, who became *čhaophrayā* Surawongwaiyawat. Prince Wǫrasak was replaced as Phrakhlang, a rather unorthodox step in Siamese history and one that may be interpreted as an indication of the power of the Bunnāk family, for his post was given to *čhaophrayā* Phanuwong, Sīsuriyawong's brother Thuam. The remaining senior ministries were left in the hands of other families: the Mahātthai remained headed by *čhaophrayā* Phutharaphai of the Bunyarathaphan family, who had held the post since 1863; the *krom* Mū'ang stayed under the direction of one of the Singhasēnĭ family; and the *krom* Nā went to a Bunlong, whose mother, however, was a Bunnāk.[10] The Bunnāks thus dominated the administration. Members of the family were spread over various departments in the capital, and in addition a beginning was made of the Bunnāk control of key coastal towns with the appointment of a younger scion, Sut Bunnāk, to the governorship of the coastal town of Samutsakhon.[11]

At the beginning of the reign another general registration of the populace was held. The last had been carried out between 1858 and 1860. Thus, during 1870 large numbers of people whose masters resided in Bangkok had to travel to the capital to receive new tattoo marks and to be put down on the rolls. Many were ordinary *phrai luang*; in 1870 there were many who paid from nine to twelve *baht* each year to buy themselves a certificate exempting them from corvée duties.[12] The tattoo marks indicated the *krom*, administrative region, and master. People whose master belonged to a right-side *krom* were tattooed on the right wrist, or on the inside of the arm not far from the wrist. If a person's master was attached to a left-side *krom* the left wrist or arm was used for the marks.[13] The royal bodyguard was tattooed on the chest, just below the left armpit.[14]

Apart from the large contingent of general *phrai luang*, many other categories of people were classified and marked. Thus there were the *phrai som*, those who were directly attached to a particular master rather than to the government, and the *thanāi*, personal assistants to men of power, who were given exemption from corvée. There were free men serving members of the royal family. Some categories had to serve fifteen days each month, some served nine months, and some were permanently in government service. The latter invariably received a yearly sum of money and other benefits such as housing and food. Yet others had borrowed money and had become legally debt-bondaged people who worked for their creditors in lieu of paying interest. These people were registered as debt-slaves, and in 1870 they were exempted from corvée provided their creditor paid a tax of one *baht* two *salu'ng* per slave per annum.[15]

The general registration of 1870 apparently was quite all-encompassing, and many *phrais* were forced into one category or another. Avoidance was widespread. Some attempted to hide in the hope that their cases would be overlooked, others considered obtaining a debt-bondage certificate. In Bangkok many Malays and Burmese tried to register themselves as aliens so as to escape this burden. The Chinese immigrant could buy himself an exemption by paying his triannual poll tax, which then stood at four *baht* and one *salu'ng*.[16]

During the 1870 registration the government made a special effort to advertise the possibility of registering for the army:

> There is just now special effort being made to create an army. Proclamations have been issued to prevail upon young unmarked men from 15 years old and upward to present themselves for this branch of government service.
>
> Those who like this prospect are voluntarily being marked for this service. Others not liking a soldier's life are concealing themselves in hopes they may escape impressment and eventually be marked for some other department of Government service, that is, the department to which their father belonged.[17]

Apparently the central government had realized the need for a professional army, and the recruitment drive of 1870 may be seen as the first formal move in the direction of creating such a force.

## Čhulālongkǭn during the Regency Period

When the young king was formally anointed on 11 November 1868, there lay before him almost five years of tutelage before his twentieth birthday would release him from his minority. Meanwhile, Sīsuriyawong and his team were responsible for governing the country. This group consisted of men who neither needed nor asked for the king's opinion when making decisions. Some twenty-five years later, King Čhulālongkǭn recalled his feelings of isolation and powerlessness:

> When I ascended the throne I was only fifteen years and ten days old. My mother [had long ago] died. Of my maternal relatives, they were either unreliable or they were in unimportant positions. My paternal relatives in the Royal Family had fallen under

the power of the Regent, and had to protect their own interests and their own lives, and most did not support me in any way. As for government officials, although there were some who were very close to me, most of these were but minor officials. Those who had important positions did not have the ability to support me in any way. My brothers and sisters were all minors, younger than I, and not one of them was able to do anything. As for myself, I was but a boy. I had no great knowledge or ability in government affairs by which I might carry out my duties except for what my father had been able to give me. I was sick almost to the point of death. I grieved constantly because of my father's death. At that time I was like a headless person, my body propped up as a puppet king . . . and there were enemies whose intentions were openly bared around me, both within and without, in the capital and abroad, and my bodily illness was afflicting and tormenting me beyond endurance.[18]

This statement expresses well what the young king may have felt, though it appears somewhat exaggerated for dramatic effect. By the time King Mongkut died, young Čhulālongkǫ̈n was recuperating from the "jungle fever" contracted two months earlier. In the beginning of October he was still weak, but not so ill as to prevent him from attending the oath-taking ceremonies when thousands of civil servants pledged their allegiance, or from receiving delegations of foreigners. At the time of the coronation he seemed quite well and was able to make public appearances.[19]

It was true that the king had no close friends among those who held most power, and gossipy tongues pointed out that during the Ayutthaya period a young king had been assassinated by a regent who carried the same name as the present one.[20] However, such gossip only alluded to a peculiar coincidence, and it may not be taken as a reflection of existing hostilities. Sïsuriywong was a perfectly honourable man who had agreed to let Čhulālongkǫ̈n become king, and he encouraged the boy to assume the royal role. The young Čhulālongkǫ̈n presided at cremation rituals for members of the royal family; he gave public audiences whenever a foreign envoy came to Bangkok; and when one of Queen Victoria's letters reached Bangkok, it was Čhulālongkǫ̈n who accepted the missive while a salute of twenty-one guns was given. Every October or November the young king would make official presentations to Buddhist monasteries in connection with the Kathin festival, and around 18 November there would be a large fireworks display in honour of the anniversary of his coronation tour. Early in 1870 he travelled to Nakhon Pathom, because at that time the gigantic pagoda his father had begun building was completed.[21] Thus the young king was able to become used to the regal role, and he often formally appeared in public as Siam's head of state.

In 1870, one year and five months after King Mongkut's death, the great ceremony of the cremation of his remains took place. This was a major state ceremony, a time when traditionally all the heads of vassal states would come to Bangkok in order to pay respect to the deceased and pay homage to the new king. The cremation may be seen as the formal farewell to the previous king, and it was a tradition that major decisions and innovations were best postponed until after the ritual. That is why the general registration of the populace in central Siam began immediately afterwards.[22] This appears also to have been the time when the young king began to show signs of wanting to be involved in the nation's affairs and to play an active and innovative role.

This was the year when the young king recruited among relatives, friends, and acquaintances for the Mahātlek, the corps of royal pages. He created as part of that department a subsection, the *kǫng* Thahān Mahātlek Raksā Phra'ǫng, or the Mahātlek Royal Bodyguard Troops, with himself taking the position of commander, with the rank of colonel.[23]

On 19 September 1870, during the festivities for the king's seventeeth birthday, there was a grand illumination. According to one of the capital's oldest foreign residents, this was by far the most glorious illumination Bangkok had seen thus far. Two days later, on the king's actual birthday, some fifty Europeans and Americans were entertained with a banquet at the palace of the *chaophrayā* Phrakhlang.[24]

Early in 1871 the young king went on his first voyage overseas, to Singapore and Batavia. This travel in foreign parts had been planned by the regent, in whose considered opinion it would be good to let the king observe the British and Dutch systems of administration. On 9 March 1871, the king, accompanied by the senior Bunnāk members of the "cabinet" and a number of others, left Bangkok, to return on

15 April. Everywhere abroad the king was lavishly entertained, and at the same time the educational aspect of the journey
was not forgotten. Čhulālongkǫn visited "post-offices, jails,
hospitals, schools, telegraph offices, fire stations,
lighthouses, botanical gardens and museums, theatres, shops
and stores, orphanages, railways and factories".[25] On his
tour, Čhulālongkǫn attended a performance of a travelling
American circus and invited the show to Bangkok, pledging a
sum of money to persuade them to include Bangkok in their
itinerary. Thus, a few days after the king returned, probably
for the first time in Siam's history a circus performance took
place at the royal palace.[26] This may be taken as a clear sign
of the young king's independent and original turn of mind.
Having greatly enjoyed his study tour, Čhulālongkǫn asked
the regent to arrange a visit to Europe. However,
Sīsuriyawong decided that a European tour was out of the
question, and suggested instead a visit to India.

Meanwhile, at the royal palace the king reorganized his
troops again, this time to form a separate *krom*, named *krom*
Thahān Mahātlek Rātchawanlop Raksā Phra'ong, or
Mahātlek Faithful Royal Bodyguard, consisting of six companies of ninety-two men each.[27] Some of the officers were
officially given a monthly salary in their letters of appointment. This represents a departure from the system of yearly
*biawat*. It indicates that the young king intended to offer, at
least to some men of rank, financial security. For the time
being, only four appointments in the Mahātlek were singled
out for this honour, and other royal appointments during
1871 and 1872 were made according to the time-honoured
principles of mentioning only the person's name at the time of
appointment, his new name, his *krom*, his *saktinā* rating, and
the date of appointment.[28]

The military character of the six new companies may have
been partly the result of wishing to imitate the "Second
King's" body of troops, the late Phra' Pinklāo's pride and joy,
troops which had been drilled on European lines. At the same
time, Čhulālongkǫn's ambitions were more comprehensive.
To the military training the young boys received was added a
programme of general instruction directed towards a career
in the government administration. At the king's instigation, a

series of new textbooks was written with which the students could gain a grounding mainly in literary expression. It was intended to make English part of the curriculum, but no suitable instructor could be found on short notice. The king decided therefore to enrol fourteen of his relatives, all boys of *mǫmčhāo* rank, at the Raffles Institution in Singapore.[29] He used the opportunity of his Indian tour to deliver this batch of Siamese students. Čhulālongkǫn's second journey abroad lasted more than three months, and during that time he visited Singapore, Malacca, Penang, Moulmein, Rangoon, Calcutta, Delhi, Agra, Lucknow, Kanpur, Bombay, and Benares.

The young king appeared greatly stimulated by his experiences abroad. He was now one of Siam's most travelled men and eager to apply all he had learnt in the improvement of the palace, Bangkok, and the country as a whole. During the welcoming reception upon his return, at the young king's express wish, not one of the guests was allowed to crouch or prostrate himself.[30] The military school in the palace was further built up with a section where English, French, and mathematics were taught under the supervision of F.G. Patterson, who was engaged for a period of three years, even though he had no previous knowledge of the Siamese language. Just as in the early experiments of this kind when King Mongkut organized English instruction for the women's section of the palace, after an initial period of enthusiasm the number of pupils rapidly declined, and by 1873 only five princes, all younger brothers of Čhulālongkǫn, still attended.[31]

During the year 1873 King Čhulālongkǫn would reach his majority, and he began preparing for the moment when he would gain formal control over Siam's destiny. By this time it had become quite clear that he was a bold and daring young man, and also that in the course of the five years preceding the "second coronation"[32] there had developed no feelings of cordiality between him and Sīsuriyawong. The two appear to have avoided each other quite studiously, and nobody dared go near the king lest he should be taken as an informer against the regent.[33] A topic that was frequently broached in the houses of many powerful men during 1873, often with a measure of trepidation, was what the king would do after gaining full power. Some time in late 1872 or early 1873 the king submitted a formal programme for reform, proposing to abolish the corvée system, slavery, and gambling, to reform the law courts, and to develop a salaried bureaucracy, a police force, and a regular army.[34] Quite understandably, these plans were rejected by the council of ministers as being impracticable, and it is with this background in mind that we must understand Bradley's conversation with one of the young princes, the gist of which was "that the young king was fully prepared to make great improvements in his administration when he comes into full power, but that now he meets with much opposition from the old fogies in high places or power, and hence he judges it best to wait quietly for his full power."[35]

## The First Reforms

In November 1873, almost two months after the king's twentieth birthday, he was formally reanointed and the period of regency came to an end. The king's first decree could have caused little surprise, because he had indicated his views quite clearly on previous occasions. It was an order that henceforth his subjects were not permitted to prostrate themselves before him. He had come to view this time-honoured Siamese practice with distaste, aware of the discomfort Europeans felt when confronted with these outward signs of a system of inequality. Possibly the king hoped that by doing away with the custom he would encourage people to stand up for themselves, to speak more openly and with more forthrightness. If those were his intentions, the measure cannot be regarded as very effective outside the group of the king's personal friends.

Almost immediately upon assuming formal control of the government, the king made a series of appointments strengthening the Mahātlek and its military branches. Most of these carried monthly salaries, an expansion of the first four salaried positions given in 1871, so that the number of people receiving money every month was raised to thirty-two.

All these positions were held within the palace organization, and for the time being the experiment was not extended over the *kroms* beyond. It is also clear from the list of appointments that the leading positions were given to young men from influential families, such as the Chūtō, Kanlayānmit, Singhasēnǐ, Khochasēnǐ, Khridet, Būranasiri, and Amātayakun families. The Bunnāk family also was well represented; among the first batch of appointments not only was young Thuy Bunnāk promoted to lieutenant in the first company and Thomyā Bunnāk as ensign, but also remarkable honours were accorded to Phon Bunnāk, who became lieutenant-colonel in the Mahātlek with the title of *phrayā* Phātsakǫrawong and a *saktinā* of 3,000 *rai*.[36] The strong representation of the regent's family in these appointments should not be seen as an attempt on the regent's part to enlarge his influence at the king's palace, because the Bunnāk family ought not to be regarded as a unified group. *Phrayā* Phātsakǫrawong appears to have been a very independent character. He was the youngest son of the late Elder *somdet*, and therefore the regent's youngest half-brother. When he was fifteen Sǐsuriyawong had sent him for four years' education in England, and at the time of King Mongkut's death he had already become a junior official in one of the king's palace departments. Probably he was the only Siamese of his time who was completely fluent in both written and spoken English. During the regency period he became a close friend of the young king, and shared and stimulated some of Čhulālongkǫn's reformist ideas. Apparently he was loyal to the king and did not hesitate to defend him strongly when the regent voiced some criticism.

*Phrayā* Phātsakǫrawong aided the king in finding a solution to the problem of the large measure of control over senior ministries still exercised by Bunnāks even after the king had formally taken on responsibility for ruling Siam. In early May 1874, Čhulālongkǫn announced the appointment of a State Council to advise the monarch in making laws. All members of the State Council were of *phrayā* rank; none of the senior *čhaophrayā*-ranking officials were included, nor did the council have any representatives from the royal family. All its members appear to have been

fairly senior officials, scions of influential families whom
the king trusted as knowledgeable, reliable, and progressive men. Naturally, *phrayā* Phātsakọrawong was included as a member. Siam's senior ministers were invited
to attend the new council's deliberations. The ex-regent did
not attend, although it is likely that he was invited. The appointment of a State Council was generally seen as a
measure intended to diminish the power of Sisuriyawong's
faction, and at first many members did not dare to attend
meetings for fear of offending the ex-regent.[37] Gradually,
however, as no drastic revenge was taken, confidence
grew.

The State Council bravely began its deliberations with two
major items. The first was the question of the control of the
country's finances. It was the council's intention to begin collecting all forms of taxation, paying all state revenue into a
central treasury. It was not long before the council met with a
direct refusal to co-operate. In July 1874 the head of the
*krom* Nā, *phrayā* Ahānbọrirak, a nephew of the ex-regent,
was reprimanded for being unwilling to disclose details regarding the collection of land tax.[38] Later that year one of the
council's committees found him guilty of misappropriation of
government funds and he was dismissed and imprisoned,
whereupon one of the members of the State Council, *phrayā*
Rātchawọranakun (Rọt Kanlayānmit) was put into the
vacant position. A second item for deliberation concerned
the gradual abolition of slavery. After lengthy discussion, it
was decided to proclaim an act providing for a new scale for
the valuation of "absolute" slaves' children, a law acting
retrospectively and including all children born as "absolute"
slaves from the beginning of the Fifth Reign onwards. These
children had a legal maximum value, which under the new
law was to gradually diminish so that by the age of twenty-
one they would automatically have lost all value and become
free.[39]

In August 1874 the king created a second committee, the
Privy Council, the members of which were to be personal advisers to the king. At first forty-nine men made up the Privy
Council. Among them were thirteen members of the royal
family, the head of the *krom* Mahātthai (*čhaophrayā*

Phutharaphai) and the head of the *krom* Phrakhlang (*čhaophrayā* Phanuwong), and many officials in less exalted positions, including some as low in the official hierarchy as *luang*.⁴⁰ All members of the State Council were *ex officio* Privy Councillors. Sīsuriyawong was invited to become a member, but he declined firmly. So did his eldest son, head of the *krom* Kalāhom. Unlike the State Council, from which members could resign, the Privy Council was thought of as "permanent", and all Privy Councillors had to swear a special oath of allegiance to the monarch. The Privy Council was created to guarantee a constant flow of information to the king and to provide a wide debating ground to discuss the ways and means for major reforms.

The fact that the king proceeded rapidly with major and fundamental reform measures that threatened to deprive the largest *kroms* of their financial independence and impinged upon their judicial powers, combined with the fact that Sīsuriyawong and his eldest son took no part in the deliberations, made for an ominous situation. Sooner or later, it seemed, the ex-regent and his party would find themselves in open conflict with the king and the reformers. This situation was to a large extent the result of Čhulālongkǫn's youthful impatience and inexperience. The ex-regent was not in principle against many of the proposed reforms, but he resented the fact that he was not given a prominent role in the process of policy-making and he decided for the time being to remain aloof.⁴¹ However, before the situation developed into a confrontation between the young radicals and the established interests, a completely different conflict, between Čhulālongkǫn and the Uparāt, decided the fate of the reformers.


## The "Palace Incident"

When Prince Wichaichān was installed as head of the Front Palace, he did not receive the quite extraordinary honours that had been given to Phra' Pinklāo in 1851. His title reverted to that of Mahā Uparāt, and the details of his anointment demonstrate clearly that his position was not as exalted as his father's had been.[42] Nevertheless, he was able to act, especially with respect of Europeans and Americans, in the manner that had become customary during the Fourth Reign. Thus he placed his seal as "Second King" upon treaties with foreign powers, he gave receptions to foreign dignitaries and freely distributed a photograph of himself, crowned and seated on a throne flanked by regalia. He received his father's income of 160,000 *baht* per annum from the Royal Treasury, and with that amount of money he was able to maintain an entourage comparable in size to that of Čhulālongkǫn. It included a number of troops, some two thousand infantry and four hundred artillery, all well armed, drilled, and trained.[43] The following account of one of the parades at the Front Palace, held early in 1872 to entertain an American visitor when Čhulālongkǫn was in India, provides an idea of their high standards:

> There were two companies of troops, which marched in quick time from their barracks. The Second King has two thousand soldiers; but these were picked men (or rather boys, for such they were), who guarded the palace and its royal occupants, and of whose proficiency in military tactics His Majesty is especially proud. They have had various instructors (drill-masters) at different times — French, English and German; the orders which we heard given were in broken German. Their uniform of white duck is patterned after that worn by the British troops in India; they wear also (*mirabile dictu*!) shoes and socks. The companies, in turn, went through the manual of arms, and performed some skirmishing in remarkably good style; the musket drill was better than that of many of our so-called "crack" regiments at home. After the parade His Majesty's own brass band played for us.[44]

The Uparāt was a busy man during the regency period. He travelled and was actively involved in the drawing up of the most accurate maps of Siam at that time.[45] He was interested in European technology and the modernization of the country, and the few accounts of him show him to be an attractive, well-educated, and mature person. Sǐsuriyawong could get along with him, and possibly the regent would have liked him to have occupied the position of monarch, a situation which was not unthinkable during the first five years of the 1870s. If a fatal accident had befallen Čhulālongkǫn, who had as yet no descendants, the Uparāt would have been in an excellent position for consideration for elevation to the throne.

Čhulālongkǫn was envious of the Uparāt's impressive little army, which outdid that of the Mahātlek. Prince Wichaichān bought with his own funds two Armstrong guns. The royal edict of September 1874, in which it was prohibited to buy or accept as a present the redoubtable Gatling gun, was directly aimed at preventing the Uparāt from obtaining this weapon "with which one man would dare to fight an army".[46] Possibly the king saw the Uparāt's presence as a threat to his own authority while the process of reform was meeting with its first opposition. When T.G. Knox, the British consul and a close friend of the Uparāt, left for six months' leave in Europe in late 1874, he asked W.H. Newman, who would be acting British consul, and F. Garnier, the French consul, to watch over Prince Wichaichān.[47] During December of that year it seemed that the king was planning to either abolish the position of Uparāt altogether or to replace Wichaichān. Rumours of the king's intentions reached the Front Palace, and Wichaichān's people felt exceedingly apprehensive. In late December the king heard that the Uparāt was arming an unusually large number of men and, before the veracity of the report could be tested, some of the king's guards were alerted. No direct communication took place between Čhulālongkǫn and Wichaichān regarding the tense situation.

On the night of 28 December 1874, a fire broke out in the gasworks of the Grand Palace, a dangerous spot not far from the gunpowder magazine, the armoury, and an oil storage, and when the fire was being extinguished, it was noted that the troops from the Front Palace had been tardy in coming to the rescue. It was assumed that the Uparāt's men had been responsible for the fire, and when they arrived later in the night to offer assistance, they were refused entry. Čhulālongkǫn treated the event as a direct assault upon himself and ordered a full alarm. On 29 December, some five or six thousand men were armed to protect the king,[48] and the Front Palace was besieged during the early hours of that day. Čhulālongkǫn wrote as letter to Sīsuriyawong, who was at his private residence in Ratburi, asking him to return to Bangkok for consultations, but before the ex-regent had time to come, the king invited Wichaichān to discuss the matter in a private audience, during which he planned to have the Uparāt arrested. However, Wichaichān declined the invitation.

On 31 December Sīsuriyawong arrived upon the scene and advised the king to negotiate a settlement. Sīsuriyawong himself became the go-between, and he presented Wichaichān with Čhulālongkǭn's terms, which were that the Uparāt should abandon the Front Palace and disband its personnel and that he should assent to a ritual purification as amends for any offence to the king's person. He would then be allowed to retain any personal servants who chose to stay with him and would be assured of sufficient income to keep them. The prince considered the proposals and eventually decided that they were unacceptable. No longer certain of Sīsuriyawong's protection, and in the face of the massive number of troops pitched against him, the unfortunate Wichaichān decided to flee, and during the night he managed to leave his palace unseen and reach the British consulate, where the acting consul-general granted him asylum.

The Uparāt not wishing to be sacrificed for the sake of national unity, had in his despair forced an international incident. All efforts to persuade Wichaichān to leave the consulate failed. There were rumours that the British would invade the country, and many people prepared for flight. It was not long before a British and a French man-of-war arrived at Bangkok. New proposals were made to Wichaichān, offering him the Front Palace and a certain amount of power, but the prince, probably aware of the widespread opinion that his flight was a treacherous act, refused to leave the safety of the British consulate. Three weeks after his arrival there, the acting consul requested Sir Andrew Clarke, the governor of the Straits Settlements, to come and assist in breaking the deadlock. A month later, the affair was settled. Clarke had decided, in accordance with general British opinion,[49] to support Čhulālongkǭn in his attempt to dismantle the Uparāt's military establishment, and at the same time he arranged for Wichaichān's safe return to the Front Palace.

While Čhulālongkǭn had succeeded in asserting himself

towards the Uparāt, it cannot be said that he had gained a clear victory over his opponent. During January 1875 it became quite clear that the crisis was seen by many as the outcome of the king's extraordinary pace in reforming the country. The pro-Western clique around Čhulālongkǫn was widely blamed for encouraging the king to act hastily. A petition was circulated in Bangkok addressed to Sīsuriyawong, asking him to drive out the king's associates, to abolish the State Council, to dispense with newfangled ideas such as allowing people to wear shoes in sacred precincts, and to abandon the recently introduced modes of address and salutation.[50] Sīsuriyawong had witnessed with growing disapproval how members of the State Council and the Privy Council, in their youthful zeal, had antagonized many people, including members of the *sēnābodī* (ministerial committee, or "cabinet") whose co-operation was necessary for efficient government. He was quite happy to lay the blame upon the reformist faction. Probably Čhulālongkǫn himself became convinced by the popular reaction against the new councils that he had been too hasty, and he asked the members of the councils to show restraint. In 1875 the Bunnāk-dominated Sēnābodī regained its authority.

During the years immediately following the "Palace Incident" both the State Council and the Privy Council continued to exist, but the king no longer attempted to force major changes by means of these institutions. It may be tempting to depict the abrupt halt in major reform measures as a triumph for the conservative factions, with Sīsuriyawong, in his late sixties, as the "arch-conservative" again in power. However, such a view would do justice neither to the king nor to Sīsuriyawong. Čhulālongkǫn appears to have been penitent and contrite. Events had shown a widespread resentment of some of his fondest ideas, and his actions had been instrumental in creating a crisis which had threatened the national peace. At the same time he had noted how many people had spontaneously rallied behind him even though they considered his clique of modernizers a bad influence. The king reconsidered his position and decided that he was king of Siam "by consent of all", and that he ought to avoid actions that would make the people unhappy.[51]

At the same time, Sīsuriyawong should not be seen simply as an intransigent reactionary. It is true that he had no sympathy with the State Council and the Privy Council, which he considered dominated by juveniles. This does not, however, preclude his broad-mindedness in other respects. Sīsuriyawong had always been in the vanguard of reformation; he had pioneered the introduction of Western technology, and he had an intelligent appreciation of the insights that could be derived from comparing foreign customs with those of one's own country. He shared many of the ideals of the group that surrounded Čhulālongkǭn in 1874, disagreeing with its members largely over the means they chose and the speed with which they wished to attain their goals. In 1876 Sīsuriyawong again had an opportunity to travel abroad when he chose to attend the large Delhi durbar on the occasion of Queen Victoria's being proclaimed Empress of India. On his way to India he spent some time in Singapore, where he was received with great honour.[52]

King Čhulālongkǭn was still a reformer, and he let it be known that he hoped to instigate many changes. However, in contrast to the year immediately after his coming of age, he now moved with great circumspection, encouraging innovation only when he had ascertained there would be no opposition from the more conservative factions. New initiatives ascribed to the king during the years immediately following the "Palace Incident" were relatively minor ones, such as a decree encouraging all royal monasteries to use the textbooks that had originally been devised for the palace school.[53] During 1877 he waxed enthusiastic over a proposal that had been put forward by Samuel McFarland for the establishment of a college of education in Bangkok. This would give both princes and nobles a chance to receive a modern education. It would be an institution where they could learn European arts and sciences. This school proved initially much more successful than the earlier one in which Patterson had taught.[54] In addition to founding this college, the king reputedly was personally involved in the ordering of a "floating fire engine" to protect Bangkok port,[55] and he described himself as having been active in encouraging the digging of new canals and the opening up of new rice land.[56]

## Towards Firmer Control of the Outer Regions

Siam's leaders were aware of the dangers inherent in the ancient system of vassal states. France's incursion into Cambodia had demonstrated the necessity for consolidation of the nation's strength in the outer regions to forestall other powers' expansionist programmes. Bangkok's control was fairly strong in most of the southern provinces. Towards the east the Siamese rule was accepted in Battambang and Angkor provinces; however, in Vientiane, Luang Prabang, and Chiang Mai and many smaller *mū'angs*, Siamese overlordship was largely a matter of ceremony. From time to time a formal tribute mission would be sent to Bangkok, and while the Siamese government had the formal right to appoint local chiefs, these *mū'angs* remained for all practical purposes independently governed territories. During the regency and the early years of Čhulālongkǫn's reign, this situation continued in the Laotian states of Vientane and Luang Prabang, but it changed considerably in Chiang Mai and its surroundings *mū'angs*. Already during 1870, in order to protect some American citizens resident in Chiang Mai, the regent had been forced to send a "royal commissioner" to the north, empowered to command Kawilōrot, the lord of Chiang Mai, to leave the resident American missionaries in peace.[57] Sometime around 1874, taking advantage of the fact that the man who had succeeded Kawilōrot was mild and rather indolent, Čhulālongkǫn appointed a permanent representative at Chiang Mai, complete with a bodyguard co-opted from troops attached to the Grand Palace.[58]

The commissioner, *phrayā* Thēpwǫračhan, had the unenviable task of being the king's representative without a clearly formulated brief. His task appears to have been mainly limited to dealing with cases involving international rights. Usually these concerned complaints by Burmese who professed to be British subjects regarding infringements upon teak-felling contracts which they had signed with local chiefs. Whenever the Siamese decided a lawsuit in favour of the Burmese, hard feelings were aroused among the local leaders, and some resentment against Siamese "meddling" was apparent. A challenge to Siam's authority came in 1878 when the commissioner adjudicated a case between the senior administrators of *mū'ang* Lampang. In this instance his decision was not respected by one of the parties, probably the ruler of Lampang himself. Soon afterwards, the king strengthened his hand by changing his appointment from "commissioner" to "governor", nominally bringing the north under direct Siamese control.[59] However, it would take several far-reaching measures more than a decade later before this nominal control was backed up by an administrative reform which would effectively bring Chiang Mai under Bangkok's sway.

Meanwhile, the Siamese leaders had been able to reassure themselves regarding their authority over the region controlled by Vientiane and Luang Prabang. In these northeastern parts there had been an insurrection caused by Chinese "Hō gangs", who had mustered an army of some four thousand men. The problem was handled effectively in a traditional manner. The northern region fell under the *krom* Mahātthai, and in late 1875 its officials raised a small army in the northern provinces and marched up to meet the enemy. The Hō chiefs decided to avoid a direct military confrontation and tendered their submission. The campaign was concluded in April 1876 apparently without a shot having been fired.

In the following year, large-scale rioting broke out in the southern provinces of Ranong and Phuket. The central government sent *chaomū'n* Samoechairāt (Chūn Bunnāk) to rally forces from various southern provinces and put down the disturbances at Phuket, and the governor of Ranong, assisted by troops from a neighbouring province, managed to restore order in his own region.[60] By the end of 1877 the government had demonstrated its ability to maintain its hold over outer provinces and vassal states, and it had been able to do so by following the time-honoured methods. Chulālongkōn played only a minor role in these affairs; the responsibility for the day-to-day decision-making had reverted to the Bunnāk-dominated Sēnābodī. The case of the ill-fated *phra'* Prīchā clearly illustrates in whose hands most power lay.

## *Phra'* Prǐchā, Čhulālongkǭn, and Sǐsuriyawong

The case against *phra'* Prǐchā was in itself not very important, and it would have run its course unnoted by historians had it not been for the passionate intervention of the British consul. *Phra'* Prǐchā was a middle-ranking government official. He was a member of the Amātayakun family, one of the leading influential families of that time. An Amātayakun (Mot) had been appointed to the State Council, one (Khlip) was governor of Prachinburi, another (Phlap) was one of Siam's chief judges.[61] Yet another Amātayakun held a senior position in the *krom* Phrakhlang.[62] *Phra'* Prǐchā was not as high-ranking as all these relatives, yet he wielded more influence than his rank would suggest, because he knew the king personally. Early in 1879 *phra'* Prǐchā was in great trouble, for he had been formally accused of embezzling funds. The accusation came from members of the Bunnāk family, at that time undoubtedly by far the most powerful in the country. In a bid to save himself, *phra'* Prǐchā married Fanny Knox, the British consul's eldest daughter. The newly forged links with the leader of the consular corps did not prevent his arrest, which took place in March 1879, not long after the marriage,[63] by which time *phra'* Prǐchā had given Fanny all his property.

In April, probably already knowing that his daughter was expecting a child, Consul Knox made a bold attempt to help *phra'* Prǐchā. He went to Čhulālongkǭn and asked him to intervene. Meanwhile, however, the investigations into *phra'* Prǐchā's past had uncovered serious malfeasances relating to the management of the Kabin goldmine in Prachinburi province. In addition he was now charged with having murdered some of the prisoners working there. The case had developed into a considerable scandal, and apart from the main culprit, *phra'* Prǐchā, other members of the Amātayakun family were arrested and held in custody. Knox reminded the king of the friendship that had existed between him and *phra'* Prǐchā and requested that the king appoint unbiased judges to examine the charges. Čhulālongkǭn assured the consul that he did not wish *phra'* Prǐchā to be punished unless he was found guilty. Realizing that the king was not willing to risk the displeasure of most of the cabinet by appointing new judges, Knox did his utmost to provoke the king to action. He depicted the charges as weapons in the hands of the Bunnāk family to destroy a rival power, and described Sǐsuriyawong and his eldest son as the king's enemies. Siam itself was enslaved to Sǐsuriyawong. Knox is reported to have continued as follows:

> I should like to see it [Siam] free for once. If Your Majesty will dismiss the Somdetch Chao Phraya [Sǐsuriyawong] and the Minister for Foreign Affairs, I will help you in every way. And Siam will be free. . . . I know for certain that that party wish to wrest the Sovereignty from Your Majesty and destroy you. If you do not act now, you will in future have no-one to help and no authority.[64]

In addition, Knox told the king that he had summoned a warship which could be of assistance. Čhulālongkǫ̌n did not take the bait and insisted that *phra'* Prǐchā would stand trial, reassuring Knox that he saw no imminent danger to his throne. Knox, a man with a formidable record in Siam, clearly had no business interfering officially on behalf of *phra'* Prǐchā, and his spirited attempt not only was firmly rejected by Čhulālongkǫ̌n but also was repudiated in London and caused him to be recalled and retired. *Phra'* Prǐchā was duly tried and found guilty. Not long before his execution, Fanny left the country, taking her newly born baby, two of *phra'* Prǐchā's children by another marriage, and a considerable amount of money and valuables.[65]

The confrontation between the British consul and the king reflects also on the relations between the king and the Bunnāk family. Knox tried to turn the enmity between Sǐsuriyawong and Čhulālongkǫ̌n to his own advantage. It was now four years since the "Palace Incident", and the king had not established cordial relations with the Sēnābodǐ. The affairs of the Grand Palace were left to Čhulālongkǫ̌n, while the government of the country remained largely in the hands of the senior ministers. Legally, Čhulālongkǫ̌n had immense powers, and gradually he was regaining some confidence in himself. However, he clearly felt in no position to provoke a direct conflict over *phra'* Prǐchā's case.

## The Tug-of-war for Manpower

Although King Čhulālongkǫn may outwardly have demonstrated a united front with the Sēnābodī, he retained and expanded his circle of "progressive modernists" and occasionally managed to favour his trusted friends with appointments. Thus, when in 1879 a mission was sent to England to conclude an arrangement regarding the status of Siam's northern vassal states, the honour of leading the mission was given to Phātsakǫrawong. Prince Sāi Sanitwong had been put in charge of the Royal Arsenal, and in 1879 he also gained the command of the Royal Yachts.[66] Čhoem Saengchūtō, another of Čhulālongkǫn's close friends, became an officer of the First Foot Guard, and when the commander was replaced on account of gross negligence,[67] Čhoem rose to be deputy-commander. He had direct access to the king and was thus able to suggest and implement reforms over the head of his commanding officer. Having been trained in the king's personal bodyguard, Čhoem found the First Foot sadly lacking. Its enrolment had dropped over the years until it had only about three hundred men under arms at any one time.[68]

> The officials tucked away the fees the commoners paid not to serve and padded the registration lists when they drew funds and supplies; with one hand they cheated their subordinates and with the other they misappropriated funds from the Royal Treasury. Many of them were incompetents who had purchased their posts which were investments made to pay by corrupt practices. The men in the ranks were poorly trained by the best Siamese standards of the day.[69]

With the king's full knowledge and backing, Čhoem began to reform the First Foot. Corrupt officers were delegated to a reserve force and more enthusiastic ones put in their positions. In order to boost the number of troops, Čhoem proposed to attract young men who were not officially registered and tattooed as being *phrai luang* or *phrai som*. The king agreed, and posters were put up asking for volunteers to join the First Foot Guard. Those prepared to enlist for five years were offered four *baht* in cash and a piece of cloth, and they were permitted to remain free of administrative tattoos.[70]

The recruiting drive was immensely successful. Over five

thousand men, mainly from the Ratburi and Phetburi regions, flocked to Bangkok. The gains to the reconstituted First Foot were, however, at the expense of the old system of *phrai som* and *phrai luang*, and state officials in Ratburi and Phetburi were faced with an acute shortage of manpower. Sīsuriyawong, who had a large estate at Ratburi, came to intercede with the king, asking him to allow the volunteers to return. The king pointed out that most of his recruits had been unregistered under the old system and that therefore they automatically fell into the category of king's men. He agreed to return the few men who had been firmly employed in Ratburi and kept the remainder.

The king's firm stance towards the ex-regent may be seen as a sign that by 1880 he had ceased to be subservient to the Sēnābodī and that he was beginning to assume a greater share of responsibility. He was able to do so for several reasons. In the first place many of his half-brothers were reaching maturity, and some of them were able and diligent men who were willing to serve their elder brother. Among these was young Prince Thēwan, who assisted the king as private secretary.[71] Secondly, over the course of time the king had been able to change the composition of the Sēnābodī. Whenever a vacancy occurred, he had been able to fill the post with someone in whom he could place some trust. In 1876 the twenty-year-old *kromamū'n* Phūtharēt was appointed to head the *krom* Mū'ang, and in 1878 the king's uncle, *kromphra'* Bamrāp (*čhaofā* Mahāmālā), became the head of the *krom* Mahātthai. Thirdly, Sīsuriyawong was growing rather old and feeble. Fourthly, the three most senior Bunnāks — the ex-regent, the Kalāhom, and the Phrakhlang — by no means formed a united family group. *Čhaophrayā* Surawongwaiyawat, the ex-regent's eldest son, who had been placed in the best position to maintain Bunnāk dominance in Siamese politics, had been a great disappointment to his father. He apparently lacked his father's integrity and administrative ability.[72] *Čhaophrayā* Phanuwong, Sīsuriyawong's half-brother, fell into disgrace in 1880 when he was unsuccessful in negotiations with the British government regarding a new treaty.[73]

Sīsuriyawong, who was not altogether unsympathetic

towards the idea of a more professional army but who did not wish to see the corvée system severely undermined, obtained permission to update the corvée lists and instigate tattooing drives, and thus many men who had not joined the new volunteer army were forced to enrol under the old system.[74] The king's innovation in allowing his new volunteers to remain untattooed caused problems, because these soldiers could now be caught and tattooed under the old system if they could not prove exemption. On the other hand, volunteers with exemption papers could desert and escape all their obligations.

Throughout 1881 there were several clashes of interest between the First Foot Guard and various provincial authorities. In that year a cholera epidemic broke out in Bangkok; hundreds of volunteers died, and thousands were allowed to flee to the provinces.[75] Later it was difficult to round them up and regroup them. In Ratburi province it was discovered that Sīsuriyawong's grandson To Bunnāk, who was in charge of the local registration, had incited soldiers of the First Foot to desert and register under the old system. One of the king's pet schemes was being undermined by a young Bunnāk, as the king was duly informed by officers of the First Foot. Those who may have hoped for a direct clash between Čhulālongkǫn and the Bunnāks underestimated Sīsuriyawong's political skill and the king's caution. Young To Bunnāk was sent to the king to offer his apologies and the king in return waived punishment.[76] In order to prevent further competition between Bangkok and the provinces over the volunteers, it was finally decided to create a new tattoo design for all members of the First Foot, including officers.[77]

## Towards Curbing the Consular Powers

Because of the Bowring treaty, Europeans could import a large number of articles at only 3 per cent duty. Consequently, Siam was opened up as a market for goods produced cheaply abroad, and the results of this could be seen all over the country. Cheap calico and various items of metal "Birmingham ware" found their way to provincial markets.[78]

Since European wines and ardent spirits were generally much more costly than the alcoholic beverages manufactured under government licences, the Siamese had not thought to make a special provision for alcohol. However, rice wines from Java and from Cochin-China could be obtained at comparatively cheap prices, and already during King Mongkut's reign the Siamese government was alarmed at the thought of foreign traders undermining the State's liquor monopoly. The consuls insisted on their rights in this matter, however, and not only imported rice wine but also issued licences to foreign nationals to trade in this commodity. Each licence created a new outlet for selling liquor, and each caused the Siamese government to suffer a reduction in income. In the 1867 treaty with France a clause had been inserted giving the right of issuing licences to the Siamese authorities. However, none of the other consuls would agree to have their powers thus curbed, and the French consul eventually did not feel obliged to heed the clause since it was prejudicial to the rights of a single country.[79]

The consuls had wide judicial powers, and they could extend their protection not only over foreign nationals but also over locals in their employ. As many consuls had little or no training in legal affairs, it was inevitable that their decisions would often encroach upon what was felt, by the Siamese authorities, to be their own domain. The liquor licensing, however, epitomized in Siamese eyes the inequalities that had emerged from the treaties, and in 1881 a major drive was launched to prevent the consuls from issuing these permits. The consuls were advised of the appointment of a Siamese envoy to negotiate with the various European governments a revision of the treaties with particular reference to the sale of spirits. The person appointed was *mǫmčhao* Pritsadāng, who, after completing his education in London, had assisted Prince Thēwan and had been sent back to Europe to guide another group of young Siamese students[80] and to carry messages and presents from King Čhulālongkǫn to various European heads of state. Pritsadāng spent many months travelling and negotiating, but all hopes of a quick settlement foundered when France insisted on introducing various political issues and making political concessions on the part of Siam a condition for an agreement on the sale of spirits.[81]

## The Kra Canal

A question that occupied many minds was the possibility of digging a canal through the Isthmus of Kra in southern Siam. The first serious estimate of the amount of work required to cut through the isthmus took place in 1843.[82] Undoubtedly it was the spectacular success of the Suez Canal, which was opened in November 1869, that rekindled interest in the possibility of creating yet another short cut in shipping routes, albeit on a much smaller scale than the Suez Canal. When in 1881 a British firm requested assistance from the British government in its application for a concession to construct the canal, the response was rather discouraging: Her Majesty's government could not recommend any particular applicants for the concession to the Siamese government.[83]

The matter became one of much greater moment when it was learnt that a French concern was interested in the scheme. By 1882 Britain and Siam were the chief powers in the Malay Peninsula; a French concession would introduce a third major party into the region. Moreover, a French-built canal would provide France with control over the shortest shipping route between Europe and China. Furthermore it would greatly stimulate French expansionist drives, one of which had just begun in Tonkin. Thus the British representative in Bangkok was instructed to ensure that a concession would only be granted to a British firm, and only after previous communication with Her Majesty's government.[84] By this time a French emissary was already on his way to Bangkok, and both *čhaophrayā* Surawongwaiyawat and *čhaophrayā* Phanuwong were supporting the French move.

In June 1882 the pressure upon the Siamese government was intensified by the arrival of François Deloncle, employed by the French Ministry of Foreign Affairs, who offered the Siamese the services of the famous Ferdinand de Lesseps.[85] Eventually the Siamese government decided to allow the

French to make a survey of the terrain where the canal was planned. To prevent international rivalry, the project was handled by the international Suez Canal Company, and the British government agreed not to offer opposition to the concession so long as British subjects and British vessels would enjoy the same rights as those granted to any other nation.[86] The survey began in January 1883, and its findings were of such a nature that they effectively put an end to the French proposal.[87]

The French had demonstrated, however, that they possessed the power and drive to force the issue, notwithstanding the king's opposition and the British moves to forestall them. The French proposal may be seen as one of the moves related to a French expansion of interests in mainland South-East Asia and China, one that would threaten Siam's very existence in the years to come.[88]

## The Bangkok Centenary

During 1882 the capital was the scene of large-scale festivities in order to mark the hundredth anniversary of its foundation by Rama I. It was a time to stress the nation's accomplishments, to rejoice, and to perform ceremonies designed to enhance the country's chances in the future. The king, now twenty-eight years old, had devised various ceremonies to celebrate the event. The most important was probably the official opening of Wat Phrakaew, or the "Temple of the Emerald Buddha" as it became known in foreign circles. This monastery had first been inaugurated at the beginning of the First Reign, but for this occasion it had been completely renovated. Čhulālongkǫn had decided upon this scheme in late 1879, and the work was done at the expense of himself and his near relatives. The various buildings in the monastery were decorated in a most lavish style so as to make the Wat a fitting symbol during the celebrations.[89]

Čhulālongkǫn used the opportunity of the centenary to complete one of his father's projects: the creation of a fully fledged system of European-style decorations to be added to the array of traditional Siamese marks of ranking. The Most

Noble Order of the Royal House of Čhakrī was reserved for senior Siamese princes and members of foreign royal families. The Order of Čhulā Chọmklāo was for presentation to Siamese princes and nobility. The Order of the White Elephant and the Order of the Crown of Siam were created for members of the wider public, for services to the State.[90]

The centenary was also an occasion for setting up a large national exhibition. The idea of such a spectacle was undoubtedly drawn from foreign examples. Ever since the first "universal exhibition" in London's Crystal Palace, great cities had vied with each other in surpassing previous displays. The Siamese National Exhibition of 1882 consisted of more than fifty sections illustrating the country's handicrafts, natural resources, and fine arts.[91] The following year a large part of this exhibition was sent to the international fair at The Hague.[92]

The Bangkok festivities were an appropriate moment to sum up the king's accomplishments during the fourteen years after his father's death. In a felicitation address five achievements were mentioned: the gradual emancipation of certain classes of slaves, the abolition of prostration before the king, granting permission for all government officers to submit written opinions to the king on any point they thought proper, the improvement in relationships with foreign countries, and the construction of Wat Phrakaew.[93] Considering that the State lacked the means of enforcing the proclamation on the gradual emancipation of certain classes of slaves,[94] that the British had not yet made up their minds whether nor not they ought to dispute Siam's rights in the Malay Peninsula,[95] and that France was threatening Siam's north-eastern vassal states, the list of accomplishments is rather meagre. However, it would be fair to add that the king had encouraged educational reform, actively sponsored the opening up of new rice-fields, and stimulated economic life by having new canals dug.

It had been the intention to mark the centenary by the inauguration of at least one telegraphic link with the international network, but the lines had not yet been completed. Similarly, a Siamese postal service to supplant the consular services which used Hong Kong and Straits Settlements stamps had been planned for this time. A general post office had been erected and all houses had been numbered in preparation for this service,[96] but it was not until August 1883 that the Siamese postal department finally began selling its own stamps and delivering its own letters.[97] The establishment of the Siamese postal service was organized by the young *kromaluang* Phānuphantuwong (Prince Phānurangsī).

## The Bunnāk Decline

In January 1883 *somdet čhaophraya* Sīsuriyawong died at the age of seventy-four. All first-hand accounts agree in describing him as one of Siam's greatest men who possessed a keen intelligence and great statesmanship. In order to assess his role in the Siamese political system, it is necessary to take into account his position in the Bunnāk family as a whole.

Sīsuriyawong was the son of the Elder *somdet*, the man who had played a decisive role in Siamese politics from the early 1820s until the mid-1850s. The Bunnāk family had been one of the families supplying the State with administrators since Ayutthayan times, but at the beginning of the nineteenth century they surpassed all other noble families in power and influence. The Bunnāks secured for themselves and their relatives the best positions, because they had great influence upon Rama III and Rama IV, and at the beginning of the Fifth Reign their hold upon the State's decision-making was supreme.

Ideally, the late-Ayutthayan and early Bangkok period system of administration was one whereby many noble families vied for lucrative appointments and the king would select from a large field of candidates. Quite often a minor official would manage to have one or more of his sons accepted in the junior ranks of the administrative hierarchy. The positions of great power were usually given to men who had considerable influence, including the right family connections. As far as can be determined, there were at that time probably about a dozen leading families who competed for the top appointments. Although the king had the right to dismiss any officer, in practice this was not often done, and under normal circumstances senior officials enjoyed the prerogatives of their office until death. In this system of competition and checks, the rise of a single family to dominate the chief executive posts must be seen as an extraordinary event.

In retrospect, it is possible to determine the set of circumstances that allowed the Bunnāks to manipulate the system in their own favour to such an extent that an imbalance was created. These arose during the Third Reign. Rama III came to depend upon two men in whom he could trust, upon whom he could rely implicitly, namely *čhaophrayā* Bǫdindechā (Sing Singhasēni̇̄) and *čhaophrayā* Phrakhlang (Dit Bunnāk). When Rama III became ill, it was apparent that nobody had been groomed for the succession. Therefore it seems that Rama III's failure to stimulate the development of a full cabinet, the sudden death of one of his trusted executives, and the succession struggle all combined to place Dit Bunnāk in the position of king-maker.[98] He himself, his brother That and his two sons Chuang and Kham gained the most powerful positions. After Dit and That's death, Chuang (*čhaophrayā* Sīsuriyawong) became the most senior member of the Bunnāk family. The Bunnāks then had considerable wealth; they possessed extensive lands, controlled a large work force, managed many lucrative tax-farms, and invested in trade. It has been remarked that Sīsuriyawong's power was also partially based upon deals with various Chinese secret societies.[99] Mongkut's personal wish to be succeeded by *čhaofā* Čhulālongkǫn played into Sīsuriyawong's hands and, in a masterly move, the head of the Bunnāk family became regent.

At the beginning of the regency period, the 1851 situation seemed to be repeated: the cabinet was stacked with Bunnāks and their men, and many promising younger Bunnāks entered government service so that yet another generation could be trained. It would seem at first sight that the regency period marked the zenith in the fortunes of the Bunnāk family.[100] Yet in reality the situation was not without ominous signs. In the first place, a feeling of cordiality and trust between Sīsuriyawong and Čhulālongkǫn failed to develop. During the first years of the Fifth Reign, when the king was still inexperienced, this did not threaten the Bunnāk fortunes, but as the king gradually became more sophisticated it became a matter of concern. A much greater problem for Sĩsuriyawong was the fact that his son Won Bunnāk, who had been groomed to succeed his father as Siam's most powerful man, turned out a great disappointment. Won has been described as a man who blatantly used his powerful position for his own private advantage, enriching himself at the cost of his subordinates,[101] and as being "a man without talent or strength of character, whose unfitness to keep up the prestige of the Sisuriyawongs was a source of unconcealed anxiety to the ex-Regent".[102] The most outstanding adult Bunnāk of the 1870s was probably Sĩsuriyawong's youngest brother Phon, but he was firmly on Čhulālongkǫn's side, and occasionally even spoke up against his brother Chuang. In addition, the Bunnāk family had been too conspicuous for too long a period, and a downturn in their fortunes would not have displeased many of the other noble familes. However, if these latter expected to gain from the Bunnāk's setbacks they were to be disappointed, because the king generally no longer gave new senior appointments to members of the nobility, preferring to select members of the royal family for such posts.

# Notes

1.  Prince Čhulālongkǫn's fifteenth birthday fell on 21 September 1868.
2.  D.K. Wyatt, "King Chulalongkorn the Great: Founder of Modern Thailand", *Asia*, supplement no. 2, 1976, p. 6.
3.  D.B. Bradley's journal, 3 October 1868.
4.  D.K. Wyatt, "Family Politics in Nineteenth Century Thailand", p. 224.
5.  See above p. 179.
6.  Bradley, journal, 22 October 1868.
7.  The standard account of the meeting is in Prince Damrong Rātchanuphāp, *Phrarātchaphongsāwadān Krungratanakōsin Ratchakān thĩ Hā*, pp. 15-25. See also Chula Chakrabongse, *Lords of Life*, pp. 216-17.
8.  Further details on currency problems at the beginning of the Fifth Reign can be found in Bradley's journal of 26 October and 3 December 1868, and in Prachoom Chomchai, ed. and trans., *Chulalongkorn the Great*, pp. 76-77.
9.  *Siam Repository* 1 (1869): 319-23.
10. Wyatt, "Family Politics", p. 228.
11. *Kāntaengtangkhunnāngthai nai samai Ratchakān thĩ Hā*, p. 12.

12. *Siam Repository* 2 (1870): 363.
13. Ibid., p. 362.
14. *Bangkok Calendar*, 1871, p. 70.
15. *Siam Repository* 2 (1870): 363.
16. Ibid., pp. 363-64.
17. Ibid., p. 364.
18. Wyatt's translation in "King Chulalongkorn the Great, pp. 6-7.
19. Bradley, journal, 3 and 12 October and 11 and 18 November 1868.
20. Chula Chakrabongse, *Lords of Life*, p. 219.
21. Bradley, journal, 28 May 1870.
22. Ibid., 11 June 1870.
23. *Prawatkitčhakānthahān samai Krungratanakōsin*, p. 44.
24. Bradley, journal, 19 and 21 September 1870.
25. D.K. Wyatt, *The Politics of Reform in Thailand: Education in the Reign of King Chulalongkorn*, p. 40; see also N.A. Battye, "The Military, Government and Society in Siam 1868–1910: Politics and Military Reform during the Reign of King Chulalongkorn", pp. 119-21.
26. Bradley, journal, 29 April 1871.
27. *Prawatkitčhakānthahān*, p. 45.
28. *Kāntaengtangkhunnāngthai*, p. 176-77.
29. Wyatt, *The Politics of Reform*, p. 70 and *Prawatkitčhakānthahān*, p. 45. This was the second group of high-ranking youths sent abroad. Already in 1871 some young students were sent to Singapore and England. The most notable among the first group were probably *mǫmčhao* Pritsadāng, who successfully completed a course at King's College, London, and *phra' ǫngčhao* Sawat, one of Čhulālongkǫn's brothers.
30. Bradley, journal, 19 March 1872. Apparently the king had begun training the members of his Royal Bodyguard with regard to the European custom of moving freely about during a reception for his birthday, not long before his departure for India; for details see Battye, "The Military", p. 122.
31. Wyatt, *The Politics of Reform*, pp. 70-71.
32. By this time, under European influence, the moment of crowning had gained considerable symbolic value so that one is more justified in speaking of a coronation rather than an anointment.
33. Prachoom Chomchai, *Chulalongkorn the Great*, p. 16.
34. For details, see Battye, "The Military", pp. 137-38.
35. Conversation with Prince Sāi Sanitwong, one of Prince Wongsāthirāt's sons (Bradley, journal, 4 April 1873).
36. Further details can be found in *Kāntaengtangkhunnāngthai*, pp. 197-202.
37. Prachoom Chomchai, *Chulalongkorn the Great*, p. 37.
38. Battye, "The Military", p. 155.
39. Prachoom Chomchai, *Chulalongkorn the Great*, pp. 50-65.
40. Ibid., p. 40.
41. On the ex-regent and his attitude towards the reformers, see the correspondence published in the *Straits Times*, 28 May and 18 and 27 July 1874.
42. Battye, "The Military", pp. 161-62.
43. Ibid., p. 164.
44. F. Vincent, *The Land of the White Elephant*, pp. 151-52.
45. Bradley, journal, 19 April and 31 May 1869.
46. Battye, "The Military", p. 169.
47. Ibid., p. 172. The following account of the "Palace Incident" is largely based on Battye's dissertation, which undoubtedly contains the most detailed account.

48. *Straits Times*, 16 January 1875.
49. Ibid., editorial.
50. Battye, "The Military", pp. 194-95.
51. W.S. Bristowe, *Louis and the King of Siam*, p. 45, citing an account of a dramatic confrontation between Knox and Chulālongkǫn in 1879. Similar sentiments were expressed on other occasions during the years immediately after the "Palace Incident" (see Battye, "The Military", pp. 209-10).
52. *Straits Times*, 9 December 1876.
53. D.K. Wyatt, "Samuel McFarland and Early Educational Modernization in Thailand, 1877–1895", *Felicitation Volumes of Southeast-Asian Studies Presented to His Highness Prince Dhaninivat Kromamun Bidyalabh Bridhyakorn*, vol. 1, pp. 1-2.
54. Ibid., *passim*.
55. *Straits Times*, 3 March 1877.
56. From King Chulālongkǫn's 1877 birthday speech, as reported in the *Siam Weekly Advertiser*, 25 October 1877, and reprinted in the *Straits Times*, 10 November 1877.
57. D. McGilvary, *A Half Century Among the Siamese and the Lao,* pp. 102-29.
58. Battye, "The Military", p. 146.
59. McGilvary, *Half Century among the Siamese*, p. 220.
60. For details, see *Prawatkitčhakānthahān*, p. 47, and the *Straits Times*, 10 November 1877.
61. *Kāntaengtangkhunnāngthai*, p. 6 and p. 184.
62. Bristowe, *Louis and the King of Siam*, p. 44. Probably this refers to *phrayā* Charoenrātchamaitrī, mentioned in *Kāntaengtangkhunnāngthai*, p. 217 and p. 219.
63. Manich Jumsai, *Prince Prisdang's Files on His Diplomatic Activities in Europe, 1880–1886*, p. 238.
64. As recounted by Bristowe, *Louis and the King of Siam*, p. 45. A much more dispassionate account of Knox's interview can be found in Chulālongkǫn's diary for 1879–80. See *Čhotmāihēt Phrarātchakitrāiwan nai Phrabātsomdet Phračhunlačhǫmklāo Čhaoyūhua Pī Thǫ Čhunlasakarāt 1241*, the entry for 21 April 1879, pp. 30-31.
65. Bristowe, *Louis and the King of Siam*, p. 46, and Manich Jumsai, *Prince Prisdang's Files*, pp. 238-45.
66. Battye, "The Military", p. 216.
67. The First Foot Guard was responsible among other things for the safety of all those taking part in royal processions. In mid-1880 there was a boat accident near the king's palace at Bang Pa In in which one of Chulālongkǫn's senior queens, his half-sister Queen Sunathā, was drowned. The accident has been wrongly taken as having occurred in 1881 by Chula Chakrabongse (*Lords of Life*, p. 221), because he took the date of the monument commemorating the event as the date for the accident. For the exact date, see *Rātchasakunwong*, p. 59.
68. Battye, "The Military", p. 223.
69. Ibid., pp. 223-24.
70. Ibid., p. 226.
71. Better known under the name of Prince Thēwawong, a name he acquired in 1881 (*Rātchasakunwong*, p. 55).
72. See, for example, C. Bock, *Temples and Elephants: The Narrative of a Journey of Exploration Through Upper Siam and Lao*, p. 15.
73. Bristowe (*Louis and the King of Siam*, p. 46) asserts that Phanuwong was

dismissed from office. This was not the case; he retained his post until his retirement in 1885.

74.  A tattooing office was set up almost immediately at Ratburi (Battye, "The Military", p. 231), and by December 1881 a traveller reported the arrival of a tattooing official in the northern town of Raheng (Bock, *Temples and Elephants*, p. 133) — undoubtedly part of the same drive.

75.  Battye ("The Military", p. 233) places the epidemic in 1882, but Bock's account (*Temples and Elephants*, pp. 60-61) would suggest that it was in 1881 that the outbreak took place.

76.  Battye, "The Military", pp. 234-35.

77.  Ibid., p. 235.

78.  Bock, *Temples and Elephants*, p. 137. On the effect of cheap imports on some of Siam's local industries, see J.C. Ingram, *Economic Change in Thailand 1850–1970*, pp. 113-21.

79.  Pensri Duke, *Les relations entra la France et la Thailande (Siam) au XIXe siècle*, pp. 58-60.

80.  Among them Prince Sawat, the only one of Čhulālongkǫn's brothers to be given an education abroad.

81.  Details can be found in Manich Jumsai, *Prince Prisdang's Files*, p. 28ff., and Pensri Duke, *Les relations*, pp. 85-89. While from Manich's account it would appear that the negotiations ended successfully in August 1885, it is clear that at the last moment the French refused to implement their ratified treaty, pending further clarification of matters relating to the protection of Annamites and the establishment of a vice-consulate at Luang Prabang.

82.  The 1843 survey was made by G.B. Tremenheere and E.A. Blundell. For references to this and subsequent efforts to examine the question of a canal, see H.B. Smith, "Historic Proposals for a Kra Canal: Their Impact on International Relations in Southeast Asia with Emphasis on British Perspectives", *Asian Profile* 3, no. 1 (February 1975): 43-58.

83.  Ibid., p. 48.

84.  Ibid., p. 47.

85.  Antoine Benoit François Deloncle was *chef de cabinet* to the undersecretary of state at the French Ministry of Foreign Affairs from 1881 to 1888. See R. d'Amat and R. Limouzin Lamothe, ed., *Dictionnaire de biographie française*, vol. 10, p. 874.

86.  Smith, "Historic Proposals", p. 51.

87.  It was by no means the last time that the idea of a canal was put forward. From time to time the matter was raised again. For some literature on more recent proposals, see H. Cucherousset, *Quelques informations sur le Siam*, pp. 97-99; J.L. Christian, "The Kra Canal Fable", *Amerasia* 1 (February 1938): 559-63; and M. Rajaretnam, *Thailand's Kra Canal: Some Issues*.

88.  Probably the best background article on Siam's international politics at this period is V.G. Kiernan, "Britain, Siam, and Malaya: 1875–1885", *The Journal of Modern History* 27, no. 1 (March 1956): 1-20.

89.  For details, see Bock, *Temples and Elephants*, pp. 385-91.

90.  One of the first foreigners to be awarded the Grand Cross of the Order of the Crown of Siam was Ferdinand de Lesseps, who received this honour in 1884, probably for having been willing to supervise the digging of the Kra Canal (see Manich Jumsai, *Prince Prisdang's Files*, pp. 72-73).

91.  Details can be found in Bock, *Temples and Elephants*, pp. 392-99.

92.  Manich Jumsai, *Prince Prisdang's Files*, pp. 117-19.

93.  For an account of the address, see Bock, *Temples and Elephants*, pp. 379-80.

94. A somewhat emotional account of the condition of Siam's slaves during the 1870s can be found in W.H. Senn van Basel, *Schetsen uit Siam*, pp. 85-99.

95. Kiernan, "Britain, Siam, and Malaya", pp. 7-8.

96. Bock, *Temples and Elephants*, p. 384.

97. P.P. Lindenberg, "The Early Postal History of Thailand", *Journal of the Thailand Research Society* 35, pt 1 (1944): 87.

98. In his seminal article on the Bunnāk family, D.K. Wyatt places the crucial point in their history early in the Second Reign ("Family Politics", p. 219). Clearly I disagree here with Wyatt. Even though Dit Bunnāk was very favourably placed in 1810, there were many scions of other families in the administration who could be elevated to senior positions. Dit's appointment as head of the *krom* Phrakhlang did not take place until 1822, and at that time he was no more than an able member of a team of state ministers.

99. Sisuriyawong's involvement with Chinese interests may have dated from the negotiations surrounding the Bowring treaty. His links with secret societies appear to have been widely known. The British consul-general reported on this in 1882 (as quoted in Bristowe, *Louis and the King of Siam*, p. 135).

100. Wyatt, "Family Politics", p. 222.

101. Battye, "The Military", pp. 138-39.

102. Report by E. Satow to the Earl of Granville, dated 26 June 1885, as reprinted in Chatthip Nartsupha and Suthy Prasartset, *The Political Economy of Siam, 1851-1910*, p. 322.

# 8

# *The Fifth Reign, Part II (1884–1910):*

# *Humiliation and the Path to Autocracy*

**Problems in the North-East**

In 1881 the French parliament had authorized renewed attacks on Tonkin. This had led, in April 1882, to the capture of Hanoi, which met with unexpectedly violent resistance. The Vietnamese, aided by Chinese troops, seriously threatened the French garrison, and substantial reinforcements were sent to the region. In 1883 the Vietnamese emperor died, and the French used the ensuing dynastic crisis to conclude an armistice whereby Vietnam became a French protectorate. Thus by late August 1883 the French had gained for themselves the right to establish forts to pacify and control the whole of Vietnam. Further reinforcements were sent in and the slow and painful conquest of the region continued, hampered not only by the fierce resistance of the local people but also by the presence of a large number of Chinese troops.

These troops, which, as noted earlier, were known in Siam as Hō soldiers, terrorized the countryside of the upper reaches of the Red River, the Black River, and the Song Ma, where many Tai-speaking groups lived. That region was not under the firm control of any of the surrounding powers, the local chieftains being aware of Hue's might, but not denying that of Luang Prabang. The Hǭ troops found the Laotian states an easy prey, and they "roamed or settled in their stockades, plundering, killing, enslaving, sometimes levying taxes and virtually ruling".[1] King Čhulālongkǭn and his advisers apparently were now reminded of their role as nominal overlords in Vientiane and Luang Prabang, and in 1883 the king announced a military expedition against the Hǭ.[2] While in the days of Rama III such a call to arms would automatically have resulted in the sending of a large expeditionary force, in the 1880s the matter was debated; and instead of a fully fledged army, it was decided to send a team of surveyors accompanied by some two hundred soldiers to map this region where Siamese power was weakest. When the surveying team left Bangkok in January 1884, the Hǭ deftly avoided a confrontation. Most of the Siamese contingent came down with malaria, and the expedition was recalled.[3]

During 1885 the French suffered heavily under attacks from Hǭ troops, and the power of the Laotian princes was so deeply undermined that a strong show of force was necessary. It was decided not to rely upon untrained corvée forces, but to send most of Bangkok's professional army, drawn from the First Foot and the Royal Household Guards, and armed with the best weapons available at that time. In November 1885 this model force, divided into two separate columns, one under the command of Čhulālongkǭn's younger brother *kromamū'n* Pračhak and the other *čhamū'n* Waiyaworanāt (Čhoem Saengchūtō), set out for the north. The campaign began very promisingly. Waiyaworanāt ventured deep into what had become Hǭ country and used his superior weapons and supplies to dislodge some Hǭs from their strongholds. During the wet season the column was forced to be on the defensive, and at one stage it was hard pressed. When the rains eased, Siamese forces again took the initiative and managed to cause many Hǭ troops to seek shelter further east and others to negotiate a truce.[4] It was not until the beginning of May 1887 that the Siamese troops returned to Bangkok, carrying with them some of the captured Hǫ leaders and some thirty young Laotian princes and noblemen as hostages to guarantee the future submission of the region.[5] The army was given a triumphal welcome back at the capital.

The military operation had taken place during a critical period when the French expansionist mood had been demonstrated not only by her tightening grip in Cambodia, Annam, and Tonkin, but also by fervent diplomatic activity. In 1885, after two years of negotiations, a commercial treaty was signed between France and Burma, and a French consul was sent to Mandalay. The French consul in Bangkok negotiated a new treaty with Siam, in which provision was made for a French consul at Luang Prabang. If this treaty, which was submitted to parliament in 1886, had been ratified, the French would have implicitly recognized Siam's suzerainty over the Laotian region.[6] When the ratification did not take place, the Siamese must have realized that the French were aiming towards a greater control over some of the Laotian territories.

Much more sudden and alarming, however, was the conflict that arose between the British and the Burmese. A court case against a British firm sparked off the British invasion of upper Burma. At the beginning of 1886 the territories that had formerly been governed by King Thibaw were formally annexed.[7] Thus, between 1882 and 1886 two major South-East Asian kingdoms, Annam and Burma, had been forced to accept European dominance, and by 1886 Siam was the only free country remaining in the whole of South-East Asia. Many people considered this an ominous state of affairs; it did not need much imagination to foresee further encroachments upon Siam's traditional sphere of influence.

## The Search for Reform

Siam's precarious position was noted with alarm by the Siamese legation in London, and the senior officials debated among themselves about how the country should attempt to maintain its independence. They drew up a lengthy document, dated 8 January 1885, which they submitted to the king.[8] In broad outline their suggestions were that it would be futile to rely upon Siam's military power or upon the strength of diplomatic links with European countries to avoid colonization. The best way to counter European expansion was to deny Westerners the opportunity to denounce Siam's government as archaic and oppressive. Therefore the signitaries argued that drastic internal reform was needed, of a much more fundamental nature than the few steps hitherto undertaken. They proposed the introduction of a constitutional monarchy in conjunction with a cabinet of ministers who would carry full responsibility. Also they suggested clarification with regard to succession to the throne so that the choice of a new monarch would become more predictable and less likely to cause an upheaval. In addition, they boldly suggested the eradication of corruption in administrative circles and the overhaul of the taxation system. They pointed out that promotions ought to be given on the principle of merit rather than being determined by family connections. Other ideas brought forward were the introduction of universal suffrage and the establishment of legal rights such as equal justice and freedom of the press. In order to make these drastic changes possible, the reformists suggested that the king first institute military reform, bringing all troops under a single high command consisting of trustworthy officials.[9]

This frank, revolutionary proposal has been described as *"lèse-majesté"*[10] and as a "treasonable challenge".[11] However, Čhulālongkǭn had specifically invited written proposals for change and the signatories had simply taken him at his word. In his reply, he first thanked them for their patriotic interest and assured them that questions of reform had often been in his mind during the past eighteen years. Also he told them that he lacked the team to carry out such drastic changes:

> That we need in this country a reform of the whole system of government I entirely agree, but then members of an effective legislative council must be independent men. Where are we to find such men? . . . The older ministers, who know their limitations, now hardly ever dare to speak. What should they do? Should they resign *en bloc*? . . . I, too, want political reforms, but at present there are other matters more pressing.[12]

Gradually, as senior posts had become available, Čhulālongkǫn had filled the ministry with men of his choice, and these were often members of the royal family. He had begun to take away some of the senior administrator's lucrative perquisites, and felt sufficiently confident to remove from the *čhaophrayā* Surawongwaiyawat (Won Bunnāk) control over the opium tax-farm and the administration of liquor licensing.[13] In 1885 his position was strengthened further when the retirement of *čhaophrayā* Phanuwǫng (Thuam Bunnāk), enabled him to appoint his close associate and trusted younger brother *kromaluang* Thēwawong to the post of Minister of Foreign Affairs.

In 1885 the Uparāt, Prince Wichaichān, died. After 1875 his powers had been so drastically curbed that in the event of the king's premature demise he would have had little chance of election to the throne. With his death, the office of Uparāt was abolished and Čhulālongkǫn took the opportunity to implement one of the reforms suggested in the 1885 petition. He announced the appointment of Siam's first *sayāmmakutrātchakumān*, or crown prince, who would bear the title of *somdetphraboromōrotsāthirāt*. The eldest of Čhulālongkǫn's sons of *čhaofā* rank, Prince Wachirunhit, at the tender age of nine, was chosen to be the heir to the throne and his investiture took place in January 1887.[14]

The appointment of an official heir was one of the many fundamental changes that swept Siam during the late 1880s. Notwithstanding the king's formal rejection of the reform programme that had been suggested by his legation in London, it was clear that he was examining the possibility of altering Siam's system of government. It is in this context that his request for a report on the working of the corvée system must be considered. In June 1885 *čhaophrayā* Mahinthon presented his assessment of the administration of corvée. From the report it is clear that various classes of people were charged different amounts. Some *phrai luang* paid twelve *baht* per year, some ten *baht*, some eight *baht* and some six *baht*. Since the Fourth Reign the general rate for *phrai som* had been fixed at six *baht,* whilst those registered as slaves were liable to pay one *baht* and two *salu'ng*. The lowest ranks of government servants were taxed at a rate of four *baht* per annum. The government kept a register, noting for how many slaves, *phrai luang, phrai som* and minor officials each prince and nobleman was responsible. It was thus possible to calculate how much money these notables ought to collect and hand over to the government. Already during the Fourth Reign the king had decided not to press his officials for payment of these sums and this had remained so during the Fifth Reign.[15] The 1885 report showed that many high officials and princes regarded the poll tax payable for all members of the lower classes under their jurisdiction as one of the perquisites of their rank and status, and the king must have realized that he could only change the corvée-linked taxation system in conjunction with a major financial restructuring of the whole civil service.

## The Politics of Gradual Reform

The changes that were to take place in 1892 have been called the "great transformation",[16] and a "general reorganisation of government",[17] statements that give the impression of a sudden metamorphosis. In actuality, the reform edict of 1892 was the culmination of a series of changes which had begun approximately five years earlier. Already in April 1887 the king had created the *krom* Yutthānathikān, or Department of the Military, which united all Siam's army and navy units. He gave his brother Prince Phānurangsī the acting command of this new government unit.[18] The new commander was assisted by his brothers Damrong and Narit, by Čhoem Saengchūtō and Prince Sāi Sanitwong,[19] a team the king could rely on; thus yet another of the reforms suggested in 1885 was established. The military reformation was largely at the cost of the power of the *krom* Kalāhom, and there can be little doubt that this led to Won Bunnāk's resignation from the Sēnābodī. During May 1887 Čhulālongkǫn created the Department of Education, and soon he added a Department of Public Works, a Department of Justice, and a Department of the Privy Seal, each of them headed by a prince.

The increasing prominence of princes in Siam's administration represents a considerable deviation from the traditional

Siamese system of government. Earlier kings had occasionally selected a prince to head an army or to supervise a particular task, but in general princes were not allowed to do the work customarily performed by senior nobles. By 1888 it had become clear to the Thai nobility that Čhulālongkǫn had no hesitation in training his brothers as civil servants and in assigning them to all the major executive posts, thus excluding all but a few trusted young nobles. The king could choose from no less than twenty-six younger brothers, now all adults, who generally looked up to him as the man who had led their family into prominence and who was now leading Siam cautiously towards a promising future.

The 1887 December decree against gambling illustrates Čhulālongkǫn's style of gradual reform. As early as the 1870s, opium and gambling had been singled out by "Young Siam" as evil practices which ought not to be fostered by the government. Yet opium and gambling licences constituted the largest sources of state revenue. While the king still espoused an abolitionist cause, he decided to leave the opium problem alone and tackle gambling dens and lotteries first. In his decree of 1887 he gave warning of the decision to close a considerable number of licensed gambling houses, leaving only sixty-seven dens open in and around Bangkok. Provincial gambling was not yet affected by this first measure. Other decrees, each of them further limiting certain types of games of chance, were issued in the years to follow.[20]

Between 1887 and 1892 reorganization is apparent in many departments, with a spate of decrees and effective measures. Thus the new Department of the Military founded a cadet school and a school for non-commissioned officers. The infantry was re-equipped with rapid-firing Mannlicher guns. A uniform code of military law was drawn up, an officers' club created, and a military journal, *Yutthakot*, established.[21] These and other reforms were inspired by both the wish to imitate the colonial powers and fear of those same powers. The addition of these newly trained troops made it possible to send small garrisons to support Siamese high commissioners in the vassal states. By sending commissioners to Chiang Mai, Luang Prabang, Nakhon Ratchasima, Nongkhai, and Ubon Ratchathani, Bangkok established a degree of control and regular channels of communication, making it more difficult for foreign powers to challenge Siamese rights there. Čhulālongkǫn's decision to have the terrain between Bangkok and various places in the north surveyed in preparation for the establishment of railway lines was also inspired largely by strategic considerations.

In April 1892 the protracted search for a new government structure and the creation of new *kroms* at the cost of established ones culminated in the appointment of a new cabinet consisting of twelve men, nine of them Čhulālongkǫn's brothers. Many of the new ministries were continuations of the previous major *kroms*. For example, the *krom* Wang simply changed its title to Ministry of the Royal Household, and the *krom* Nā became Ministry of Agriculture. The main administrative innovation was the creation of a powerful Ministry of the Interior to supersede the old *krom* Mahātthai and the *krom* Kalāhom and to absorb some of the functions of the previous *krom* Phrakhlang. All revenue collection was centred in the Ministry of Finance, all military affairs in the Ministry of Defence, and all legal affairs in the Ministry of Justice, in accordance with the structural changes brought about earlier in the reign.

However, while creating a new cabinet the king did not delegate any of his powers; none of the ministers could make policy decisions without his formal approval. The whole cabinet consisted of "king's men", chosen because Čhulālongkǫn trusted their personal loyalty. They could be seen primarily as extensions of the king. When Thēwawong was sent to England as the king's representative at the celebrations for Queen Victoria's jubilee, he had to collect ideas about government administration for submission to his elder brother. Similarly, Prince Damrong's visit to Europe in 1891 and 1892 was to gather ideas on various ways of organizing an education system. To Damrong's consternation, he learnt upon his return that he had been transferred to the new Ministry of the Interior, because the man who by rights ought to have inherited the office, *čhaophrayā* Ratanabǫdin (Rǫt Kanlayānmit), had become seriously ill.

Loyalty to the king appears to have been the overriding criterion for allocation of cabinet posts, and little thought seems to have been given to other qualifications. The result was an ill-assorted group of people who had little experience in co-operating with each other and with working as a team. The cabinet formed in 1892 "proved to be not a deliberative and administrative body which could forge a common policy of internal modernization and united resistance to Western pressures, but rather a battleground for personal, intra-family 'cabals and recriminations' ".[22] Several serious disputes did in fact mar the atmosphere within the cabinet. Tension had arisen between *čhaophrayā* Phātsakǫrawong, since 1888 in charge of the *krom* Nā, and the Siam Land, Canals and Irrigation Company, a private enterprise which had obtained the rights to virtually all canal and land developments projects in the country. The company accused the chief of the *krom* Nā of being more interested in his relatives' speculation than in Siam's development, and Phātsakǫrawong was moved to the Ministry of Public Instruction. Čhoem Saengchūtō, now *čhaophrayā* Surasak, replaced him.[23] Some time earlier, Surasak had resigned angrily from his army command after he had lost a dispute with the Treasury over army expenditure.[24] Prince Narāthip, the Treasurer, quarrelled with Prince Phānurangsī, the new Minister of Defence, on matters concerning the future of corvée and conscription, and Phānurangsī threatened to resign. Čhulālongkǫn backed Phānurangsī, who was given the right to prepare a draft conscription law. When in September 1892 this draft was ready for discussion, *čhaophrayā* Surasak found much to criticize, and the cabinet could not come to a decision on the matter.[25] Meanwhile, it became increasingly apparent that Prince Narāthip was not a good Treasurer and, early in 1893 after an audit of the accounts by four of his brothers, he was dismissed and replaced by Prince Narit.[26] This was not the type of cabinet to be helpful in a serious crisis, and the squabbling among the king's senior advisers may have contributed to some of the ill-thought-out decisions of 1892 and 1893 in response to the French expansion westwards.

## The Crisis of 1893

In the late 1880s several French colonialists noted with dismay how the Siamese were proceeding to consolidate their hold upon the Laotian vassal states. The regions known as the Sibsong Chao Thai and the Hua Phan Tang Ha Tang Hok threatened to fall under Siamese rule, at least in the eyes of the French consul.[27] Some sort of delineation between the French and the Siamese sphere of influence had to be made also with respect to the territory more directly ruled from Luang Prabang and Nongkhai. The idea that the whole region east of the Mekong River could be brought under French control had passed through the minds of many officials convinced of the superior blessings of French culture.[28] In 1887 the French and the Siamese each had sent commissioners to explore the border regions. The Frenchman, Auguste Pavie, used the opportunity to make contact with local chiefs and to consider the possibilities of "pacification" under the French flag.[29] The Siamese heard that a French occupation of *mū'ang* Theng (Dien Bien Phu) was imminent and hastened to send reinforcements. In December 1888 French and Siamese troops confronted each other, and the Siamese were forced to retreat, leaving the Sibsong Chao Thai in French hands. This event pushed Tonkin's border deep into Laotian territory.

The French consul in Bangkok had asked the Siamese to recognize that the Annamite empire used to dominate the whole region up to the Mekong River, but this claim was dismissed by Prince Thēwawong. The two governments agreed, however, to establish a joint committee to collect evidence upon the basis of which a border could be fixed. Meanwhile, the Siamese set up many military posts between the Mekong River and the Annamite Cordillera, and the restoration of Luang Prabang became a matter of priority. The French proceeded with establishing trading posts along the Mekong River and asked the Siamese to cease collecting taxes on certain products in that region, an issue the Siamese relegated to the frontier question.

Siamese tempers rose when a French member of the joint commission appointed a Laotian as French representative of one of the Mekong River posts. When the official protest did not have the desired effect, the Laotian was arrested and his post's flag and weapons were captured. In another incident, which took place in 1892, two French traders who refused to wait for local Siamese travel permits and who had not obeyed Siamese tax regulations were arrested and their goods confiscated. Late in 1892 the French agent at Luang Prabang died, and it was rumoured that he had committed suicide as a result of the tense political situation.[30] Such problems were the inevitable outcome of the differing aims of the French and Siamese agents entering the region. Some of the incidents caused alarm and consternation in France, and demands were made that the Siamese be taught a lesson.

The Siamese were aware that a dangerous situation had developed. It may be asked why they were not more willing to accommodate the French and suggest certain territorial concessions in exchange for a more secure border. In the first place the Siamese were convinced of their rights in this matter: Siam had a better claim on Lao territory than Annam; Siamese suzerainty had been reaffirmed many times during the previous hundred years. Secondly, the Siamese military appeared stronger than ever before. This had been demonstrated by the second expedition against the Họ troops, and again later in the suppression of Chinese riots in Bangkok, Ratburi, and Nakhon Chaisi.[31] Thirdly, France's position did not appear to be very strong. France had virtually no troops in the disputed territory, and the French demands were not very forcefully expressed. Fourthly, the Siamese were actively engaged in proposing a treaty in London whereby Great Britain would agree to protect Siam against the dangers of losing territory by annexation on the part of any foreign power.[32] They did not realize that British anxieties mainly centred upon what was going to happen further north, in the upper reaches of the Mekong, where Burmese, Chinese, and Siamese interests met and where a French expansion in the region was rapidly complicating the problems of an unsettled border.[33]

The British reluctance to become involved with Siam's border dispute, combined with Siamese "provocations", provided the French with the opportunity to press their claims vigorously. In April 1893 Prince Thēwawong, the Minister of Foreign Affairs, again offered to submit the whole border question to international arbitration, but the French rejected that offer, asking for immediate concessions, and they increased the pressure by adding the *Comète* to the man-of-war *Lutin* already stationed at the mouth of the Chao Phraya River. The Siamese became seriously alarmed. The French were asked not to proceed up-river, and the fortresses at Paknam were alerted and reinforced. Once again the Siamese beseeched the British to intervene and also sent an emissary to Washington for help; meanwhile, a brave front was shown at home. In May skirmishes broke out at Khong, an island in the Mekong River near the border with Cambodia, in which several French officers were killed and a senior officer captured. From then on the situation worsened; clashes broke out at various points along the left bank of the river, and reinforcements were sent. By June a formal declaration of war seemed imminent. As the Siamese did not seem prepared to back down, they provided the French with an opportunity to press their case even further. Pavie wrote on 28 June 1893 to the French Foreign Minister: "Events have taken a turn which permits us to make the greatest demands and which makes even the foreigners envisage the inevitable solution as being the establishment of our Protectorate over the whole of Siam."[34] The Siamese government, however, still hoped to dissuade the French by raising a daunting force, and a general mobilization of the masses was ordered.[35]

On 10 July Pavie reported to Thēwawong that he planned to call two gunboats, the *Comète* and the *Inconstant*, to Bangkok to join the *Lutin* already there in order to protect French subjects during the emergency. The Siamese protested that the French were exceeding the provisions of the Franco-Siamese Treaty, and the king warned that the fortress would fire upon warships attempting to cross the bar at Paknam. For a moment it seemed that the Siamese protests were effective, for the French government sent assurances that the gunboats would not cross the bar of the Chao Phraya River. For reasons that are not absolutely clear, however, the chief officers on the French boats did not receive clear instructions on this matter. The possibility that Pavie deliberately enticed the commanders to proceed, thus provoking an incident, may not be ruled out. The Frenchmen had brought their own pilot, the captain of the small steamer *Jean-Baptiste Say*, and during the evening of 13 July, when the tide and weather were favourable, a small convoy, consisting of the *Jean-Baptiste Say*, the *Inconstant*, and the *Comète* went over the bar and proceeded up-river. The Siamese fired warning shots from a fortress. When these had no effect, Siam's largest warship, the *Coronation*, which lay in midstream, opened fire. However, when its second projectile was launched, its largest gun exploded, and in the ensuing confusion the *Inconstant* narrowly avoided colliding with it. Meanwhile, the batteries on the river bank fired and the French returned fire, all the time moving full-speed further up-river. Eventually the two French gunboats joined the *Lutin* at anchor opposite the French consulate; the *Jean-Baptiste Say* lay in the mud at the side of the river with a large hole in her side.[36]

The leaders in Bangkok were in a quandary over how to react. Some contemplated attacking the three ships in front of the consulate; others argued for caution. The Bangkok populace was deeply perturbed, and there was some looting of shops. Many feared that the Chinese would revolt.[37] Eventually caution prevailed, and an uneasy calm reigned while people awaited further French reaction.

Circumstances had played into France's hands. Siam could be accused of having violated the 1856 treaty and of having fired at French ships, killing some of the crew. Moreover, the failure to stop the ships from entering the river greatly assisted in demoralizing the Siamese military, because they had proudly believed in the indomitability of the new fortress at Paknam. A British offer to mediate was rejected by the French. The French consul was authorized to present the Siamese with an ultimatum on 20 July 1893, asking the Siamese to withdraw from east of the Mekong River, to punish all those who had caused belligerent incidents, to pay two million *francs* indemnity, and to deposit a further three million as guarantee, or instead of the latter clause, to allow France to appropriate the customs revenue of Battambang and Siemreap provinces. If the Siamese did not agree within twenty-four hours, France would close Bangkok harbour by a naval blockade. When the Siamese attempted to negotiate, France proceeded with the blockade until 29 July, when the Siamese agreed not only to all the terms of the original ultimatum but also, during the following days, to a temporary French occupation of Chanthaburi, to the Siamese withdrawal of military posts from Battambang and Siemreap, and to the Siamese withdrawal from a twenty-five-kilometre zone along the west bank of the Mekong River.

Probably afraid that even more terms would be added, and not aware that British diplomats, alarmed at the extent of French gains in a country where the British had considerable trade interests, were negotiating more favourable conditions,[38] the Siamese abruptly signed their new treaty with France in October 1893. The treaty still did not satisfactorily determine the border between French and Siamese territory, and it extended the status of "French subject" to numerous residents of Vietnamese, Cambodian, and Lao origin, which created the likelihood of many further "incidents" involving the two countries.

## After the Debacle

It was quite clear that the Siamese government had not handled the situation well. There had been an underestimation of the French appetite for conquest, coupled with an over-optimistic view of Siam's own military might. At the same time too much hope had been placed on Britain's power and on the idea that justice was on the side of the Siamese. Čhulālongkǫn could now see that he should have been more prudent and not have relied upon those who had advocated military resistance. He realized that he was personally responsible for Siam's humiliation and for the excessive loss of territory.[39] Before the confrontation he was already ill, but at the time of the ultimatum and blockade he collapsed and left the country's daily affairs in the hands of his cabinet. He took matters so to heart that he refused to eat and to meet people, and it was widely expected that he would die, his spirit broken.

The king's grave illness caused a serious succession crisis.

The crown prince was still a teenager, and it was difficult to decide who ought to be regent in the case of Čhulālongkǫ̈n's death. The king's brothers could not agree upon a candidate for that important office, some rallying behind Prince Phānurangsī, others preferring Prince Thēwawong.[40] Late in 1893, however, the king's health began to improve and the king's brothers could stop wrangling over the position of regent.

Meanwhile, the cabinet, urged on by Phānurangsī, reacted in its own way to the disastrous confrontation with the French. It was clear that Siam needed a complete overhaul of its defence system. A plan was drawn up by which army and navy would fall under a single command and the provinces would be included in the defence plan of the country as a whole; various other administrative changes also were proposed.[41] This plan was submitted to the king in April 1894, but before it could be discussed the king caught a fever and in his weakened state he was not expected to recover.[42] Again the court was divided over whom should be called upon to become regent; again the king rallied. By late 1894 he was beginning to emerge from his deep depression and to show signs of interest in the debate on how best to safeguard Siam's independence. Many people feared at that time that sooner or later the country would become a French colony.[43] While accepting some of Phānurangsī's proposals for military reform, the king was no longer interested in creating a major modern army. He saw more merit in plans put forward by Damrong and Gustave Rolin-Jaequemyns, a Belgian lawyer who in 1892 had been appointed as Siam's General Adviser and who had rapidly established himself as a man with Siam's interests at heart.[44] Damrong's plan consisted of a series of government priorities for the years to come, namely, the maintenance of peace and order in the whole territory that remained under Siamese rule, the strict avoidance of conflicts involving foreigners and foreign interests, and the drawing up of plans for internal administrative reforms. A modern army was no longer regarded as an effective means of halting foreign incursions. In January 1895 the court was shocked to learn that the crown prince had died, but the king rapidly appointed fourteen-year old Wachirāwut to the position.[45]

## The Creation of the Buffer State

The French territorial conquests in the region had caused some anxieties about safeguarding British interests, and the problem of French-held territory coming uncomfortably near that under British control had lead to considerable diplomatic activity. Already in July 1893, at the end of the French blockade of the Chao Phraya River, the French and the British "agreed to recognise the necessity of constituting, by means of mutual sacrifices and concessions, a neutral zone between their possessions".[46] The subsequent negotiations centred upon the Shan state of Keng Cheng, which straddled the Mekong River. Throughout 1894 it was not clear what Keng Cheng's fate would be. Although Britain maintained it had inherited the state as part of Burma's sphere of influence, France claimed at least that part of the state which lay east of the Mekong River, a part which, incidentally, included Keng Cheng's capital town, mü'ang Sing. At the same time Siam hoped to be given Keng Cheng, and thus create a neutral zone between the French and the British. Britain, however, was discouraged by the news of Čhulālongkǭn's ill health and Siam's apparent instability. In early 1895 the British decided to leave no doubts about their superior claim to Keng Cheng and set up a military post at mü'ang Sing, but soon afterwards they withdrew again when agreement had been reached to split up Keng Cheng between themselves and France, making the Mekong River the actual border. In return for this concession, the way was opened for a more satisfactory arrangement regarding the status of Siam.

The British perceived three options: they could leave Siam to be taken by the French, in which case they would have to ensure that the whole Malay Peninsula would come under British control; they could declare Siam to be a British protectorate, whereby they would face the French along a vast stretch of the Mekong River; or they could negotiate for an internationally guaranteed, independent Siam.[47] The latter option was considered preferable, and after further negotiations this was achieved. In January 1896 an agreement was reached which guaranteed the inviolability of the Chao Phraya River basin; a stretch of Siamese territory, ranging from Chiang Rai in the north to a point not far south of Prachuap Khirikhan in the south, was designated as the guaranteed portion of Siam. Not included in the portion was the whole of the Khorat plateau, the provinces neighbouring Cambodia, and most of the Siamese portion of the Malay Peninsula. Naturally, after the traumas of 1893, the Siamese initially regarded the declaration as a direct threat to all the territories not guaranteed and feared that soon they would be left only with the Chao Phraya River basin. In due course, however, it became clear that the British and French had indeed agreed to allow Siam to remain independent. Siam's leaders began looking more hopefully to the future.

## Renewed Initiatives

Throughout the period of almost three years of uncertainty about Siam's status and prospects, ordinary life had largely continued. The Siamese economy went on expanding, and various major projects continued. The Siam Land, Canals and Irrigation Company proceeded with the opening up of large stretches of land to the east and north-west of Bangkok. In 1888 the surveyor James McCarthy had been just east of Bangkok and had reported "no cultivation" to the north of the Saen Saeb Canal. In 1895 he noted: "I was astonished at the change that had taken place. In every direction the land was cleared of the heavy jungle grass which afforded shelter to wild elephants."[48] It has been estimated that during the 1890s more than a hundred thousand people came to farm in the Rangsit area alone,[49] and it can thus be said that although the central government was incapable of effective leadership, a "quiet revolution" took place in the countryside which began to have a major effect upon Siam's economy by the turn of the century.[50]

Similarly, the years of despondency between 1893 and 1896 should not obscure the fact that Siam's first railway was steadily being constructed. The contract for the Khorat line from Bangkok to the north-east had been signed in December 1891 and, notwithstanding considerable problems, large stretches of this "pioneer railway of Siam" had been completed. In November 1895 King Čhulālongkǫn, still showing signs of having suffered deeply, travelled several sections of the new line still under construction.[51] This line was built with German technical personnel and large numbers of Chinese labourers.

During the early 1890s there were more than a hundred foreign technical specialists in Siam assisting with a wide range of development projects. Most of them were British, Danish, and Germans. Other nationalities were represented in much smaller numbers. The French had some missionaries and consular representatives, but no technical advisers in Siam.[52] In 1897 the foreigners in state service were: fifty-four Englishmen, twenty Danes, eighteen Germans, nine Belgians, seven Italians, and a few Dutchmen, Austrians, Americans, Portuguese, and Swiss.[53]

In 1896 the king resumed active control over the senior administrators and reshuffled cabinet. The chief posts were given to the king's brothers Damrong (Interior), Mahit (Finance and Agriculture), Phithayalāp (Palace and Public Works), Thēwawong (Foreign Affairs), Narit (Army), and Narēt (Local Government). A new face in the Siamese administration in 1897 was young Prince Rātburi (Rātchaburidirēkru't) freshly returned from his studies in Oxford, the first of Čhulālongkǫn's sons to gain ministerial rank. Most of the king's advisers were progressive reformist in outlook, and under the by now experienced hand of the king, many new initiatives were broached. Thus during 1896 plans for the new King's College, an English school for the country's prominent youth, gained cabinet approval. It was given Sīsuriyawong's old residence as its temporary quarters.[54]

The king's renewed interest in administrative reform is also apparent in the fact that he asked his newly appointed Financial Adviser, A. Mitchell-Innes,[55] to make a report on the nature of Siam's financial system and to suggest alterations and improvements. The Mitchell-Innes report provides an excellent means by which to note how the system of taxation had developed since the Fourth Reign.[56] The range of taxable goods and property was at least as wide as that under Mongkut. There were more than twenty different types of land tax, more than twenty types of fruit trees upon which taxes were levied, more than seventy types of excise, as well as house tax, boat tax, fishing tax, and other taxes. Many of these were still being collected by intermediaries — the tax-farmers, usually Chinese — a system considered particularly odious by Mitchell-Innes. In general, the role of the tax-farmers seems less prominent than during the Fourth Reign. In the Fifth Reign the Ministry of Finance, the Ministry of the Interior, and the Ministry of Agriculture sent out their own tax collectors.

From the Mitchell-Innes report it is possible to obtain a fairly clear picture of the state of the corvée system. This appears to have hovered between being a poll tax and a forced labour system. The amount a *phrai* would pay in order to be exempt from corvée varied greatly and was usually determined by what his father had paid and whether he was attached to a certain *krom* as a *phrai luang* or to a private person as a *phrai som*. Whenever the tax was not paid, it was converted into corvée. For an ordinary man it depended therefore greatly on the type of *krom* or master to whom he was assigned. If a man belonged to the *thahān ru'a*, or navy, it was likely that he would have to serve the state. If he belonged to a *krom* not in need of manpower, he could pay the poll tax.

An interesting development was taking place with regard to the collection of the tax on rice land. Until 1896, officers of the Ministry of Agriculture would be sent out every year to collect moneys due on the rice lands. They were paid 6 per cent on the amount they brought in, and another 6 per cent went to various other officials. However, in 1896, by way of experiment, the rice-land tax collection was transferred to the Ministry of the Interior, which gave the responsibility for the tax collection to the provincial administrators. This, undoubtedly, was one of the measures devised to bring all parts of the kingdom under effective control.

During the year 1896 Siam's government moved to prevent a recurrence of the shameful breaching of Bangkok's outer fortifications. With the assistance of Rolin-Jaequemyns, the services of the famous Belgian defence specialist General Brialmont were secured and plans for three new fortresses at the first bend of the Chao Phraya River were drawn up and handed over to the Siamese envoy in 1895.[57] By 1896, engineers had arrived to examine the site and prepare a draft of a project that would bring Bangkok's defence up to modern standards.[58]

## Čhulālongkǫn's First European Visit

By late 1897 the situation in the region appeared relatively stable. Siam's position in the Malay Peninsula was being clarified with Britain, and the hostilities between Siam and France were mainly concerned with the vexed problem of the status of people of Cambodian, Laotian, and Annamite descent.[59] In fact, the problem of identifying French protégés was one of the reasons for Čhulālongkǫn's European travel in 1897. He hoped that a state visit might be an opportunity to ask for the abrogation of the clause concerning Laotians, Cambodians, and Annamites.

The king had always been keen on travelling. Already in 1871, upon his return from Singapore and Batavia, he had attempted to persuade Sīsuriyawong to send him to Europe on a study tour. Later, in 1880, a state visit to America and Europe had been organized, but this had had to be cancelled when Sīsuriyawong was suddenly taken ill. This time there were no insurmountable problems. At the last moment the king was able to clear his desk, signing the secret convention with Britain[60] and officially opening the first part of the Khorat railway[61] before embarking in early April 1897 on the royal steamer *Mahāčhakrī* for a journey which would last nine months. During his absence, Queen Saowaphā was appointed regent, an unprecedented move in Siam's history. The queen had to undergo a ceremony similar to that of the installation of a crown prince; she had to take an oath of allegiance, and during the regency she was entitled to be addressed as *čhao phaendin* (the country's overlord). It is not known for certain why Čhulālongkǫn decided to elevate his queen to the regency. It is likely that the choice was prompted by the fact that there was no suitable elderly member of the royal family who could fill the post. In addition, the choice of a woman absolved the king from the difficult task of singling out one of his able brothers. Throughout the long voyage the king kept regular contact with his regent by telegram and letter.[62]

After a fairly uneventful journey via Colombo, Aden, and Port Said, the king and his entourage arrived in Venice on 14 May 1897. During the following months the king visited Geneva, Turin, Florence, Rome, Vienna, Budapest, Warsaw, Saint Petersburg, London, Hamburg, Essen, The Hague, Brussels, and Paris, as well as many smaller cities. A sovereign of an Asian country was a rarity in Europe, and Čhulālongkǭn's travels aroused considerable interest. He was quite warmly welcomed by European royalty. Although he was received at Buckingham Palace by the Prince of Wales, Queen Victoria excused herself,[63] a circumstance which must have distressed King Čhulālongkǭn. In September he was treated with full honours by the French, but unfortunately was unable to obtain abrogation of the troublesome clause regarding people under the French consul's protection.[64] After a final visit to European health and holiday resorts, an envigorated king, enriched by a first-hand knowledge of a wide range of European cultural traditions, began the long voyage home on the *Mahāčhakrī*. His arrival in Bangkok on 16 December was the occasion of a splendid welcome.[65]

The king's improved health and vigour, and the stimulus of returning after a prolonged stay abroad, are reflected in some of the decisions of 1898. Thus an assessment was made with regard to the effectiveness of earlier measures which had been intended to draw the northern semi-independent states of Chiang Mai, Lampang, Lamphun, Nan, and Phrae closer into the Siamese administrative system. The local traditional rulers had been discouraged from using Chinese tax-farmers and invited to use the services of state employees instead. When this plan failed, it had been decided in late 1895 or early 1896 to give the responsibility for collecting state revenue to committees comprising both local leaders and the Siamese commissioner. Some local leaders resented this intrusion and there were signs of a growing hostility against Bangkok.[66] Up till 1898 the Siamese had attempted gradually to introduce changes in the north, treating the northern rulers with great respect and heeding their interests. From 1898 onwards, however, a firmer line was taken after a thorough tour of inspection by the Minister for the Interior, Prince Damrong, himself. A missionary likened the effect this tour had on the local nobles to that of "a whiff of ozone".[67] The inspection tour resulted in a deeper awareness in Bangkok of the need to win the local nobles' co-operation. It was decided to create consultative bodies comprising both Siamese and "Lao" and to increase the salaries of the local chiefs. In 1899 a special commissioner for the north was appointed to implement the reforms.[68]

When the king was in Europe, he had personally inspected the schooling of many younger members of the royal family and had discovered that they were usually ill-prepared to benefit from a Western education. The king asked *phrayā* Wisut, the Siamese ambassador in London, to prepare a report on foreign education. *Phrayā* Wisut suggested sweeping reforms of Siamese education, including the translation and distribution of large numbers of simple foreign textbooks, the introduction of English as part of the curriculum in many schools, and the adjustment of the Siamese system better to fit in with that of the British. In April 1898 the report was submitted, and the king demanded a speedy reaction from *čhaophrayā* Phātsakǫrawong, the Minister of Public Instruction. The minister responded with the complaint that his officials had in the previous six years come up with innovative plans, many of them along the lines suggested by Wisut, which had had to be abandoned because of lack of funds. There had thus far been little enthusiasm for education, but now suddenly reform appeared to be coming at too great a speed: "Education is not like the construction of buildings, which can be quickly accomplished. It is rather like the planting and felling of trees. Education is like the slow growth of the great tree of the forest. If it is properly nourished with foods, it will yield its fruit in due course."[69]

In September 1898 the king convened a meeting with senior officials of the Ministry of Public Instruction to which his brothers Damrong and Wachirayān were also invited.[70] The latter was a Buddhist monk, abbot of Wat Bowoniwēt, and he had proved himself to be an able administrator and organizer of the Mahāmakut religious academy.[71] The king openly criticized the Ministry of Public Instruction for having failed to raise the standards of Siamese schools, and listened with approval to Damrong and Wachirayān, who proposed to set about providing all existing monastery schools with modern textbooks, not books translated from foreign sources, but written by Siamese, and from a Siamese perspective. The king ended the ensuing discussion by handing over the responsibility for curriculum development for all schools in the provinces to Damrong and Wachirayān. Only Bangkok schools would henceforth remain under the Ministry of Public Instruction; the bulk of the nation's educational institutions were transferred to Damrong's Ministry of the Interior.

The king's decision became law in November 1898, and for a period of four years the administration of Siam's education remained split between two separate organizations. The provincial schools were given to the Buddhist monks, and a programme was devised to standardize and improve the thousands of existing monastery schools. In Bangkok, however, educational reform was modelled on the British education system. Each of the systems had its merits and faults, and in 1902 the whole of Siam's educational goals were again re-examined and a completely different administrative structure was devised. This episode serves to illustrate the king's almost unlimited power. Not since the time of Taksin had a king been able to act so freely. After his first European journey, Chulālongkǫn was fully in command, and his word was law. Inevitably this situation stifled debate and encouraged the writing of reports which were drafted with the specific aim of pleasing the monarch.

The king's confidence was further boosted by the fortuitous discovery in India of a stone coffer containing what was accepted to be the bones and ashes of the Buddha himself. The king of Siam, as the only remaining Buddhist monarch, was invited to receive the relics, provided he was willing to share them with Buddhists in Burma and Ceylon. Naturally this was a great honour, and to commemorate the occasion it was decided to erect a monument at Bangkok's highest point, the mount near Wat Saket.[72] Apart from this welcome event, there were signs that the government would have much more money to spend than it had had formerly. In 1898 state revenue had increased greatly to more than 34 million *baht*, and after taking into account an increased expenditure, the surplus for 1898 was still a healthy 4.5 million *baht*.[73]

Administrative reform affected most government departments. Apart from the changes mentioned above, there was an improvement in the police service and in post and telegraph services. An important aspect of the reform movement was the implementation of the 1896 Law of Provincial Courts, which reorganized the workings of the entire judiciary at the provincial level.[74] A committee of senior men had been appointed to direct the implementation of the provincial law reform, and in the late 1890s most of the country's legal processes were gradually brought under direct Bangkok supervision.[75]

With so many features of Siamese administration under review, it should not come as a surprise that in 1900 Čhulālongkǫn reassessed Siam's military forces and decided that a larger share of the budget ought to be spent on Siam's defence. The king feared the imperialistic aims of Britain and France, aptly illustrated by the manner in which they took advantage of China's weakness to gain "concessions".[76] The king was inspired by his young son Prince Čhiraprawat, who had successfully completed a course at a Danish military academy and who was rapidly promoted to be Siam's army commander-in-chief.[77] By 1901 Čhiraprawat, Damrong, and the king had agreed to move in the direction of developing a large army based on universal conscription. It was decided to begin conscription in Nakhon Ratchasima and Ratburi, provinces where the government was conducting an experiment relating to the abolition of corvée. In these two provinces, notwithstanding the local nobles' opposition, a flat poll tax was levied upon all eligible men and personal service had officially been abolished. If the government were reasonably successful in collecting the universal poll tax, the plan was then to proceed with universal conscription, whereby the government would supply and pay the serving conscripts.[78] When the king decided to go ahead with the formation of a conscripted army to defend Siam against foreign aggressors, he had chiefly the French in mind, with whom protracted negotiations were in train for the settlement of various matters arising from the agreement of 1893. However, before these negotiations were concluded, domestic crises broke out which placed a completely different perspective upon the question of Siam's military power.

## The 1902 Uprisings

Early in 1902 a growing excitement swept through many villages and towns in north-eastern Siam. A cataclysmic disaster was expected in the middle of the fourth lunar month (March–April), to be followed by evil times. Messages were circulated in which people were exhorted to take magical precautions. A holy man who claimed to be the intermediary for the god Indra would lead the faithful during the predicted troubles. He promised great wealth to all those who would follow his instructions.[79] Other documents of a similar kind were passed around,[80] but because of their mystical and vague character they did not unduly alarm the authorities.

However, in March a certain Ǫng Man claimed to be the awaited prophet and, followed by a band of armed men, began a march upon Ubon Ratchathani, the seat of government of his region. On the way, the party met a local garrison and put it to flight, killing two officials and capturing the governor of Khemmarat. The king's commissioner at Ubon, Čhulālongkǫn's brother *kromakhun* Sanphasit, telegraphed the army post at Nakhon Ratchasima, and reinforcements were sent. Meanwhile, more people joined Ǫng Man's band, and by the time he had won another skirmish, there were several thousand rebels. Sanphasit set up artillery at a strategic point, and when Ǫng Man walked into the ambush more than three hundred rebels were killed and four hundred captured. The leaders escaped into French-held territory, where they continued organizing resistance.[81] These events were viewed with some concern in Bangkok. They occurred close to the demilitarized zone between Siam and French Indo-China, and if the Siamese had not been able to demonstrate their ability to quell the uprising, it would have detrimentally affected the Siamese-French negotiations on a new treaty. Almost at the same time there were reports of rebellion in the Malay provinces, but these proved to be of no great concern for the central government.[82]

Much more important was the "Shan Rebellion", which broke out in late July of that year. It began when a large police force failed to apprehend and arrest a band of Shan robbers and abandoned their weapons and ammunition.[83] Many Shans joined the outlaws, and more than a hundred men attacked *mū'ang* Phrae, sent the Siamese troops fleeing, and seized the town. Looting took place, and government property was seized. The Shans obtained the co-operation of some local leaders in arresting and killing Siamese government officials who had attempted to hide. The idea of routing all Siamese caught their imagination. In a few days a large group of rebels marched up to Lampang, the town halfway between Phrae and Chiang Mai, while another moved in a southern direction as a defence against possible Siamese reinforcements. At Lampang, however, local police and hastily armed farmers, under the command of the Danish adviser H.M. Jensen, made a stand. On 3 August they drove off the Shans, killing the rebel leader. Soon afterwards, on 14 August, the rebellion was totally crushed by large numbers of locally mustered troops and subsequently by a royal army of some two thousand men sent up under the command of *čhaophrayā* Surasak.

Altogether the Shan rebellion had lasted less than three weeks. Notwithstanding Bangkok's successful suppression of the civil disturbances, the events created apprehension among many administrators. Most of the Bangkok standing army was used in the occupation of the north in the aftermath of the rebellion, and it was clear that Siam's military resources would be insufficient to handle a larger-scale emergency. As a result of the 1902 uprisings, the conscription experiment was extended to the north and north-east, and the Siamese tightened their control over the northern states, especially over Phrae, which was henceforth administered like an "inner province".

The disturbances in the north-east may also have served to hasten protracted negotiations with France regarding a "definitive" border settlement. In October 1902 a document was signed in which Siam agreed to allow France rights over the trans-Mekong part of the old kingdom of Luang Prabang as well as a portion of land along the border with Cambodia. In return the French would retreat from Chanthaburi, they would no longer insist on a demilitarized zone along the Mekong, and they would limit the classes of people who would be able to claim French legal protection.[84] The October agreement met with opposition in France and was never ratified. New negotiations were begun, and a treaty that was still more favourable to France was drawn up and signed in February 1904. Even that proved insufficient to satiate the colonialists' appetite for expansion.

The Shan rebellions may also have served to spur on the central government to proceed with the long-planned railway to Chiang Mai.[85] In each of the following years several million *baht* were set aside for its construction. In January 1908 the king opened the first half of the line reaching Phit-sanulok.[86]

## Rice and Irrigation

For as long as people could remember, the price of rice had remained remarkably stable, especially when compared with sugar, pepper, cotton, and other commodities.[87] A growing farming populace, abundant land, an ever-increasing system of canals, roads and railways, combined with an efficient class of traders, middlemen, millers, and merchants, provided the circumstances under which jungle was cleared and marshland was transformed into rice-producing land. Though the yield varied from year to year, there was a steady increase in the amount sold on the international market. The annual growth rate of rice exports in the half-century between 1860 and 1910 was approximately 5.2 per cent.[88] In the first decade of the twentieth century, rice exports formed some 80 per cent of the total value of the nation's export; teak accounted for another 10 per cent, while all other products made up the remainder.[89] Meanwhile, however, the grand plans for opening up new tracts in the Chao Phraya delta, undertaken by the Siam Land, Canals and Irrigation Company during the 1890s, were proving less successful than originally hoped. On the Rangsit project, for example, newly dug canals had been silting up, and by the turn of the century less than 40 per cent of the entire area opened up by the project had been cultivated.[90] In line with Čhulālongkǫn's general policy of obtaining the services of foreign technical experts, a Dutchman, J. Homan van der Heide, was persuaded in 1902 to become adviser to the Ministry of Agriculture. He and a team of Dutch engineers compiled a comprehensive report, proposing the construction of a large dam across the Chao Phraya River near Chainat, as well as a network of irrigation canals and a great number of additional water-control measures. The government decided that in principle future hydraulic works had to be constructed in such a manner that they would fit in with the proposed overall scheme. However, the adoption of the whole plan would involve a massive capital investment, estimated to be 47 million *baht* over a period of twelve years, a cost comparable to that of the current railway-building programme. A newly appointed British Financial Adviser to the government flatly rejected the scheme:

> Before we can think of a great Irrigation scheme we must provide funds for the strategic Railways which are essential if the outlying Provinces are to be properly governed. Those Railways must be constructed out of borrowed capital and I am altogether averse to borrowing money for Irrigation at present in addition to money for Railway Construction. Such a course would be rash in the extreme.[91]

At that time the king and his ministers were adjusting themselves to the idea of borrowing money for the railway, rather than financing it from government revenue. In addition, it had just been decided to base Siam's currency upon the gold standard, and the ensuing revaluation had caused some financial problems.[92] Van der Heide's proposal therefore came at an awkward moment. He proceeded to develop several less expensive alternative plans and fought hard to have them adopted. In 1906 and in 1908 the whole question was reviewed, but the scheme failed to pass the council of ministers, who could not see how to raise the money. In 1909 all plans for large-scale irrigation works were abandoned and van der Heide resigned.

The restraining and conservative advice of financial advisers played a role in the rejection of an imaginative plan,[93] the adoption of which would have benefited millions of Siamese.[94] Yet it seems wrong to assign the full responsibility to such advisers. The council of ministers and the king were not convinced of the merits of the scheme. If Čhulālongkǫn had shown enthusiasm for the irrigation plans and had wished their implementation, special loans could have been raised, especially when the 1905 and 1907 loans in Europe were oversubscribed and it had been proved that Siam was able to raise foreign capital for its development.[95] Siam's reform measures during this period showed but little imagination. One of the reforms was the 1905 extension to the provinces of the limitations on gambling.[96] To make up for the accompanying loss in government revenue, a heavier land tax was established.[97] This was also the year during which the general conscription edict was proclaimed, formally abolishing the remnants of the corvée system.

## The Monarchy

At the beginning of the twentieth century King Čhulālongkǫn held sway over Siam as no Siamese monarch had done before. Most of the key executive positions were occupied by the king's younger brothers and sons. All policy decisions had first to gain the king's approval before they could be implemented, and he could at any time overrule existing legislation and introduce new ideas. At the same time the king controlled a large proportion of Siam's revenue, an amount estimated to have been as large as one-sixth of the nation's annual income.[98] During his long reign, the royal family attained considerable financial security. The king invested money, especially for the benefit of the higher-ranking princes and princesses.[99]

Although the king's power was unparalleled in Siamese history, this did not diminish his popularity. Čhulālongkǫn was revered by large sections of the populace. In general he was considered an enlightened monarch, a king who, like his father, had the nation's welfare at heart and who was guided by high personal standards. There was no sign of public opposition to the king's spending, even when it concerned projects such as the creation of the Dusit pleasure grounds, which cost many millions of *baht*, and through which large tracts of productive rice-fields were converted into a park.[100] To begrudge the king his lavish lifestyle would have been felt tantamount to denigrating the nation's wealth and prosperity. The country was stable, many people were earning more than before, and this was seen to be directly linked to the fact that the country had a virtuous king. His display of wealth was a symbol of Siam's well-being. The king was aware of this general feeling and rejoiced in it.[101]

Some Siamese intellectuals, especially those who had studied abroad or who otherwise had first-hand experience of foreign attitudes, occasionally had ambivalent feelings towards the monarchy. On the one hand, most prosperous, leading countries did not allow a monarch to have such a measure of influence; in this respect, Siam appeared to have an outmoded form of government. On the other hand, the king was widely acclaimed as an able monarch who managed the country in an admirable fashion. The most intellectuals such as Thienwan could do was hint at the possibility of other forms of government.[102] Clearly, the initiative for a system of shared responsibilities should have come from the king himself, because Čhulālongkǭn was quite knowledgeable about various systems of government. In fact, however, he decided to strengthen rather than weaken his own position. He relied upon the argument that the Siamese were not ready for a constitution and that a long period of education was yet needed before any fundamental changes could be contemplated. Meanwhile, he actively fostered the idea that the king occupied the position of "father of the nation".

Publicly the king was enjoying both great power and a wide popularity, yet in his private life all was not well in the years between 1904 and 1907. In the first place it had become clear that the young man who had in 1895 been elevated to the position of crown prince was not altogether living up to his father's expectations. When Prince Wachirāwut returned in 1904 from England, where he had completed his education, he did not conduct himself fully in the manner expected of the heir to the throne. He shunned court life and did little to make himself liked in the royal family; he limited his personal contacts largely to a circle of intimate friends who shared his artistic tastes.[103] If at this stage the king had felt free to choose a different crown prince from among the *čhaofā* princes, he would probably have selected Čhakraphong, who was lively, intelligent, and gregarious and who displayed an easy charm.[104] In 1906 this favourite prince finally returned to Siam, having successfully completed his military education in Russia. Soon, however, gossip would have it that Čhakraphong had secretly married a Russian woman who was being kept in hiding at Singapore. When the fact emerged that the Russian bride really existed, Čhulālongkǭn was very angry with his son, whom he regarded as second in the line of succession.[105] During the remaining years of his life, Čhulālongkǭn refused to meet the foreign woman. These family troubles regarding the succession were further compounded by the king's ill health. The king suffered from diabetes and chronic interstitial nephritis,[106] and his doctor suggested a sojourn in a different climate. This took the shape of a tour in Europe, Čhulālongkǭn's second one, which lasted almost eight months, from March to November 1907.

When it became known that the king was preparing for a long voyage, all urgent state business was quickly settled. It was during this period that the French plenipotentiary, Colonel F. Bernard, contacted the king and asked him to discuss the final settlement of border problems between Siam and French Indo-China. A joint committee had been preparing reports on these since the treaty of 1904. A few days later an agreement was reached. France would cede a small strip of land north of the village of Dan Sai, near the Laotian border, and also return the strip of coastal land near the town of Trat. In addition, France would relinquish judicial rights over French protégés while retaining full jurisdiction over French nationals. In return for these concessions, Siam ceded the provinces of Battambang and Siemreap.[107] The extraordinary haste with which the 1907 treaty was drawn up and the ease with which Siam had made great land concessions took everybody, including the French consul, by surprise.[108] The French were delighted to receive Battambang and Siemreap in return for two small strips of land and some legal concessions.[109] Bernard had taken advantage of the king's illness and his wish to clear his agenda and achieved a great diplomatic success. For Siam it was a disadvantageous step, closely watched by Britain. Soon after the king's return from Europe, the British emulated the French and offered to relinquish some of the British consul's extraordinary legal rights in return for Siam's abandoning all claims on Kedah, Perlis, Kelantan, and Trengganu, as well as the adjacent islands.[110]

During Čhulālongkǫn's second European tour, Crown Prince Wachirāwut was appointed regent. However, just as during the voyage of 1897, Čhulālongkǫn did not really delegate his authority; all policy decisions had to be submitted to him telegraphically for approval.[111] The king's return in November 1907 was the occasion of festivities on an unprecedented scale. The parkway that led from the river to the Dusit palace was decorated with the help of some fifteen thousand soldiers, and half a dozen beautifully embellished "gates of honour" were erected for this occasion. There were speeches, blessings from a chapter of Buddhist monks, processions, a general illumination, fireworks, a military parade, and large-scale parties.[112]

The negotiations for the new treaty between Siam and Britain lasted through most of 1908. Britain obtained Siam's withdrawal from the above-mentioned Malay states, a Siamese promise not to cede or lease any territory south of Ratburi (a clause inspired by fears of the creation of a Kra canal), and the rights to build a railway through the remaining Siamese part of the Malay Peninsula.

The latter clause was prompted by intense international rivalry between the three largest European countries for a share in Siam's imports. After 1904, the French had partly succeeded in overcoming the Siamese government's reluctance to develop closer contacts. They had gained an advisory position in the sanitary department and had opened a bank in Bangkok. The Germans controlled the railway department and thus were able to secure many contracts for their compatriots. Moreover, German shipping was competing seriously with that of the British. Britain still had most advisers in Siamese government service. In 1908 there were altogether 110 Englishmen employed by the Siamese. They dominated the Siamese departments of survey, mining, police, education, justice, and customs. In that same year there were forty-five Germans, mostly railway engineers; forty-two Danes, dominating the naval section; thirteen Italians, mainly in public works; eight Dutchmen, in irrigation; seven Frenchmen, who were judges and civil engineers; and three Americans, one of whom was the nation's General Adviser.[113] The Siamese-British treaty, which was ratified in 1909, effectively split up the railway department into a northern and central section still under German control, and a southern one supervised by the British.

Apart from the painful concessions to the British, in 1908 there were also financial difficulties. During 1906 and 1907 the Ministry of Finance was headed by *phrayā* Suriyā, who abandoned his predecessor's cautious policies and pressed for a series of rapid revaluations of the *baht*. While in November 1905 one pound sterling was worth 16 *baht*, in December 1906 it was worth only 13 *baht*.[114] This massive revaluation caused export trade problems, and the ministry was forced to sell a major portion of its sterling reserves in order to support the *baht*.[115] The king asked his General Adviser, Edward Strobel, to suggest what action should be taken. Strobel replied that a devaluation at that moment would severely undermine trust in the currency and that the government ought to assert its intention to maintain the going rate. In 1906 there existed an alternative course of action — to reduce the silver content of the *baht*, a measure that had been taken in the Philippines and in the Straits Settlements that year. However, *phrayā* Suriyā rejected that alternative because he feared a general loss of faith in the *baht*, which would have become a mere token coin.[116] *Phrayā* Suriyā resigned early in 1908, and the king appointed his son Prince Čhanthaburĭ as the new Minister of Finance. The run on the *baht* continued during that year, and the ministry again had to spend large sums to support the currency.[117]

On the suggestion of the Financial Adviser, it was decided to reaffirm the government's position. In November 1908 this was demonstrated by the promulgation of the Gold Standard Act, whereby the value of the *baht* was determined in centi-grammes of gold.[118] Bolstered by a buoyant economy, Siam weathered the storm.[119]

While it is true that Siam would have been better served by a drastic reduction in the *baht*'s silver content, the ministry's reluctance to countenance this is quite understandable. The government had repeatedly been forced to withdraw or amend measures intended to change and streamline the na-tion's currency. At the very beginning of the reign, as has been mentioned above, the copper and tin coins were devalued as a result of widespread panic. Paper notes had been introduced in September 1902, and initially they had had a good reception, especially in the business world. However, in 1903 forged twenty-*baht* and hundred-*baht* notes began to appear, and for many months the public refused to put trust in the paper money.[120] At the same time the government had attempted to simplify the system of small coins by introducing a decimal system, creating the *satang*, one-hundredth of a *baht*. That attempt failed, mainly because people did not take to the newfangled coins. The old system — with copper half-*at* and two-*at* pieces, and silver eight-*at* and sixteen-*at* coins remained the basic one, with four of the sixteen-*at* coins equivalent to one *baht*. In con-junction with the gold-standard edict of 1908 came a renewed drive to introduce *satangs*, and great amounts of one-, five-, ten-, twenty-five-, and fifty-*satang* pieces were put into cir-culation.[121]

In June 1908 the king had the satisfaction of promulgating Siam's new Criminal Code, the culmination of many years' experimenting and drafting, an undertaking likened by the king himself to that just over a century earlier during the First Reign.[122] It was, however, essentially the result of a quite dif-ferent type of inquiry. The legal revision under Rama I was intended to provide the most authoritative version of the ancient Siamese code; the 1908 laws were an attempt to provide a modern set of rules which could be applied in Siam's changed circumstances. The legal code was drawn up with the assistance of foreign experts, and its promulgation was loudly heralded so as to convince foreigners of Siam's ability to rule itself and thus pave the way for future action against the iniquitous extraterritorial rights of foreign consuls and their charges.

In November 1908, a year after his return from Europe, there was yet another massive ceremony in honour of the king, this time the celebration of his fortieth anniversary as ruler. Apart from a military parade and a festive ball, the occasion was marked by the unveiling of an equestrian statue of Čhulālongkǫn, paid for by voluntary public subscription.[123] On this occasion the king gave a speech in which he looked back on his long reign. As the major feature of his times he chose the political transformation of the whole region, where all independent states except Siam had been changed into colonies. It was the king's duty to retain his country's independence, and in order to do so he had opened up Siam to Western innovation, while at the same time not denigrating time-honoured Siamese customs. He felt that by doing so he had followed the right path.[124] This speech seems to have set the pattern for general assessments of Čhulālongkǫn's reign: that of a wise man steering deftly, playing off one nation against another, sacrificing the outer regions in order to preserve the nation's independence.[125]

In this chapter it has been seen that Siam's independence was primarily decided by the 1896 agreement between France and Britain: Siam's fate was discussed and determined without Siamese being present to influence the course of events. The crisis that arose in 1893 could have been prevented, and Siam appears to have lost considerable tracts of land by being obdurate and by attempting to fight the French, giving them a chance to press for more than they had originally envisaged taking. After the 1893 debacle the king proceeded with laudable caution, but it has been shown that the final settlement of 1907 was unnecessarily generous towards his adversaries and that this probably detrimentally influenced the ensuing negotiations with Britain. While there can be no doubt about King Čhulālongkǫn's good intentions, and while he must be regarded as a leader who kept Siam's interests at heart, in face of the available evidence it is difficult to maintain the image of a skilled diplomat.

During the year 1908 there were many other events that needed the king's personal attention. A new section of railway had to be opened; journeys had to be made in the southern provinces and to the northern part of the central plain. Every major problem that required cabinet action eventually reached the king. Probably 1908 was an exceptionally heavy year for Čhulālongkǫn because there had been a backlog of work upon his return from Europe, and the financial difficulties that arose must have involved many meetings and reports. Even during an ordinary year the tasks of an absolute monarch were immense. With the country rapidly adopting innovations, with an ever-expanding economy and increasingly complex problems, the duties probably became too onerous for a single person to carry.

A government decree in March 1909, which changed the triannual poll tax on Chinese into a yearly capitation tax in line with that applying to the Siamese, caused unexpected troubles.[126] The 1909 collection proceeded without undue stress, but when in 1910 it became clear that government officials would proceed to tax the Chinese again just like other members of society, there was widespread dissatisfaction in the minority group. The Chinese secret societies decided to force the Siamese government to desist. In order to bring this about, a general strike was organized for 1 June 1910. At first it seemed that the strike was a resounding success; all Chinese business came to a halt for several days, and food became expensive. However, Siamese police, reinforced by troops, managed to make their presence felt; when disorders occurred arrests were made. After three days some shops reopened, and by the fifth the strike was over, leaving the government in a stronger position than before. Once again it had been demonstrated that the Siamese could handle a local emergency. At the same time, the strike served as a warning to the Siamese, for it showed that many Chinese were not integrated into Siamese society and that they formed a potential danger to the nation. The strike also strengthened anti-Chinese feelings among certain groups, especially among some of the Western-educated nationalistic Siamese. Čhulālongkǫn himself did not agree with anti-Chinese views; his policy was always to guide them into becoming an integral part of the nation.[127]

The king's health remained poor. His second European trip had not succeeded in restoring him to full vigour. He therefore began to prepare for his retirement and made known his intention to step down in 1913, when he would be sixty, in favour of the crown prince. He built himself an estate where he hope to spend his later years. He imagined that he could still be of use to the country by breeding leghorn chickens and helping improve the country's poultry stock.[128] Before these plans could be put into action, however, the king fell sick, his kidneys failed and on 23 October 1910 he died of uraemia, at the age of fifty-seven. He had been Siam's king for almost forty-two years.

The Fifth Reign thus encompasses a very long period. It may be assessed from various angles. The Siam of 1910 was a very different country from that of 1868. The population in the central region had greatly increased, and the country's wealth was much augmented. Siam had lost nominal control over large tracts of land, but the remaining region had been more effectively brought under Bangkok's suzerainty. While in 1868 the Bunnāk family held the chief executive positions, in 1910 it was royalty who filled the most important posts.

General assessments of this reign often stress the positive and laudable aspects, and in retrospect the Fifth Reign has assumed the glow of a golden age. In this and the preceding chapter several of the well-intended, helpful, and progressive governmental reforms have been described. Čhulālongkǫn attempted to be a "father of the people", a wise and autocratic figure who acted in the interest of the community at large. As he grew older and more experienced, he played that role very well. He became an able administrator and an admirable head of state. During the years he won the respect and loyalty of a great number of people. Yet these and other rare personal qualities ought not to blind us to the fact that the concentration of power and responsibility in a single individual carried severe risks. Even a king as experienced as

Čhulālongkǫn could make hasty decisions, and it is likely that his unsatisfactory health contributed to his making some ill-considered resolutions of far-reaching consequences. Finally, the king's refusal to create a system in which he would have to delegate a measure of his authority put an extraordinarily heavy burden upon his young successor, to whom he handed all the power and prestige it had taken him a lifetime to accumulate.

## Notes

1. N.A. Battye, "The Military, Government and Society in Siam, 1868-1910", p. 251.
2. Ibid.
3. Details of the survey can be found in W.S. Bristowe, *Louis and the King of Siam*, pp. 50-54. Bristowe drew his information from J. McCarthy, *Surveying and Exploring in Siam* (London: John Murray, 1900), which I have not been able to obtain.
4. Battye, "The Military", pp. 251-59, and *Prawatkitčhakānthahān samai Krungratanakōsin*, p. 50.
5. A. Pavie, *Eine friedliche Eroberung, Indochina 1888*, p. 98.
6. Pensri Duke, *Les relations entre la France et la Thailande (Siam) au XIXe siècle*, p. 121. *Luang* Vichitr Vadakarn, *Thailand's Case*, pp. 31-32, gives the details of the 1886 convention but omits to mention that this treaty was never ratified and that neither country ever felt bound to adhere to its provisions.
7. For details, see Muang Htin Aung, "Three Unpublished Papers by Harvey, Introduced, Explained and Commented Upon", *Journal of the Burma Research Society* 63, pt 1 (1975): 1-52.
8. D.K. Wyatt (*The Politics of Reform in Thailand*, p. 89) dates the document 8 January 1887. However, other sources (Battye, "The Military", p. 263; Manich Jumsai, *Prince Prisdang's Files on His Diplomatic Activities in Europe*, p. 257) place it two years earlier, while Chula Chakrabongse (*Lords of Life*, p. 261) says 1886. Thus far I have not been able to examine Wyatt's source, but since it is the same as that mentioned by Battye, and from internal evidence relating to the question of the succession, it appears that 1885 is the accurate date.
9. This summary is based upon the sources mentioned in footnote 8 above.
10. Chula Chakrabongse, *Lords of Life*, p. 261.
11. Wyatt, *The Politics of Reform*, p. 90.
12. Chula Chakrabongse, *Lords of Life*, pp. 262-63.
13. See Satow's letter to the Earl of Granville, dated 26 June 1885, reprinted in Chatthip Nartsupha and Suthy Prasartset, eds., *The Political Economy of Siam, 1851-1910*, p. 322.
14. For details of the ceremony, see *Somdetphraboromōrotsāthirāt Sayāmmakutrātchakumān*, pp. 31-33.
15. The report has been translated and printed in Chatthip Nartsupha and Suthy Prasartset, eds., *Socio-economic Institutions and Cultural Change in Siam, 1851-1910*, pp. 12-16, and reprinted in their *Political Economy*, pp. 249-55.

16. F.W. Riggs, *Thailand, The Modernization of a Bureaucratic Polity*, p. 117.
17. Rong Syamananda, *A History of Thailand*, p.130.
18. *Prawatkitčhakānthahān*, pp. 51-53.
19. For details, see Battye "The Military", p. 276.
20. Prachoom Chomchai, *Chulalongkorn the Great*, pp. 66-72.
21. Battye, "The Military", pp. 291-96.
22. Sir Henry Norman, *The Peoples and Politics of the Far East* (New York, 1895), as quoted by Wyatt, *The Politics of Reform*, p. 95.
23. D.B. Johnston, "Opening a Frontier: the Expansion of Rice Cultivation in Central Thailand in the 1890's", *Contributions to Asian Studies* 9 (1976): 32-33.
24. Wyatt, *The Politics of Reform*, pp. 96-97.
25. Battye, "The Military", pp. 306-8.
26. Wyatt, *The Politics of Reform*, p. 97.
27. Dispatch by the French consul, 2 July 1887, quoted in Pensri Duke, *Les relations*, pp. 122-23.
28. The idea was part and parcel of the French proposals to Britain in 1889. See Jeshurun Chandran, *The Contest for Siam 1889-1902: A Study in Diplomatic Rivalry*, pp. 5-6.
29. See Pavie's diary, 27 June 1887, *Eine friedliche Eroberung*, pp. 136-37.
30. For these and other conflicts, see Pensri Duke, *Les relations*, pp. 133-39.
31. Battye, "The Military", p. 297.
32. Chandran, *The Contest for Siam*, p. 33.
33. C. Hirshfield, "The Struggle for the Mekong Banks, 1892-1896", *Journal of Southeast Asian History* 9 no. 1 (1968): 25-31; Chandran, *The Contest for Siam*, pp. 52-54.
34. In Pensri Duke, *Les relations*, p. 152, the letter is quoted: ". . . les événements ont pris une tournure qui nous permet les plus grandes exigences et fait envisager la question par les étrangers même, comme devant avoir pour solution fatale l'établissement de notre Protectorat sur le Siam tout entier."
35. For details, see Battye, "The Military", pp. 338-55.
36. For details, see O.J.A. Collet, *Étude politique et économique sur le Siam moderne*, pp. 26-30; and especially Chaen Patčhusānon and Sawat Čhanthanī, ed., *Kǫraniphiphāt rawāng Thai kap Farangset lae Kānrop thī Pāknām Čhaophrayā samai* r.s. 112.
37. L. Weiler, *Anfang der Eisenbahn in Thailand*, p. 49; Battye, "The Military", pp. 350-52; and B.A. Smith, "The King of Siam", *Contemporary Review* 71 (January-June 1897): 891.
38. Chandran, *The Contest for Siam*, pp. 82-3.
39. At the same time, in these days of turbulence the king considered his children's welfare, and secretly deposited a large sum of money in England on their behalf (W.F. Vella, *Chaiyo!: King Vajiravudh and the Development of Thai Nationalism*, p. 12).
40. Battye, "The Military", pp. 372-74.
41. The full text of the proposal can be found in *Prawatkitčhakānthahān*, pp. 58-63.
42. Weiler, *Anfang der Eisenbahn*, p. 68; the author's diary entry for 28 March 1894 mentions that the king could hardly move about without help and that there were grave doubts whether he would ever recover. See also J. MacGregor, *Through the Buffer State: A Record of Recent Travels through Borneo, Siam and Cambodia*, p. 56.

43.  Chandran, *The Contest for Siam*, p. 125; Weiler, *Anfang der Eisenbahn*, p.79. MacGregor, *Through the Buffer State*, p. 56.
44.  For details see C. de Saint-Hubert, "Rolin-Jaequemyns (Chao Phya Aphay Raja) and the Belgian Legal Advisers in Siam at the Turn of the Century", *JSS* 53, pt 2 (1965): 181-90, Kanlayā Chunnuan, comp., *Chaophrayā Aphairātchāsayāmanukūnkit (Khutsatāp Rolin Yakhmin).*
45.  Prince Wachirunhit died on 4 January 1895 and not in 1894 as Battye would have us believe ("The Military", p. 377 and p. 394). Rong Syamananda also wrongly took Wachirāwut's appointment to have occurred in 1894 (*A History of Thailand*, p. 146); in fact it was 17 January 1895. See *Somdetphraboromōrotsathirāt Sayāmmakutrātchakumān*, p. 88; *Rātchasakunwong*, p. 76 and pp. 78-79; and Smith, "The King of Siam", p. 887. His formal installation took place on 8 March.
46.  Chandran, *The Contest for Siam*, p. 71.
47.  Ibid., p. 116.
48.  Letter from McCarthy to Surasak, 6 April 1895, quoted by Johnston, "Opening a Frontier", p. 35.
49.  Ibid.
50.  The standard source on Siam's economic change, Ingram's *Economic Change in Thailand, 1850–1970*, depicts a consistent and steady growth in Siam's rice exports between 1880 and 1895, and accelerated growth between 1895 and 1905 (see pp. 38-39). The table and graph tend to obscure the fact that there seems to be an abrupt change in 1900. According to Dilock's figures, Siam's rice exports for the years between 1896 and 1900 were 7.6, 9.8, 8.6, 7.1, and 6.8 million piculs respectively, while in the subsequent five years the figures were 11.1, 13.0, 9.5, 13.5, and 13.2 million piculs (Dilock, *Die Landwirtschaft in Siam: Ein Beitrag zur Wirtschaftsgeschichte des Königreichs Siam*, p. 191.
51.  Weiler, *Anfang der Eisenbahn*, p. 85.
52.  Ibid., pp. 76-77.
53.  As reported in the *Siam Free Press* quoted by Weiler, *Anfang der Eisenbahn*, p. 102.
54.  The school was officially opened in early 1897 and turned out to be Siam's most successful venture in this type of education. For details, see Wyatt, *The Politics of Reform*, pp. 183-84.
55.  Mitchell-Innes, with four years' experience in Egypt, took up his duties in Siam in June 1896. See I. Brown, "British Financial Advisers in Siam in the Reign of King Chulalongkorn", *Modern Asian Studies* 12, no. 2 (1978): 196.
56.  The full text of Mitchell-Innes's report is reproduced in Chatthip Nartsupha and Suthy Prasartset, *Policical Economy of Siam*, pp. 269-90; further details can be found in Piyachat Pitawan, *Kānyokloekrabopphrai nai Ratchasamai Phrabātsomdetphra' Chulachōmklāo rawāng Ph. S. 2411-2453*.
57.  Saint-Hubert, "Rolin-Jaequemyns", p. 185.
58.  Weiler, *Anfang der Eisenbahn*, p. 93.
59.  *Revue Politique et Parliamentaire* 12 (April, May, June 1897): 658-59.
60.  Thamsook Numnonda, "The Anglo-Siamese Secret Convention of 1897", *JSS* 53, pt 1 (1965): 45-60.
61.  *Annual Register*, 1897, p. 366.
62.  See *phrabātsomdetphra'* Chunlachōmklāo *chaoyūhua Phrarātchahatlēkhā mu'a Sadetphrarātchadamnoen Praphāt Yurōp Ph. S. 2440.*
63.  Chula Chakrabongse, *Lords of Life*, p. 254.
64.  *Annual Register*, 1897, p. 366; Pensri Duke, *Les relations*, p. 228.
65.  Weiler, *Anfang der Eisenbahn*, p. 105-6.

66. For details, see Tej Bunnag, *The Provincial Administration of Siam, 1892-1915: the Ministry of the Interior Under Prince Damrong Rajanubhab*, pp. 116-17; J.A. Ramsay, "The Development of a Bureaucratic Policy: The Case of Northern Siam", pp. 164-77.

67. L.J. Curtis, *The Laos of North Siam*, p. 128.

68. For details, see Ramsay "Development of a Bureaucratic Policy", pp. 178-83.

69. A letter from Phātsakǫrawong to the king's secretary, dated 21 June 1898, translated and quoted by Wyatt in *The Politics of Reform*, pp. 213-14.

70. For a detailed discussion, see Wyatt, *The Politics of Reform*, pp. 217-29. See also Wuthichai Mūnsin, *Kānpatirūpkānsu'ksā nai Ratchakān thī 5*, pp. 121-23.

71. A background to Prince Wachirayān's early life can be found in C.J. Reynolds, trans. and ed., *Autobiography: The Life of Prince-Patriarch Vajirañāna of Siam, 1860-1921*.

72. *Annual Register*, 1898, p. 341; Prachoom Chomchai, *Chulalongkorn the Great*, p. 102.

73. Figures taken from the *Annual Register*, 1898, pp. 341-42, and converted to *baht*, taking one pound sterling to be worth 17.40 *baht* for the year 1898 (Ingram, *Economic Change*, p. 337).

74. D.M. Engel, *Law and Kingship in Thailand During the Reign of King Chulalongkorn*, p. 70.

75. Ibid., p. 72.

76. Battye, "The Military", pp. 401-2.

77. Also known as *kromamu'n* Chaisi (*Rātchasakunwong*, p. 75). King Čhulālongkǫn, imitating an aspect of the British system of peerage, had established the custom of attaching the name of a Siamese province to his sons' titles when he elevated them to *krom* rank.

78. Battye, "The Military", pp. 403-11.

79. Chatthip Nartsupha and Suthy Prasartset, *Political Economy of Siam*, pp. 361-65.

80. J.B. Murdoch, "The 1901-1902 'Holy Man's' Rebellion", *JSS* 62, pt 1 (1974): 57; and Yoneo Ishii, "A Note on Buddhistic Millenarian Revolts in Northeastern Siam", *Journal of Southeast Asian Studies* 6, no. 2 (1975): 121-22.

81. Murdoch, " 'Holy Man's' Rebellion", p. 60.

82. Battye, "The Military", p. 415.

83. Accounts of the Shan rebellions can be found in Ramsay, "Development of a Bureaucratic Policy", pp. 217-34; *Prāp Ngiew Ton Thī 1, PP*, pt 75; Battye, "The Military", pp. 416-18, and Bristowe, *Louis and the King of Siam*, pp. 107-21.

84. Pensri Duke, *Les relations*, pp. 239-51; M.F. Goldman, "Franco-British Rivalry over Siam, 1896-1904", *Journal of Southeast Asian Studies* 3, no. 2 (1972): 218.

85. Apparently the decision was taken in late 1902 (see I. Brown, "British Financial Advisers", p. 218).

86. *Volkswirtschaftliche Chronik für das Jahr 1908*, p. 125.

87. N.G. Owen, "The Rice Industry of Mainland Southeast Asia, 1950-1914", *JSS* 59, pt 2 (1971): 91.

88. Ibid., p. 95.

89. See, for example the export figures in Dilock, *Die Landwirtschaft*, p. 191; and *Volkswirtschaftliche Chronik für das Jahr 1906*, pp. 212-13.

90. L.E. Small, "Historical Development of the Greater Chao Phya Water Control Project: An Economic Perspective", *JSS* 61, pt 1 (1973): 2. The problems of the Rangsit scheme are well illustrated by the report dated 4 May 1906,

published in Chatthip Nartsupha and Suthy Prasartset, *Political Economy of Siam*, pp. 333-37.

91. Memorandum by the Financial Adviser, 1903, quoted by J.C. Ingram in *Economic Change in Thailand 1850–1970*, p. 197.

92. For details, see I. Brown, "Siam and the Gold Standard, 1902–1908", *Journal of Southeast Asian Studies* 10, no. 2 (1979): 385-86.

93. Ingram, *Economic Change*, p. 198; Brown, "British Financial Advisers", p. 202.

94. Van der Heide's plans seem to have much in common with the Greater Chao Phraya River Irrigation Project, which was adopted after the Second World War.

95. Brown, "British Financial Advisers", pp. 205-6.

96. Prachoom Chomchai, *Chulalongkorn the Great*, p. 71.

97. Brown, "Siam and the Gold Standard", p. 388.

98. See C.J. Rivett-Carnac's memorandum on the expenditure of the royal household, Chatthip Nartsupha and Suthy Prasartset, *Political Economy of Siam*, pp. 291-94.

99. A full picture of the royal finances is not available. Glimpses of the king's investments are given in Chatthip Nartsupha and Suthy Prasartset, *Political Economy of Siam*, pp. 305-7 and M. Collis, *Wayfoong, the Hongkong and Shanghai Banking Corporation*, p. 91. In 1889 the king deposited 960,000 Mexican dollars with the Hongkong and Shanghai Bank in the understanding that this money would not be withdrawn for many years. See Paul Sithi-Amnuai, *Finance and Banking in Thailand: A Study of the Commercial System, 1888–1963*, p. 139. The king's personal wealth was such that he could buy Queen Saowaphā a necklace valued at £100,000 (M. Smith, *A Physician at the Court of Siam*, p. 111). The king bought tracts of land for his dependents. Queen Saowaphā's income was estimated to have been between £80,000 and £90,000 a year (ibid., p. 109), and Prince Čhakraphong apparently received £20,000 annually from "his Bangkok estate" (Chula Chakrabongse, *The Twain Have Met, or An Eastern Prince Came West*, p. 64).

100. Weiler, *Anfang der Eisenbahn*, p. 122.

101. Sir Josiah Crosby, *Siam: the Crossroads*, p. 32.

102. K. Rosenberg, *Nation und Fortschritt*, pp. 103-4.

103. Vella, *Chaiyo!*, p. 8.

104. Smith, *Physician at the Court*, p. 115.

105. Chula Chakrabongse, *The Twain Have Met*, p. 62.

106. M. Smith, "The Families of the Kings of Siam of the House of Chakri", *Annals of Eugenics* 12 (1943–45): 153. See also *Physician at the Court*, pp. 93-94.

107. Further details in Pensri Duke, *Les relations*, p. 266 and pp. 294-95.

108. Weiler, *Anfang der Eisenbahn*, pp. 149-50.

109. *L'Asie Française*, 1910, p. 418.

110. Weiler expressed his dismay in his diary entry for 7 April 1907 and rather prophetically wrote that it would not surprise him after this to hear soon of the cession of some of the Malay sultanates to England (*Anfang der Eisenbahn*, pp. 149-50).

111. Vella, *Chaiyo!*, p. 3.

112. For details, see Weiler, *Anfang der Eisenbahn*, pp. 156-58.

113. Ibid., pp. 169-70.

114. Brown, "Siam and the Gold Standard", pp. 389-91.

115. Ibid., p. 392.

116. Ibid., p. 395.
117. Ibid.; see also Weiler, *Anfang der Eisenbahn*, p. 163.
118. According to Brown ("Siam and the Gold Standard", p. 396), the gold *baht* was set at 56.25 centigrammes of gold; Weiler (*Anfang der Eisenbahn*, p. 169) mentions 55.8 centigrammes.
119. For the general state of the Siamese economy between 1908 and 1911, see *L'Asie Française*, 1911, p. 463.
120. Prachoom Chomchai, *Chulalongkorn the Great*, p. 83.
121. Weiler, *Anfang der Eisenbahn*, p. 175.
122. Engel, *Law and Kingship*, p. 75.
123. Vella, *Chaiyo!*, p. 141; Chula Chakrabongse, *Lords of Life*, p. 266.
124. Weiler, *Anfang der Eisenbahn*, pp. 167-68.
125. See, for example, Rong Syamananda, *A History of Thailand*, p. 144.
126. G.W. Skinner, *Chinese Society in Thailand*, pp. 162-63.
127. Ibid., pp. 161-62.
128. Chula Chakrabongse, *Lords of Life,* pp. 260-61, and *The Twain Have Met*, p. 64.

# 9

# The Sixth Reign: The King, Nationalism, and the Alienation of the Bureaucracy

Not long after Čhulālongkǫn's death the cabinet met and confirmed Wachirāwut's succession to the throne. For more than fifteen years this prince had been officially recognized as Čhulālongkǫn's heir. At the time of his investiture as crown prince in 1895, he was in England, where the ceremony took place at the Siamese legation. After some years of private tuition the Siamese crown prince qualified for admission to the Royal Military College at Sandhurst, where he followed several courses. Then for a while he went to Oxford University, but came down without a degree and returned to army training. Altogether, Wachirāwut spent just over nine years abroad from the age of twelve to twenty-one. He was one of many who had been sent abroad by Čhulālongkǫn.

Although Wachirāwut had become intimately acquainted with European culture and had acquired much military knowledge, the two other *čhaofā* princes who were almost his contemporaries had distinguished themselves more. *Čhaofā* Boriphat (Prince Nakhǫn Sawan) had gone to school in Germany and graduated from the military academy at Kassel.

*Čhaofā* Čhakraphong had been sent to Saint Petersburg, where he studied successfully at the military academy, gaining great distinction.[1] Upon their return to Siam, these three princes had been given high ranks and titles: Wachirāwut was given the post of Inspector-General of the Army, Boriphat became Chief of the General Staff, and Čhakraphong, several years younger than Boriphat, his deputy chief.

On 11 November 1910, Wachirāwut was solemnly crowned King of Siam and became officially known as *phrabāt-somdetphra'* Mongkutklāo *čhaoyūhua*. He reaffirmed Čhulālongkǭn's policy by proclaiming Queen Saowaphā's male children to be in line for the succession, at least until he himself had sons. At the age of twenty-nine Wachirāwut was still unmarried, an oddity at the Siamese court. Therefore his younger full brother Čhakraphong automatically became heir-apparent, but it was understood that the prince's children by his Russian wife would not be eligible for the throne.[2] During the previous reign, the monarchy of Siam had gained immensely in both power and popularity. Wachirāwut, who never had been very popular and who was rather shy and retiring, and particularly deficient in social graces and unable to make many people feel at ease,[3] was likely to disappoint many people.

## The Wild Tiger Corps

During the first months it was not immediately clear how Wachirāwut would adjust to the role of monarch and what changes he would bring about. The first months were taken up with routine matters of state, and the king was also preoccupied with the preparations for his father's cremation, which took place in March 1911. Not long after this ritual farewell to the previous king, in May, Wachirāwut made his first major original contribution to the Siamese political scene when he created the Wild Tiger Corps (*su'a pā*),[4] an organization of Thai citizens of good character, united to further the nation's cause. The king and some of his intimate friends who had worked out the idea had drawn up a list of prominent Siamese who might wish to join — men who would gladly sacrifice the entrance fee of fifty *baht*[5] and regularly take part in exercises designed to strengthen the body and to inculcate a team spirit and pride in the nation. Each member had to swear allegiance to the king and purchase a spectacular uniform in black and yellow with a wide-rimmed black felt hat.[6] The king spent much time on the development of the Wild Tiger movement, setting up a para-military organization, devising badges, signs, mottoes, drills, marching orders, and war games. Three months later he founded the Tiger Cub (*lūk su'a*) branch, almost a replica of the Wild Tiger organization: "Boys in their adolescent years should also receive both physical and mental training of the sort given Wild Tigers so that when they become older they will know their proper duties as Thai men. Everyone should do what is useful to the nation and country, to the land of one's birth."[7]

W.F. Vella, who studied Wachirāwut's Wild Tigers and Tiger Cubs, has stressed that Wachirāwut's movement ought not to be confused with Baden-Powell's Boy Scout organization. "Baden-Powell's organisation came too late to have been responsible for the Wild Tiger idea, and the Wild Tiger concept was certainly not a literal or even a close approximation of the entirely youth-directed, essentially non-military concept of the Boy Scouts."[8] This view, which assigns an extraordinary high degree of orginality to the Siamese king, can be challenged. Baden-Powell's organization dated from January 1908, and it had become a widely publicised, internationally known movement. The non-military nature of the Boy Scout movement had not yet been fully determined. The original idea had evolved from the para-military duties given to young boys in India and South Africa; Baden-Powell, the Chief Scout, was until May 1910 a lieutenant-general in active service. In Baden-Powell's original draft of *Scouting for Boys* he had written, "So long as war remains possible, it is the duty of every man and boy to prepare himself to defend his country in case it should unfortunately become necessary." While this sentence did not appear in the printed version,[9] in 1910 it was still not certain how far there was a military side to the Scout movement.[10] The king, who regularly kept himself informed of British news, must have been aware of Baden-Powell's Scouts, who frequently came before the public eye during the early years. Boy Scouts were on duty at the funeral of Edward VII in 1910 and during the coronation of George V in 1911.

However, King Wachirāwut incorporated many of his own ideas in the Siamese Wild Tiger movement and deliberately stressed its military aspect. The king saw it as an opportunity to create a bond between himself and loyal citizens; a volunteer corps willing to make sacrifices for the king and the nation. With a keen sense of the theatrical, the king proclaimed that the concept of staunch and loyal Wild Tigers was one that went back to olden times when the ordinary citizen was trained for warfare and belonged to detachments used to guard Siam's frontiers.

All people of good name and standing could volunteer for the corps, but rank and position did not automatically lead to an appointment to officer rank in the Wild Tigers. The king conferred status in this new organization according to his personal inclination. Among the first 122 appointments in May 1911 there were nineteen officers, of whom only one was a prince of *krom* rank, the others being various nobles with titles below *čhaophrayā*. The lower ranks, however, boasted one *čhaophrayā* and nine *krom* princes.[11] *Čhaofā* Boriphat and *čhaofā* Čhakraphong, probably the country's highest-qualified military leaders, were only given the status of subalterns in the Wild Tigers.[12] The king made the Wild Tigers his personal concern, and in Bangkok he commanded the Wild Tigers' first company, an élite group often on parade when the king performed public duties.

While at first the Wild Tigers were drawn from the king's personal entourage and it is likely that many joined in order to gain favour with Wachirāwut, the idea rapidly caught on. A genuine widespread enthusiasm for the Wild Tigers and the Tiger Cubs arose. In September 1911, just over five months after the inauguration of the scheme, Weiler described them:

> This is a troop of volunteers in black uniform, drilled in a more or less military fashion, but without weapons. The British Scouts are apparently the paradigm for the Tiger Corps. In the whole country, at the most far-away places, units of this corps are being set up. One would hardly recognize the quiet and phlegmatic Siamese. The oldest people, of high and low status,

join the corps and take part in the exercises, which have been changed to the evening hours from 4 to 6 p.m. in order not to clash with the ordinary duties of life. The king himself prefers to appear in the Wild Tiger uniform. The princes must, of course, follow his example.[13]

What originally had been a local idea directly emanating from the king and his entourage had rapidly evolved into a nationwide movement. Old and young joined in the regular drill and were proud to swear their new oath of allegiance to the king, the nation, and religion. Both Mongkut and Čhulālongkǭn had gained strength through creating links between the monarch and the common people, but Waichirāwut established a truly nationalistic organization which made people feel that they were part of the Siamese nation and bonded to the monarch himself.

## The Second Coronation

The king was an accomplished actor and playwright. Between 1903 and 1910, while living at Saranrom Palace, he had written at least four full-length plays and had directed and written texts for his own troupe of classical dancers. He shocked some people, notably his mother, Queen Saowaphā, by taking roles and appearing on stage.[14] Acting, it was widely felt, was a fine and honourable art form, but not one a *čhaofā* prince ought to practise. Wachirāwut, however, was not to be discouraged and persisted in taking part in dramatics, even after he became king. This taste for drama can be seen in the king's preoccupation with the Wild Tigers, for whom he designed uniforms, flags, and banners, as well as manoeuvres and war games. It was the same gift for drama which inspired him to order the preparation of a second coronation, one that would surpass all previous coronations and impress the international aristocratic world.

A second, more formal inauguration had been held by Wachirāwut's great-great-grandfather, the founder of the dynasty. The coronation of November and December 1911 was such a traditional event, beginning with the consecration of *abhisēka* water in seven shrines, lighting of the victory candle and rituals guided by court Brahmans and Buddhist monks. It included the ritual on the octagonal throne, a royal procession and vows of allegiance by palace servants. It was concluded on 4 December by a royal procession around the city and a formal boat procession.[5] This elaborate Siamese ritual lasted almost four weeks and was followed by another six days of festivities devised by the king. Apparently inspired by European royal accession ceremonies, which Wachirāwut had attended when still a crown prince, invitations to attend the coronation festivities from 5 to 10 December were personally delivered by Prince Čhakraphong to heads of state and royalty around the world. As a result, a large number of countries sent high-ranking representatives. There was Prince Hiroyasu Fushimi from Japan, a Mr Hamilton deputising for the President of the United States, and a virtual constellation of princes, princesses, a grand-duke, a count, a duke, a baron, and a marquis, together with their suites, from a dozen European countries.[16] No expense was spared to receive the foreign guests in European style; some 750 tons of furniture was bought from abroad "to provide the guests with nothing but the best".[17] During the European part of the coronation festivities the king himself provided ample entertainment. There was a formal reception, a presentation of new colours to the army, a grand troop review, an excursion to the royal palace at Bang Pa In and to Ayutthaya, and a great muster of the Wild Tiger Corps. One evening there was a theatrical and classicial dance performance; on another, fireworks.

The ceremony was hailed as a great success. The foreign guests had been well entertained. At the same time, it had been extremely costly. In fact, the king had grossly overspent. While some 450,000 *baht* had been allocated in the budget for this purpose, more than 4½ million was used, or nearly 8 per cent of the national budget of just over 60 million.[18] The lavish spending may have served to impress many people with the new monarch's grandeur, but if the king had entertained the thought that it would make him universally liked, he was suddenly made aware of considerable opposition, which became apparent when in late February 1912 a plot to overthrow his regime was discovered.

## The Abortive Plot

Since the beginning of February 1912 the king had been on manoeuvres at a camp near Ban Pong with his Bangkok Wild Tigers, who, reinforced by the Ratburi contingent, contended with the Nakhon Chaisi Wild Tigers. The king's party were declared victors, even though at one stage the king had been "taken prisoner" by the opposing group.[19] While Wachirāwut was thus engaged, Prince Čhakraphong was informed by an army officer that many people were preparing to stage a coup d'état. Čhakraphong acted fast, and 106 conspirators and sympathizers were arrested.

There was indeed a group of young army officers discussing ways and means of overthrowing King Wachirāwut. They had only recently begun sounding out officials in various government departments and had met with quite a positive response. Although the arrests took place on 1 March 1912,[20] it was not until 4 March that the *Bangkok Times* noted that there had been an attempted "mutiny". After the press had revealed the plot, Prince Čhakraphong issued a formal statement disclosing that there were three separate parties who had been formally in contact for less than two months. One was led by a medical officer and consisted of Siamese of Chinese descent, another was led by an officer in the Judge Advocate's Department, and the third by an officer on the General Staff. The first group advocated changing Siam into a republic, with Prince Rātburi as Siam's first President. The second group wanted a constitutional monarchy under *čhaofā* Boriphat, while the third also aimed at a constitutional monarchy, but under *čhaofā* Čhakraphong. At the moment when the plot was revealed, the first group seemed to have been strongest, and in order not to dissipate the initial thrust, all parties had agreed to pursue the first group's aims.[21]

When the plot was discovered, the conspirators had just reached the stage of deciding upon practical measures. The best moment, it was thought, would be the April ceremony of the swearing of the oath of allegiance, when all important people would be at the Temple of the Emerald Buddha. All key members of government would be arrested. However, long before any member of the government was in danger, the whole affair was over. Prince Čhakraphong, who was in charge when the plot was uncovered, decided to dismiss it as one of minor importance, just a group of misguided young men who did not really understand grave matters of state. However, it must have been noticed that the movement appeared to have rapidly gained support among young and progressive government officials and that there was a keen interest in the idea of a change of government.

There were both external and domestic factors that stimulated such a movement. Abroad, there was the example of Turkey, where in 1908 young army officers, the so-called "Young Turks", had overthrown Sultan Abdul Hamid II's regime. Even more important was Sun Yat-sen's revolutionary republican movement in China, which in 1911 had led to the formal secession of various southern provinces and, on 1 January 1912, to the proclamation of the Republic of China. At home, Siamese intellectuals had for some time been considering alternatives to the absolute monarchy. King Čhulālongkǫn had once favoured a more broadly based form of government, but with increasing age and experience had decided to retain personal control of all policy decisions. The accession of a new king, the first to have received his education in a country with a system of parliamentary democracy, was in itself sufficient reason to reopen the debate on Siam's form of government.

All these factors played a role, but the chief impetus for a revolutionary movement in Siam probably was a widespread disenchantment with the new king. The fact that of the three "branches" in the movement, two subscribed to a constitutional monarchy headed by a king other than Wachirāwut, testifies to antipathy against the man who succeeded Čhulālongkǫn. Some young military officers held a grudge against Wachirāwut because in 1909, when he was still crown prince, he had insisted upon a humiliating public flogging of some military men, among them two junior officers, who had been involved in a fight with several of his personal pages.[22] Others feared that Wachirāwut lacked statesmanship, for he had bestowed rank and honour on personal friends who were widely held to be unworthy of such an increase in status.[23]

Among the military in particular there was resentment of the king's manifest preoccupation with the quasi-military Wild Tigers. In addition to these factors was the king's strangely undignified personal behaviour. Instead of settling down to a traditional royal family life, he remained a bachelor and, together with his bachelor friends, engaged in artistic pursuits, including appearing on the stage in a wide variety of roles. At the time of the plot it was also quite clear that the king had a strong and wilful character and that he was not willing to seriously consider any fundamental change in the system of government.

The king realized that the plot was partly directed against his person and his way of governing, and when he returned from some two months of the Wild Tiger exercises, he did not wear his customary Wild Tiger uniform.[24] In a move apparently designed to protect himself and to counter criticism against his personal lifestyle, the king issued a decree stating that all palaces and palace grounds were the king's private domain and that access to the king was restricted. In an oblique reference to the plot he stated:

> . . . the number of government servants is increasing, but their awareness of the fact that they are servants of the king has been decreasing. For one thing, they have the false idea that their places of work are public property and from this they proceed to take the king's palaces also to be public places. This, however, is a completely wrong idea. The king still has absolute power and it is he who shall allow or forbid people to enter royal palaces. He may even refuse all access.[25]

Just over two months after the plot had been discovered, a special court passed sentence. Three men were sentenced to death and twenty to life imprisonment, thirty-two received gaol sentences of twenty years, seven fifteen years, and thirty twelve years. The king commuted the sentences, however, so that only the first two categories (involving twenty-three men) were put in gaol.[26] The king regarded the episode as a serious warning, and for the time being gave heed to his personal security. The daily Wild Tiger exercises were reduced to once a week. With respect to placing himself under the guidance of a parliament, Wachirāwut considered the time inopportune. He continued to be the final authority in all matters of state, and liberalized only to the extent of frequently following the recommendations brought forward by the chief advisory committees.

## The King's Style of Government

It has often been remarked how Wachirāwut's style of government differed from that of his father, and that a main feature of his reign was that he decided no longer to rely upon his many brothers and uncles who had been placed in executive positions.[27] While there are grounds for this general statement, what is usually overlooked is that the shift away from the princes occurred only gradually. At the beginning of 1912 the cabinet of twelve still included seven princes of *krom* rank, and several of the remaining posts were also occupied by men who had been appointed by Chulālongkǫn.[28] Notable among the latter was the head of the Ministry of Municipal Government, *čhaophrayā* Yomarāt, under whose unassuming but at the same time firm leadership various schemes to improve Bangkok were completed. New roads were built, a tramway was set up, and a large number of wooden bridges were replaced with reinforced concrete ones. During 1912, 1913, and much of 1914 Bangkok was provided for the first time with a regular water-supply system. Yomarāt has been described as Bangkok's most popular personality.[29]

Wachirāwut continued to use Chulālongkǫn's team, and there was no sudden break in the daily routine of government; nor was there widespread anxiety about tenure of office. It was only when a vacancy occurred through death, retirement, or resignation that the king would fill a senior post with one of his coterie. Much of the running of daily affairs was therefore in the hands of experienced men. To them and their staff Siam owed many progressive steps, such as the development of a national plan for the education of the whole populace, the setting up of clinics in Bangkok and some of the provinces, where free vaccination was given against smallpox, and the continuing investment in the building of railways. During 1913 the northern line reached as far north as Ban Pak Tha in the province of Lampang, and the construction of a southern line was proceeding satisfactorily.[30]

In 1913 the Siamese government managed to control and overcome a serious financial crisis which began when the Chino-Siam Bank collapsed. This bank was under Chinese management and had been engaged in financing much of the rice trade with Hongkong. It had apparently also been providing funds for the Chinese revolutionary forces, and the 1913 split among these revolutionaries and Sun Yat-sen's flight to Japan were undoubtedly related to the bank's failure. The government-sponsored Siam Commercial Bank came to the rescue, but when various malpractices were uncovered, not only did the Chino-Siam suspend payments, but also there was a run on the Siam Commercial Bank itself. The government had to intervene and spent large amounts of money to restore a measure of confidence in the Siamese banking system.[31]

The king's personal style of government can be seen most clearly in his decree of 22 March 1913 regarding the use of surnames. Up until 1913 most Siamese were known only by their personal name, often a monosyllabic "nickname", but mostly among the prosperous, a pleasant-sounding polysyllabic "real name". Both "nickname" and "real name" referred to the individual, and it was impossible to decide from these names who was related to whom. Family names had long been in use, but generally only by the *phūdī*, people of rank and refinement. There were signs that the number of people adopting surnames had been steadily increasing, but they remained limited to those who had distinguished themselves somehow and who had achieved a measure of wealth and influence. In the 1913 decree, it was stipulated that all heads of families were given six months from 1 July in which to choose and register their surnames. The king, who was of no mean literary talent, devised lists of well-sounding names from which the general populace might choose.[32]

The measure was obviously inspired by European practices. Like many other measures which were directed "from above", the decree did not immediately achieve the intended results. The idea of choosing a surname seemed unnecessary to many farmers who would have no need to distinguish themselves in this manner and who felt that, even if a surname were chosen, it would soon be forgotten. Throughout the reign the central government, prompted by the king, made various efforts to implement the decree, but the universal adoption of surnames was not achieved during the Sixth Reign.[33]

In his public review of the year 1914, the king was happy to mention many projects which were helping Siam along the path of progress, such as the completion of the capital's water-supply system, the opening of a government electrical power station, the continuation of work on the northern and southern railway lines, and educational and legal reform. Meanwhile, war had broken out in Europe and, though it seemed unlikely directly to affect Siam, this stimulated Wachirāwut's interest in Siam's defence. In a move reminiscent of his establishing of the Wild Tigers, he devised a scheme by which the general public would be given a chance to be personally involved in the nation's defence. He founded the Royal Navy League of Siam,[34]

> the first object of which is to invite the Siamese people to subscribe for King and country money for acquiring a warship for the Navy to serve as a protection for King, country and religion. I am happy to associate myself with and to take a deep interest in the success of this laudable object, which is an evidence that the Siamese people are determined, like their ancestors, to show their affection and loyalty to their Sovereign, to preserve the independence of the nation, and to uphold our Holy Religion, which has been the precious emblem and moral support of the Siamese race for many generations.[35]

The king's rhetoric knew no bounds when it came to an attempt to rouse the nation into participating in this scheme. He set his heart upon acquiring a light cruiser and in the following years he instigated many campaigns to raise funds. State officials throughout the country were ordered to co-operate. Writing under a pseudonym, Wachirāwut praised the cruiser-fund; he wrote several plays intended to increase people's enthusiasm, caused street signs to be erected exhorting people to contribute, and placed large advertisements in the papers. Helped by large donations from the king himself, the fund got off to a grand start, but soon the rate of contributions slowed down, and it was not until 1920 that it was used to help buy a Siamese warship.[36]

By 1915 Wachirāwut's style of government was clearly established. This is apparent, for example, from an examination of the composition of the cabinet. In 1912 this consisted almost wholly of King Čhulālongkǭn's appointees; three years and several shuffles in senior positions later, half the cabinet consisted of new faces. Notable was Prince Damrong's absence. He resigned in 1915 from his post as Minister of the Interior, officially because of ill health, but in actuality because of friction between himself and the king. Wachirāwut was proving to be a difficult leader, a man who discouraged personal contact with many of his chief administrators, preferring to keep them at a distance. His shyness caused him to avoid speaking directly to people, and he often resorted to sending written instructions. On some of the rare occasions when he had to receive European guests, this awkwardness was "distressing to witness".[37]

Commentators have attributed Waichirāwut's strained relationship with most members of the royal family to the fact that he had spent many of his "impressionable and formative years" abroad.[38] These commentators politely omit to mention that Wachirāwut returned from England with a decided preference for male company and demonstrated this by refusing to marry, not even agreeing to a *pro forma* marriage. In 1915 he was already thirty-four years old and still a confirmed bachelor who relaxed only within a circle of intimate friends who readily accepted him. There can be little doubt that many of Wachirāwut's personal communication problems stemmed from his awareness of criticism of his homosexual leaning.

The resulting stress and isolation must at least partly account for his attempts to reach out to "his nation", to appeal directly to the general public, to lead and direct the Siamese people. Wachirāwut's nationalism, his writings under the name Asvabāhu in the *Siam Observer*, his fervent speeches to the military, and his setting up of a warship fund were all measures that seemed to have been devised largely by the king and his circle of personal friends.

One of Wachirāwut's more popular programmes was his

encouragement of sports and athletics, at first within the Wild Tiger movement, but later also in schools and among the military. From 1913 onward the king went once a year to Suan Kulāp School to view athletic events and to award prizes, and other schools began to emulate these sports days. By late 1915 sporting events had gained some passionate support, as witnessed by an indignant European resident:

> On 4 November, going for an evening drive, at the great Pramaen Place in front of the Maha Chakri Palace I came across a disorderly mass of maybe a hundred sailors and marines who were pushing their way through the streets, lifting their caps and hurling them in the air, cheering, followed by half a dozen cars packed with navy officers. I had to make my way to the side of the road and stop my car in order to let the mass of people pass. At first I could not imagine what could have caused this unusual occurrence. The next day I read in the court news that the king had personally handed over a gold cup to the navy cadets as a sports trophy, and that this had been carried in triumph by the champions to the navy school.[39]

This gold cup was Siam's first football trophy. The king had himself organized that year's competiton, which proved a resounding success.[40]

In yet another respect Wachirāwut influenced the lives of a great number of Siamese, namely in proclaiming public holidays. To the traditional holidays such as Siamese New Year in April, and holidays related to the yearly cycle in the nation's Buddhist monasteries, the king added various nationalistic festivals which were widely celebrated at least in Bangkok. The twenty-third of October was Čhulālongkǭn Day, commemorating that king's death. The eleventh of November was Wachirāwut's accession day, sufficient reason for three days of festivities. The first of January was the King's Birthday, and that needed another three days' holiday, complete with a great illumination of the city.[41] On 11 November 1916,[42] the sixth anniversary of his accession, the king announced a simplified, Western-style system for referring to the various kings in the Čhakri dynasty. The well-established names, such as Phraphuthayǭtfā, Phraphuthaloetlā, and Phranangklāo, were still to be recognized, but the whole dynasty was given the name of

Rāmāthibodī. Wachirāwut himself therefore became King Rāmāthibodī VI. It was permitted to abbreviate the dynastic name to Rama. The practice never became popular among the Siamese, but it was readily adopted by Western authors, often troubled by the elaborate Siamese terminology.

Another Wachirāwut brainwave was his scheme for radical reform of the Siamese system of writing, proclaimed in April 1917. Instead of the existing method of placing vowels in various positions around consonants, they were to be written immediately after the appropriate consonant. In addition, Wachirāwut suggested that spaces be left between words. The Wachirāwut system would have simplified Siamese for those learning for the first time to read and write it, notably Europeans and young children.[43] The abolition of cumbersome obsolete practices is in the interest of future generations, and this scheme would have been a most suitable one for a benevolent absolute monarch to execute. However, Wachirāwut did not possess the full control over all administrators which was needed to implement the idea. He relied upon the hope that the reform would trigger off a broadly based supporting movement, just as the Wild Tigers and football competition had done. In this case, however, he soon discovered that the general public did not clamour for spelling reforms, and his system was soon forgotten.

## Siam and the World War

From a Siamese perspective, the First World War initially was simply a European conflict, and in August 1914 the Siamese government readily proclaimed its strict neutrality. Although the British constituted the leading foreign community in Bangkok, the Germans had established themselves as a major force. At the beginning of the war the Germans had by far the largest shipping interests, carrying much of Siam's imports and exports.[44] Throughout the first years of the war, neutrality was maintained.

The suggestion to consider joining the allied forces came from Prince Thēwawong, Siam's experienced Minister of Foreign Affairs, only in February 1917 after the United

States had broken off diplomatic relations with Germany. Should the United States declare war, Siam might consider doing the same, Prince Thēwawong thought. However, he advised caution and preferred Siam to sever relations rather than declare war. After April, when America did enter the war, Siam's position was further debated between Prince Čhakraphong and Prince Thēwawong; Čhakraphong advocated war, and Thēwawong argued for continued neutrality. Realizing that the Germans were now likely to be defeated and that Siam might derive benefits from joining the winning side, the king decided on a declaration of war, but waited for an opportune moment to declare this. Throughout June and most of July preparations were made, which included plans to seize German ships and arrest and intern German nationals. The king himself, under the pseudonym Rāmāchitti, published in a newspaper a series of articles setting out the moral reasons for entering the war.[45]

The official declaration of war, on 22 July, therefore came as no surprise. This should not imply however that it was a popular decision. The Germans had a good record in Siam. Unlike Britain and France, Germany had never threatened Siamese-held territory. Some leading princes, notably Boriphat and Dilok, had completed their education in Germany. While most ordinary Siamese had little interest in the war, among Siamese intellectuals there was debate on whether or not a declaration of war was the right decision. Prince Boriphat was clearly distressed at the move to abandon neutrality, and he showed his disapproval by being absent from cabinet meetings in May and June 1917. There even developed a plot on the part of some army and naval officers to overthrow Wachirāwiut and replace him with Prince Boriphat, a plot that was suppressed and long kept secret.[46]

The arrest and internment of the new "enemies" went smoothly, and with one stroke Siam cancelled the existing, unequal treaties with Germany and Austria.

There are several reasons why Siam declared war. By entering the war, the French and Russian diplomats had assured the Siamese, Siam would be greatly helped in future treaty revisions and the restrictions on customs duties might be lifted.[47] Apart from these legal benefits, there was for King

Wachirāwut a great attraction in that he could forge a closer link between himself and his people by personally leading them on a course towards battle. Before announcing that Siam had entered the war, he underwent the appropriate state ceremony for a king about to lead an army, and, dressed in the appropriate scarlet robe, he then made the public declaration.[48] In September 1917 it was decided that an extraordinary force should be dispatched, consisting of some thirteen hundred men, representing the most modern developments in the Siamese army. Siam decided to send a flying squadron and an ambulance corps with drivers and mechanics. A call for volunteers was issued. The response was quite gratifying, and between October 1917 and June 1918, under the personal supervision of the king, the troops were selected, equipped, and trained in such a manner that they would do honour to Siam.[49]

The Siamese expeditionary force arrived in France in late July 1918, when the final offensive under Marshal Foch was already under way, and when the Siamese motorized unit finally arrived at the front in September they were just in time to witness the end of the hostilities, because a newly formed German government began negotiating for peace on October 4. In November King Wachirāwut could proudly announce that Siam belonged to the victorious nations, and he led thousands in chanting prayers of thanksgiving. The general public was reminded of Siam's victory in the king's birthday speech, by the festive reception given to the returning aviation corps (who had not had a chance to go into action), and by the fact that Siamese troops marched in three gala victory parades, in Paris, London, and Brussels. In September 1919 the victorious ambulance corps finally returned and received a true hero's welcome, with three days of banquets, decorations, fireworks, and nationalistic speeches. Though Siam had not lost any troops in battle, there had been nineteen casualties. These dead soldiers were solemnly honoured by having their ashes placed in a large monument.[50]

All the speeches and pathos could not, however, hide the fact that Siam had entered the war at a rather embarrassingly late stage, that its role had been largely ceremonial, and that the troops had gained no military experience. In addition, it soon became clear that Siam was not accepted as an equal partner in the post-war international negotiations. It had been hoped that the inequitable foreign treaties would rapidly be revoked. Only the United States, whose president had been an ardent advocate of the rights of smaller nations, was willing to draft a new treaty; but the negotiations with other nations did not proceed well. It was only near the end of the Sixth Reign, six years after the end of the world war, that, mainly through the able work of F.B. Sayre, treaties were renegotiated and Siam gained international autonomy. Sayre's success was not based upon Siam's participation in the war, and it would have been no more difficult to achieve had Siam remained neutral. To a considerable extent the "joining the cause of justice" was intended for home consumption. It was used by the king to enhance nationalistic feelings and to strengthen the ties between monarch and people.

## Dusit Thāni

While the Siamese expeditionary force was on its way to Marseilles in July 1918, the king began the construction of a miniature town in his private gardens behind the royal palace. "It contained houses, palaces, temples, roads, rivers and canals, trees and parks, fountains, waterfalls, and electric lights — an enchanted fairyland by more than one account."[51] The king and his circle of personal friends created there a world of their own, called Dusit Thāni, or "Dusit City". They devised their own system of government, under a *nakhonāphibān* or "town caretaker". On 7 November 1918 they drew up an elaborate town constitution with fifty-one provisions.[52] The town caretaker would govern for a period of one year only, and he would not be eligible to stand again until another person had served.[53] The miniature town was organized along modern lines, with a fire department, an electric company, a sewage department, and a health department. Dusit Thāni was an elaborate game, where courtiers could express themselves on matters of language and society, on government and modernization, stimulated by the setting of the miniature city. Dusit Thāni also provided tremendous fun. During 1919 there were frequent boat-races with miniature boats on the miniature river.[54] Before the end of 1918 Dusit Thānī had its own fortnightly paper,[55] the *Dusit Samit* (Dusit United), and before long it also boasted a daily.[56]

When Queen Saowaphā, the queen mother, died in October 1919, Wachirāwut decided to move to her palace. As he enjoyed his miniature town so much, he decided to transfer it to his new residence, and in December 1919 the ceremony of the placing of a founding "city pillar" took place.[57] In the miniature city, with his few hundred associates, Wachirāwut instituted an elaborate political game, he himself being the leader of one of the two parties formed.

Authors sympathetic to Wachirāwut have suggested that the ultimate purpose of Dusit Thānī was to provide a testing-ground for democratic experiments on the national level.[58] As Vella rightly points out, there is little or no evidence for this idea.[59] At first sight Dusit Thānī resembles the *Suan Khwā* (the Garden on the Right) during the reign of Rama II. The *Suan Khwā*, like Dusit Thānī was built for the king's pleasure; it was a place where the king and his artistic courtiers could write, recite, and act. Dusit Thānī, however, was not just a setting for plays; it was a utopian model world, where beauty and friendship flourished. In spite of all its constitutional rules and regulations, there was never any doubt that it was Wachirāwut's creation. At any time he could overrule decisions by the elected "town caretaker".

For an assessment of the role of Dusit Thānī, it is necessary to make a judgement regarding Wachirāwut's personality, his position in relation to senior administrators, and his relationship with various members of the royal family. Wachirāwut's strained relationship with many people of experience and rank led him gradually to withdraw from matters of administrative routine which would have brought him in contact with his critics.[60] By creating a friendly and harmonious Dusit Thānī, where he was appreciated and where he was the undisputed leader, Wachirāwut was able to fulfil the role of absolute monarch. The fact that it was a world of make-believe, a fairly secret and sheltered world, suited

Wachirāwut's thespian inclinations. Dusit Thānī complemented the king's personal interest in his ceremonial role. In the outside world, Wachirāwut continued to make speeches and design uniforms and insignia, but the number of his public appearances declined.

## Siam's Financial Crisis, 1919–23

As early as 1916, when the price of silver began to rise, the Financial Adviser warned that Siam's silver coins soon could become worth more than their face value and that the danger would arise of people melting down the coins and exporting them. He recommended debasing the *baht* by reducing its silver content,[61] a measure that had been adopted as early as 1906 in the Philippines and the Straits Settlements.[62] The Siamese government, in line with earlier decisions with respect to the *baht*, refused to act other than by moving to officially prohibit all export of silver.

As a result, in 1919 a serious financial crisis developed. In the first place the price of silver, which had been steadily rising since 1916, and which had long since pushed the actual value of silver coins above their face value, went much higher, and it became more and more profitable to smuggle silver out of Siam. The government decided to revalue the *baht*. Late in 1919 the exchange rate was gradually raised from 13 *baht* per pound sterling to 9.54 *baht*. Earlier in the year, an unprecedented increase in the price of rice had caused a shortage of currency, and the Siamese Treasury had printed massive amounts of banknotes.[63] By the end of the year it became also apparent that Siam's rice crop was failing. The king was forced to prohibit all export of rice, to take measures to prevent smuggling, and to intervene in the crisis and buy and distribute rice.[64]

The combination of factors proved very damaging to Siam's economy. In 1920/21 the value of export trade dropped to almost half that of the previous year, a direct result of the ban on rice export. At the same time the value of imports rose to an unprecedented level, much of the increase caused by the revaluation of the *baht*. The price of silver rose even higher, but the government could no longer follow its policy of increasing the value of the *baht* at a time when only a massive devaluation could have prevented a run on the currency. With the exchange rate not high enough to make smuggling of silver unprofitable, and too high for the international currency market, Siam's wealth was eroded on several sides.[65] Siam's administrators decided to weather the storm and hoped that the next crops would be abundant, that the price of silver would drop, and that the financial troubles would soon disappear.

The rice exports were resumed, and the price of silver finally dropped, but as time went on it became clear that the exchange rate of 9.54 *baht* per pound sterling was too high. Throughout 1920, 1921, and 1922 the Treasury had to shore up the *baht* by purchasing sterling. Finally, on 3 January 1923, the decision was taken to devalue the *baht* to the rate of 11 *baht* per pound sterling, and for the time being the financial troubles were over.

The financial crisis had cost the country much revenue, foreign loans had to be raised, imports became more expensive, and the revaluation costs were partially borne by the rice farmer. King Wachirāwut, in theory, had the power to change the nation's financial policies, and he could have decreed a lessening of the silver content of the *baht*, a measure that would have freed the Treasury to determine a realistic currency rate. There is no evidence that the king even considered such a step. He retreated more and more into his fantasy world, leaving government affairs to the administrators. Moreover, he tended to regard foreign advisers with suspicion and had reduced their numbers and influence,[66] so that he may not have given the Financial Adviser's warnings the consideration they deserved.

## The King and the Government

In the early 1920s it became more and more clear that the king wished to have little to do with administrative routine.[67] The leadership of the cabinet rested largely upon *čhaophrayā* Yomarāt, who in 1915 had been appointed to the Ministry of the Interior but who had retained the post and title of Minister of Local Government, which he had been given at the end of the Fifth Reign. A man with even longer experience in the cabinet was Prince Thēwawong, who was responsible for Siam's foreign affairs, and who in 1922 or early 1923 was given the power to supervise the Treasury as well.[68] Not long before his death he was given a special honour which, the king not being in good health and not often attending cabinet meetings, amounted to that of being appointed Prime Minister.

Prince Thēwawong's death in June 1923 came at a time when the country's finances were causing some alarm. In 1922 it had become necessary to increase Siam's external debt by borrowing two million pounds sterling at, for that time, the high interest rate of 7 per cent. The budget continued to show a deficit, and early in 1924 a committee consisting of the princes Damrong, Narit, and Phānurangsi was appointed to study the situation. During 1924 another massive loan of three million pounds at 6 per cent interest was floated. Early in 1925 Siam's economic position seemed weaker than ever. The cabinet met repeatedly to consider the situation. It demanded a report from the new Financial Adviser, Sir Edward Cook. The government was spending too much and was using up its international reserves. Cook pointed out that an excessive amount was spent on defence (23.3 per cent of the national budget) and on royal expenditure (10.7 per cent). As a matter of fact, even the official amount of royal expenditure did not cover all that was used by the king, several items of Wachirāwut's spending being placed under various other headings in the regular budget.[69]

The cabinet, fortified with these figures, decided to approach the king and ask him to curb his expenses as part of the measures to improve the country's finances. In July 1925 Wachirāwut flatly refused to accept their recommendation. He reminded cabinet that he was the head of government and that the budget committee was only advisory; he had no intention of handing over any of his powers and was not willing to show restraint regarding royal expenditure. Indeed, the king would soon need more funds than ever for the preparation of the Siamese Kingdom Exhibition. Apparently it did

not concern him that there was no money for public works.[70]
Clearly, an impasse between king and almost all senior administrators had been reached. A situation developed in
which at least part of the king's powers were likely to be stripped away. However, before long Wachirāwut died a natural
death, which provided an easy way out of the stalemate.

While the king had abandoned many of his responsibilities,
he was by no means an idle man. He maintained his direct
and indirect links with the general public. He was still the
leader of the Wild Tigers and the Tiger Cubs. The Tiger Cub
organization had gradually grown into a separate form of the
Boy Scout movement. Most schools of renown had their own
corps. Whilst the number of Tiger Cubs was just over 8,800
in 1917, by 1922 it had grown to almost 21,500 young par-
ticipants,[71] and in 1924/25 the total number was reported as
38,735.[72] At the annual army manoeuvres the king would invite delegations of Tiger Cubs to take part. Wachirāwut also
continued to promote competitive sports. In the 1920s
Bangkok boasted golf courses, tennis courts, and almost
monthly horse races alternately at the Sports Club and the
Turf Club; there were football, hockey, Rugby, and cricket
matches, though the latter two sports did not attract much attention.[73]

The king's most important pursuit, however, was that of
writing for the benefit and education of the Siamese people.
Unlike some of his predecessors, he rarely chose the medium
of the formal royal decree, but communicated by means of
short articles, generally written under a pseudonym, and
plays, usually written under his own name. Wachirāwut's
literary output was phenomenal. For the theatre alone he
wrote thirty-four original dramas and translated and adapted
a further twenty-six plays. Many of his plays were intended to
propagate his messages to his people. The hero on stage
would exhort the audience to love and respect the king, and
nation and their religion. Some plays were written specifically
to foster a cause: to be respectful to military virtues, to give
to the Navy League fund, to rally behind Siam's involvement
in the First World War, or to sponsor a Wild Tiger fund. The
king did not write solely for didactic purposes, however, and
many of his writings for the stage appear to have no other

aim but to thrill and entertain.[74] When the king was ill and doctors prescribed a long rest, he would spend most of his time writing. Thus during much of the time between July and October 1925 Wachirāwut translated into English the play he had written during another illness two years earlier, but died before he could finish it.[75]

On 11 November 1925 the king left his sickbed to attend some of the celebrations for the fifteenth anniversary of his coronation, but by the evening he felt so unwell that he took to his bed again. As part of the celebrations he had devised an event on a massive scale: a Siamese Kingdom Exhibition to be held in January 1926. For this purpose the king had presented the nation with a large piece of land which he named Lumbini, after the Indian pleasure garden where the Lord Buddha had been born. The exhibition was to present Siam to the world as never before. During the first week it was planned to organize an international Boy Scout jamboree. Hotel accommodation was expanded by the king's lending a palace to the Railway Department. Meanwhile the proffered grounds became the scene of frantic building activity between September and mid-November 1925, when a violent storm broke over Bangkok, destroying eight newly erected buildings in the exhibition grounds. At the same time the king had become seriously ill, and was operated on for an abdominal abscess. In the evening of 25 November he lost consciousness, dying early next morning. One of the first acts of the new government was to cancel the grand exhibition.[76]

## The Succession

At the beginning of the reign it had been publicly announced that if the king should die without male issue, the succession to the throne would pass presumptively through the line of the queen mother's other sons according to their respective ages. Prince Čhakraphong had therefore been automatically the heir to the throne, and since his elder brother Wachirāwut had often been ailing, notably in 1918, Prince Čhakraphong had been widely regarded as the nation's hope, and it had been expected that he would become a good and popular king. It had therefore come as a severe shock when Čhakraphong died on 13 June 1920, at the age of thirty-eight. One author has repeated the gossip that he was poisoned by an unseen hand.[77] However, there seems no grounds for this. Prince Čhakraphong had become ill with influenza while travelling with his family to Singapore; this had turned into the pneumonia from which he died in spite of the best medical care available, surrounded by family and friends.[78]

His brother's unexpected death, probably coupled with the realization that he himself would soon be forty, caused Wachirāwut to seriously consider the succession. His three remaining younger brothers, the princes Atsadāng, Čhuthāthut, and Prachāthipok, may have appeared unsuitable compared with the firm, strong, and able Čhakraphong, and this could have been the reason why Wachirāwut decided to create a family of his own. On 10 November 1920, on the eve of the festivities for the tenth anniversary of the king's reign, he announced his engagement to *phra' ongčhao* Wanlaphāthēwī. However, owing to "incompatibility of temperament", the betrothal was officially annulled some four months later.[79] In 1921 a new bride was found; she received the name of Laksamīlāwan and officially became the king's consort in August 1922. Meanwhile the king's desire for an heir caused him to set aside his earlier views regarding the benefits of monogamy and take as concubines two sisters, *phra'* Sučharit and *phra'* Intharasak. The younger sister, *phra'* Intharasak, reportedly became pregnant and was elevated to the rank of queen. However, this and other pregnancies ended in miscarriages, and in July 1923 the king was still without children when his younger brother Čhuthāthut died. In February 1925 yet another of the late Queen Saowaphā's sons died, and only Prince Prachāthipok remained in the first line of succession. During 1925 another consort, Suwathana, emerged. During the eighth month of her pregnancy she replaced Intharasak as queen in anticipation of the birth of an heir. On 24 November 1925 a daughter was born to the king, who was dangerously ill, and the baby was shown to him on the following day. A short time afterwards the king sank into the coma from which he did not wake.[80] Wachirāwut had left instructions that if the child was male Prachāthipok should be appointed as head of the council of regency.

## Assessment

The Sixth Reign had lasted fifteen years. Wachirāwut had been a controversial figure when he came to the throne; by the end of his reign it was almost universally accepted that he had not made a good king. Prince Damrong summed up the situation as follows: "The authority of the sovereign had fallen much in respect and confidence, the treasury was on the verge of bankruptcy, and the government was corrupted and the services more or less in confusion."[81]

It was not that Wachirāwut lacked intelligence or sensitivity. He undoubtedly was a very gifted man, an innovator in many respects. Nor could he be accused of unbridled selfishness; many of his projects were intended to educate and advance the Siamese people. He attempted, not without success, to instil in the masses a heightened awareness of Siam's great history and the strengths of its civilization. Wachirāwut demonstrated for the first time that the Siamese people could become aroused and enthusiastic about nationalistic ideals.

Yet King Wachirāwut lacked a dimension that would have enabled him to become a truly nationalistic leader: he had little personal charm, and he could not easily relate to other people. His social awkwardness was a constant embarrassment to himself and to many who came in contact with him. It caused him sometimes to be brusque and undiplomatic, and it made him retreat from much of the daily administrative routine through which an absolute monarch keeps in touch with reality. Increasingly the king slipped into a fantasy world, one of his own creation. With immense sums of money he bought the favour of all close to him, thus creating around his immediate presense an atmosphere of popularity and good cheer. His confrontation with the cabinet in July 1925 threatened to undermine the basis upon which his masquerade was built, and therefore he was compelled to reject the cabinet's suggestions forcefully. He died a rather pathetic figure, a man whose impersonation of a popular ruler had long ago ceased to impress his associates.

## Notes

1. N.A. Battye, "The Military Government and Society in Siam, 1868–1910", pp. 509-16.
2. L. Weiler, *Anfang der Eisenbahn in Thailand*, pp. 197-98.
3. Ibid., pp. 187 and 199.
4. The inauguration is described in *The Souvenir of the Siamese Kingdom Exhibition at Lumbini Park B.E. 2468*, pp. 149-50.
5. W.F. Vella, *Chaiyo!: King Vajiravudh and the Development of Thai Nationalism*, p. 36.
6. For posed photographs of Wild Tigers in full uniform, see *The Souvenir of the Siamese Kingdom Exhibition*, pp. 149, 185, and 237; and for a rare action picture of Wild Tigers on parade, see I. de Schaeck, *S.A.I. le grand-duc Boris de Russe aux fêtes du Siam pour le couronnement du roi*, opp. p. 120.
7. As cited by Vella, *Chaiyo!*, p. 42.
8. Ibid., p. 29.
9. E.E. Reynolds, *Baden-Powell: A Biography of Lord Baden-Powell of Gilwell*, pp. 157-58.
10. Ibid., p. 154.
11. Vella, *Chaiyo!*, pp. 36-37.
12. De Schaeck, *Fêtes du Siam*, p. 119.
13. Translated from Weiler, *Anfang der Eisenbahn*, p. 199.
14. Vella, *Chaiyo!*, pp. 7.
15. *Programme of the Coronation of His Majesty Vajiravudh, King of Siam.*
16. A list is given in *The Souvenir of the Siamese Kingdom Exhibition*, pp. 175-76.
17. Vella, *Chaiyo!*, p. 19.
18. Ibid., p. 25 ("nearly 8 per cent of the national budget"). On the size of the budget, see *L'Asie Française*, 1911, p. 463.
19. *L'Asie Française*, 1912, p. 124.
20. Thaemsuk Numnon, "Khabuankān r.s. 130", *Wārasān Thammasāt* 8, pt 2 (October-November 1978): 2-7.
21. See Prince Čhakraphong's interview, reported in the *Straits Times*, 18 March 1912. This is basically also the version in Weiler's diary, dated 28 March (see *Anfang der Eisenbahn*, pp. 208-9).
22. Rian Sičhan and Nēt Phūnwiwat, *Kabot r.s. 130 (Kānpatiwat khrang rāēk khŏng Thai)*, pp. 2-5.
23. Weiler, *Anfang der Eisenbahn*, p. 209.
24. Ibid.
25. *Phrarātchaniyom nai Phrabātsomdet Phramongkutklāo Čhaoyūhua*, pp. 14-15.
26. Thaemsuk Numnon, "Khabuankān r.s. 130", p. 7.
27. For example, Phra Sarasas, *My Country Thailand (Its History, Geography and Civilisation)*, p. 131.
28. Prince Čhakraphong (Defence), Prince Boriphat (Navy), Prince Thēwawong (Foreign Affairs), Prince Narēt (Public Works), Prince Damrong (Interior), Prince Sanphasit (Palace), Prince Čhanthaburī (Treasury), mŏmčhao Čharūn (Communication), čhaophrayā Yomarāt (Municipal Government),

*čhaophrayā* Wongsā (Agriculture), *mǫmrātchawong* Piya Mālākun (Justice) and *phrayā* Surasēnā (Chamberlain). Source: *Phrarātchaniyom nai Phrabātsomdet Phramongkutklāo Čhaoyūhua*, pp. 21-22.

29. Weiler, *Anfang der Eisenbahn*, pp. 214-15.
30. *Souvenir of the Siamese Kingdom Exhibition*, pp. 180-81.
31. Further details on the financial crisis can be found in W.A. Graham, *Siam: A Handbook of Practical, Commerical, and Political Information,* vol. 1, pp. 342-43; G.W. Skinner, *Chinese Society in Thailand,* p. 158; *Souvenir of the Siamese Kingdom Exhibition,* p. 182; and especially Chatthip Nartsupha, Suthy Prasartset, and Montri Chenvidyakarn, eds., *The Political Economy of Siam, 1910–1932,* pp. 19-20 and 125-38.
32. Vella, *Chaiyo!*, pp. 128-36.
33. The Personal and Family Names Act was finally enforced in 1941. See the *Bangkok Chronicle,* 16 October 1941, p. 5. It is interesting to note, however, that surnames never achieved the same status as European ones. The Siamese still generally prefer to be addressed personally by their "real names", and the Bangkok telephone directory lists people under these.
34. Officially it was stated that others came and persuaded the king, but there can be little doubt that the whole idea was Wachirāwut's (see Vella, *Chaiyo!*, p. 97.)
35. *Souvenir of the Siamese Kingdom Exhibition*, p. 189.
36. Vella, *Chaiyo!*, p. 120.
37. M. Smith, *A Physician at the Court of Siam*, p. 114.
38. Ibid., and Vella, *Chaiyo!*, pp. 264-65.
39. Translated from Weiler, *Anfang der Eisenbahn*, p. 273.
40. For details, see Vella, *Chaiyo!*, pp. 144-51.
41. Weiler, *Anfang der Eisenbahn*, p. 278.
42. Vella, *Chaiyo!*, pp. 136-37; H. Cucherousset, *Quelques informations sur le Siam*, p. 32, gives the date a week earlier, 4 November.
43. Vella, *Chaiyo!*, pp. 241-42.
44. See, for example, the table in *L'Asie Française*, 1911, p. 465.
45. Vella, *Chaiyo!*, pp. 104-10; *L'Asie Française*, 1917, pp. 124-25.
46. B.A. Batson, "The End of the Absolute Monarchy in Siam", pp. 22.
47. Vella, *Chaiyo!*, p. 106.
48. *Souvenir of the Siamese Kingdom Exhibition*, p. 181.
49. A series of statements issued by Wachirāwut regarding the great heroic role of the troops being sent to Europe can be found in Prayut Sitthiphan, *Phramahāthirarātčhao*, pp. 117-49.
50. Vella, *Chaiyo!*, pp. 119-20.
51. Ibid., p. 75.
52. The full text of the constitution can be found in Prayut Sitthiphan, *Phramahāthirarātčhao*, pp. 182-92.
53. Ibid., p. 185.
54. Vella, *Chaiyo!*, p. 75.
55. Vella (p. 75) appears to be mistaken in calling it a weekly; see Prayut Sitthiphan, *Phramahāthirarātčhao*, pp. 201-4.
56. There were two dailies, the *Dusit Samai*, and the *Dusit Sakkhī*. The *Dusit Samai* appeared in B.E. 2462 (1919/20). The National Library in Bangkok has no holdings of *Dusit Sakkhī*.
57. Vella, *Chaiyo!*, p. 288.
58. For example, Amǫn Darunrak, *Dusit Thāni*, quoted by Vella, *Chaiyo!*, p. 76.
59. Ibid., p. 76.
60. V. Thompson, *Thailand, the New Siam*, p. 55.

61.  J.C. Ingram, *Economic Change in Thailand, 1850–1970*, pp. 156-57.
62.  I. Brown, "Siam and the Gold Standard, 1902–1908", p. 395.
63.  Ingram, *Economic Change*, pp. 156-57.
64.  For details, see the king's anniversary speech, 1 January 1920, as reported in *The Souvenir of the Siamese Kingdom Exhibition*, pp. 224-25.
65.  Graham, *Siam*, vol. 1, p. 348; Ingram, *Economic Change*, p. 157.
66.  Thompson, *Thailand, the New Siam*, p. 54. The king's attitude towards foreign advisers was quite clear. See W.F. Vella, "Siamese Nationalism in the Plays of Rama VI", p. 5; and S. Greene, "King Wachirawut's Policy of Nationalism", in Tej Bunnag and M. Smithies, ed., *In Memoriam Phya Anuman Rajadhon, Contributions in Memory of the Late President of the Siam Society*, p.255.
67.  Thompson, *Thailand, the New Siam*, p. 55.
68.  *Rātchasakunwong*, p. 56.
69.  For details, see Batson, "End of the Absolute Monarchy", pp. 26-31.
70.  *Straits Times*, 9 October 1925.
71.  Cucherousset, *Quelques informations*, p. 48.
72.  *The Directory for Bangkok and Siam*, 1928, p. 128.
73.  Information on sports in Bangkok can be found in the *Straits Times*, 23 June 1923 and 22 October 1925; *Souvenir of the Siamese Kingdom Exhibition*, pp. 248-52; and Vella, *Chaiyo!*, pp. 144-51.
74.  Vella, "Siamese Nationalism", pp. 7-8.
75.  H.H. Prince Dhani Nivat, "King Rama VI's Last Work", *Collected Articles*, pp. 121-27.
76.  Vella, *Chaiyo!*, p. 258.
77.  Phra Sarasas, *My Country Thailand*, p. 135.
78.  See the accounts in the *Straits Times*, 14, 15, and 16 June 1920; and Chula Chakrabongse, *The Twain Have Met*, pp. 112-13.
79.  Wachirāwut's unsuccessful attempts to produce an heir are reported in Prayut Sitthiphan, *Phramahāthīrarātčhao*, pp. 219-20; and Vella, *Chaiyo!*, pp. 157-8.
80.  See the account in the *Straits Times*, 3 December 1925.
81.  Prince Damrong's words are quoted in Batson, "End of the Absolute Monarchy", p. 33.

# Restoration, Revolt, and the Rise of the Military

Siam's history between 1925 and 1942 can be divided neatly into two periods. The first, lasting less than seven years, is marked by attempts to restore faith in the system of government prevailing towards the end of the Fifth Reign. The second, from 1932 to 1941, is characterized by the growth of the military, beginning with a coup d'état and an attempted counter-coup, and leads up to the Japanese invasion. This is the time when a new élite comes into power and Siamese nationalism gains unprecedented support among the people.

## THE RESTORATION

### The New King and His Council

When Wachirāwut died in November 1925, his youngest full brother Prachāthipok was just thirty-two years old, the youngest of Čhulālongkǭn's seventy-seven children still alive. Although he was of *čhaofā* rank and had always known he was in the line of succession, others had been closer to the throne, and during most of his youth he had neither expected nor aspired to succeed to the throne. It was only after Prince Atsadāng died, in February 1925, that he came to be regarded as the official heir apparent, and only from that time dated his appointment to senior government committees. With less than a year's experience in statecraft and a deplorable inheritance from his elder brother, young King Prachāthipok relied upon the respect, the knowledge, and the experience of senior members of the royal family, several of whom had already been called in to deal with the growing conflict between Wachirāwut and his government.

Three days after Wachirāwut's death, the new king announced the appointment of a Supreme Council of State, an advisory body consisting of five princes, all experienced men who had expressed concern at the way Siam was governed during the Sixth Reign. In order of age they were the new king's three uncles, the princes Phānurangsī, Damrong, and Narit, and his half-brothers Kitiyākǭn (better known as Prince Čhanthaburī) and Boriphat. Although the role and the duties of members of the Supreme Council were never specified, it was clear from the outset that they would be a sort of "super-cabinet", that all matters of importance would be discussed between the king and his five relatives, and that under normal circumstances he would follow their advice.

In February 1926 the new king was formally crowned, and a month later the remains of his predecessor were cremated. By this time the king and the Supreme Council had worked out the composition of the new cabinet and the government's priorities.[1] All those closely associated with the previous reign, from the mighty *čhaophrayā* Yomarāt downward, were dropped from the executive. The new ministry consisted of seven princes and four nobles. Only three members of the previous cabinet were retained. The changes therefore represented a sudden shift in direction, the greatest about-face since the accession of Rama I. The king obviously wanted to demonstrate a clear break with the discredited Sixth Reign, and the choice of men to fill the top positions appeared to be guided largely by a wish to restore a Čhulālongkǭn-type government.

The preparation of the budget for 1926/27 also represented a dramatic break with the past. Royal expenditure was drastically curtailed, the number of ministries was reduced by two, and the number of administrative divisions (*mon-thons*) from eighteen to fourteen. Virtually every government department was forced to retrench and dismiss a number of officials.[2] Several of the king's advisers suggested that the largest cuts be made in the military budget. Siam's armed forces had grown sufficiently to deal with possible internal emergencies. The country would never be able to afford to develop and maintain an army that could stand up against its colonial neighbours, however, and with the passage of time and with Siam's good international record, it was most unlikely that a large-scale armed conflict would arise between Siam and France or Siam and Britain. The king was aware of these views and was inclined to agree with them; in a letter summing up Siam's problems, he admitted as much. Yet cutting defence costs, he felt, was a very serious matter which very few people would dare to advocate; it might encourage foreign incursions.[3] In addition, the king could have mentioned that Prince Boriphat, who was not only a member of the Supreme Council but also Minister of War, would not allow defence to be seriously undermined.

The letter in which Prachāthipok gives first one argument and then its opposite may be seen as indicative of the style of government during the seven years that preceded the coup d'état. The king was painstaking and conscientious; he would elicit comments and suggestions from a range of experts and study them assiduously, noting the good points in each submission, but when various options were available he would seldom be able to select one and abandon others. He would often rely upon the Supreme Council to persuade him in a particular direction. This meant that in practice for day-to-day decision-making Siam depended upon a royal oligarchy. Yet Prachāthipok did not institutionalize this situation; he did not formally relinquish any of the powers of the absolute monarch.

Unlike his predecessor, the king diligently read virtually all state papers that came his way, from ministerial submissions to petitions by citizens. Late in 1926 or early in 1927 he received a petition from the father of Pridī Phanomyong (*luang* Praditmanūtham) about Pridī's recall from France.

Pridi was the principal force behind a petition from the organization of Siamese students in France to have their allowances increased. The Siamese minister in France had asked for his recall, mentioning among other things that Pridi was dangerous, so proud of his own cleverness that he would "go his own way whether right or wrong", of a class the minister considered "the danger of Siam in the future, namely, the half educated class".⁴ The king was swayed by Pridi's father's petition and countermanded his earlier telegram ordering recall, and Pridi was allowed to complete his studies. "Once he enters the government in a responsible position", the king said, "he will probably work well, and I don't much believe that he will become a 'serious danger to the government' as Prince Charoonsakdi has reported".⁵ Ironically, Pridi, after obtaining a very responsible position, did not abandon his critical stance. He became one of the leaders of the movement for drastic government reform and played an important role in the coup d'état of 1932.

## Consideration of Population Representation

Already before his accession, Prachāthipok had been aware of weaknesses in Siam's system of government; indeed, he had already discussed the idea of a Supreme Council before Wachirāwut died. This committee of senior princes was created as a safeguard against the potential mistakes and excesses of a "bad king". Prachāthipok received many petitions for more fundamental changes, and as early as July 1926 he sought the opinion of one of the most honoured and prestigious foreigners, Francis Sayre,⁶ asking him *inter alia* whether Siam ought to have a constitution, how the succession ought to be regulated, what the role of the Supreme Council ought to be, whether a prime minister ought to be appointed immediately, and whether there should be a legislative council. The king indicated that he himself was firmly of the opinion that Siam was not ready for a representative form of government. Sayre, who believed that some such form of government would eventually come about, agreed with the king that the country was not yet ready for it, as did Prince Damrong, who joined the debate.[7]

Early in 1927, however, spurred on by agitation for radical constitutional change, the king appointed a committee under Prince Boriphat to study the possibility of creating an advisory body which would be more representative than the Supreme Council and less unwieldy than the Privy Council. The Privy Council had survived since the early days of the Fifth Reign but had ceased to have any administrative function; membership of it had developed into one of the many types of honours a king could distribute, and in 1927 there were more than two hundred men who had earned that honour. The king ruled out a parliamentary form of government not only because the country had not reached the required stage of development but also because he could foresee that under it Siamese politics would be entirely dominated by the Chinese. Even if the Chinese were formally excluded from the political process, through their financial power they could still be expected to dominate the situation.[8] Fear of the increasing power of the Chinese seems also to have been the reason why in 1927 the Siamese government passed a law restricting immigration.

A parliament having been ruled out, the king favoured the creation of a *Kammakān Ǫngmontrī*, a committee selected from Privy Councillors who could practise the methods of parliamentary debate and whose views might reflect something of the general public opinion. This Privy Council Committee consisted of forty senior men, including some members of the royal family and former ministers of state. The committee had the right to select its own chairman, and at any time a group of members could request the king's permission to discuss a topic that had not yet been placed on its agenda. The committee was in due course given a number of minor laws to discuss, but there was little advance in the process of education in parliamentary debate. By 1932, when drastic changes were brought about through the coup, the Privy Council Committee had still not developed into a widely known forum, nor did it appear to reflect public opinion.

The Privy Council Committee was not the only place where

the Siamese people were given a chance to gain experience in self-government. From 1926 onward there were moves to develop the concept of *prachāphibān*, or "municipality", which had emerged late during the Fifth Reign in a law regarding sanitation. Information was obtained regarding local self-government in surrounding countries, and proposals to allow certain municipalities to raise local taxes and manage their own budgets were drawn up. There were two main problems militating against the success of this administrative venture. Firstly, it was thought that in the provinces the public was not sufficiently educated to make the scheme work. Secondly, it was feared that in Bangkok a freely elected representative body would be dominated by the Chinese.[9] Nevertheless, the idea of teaching the Siamese the concept of democracy through a measure of decentralization of power in municipalities had become, in the king's mind, fundamental to future policy-making.[10] Before practical steps could be taken, however, the days of the absolute monarchy were over.

## The King's Travels

Early in his reign, during January and early February of 1927, King Prachāthipok went with his wife, Queen Ramphai, on an official state visit to the north. The royal train took him via Phitsanulok, Phrae, and Lampang to Chiang Mai, and he went by car further north to Chiang Rai and Chiang Saen.[11] A royal voyage to Singapore and the Dutch East Indies was planned to follow, but, because of the death of Prince Phānurangsī in June 1928, it was postponed. Phānurangsī, as the eldest *čhaofā* prince and a member of the Supreme Council, was the most senior member of the royal family, and his cremation entailed full state involvement. Eventually the tour to Singapore, Java, and Bali took place in mid-1929, lasting more than two months. While the king was abroad, Prince Boriphat acted as regent.

Boriphat had emerged as the strongest and most forceful member of the Supreme Council, the only one of that body also to hold a cabinet post. In a cabinet shuffle in March 1928 he had been moved from the War to the Interior portfolio, a promotion that had made him in all but name the country's prime minister. His post as minister of war had been given to Prince Boworadet, another forceful and able man whose career had been interrupted during the Sixth Reign and who was recalled from retirement to serve Prachāthipok.[12]

The state visit by the Siamese king and queen was quite a diplomatic success. Various favourable reports on Siam and its good immediate prospects were published.[13] Indeed, the Siamese leaders had reason to regard the Seventh Reign as being generally successful. The economic problems of the early 1920s had been overcome, the country's balance of payments showed a healthy surplus, and by 1928 there was no longer any thought of retrenchments or cutbacks in government departments. Suddenly there was scope for initiative, and investment and the future could be faced with optimism, a situation which lasted until the serious economic crisis which began in 1930.

In April and May 1930 the king and queen made a state visit to French Indo-China, and Boriphat again became regent. Meanwhile, the king was worried by the state of his health, especially his failing eyesight and threatened blindness. Various proposals were considered, such as to invite an ophthalmologist to Siam or for the king to visit a clinic in France. Finally, however, the king decided that he would rather travel to the United States.[14] The king and queen spent most of 1931 overseas, travelling to Japan, Canada, and the United States. Again Boriphat was regent, this time during a period when Siam's financial problems rapidly worsened and some difficult decisions had to be made. When the king returned in mid-October 1931, the economic crisis had reached a stage where firm and decisive measures were needed, measures apparently beyond the powers of a man of Prachāthipok's character and constitution.

Between late 1925 and early 1932 King Prachāthipok had travelled through most of Siam and also extensively abroad. Though some of the journeys were primarily undertaken for reasons of health and recuperation, most of them were official state visits. Prachāthipok considered these formal visits to be an intrinsic part of his duties as king. As such, they may be seen as consistent with his general policy of restoration and emulation of his father's most popular actions. At the same time the frequency and long duration of some of the voyages may be seen as an indication of the king's willingness to drop the executive burdens of the absolute king. *En route*, Prachāthipok did his duty towards his country, by listening to innumerable speeches and complying with the programmes devised by local committees. Meanwhile, he relied heavily upon his uncles and brothers to handle affairs of state in Siam.

## The Economic and Domestic Crisis

Whereas the economic difficulties at the beginning of the Seventh Reign had been largely the result of domestic imbalances and relatively easily remedied, the crisis that began in 1930 was essentially an international crisis which had suddenly emerged in October 1929 with the collapse of the American stock market.

A combination of a bad rice crop and falling prices for some other commodities and a slackening off in trade made it clear by the end of 1930 that the Siamese government could expect a drop in revenue. In order to balance the budget for 1931/32 it was decided to cut all official salaries.[15] The budget for defence was severely slashed by one-third, a remarkable feat considering that the responsible minister, Prince Boworadet, had during the preceding year bitterly fought to safeguard and even increase funds for military expenditure. Indeed, it soon was apparent that Boworadet did not intend to adhere to the spirit of economic restraint, because in May 1931 he told cabinet that he had promoted more than two hundred officers, who would thus receive an increase in their salaries, and that he had also decided to offer salary increases without promotion to another ninety-one officers. In the ensuing debate, cabinet decided to cancel the ninety-one raises and Boworadet offered his resignation. The

Supreme Council decided to contact the king, who was recuperating from his eye operation in New York, recommending that he accept the resignation, to which the king reluctantly agreed.[16]

In September 1931 Britain abandoned the gold standard and devalued the pound by 30 per cent. Despite the fact that Siam's foreign holdings were mainly in sterling, that the bulk of its imports originated in Britain, that much of its exports were to British-held regions, and that British firms dominated the teak and tin industries, the (British) Financial Adviser, E.L. Hall-Patch, advocated that Siam break its link with the pound sterling and retain its own gold standard. By October there was a run on the *baht*, and an increasing number of sources publicly doubted whether Siam could hold out. This was the situation when in mid-October the king returned to Siam. Hall-Patch advocated new taxes, especially taxation of the richer classes, in conjunction with further cuts in government expenditure, while the Supreme Council had come to favour devaluation. The debate continued until March 1932, over five months, in which the king desperately sought a solution that would satisfy all opposing parties. Repeatedly he publicly made what amounted to an apology for not making a decision:

> The financial war is a very hard one indeed. Even experts contradict one another until they become hoarse. Each offers a different suggestion. I myself do not profess to know much about the matter and all I can do is listen to the opinions of others and choose the best. I have never experienced such a hardship; therefore if I have made a mistake I really deserve to be excused by the officials and people of Siam.[17]

The falling price of rice meanwhile seriously affected the farmers, and during the first months of 1932 the government received a large number of petitions for relief from economic hardship. Finally, in March 1932, after the purchasing power of the *baht* had been artificially maintained long after public confidence had fallen, the decision to abandon the gold standard was made. The king's wavering attitude had undoubtedly contributed to the depletion of Siam's foreign reserves.

Soon afterwards some new taxes were announced. During the previous months the prospect of increased taxation had been widely debated, and taxes on the wealthy and on businesses had been suggested in the local press, measures that had found little favour in the Supreme Council. Of the new taxes announced in April 1932 the most important was a tax on salaries, effectively reducing even further the income of government officials who had borne the brunt of the cost-saving exercise of the previous year. Royalty and the higher nobility also were to be taxed on their salaries, but since they often derived much of their income from other sources, they again escaped relatively unscathed. Among middle-ranking officials and intellectuals this was felt to be unfair and iniquitous. The enactment of this tax law must have strengthened the resolution of the parties busily devising a scheme to overthrow the government.

## The Sesquicentennial

Prachāthipok knew that during the seventh year of his reign, in 1932, the city of Bangkok would be 150 years old, and during the years of economic prosperity between 1928 and 1930 he had begun planning for the event. In one of his rare strong and decisive moves, he decided to neglect the advice of a special committee and ordered the construction of a new bridge to span the Chao Phraya River. In 1927 he had already opened a railway bridge, a project that had been started during the Sixth Reign, and he decided that the 1932 memorial bridge would be the first for general traffic. He donated considerable funds towards the construction. The bridge was called Phraphuthayọtfā Bridge, in honour of the founder of the Čhakrī dynasty, and it was duly opened on Čhakrī Day, 6 April 1932, with appropriate pomp and ceremony and a military parade.[18]

The celebrations for Bangkok's sesquicentennial were somewhat overshadowed by the worsening economic crisis. The official announcements made on the occasion may also have come as a disappointment to many. Ever since his return from the United States, the king had intended, as part of the sesquicentennial celebrations, to present the nation with its first constitution. His advisers had drawn up a first draft, which had in early March 1932 been submitted to the Supreme Council, and which provided for a prime minister and a legislative council.[19] Apparently the proposal met with opposition from the princes, and the king, true to his own assessment of himself as a person who saw both sides of every question,[20] allowed the sesquicentennial to pass without alluding to a more democratic form of government.

The organizers must have breathed a sigh of relief when the celebrations passed without incident. The economic depression and the concomitant hardship had created a political climate in which there was among many educated Siamese a resurgence of the debate on alternative forms of government. In March 1932 a senior adviser mentioned to the king that there were rumours of an attempt to overthrow the government.[21] These rumours were partly based upon an old prophecy, reputedly stemming from King Rama I, saying that his dynasty would last but 150 years.[22] At this time of economic troubles such a prophecy could be regarded as a factor adding to the general instability.


## REVOLT AND THE RISE OF
## THE MILITARY


### The Coup d'État

Just as Prince Čharūn, the Siamese minister in France, had predicted, *luang* Pradit (Pridī Phanomyong), having completed his studies and having returned to Bangkok to teach law at the university, continued to criticize the Siamese system of government and to disseminate revolutionary ideas. Gradually he became the undisputed leader of a group of idealists who all agreed to co-operate to bring about a drastic change in the system of government. Prĭdĭ's friends from the time he was in France were among the core of this group. They included some young military officers such as Plaek Khittasangkha (*luang* Phibūnsongkhrām), Thatsanai Mitphakdĭ (*luang* Thatsanainiyomsu'k), and Prayūn Phamonmontrĭ, with whom he could practise speaking French and share reminiscences of the exciting days when they were all studying abroad. Most members of this group hoped that democracy would put a stop to the abuses of a privileged class and lead to greater prosperity. They had sworn secrecy, knowing that their discussions often touched matters which, if publicized, would harm their careers. Yet, up to 1931 this group had not developed a practical plan of action, not conceiving how to accomplish violent change. If King Prachāthipok had proceeded to announce his plan for a constitutional monarchy, it would have satisfied at least some of *luang* Pradit's fellow-conspirators.

The situation changed during the second half of 1931, when several senior army officers who had heard about the growing numbers of young officers and civil servants wishing to overthrow the government decided to join forces with them. The two most important of these were Phot Phahonyothin (*phrayā* Phahonphonphayuhasēnā, usually known as *phrayā* Phahon) and Thēp Phanthumasēn (*phrayā* Songsuradēt), both colonels who had studied in Germany. The former was deputy-inspector of the Bangkok artillery and the latter headed the educational section of the Military Academy. The senior army officers and their friends appeared to have been motivated both by personal grievances and by more general dissatisfaction with the way in which Siam was ruled. Some were influenced by the Supreme Council's lack of support for Boworadet, the Minister of War, who resigned over the case for salary increase. Others felt frustrated in their career prospects because preference was often given to members of the royal family. Again others disagreed with some of the measures taken by the country's executive in a time of a worsening economic climate.[23]

It was these senior officers and their friends who finally devised the plans for the overthrow of the government, *phrayā* Songsuradēt being the general co-ordinator. Details of the overall plan were kept from most of the coup sympathizers, and so efficient was the preparation that the coup took everybody by surprise. On the night of 23 June 1932 the telephones of senior government ministers were quietly disconnected and naval units, acting on false orders to suppress Chinese riots, were mobilized, armed, and transported to the vicinity of the throne hall. A gunboat took up position opposite Prince Boriphat's residence. Boriphat was the acting head of government, because earlier during that month the king had gone to his seaside resort at Huahin. In the early hours of the morning all key government members were arrested and brought to the throne hall. The coup was officially announced to the unsuspecting public by means of proclamations from the Khana Rātsadon, or People's Party.[24] The first public announcement drawn up by *luang* Pradit contained a strongly worded denunciation of the Čhakrī dynasty and the Prachāthipok government. It was probably intended to arouse the population and elicit spontaneous support. The people, however, not knowing the character of the new party, generally reacted with restraint, awaiting the reaction of the forces that were being ousted.

Prachāthipok had meanwhile received a message from the coup leaders informing him of the fall of his government, and that hostages were being held, and asking him to return to Bangkok as a constitutional monarch. Some of the king's advisers urged him to march up to the capital and fight, but Prachāthipok decided, after some hesitation,[25] that the best course of action was to accept the offer. On 26 June the leaders of the People's Party met the king, who appeared genuinely happy with the idea of relinquishing much of his power, a move he had come close to implementing himself. *Luang* Pradit, the author of the anti-monarchial statement, formally apologized, and the king forgave all coup members for having acted contrary to the existing laws. Prachāthipok accepted a draft constitution by which executive authority was given to an Assembly, and the Supreme Council and Privy Council were dissolved. In return, the hostages were released, Prince Boriphat agreeing to go abroad.

The leaders of the People's Party rapidly proceeded to nominate an Assembly, consisting of seventy members, which in its turn chose a leader, *phrayā* Manopakǭn, a lawyer who had come to the fore because he had recently proposed in the Privy Council Committee that there be a cut in the annual princely allowances.[26] *Phrayā* Manopakǭn then chose fourteen members of an Executive Committee, consisting of the most influential members of the coup party, and on 29 June a small cabinet of seven ministers was announced.[27] The Executive Committee and Cabinet formed an interim government to implement the first measures in accordance with the policies of the People's Party; a special committee set about creating a "final" draft of the constitution.

The first priority was given to the nation's economic situation. In July 1932 it was decided that the depressed state of the economy was mainly the result of international forces which the government could not control. It was also clear that the situation in Siam was far from bad. Rice and teak, the main export items, were still finding buyers.[28] The previous government's controversial salaries tax was changed into a more general tax on incomes and businesses. Various other taxes that were particularly burdensome to the poorer people were reduced and some even repealed. The most sweeping reform took place in the military, where practically all high-ranking officers were retired, making way for coup members and their sympathizers. Although there were voices urging the confiscation of all princely fortunes, *phrayā* Manopakǭn opposed such a drastic move, and various members of the royal family were even allowed to continue holding government positions.

By the end of November 1932 the constitutional committee had managed to produce a text that was agreeable to Prachāthipok and to the Assembly, and on 10 December it was formally approved. It provided for a new National Assembly, with half its members to be appointed and half to be elected, in a two-tiered election process; eventual development of a fully elected Assembly was foreseen. According to this constitution, princes were deemed to be "above politics", a measure that was understood to mean they were not to engage in political activities and were barred from holding ministerial positions. By the end of 1932 it seemed that the coup had been eminently successful. With little violence, an outmoded oligarchical system had been overthrown and Siam had, at least from a political point of view, joined the countries where power would be exercised by people responsible to the elected representatives of the people.

Early in 1933, however, a serious rift developed between the more radical idealists and the more conservative members of the Assembly over the issue of *luang* Pradit's far-reaching national economic policy plan. He suggested that the government pay monthly wages to all citizens; that farmers should no longer work individually, but as members of government-supervised co-operative societies; and that the government should control all productive land and machinery and work towards abolishing private enterprise.[29] The plan, which in *luang* Pradit's words followed "the socialist pattern with an admixture of liberalism",[30] passed the committee stage with a dissenting minority opinion. Among the dissenters were *phrayā* Manopakǫn and *phrayā* Songsuradēt. When the controversial plan reached the Assembly, heated debate took place and fundamental differences of opinion became clear. Late in March 1933 *phrayā* Manopakǫn prorogued the Assembly; not long after, it was dissolved. A new State Council, without *luang* Pradit, who had been sent to Europe into what amounted to exile, ruled the country. At the same time an "anti-communistic" law was proclaimed, making it illegal to advocate doctrines implying nationalization or impinging upon the right to private property. To counter possible criticism that the government had no firm economic policy at all, an economic council was appointed, including some foreign advisers.[31]

Even without *luang* Pradit and some of his radical friends, and with a no longer unruly Assembly, the governing body soon split up. On 10 June 1933 the four senior military officers in the State Council submitted their resignations. One of these disgruntled men, *phrayā* Phahon, was persuaded by a group of younger army officers under the leadership of *luang* Phibūnsongkhrām, to stage another coup. On 20 June this took place, and *phrayā* Manopakǫn's government collapsed in the face of a military threat. Ironically, again King Prachāthipok was at his seaside palace at Huahin when he received the request from the coup leaders to recall the (provisional) Assembly. *Phrayā* Phahon formed a new cabinet, and *luang* Pradit was invited to return to Siam. It was made clear, however, that his economic plan would not be considered. Nevertheless, *luang* Pradit remained the symbol of revolution, and his return in late September contributed to the unsettled atmosphere which preceded yet another attempt to change the government by force.

## The Rebellion

On 11 October 1933 a full-scale rebellion broke out in the provinces. Under the leadership of the former Minister of War, Prince Boworadet, the garrisions of Nakhon Ratchasima, Ubon Ratchathani, Prachinburi, Saraburi, Ayutthaya, Nakhon Sawan, and Phetburi declared themselves in favour of a rebellion against the Bangkok government. Troops from the north-east of the country marched on Bangkok, seized the airport, and entered the northern suburbs. The commander-in-chief of the navy declared himself neutral and withdrew his battleships from the capital. The rebels sent an ultimatum, threatening to seize Bangkok by force if the government did not resign.

At this stage, Boworadet, who reputedly espoused a democratic-royalist cause, probably hoped that at least some Bangkok army units would join him and that the king would show his preference by remaining strictly neutral and non-committal. In actuality, however, none of the Bangkok garrisons revolted. The government declared martial law, and *phrayā* Phahon revealed that the king had declared himself against the action of the rebels, who meanwhile had let their ultimatum drop and had sent a much milder set of suggestions. *Luang* Phibūnsongkhrām became field commander, and during the evening of 13 October he opened a heavy artillery attack on the rebels' positions. For three days the two opposing parties shelled each other, causing many casualties and great damage. The government force, better supplied and aided by fresh reinforcements from the city, then recaptured the airport and forced the rebels to retreat. An attempt by Phetburi troops to come to Boworadet's aid failed, and by the end of October, after several skirmishes in the provinces, the central government was again firmly in control. Most of the rebel forces surrendered. Of the leading figures, some had been killed in action and seventeen were captured. These latter were sentenced to death, but later all the sentences were commuted, and no executions took place. Twenty-two officers, including Boworadet himself, managed to flee the country and find asylum in French Indo-China.[32]

The October rebellion had been an ambitious and daring attempt by Boworadet and various senior officers to seize power. At one moment the fate of the uprising seemed to hang in the balance. The government had not panicked, however; it was given time to organize resistence, and, through *luang* Phibūnsongkhrām's military action, it had gained a resounding victory. The result of the Boworadet uprising was a severe setback to many princes, together with their known supporters among the prestigious noble families. Some were arrested, some exiled, and some were retrenched.[33] In addition, some senior officers, such as *phrayā* Songsuradēt and his friends, who had kept aloof from the military conflict, obviously hoping that *phrayā* Phahon and *luang* Phibūnsongkhrām would be toppled, found their hopes of power and influence dashed. *Luang* Phibūnsongkhrām had now emerged as a real force. While in 1932 he had been simply one of the junior coup members, he had now risen to prominence and was put forward as the saviour of the country.

## King Prachāthipok's Position

As if to demonstrate its post-uprising confidence, in late 1933 the government held the nation's first elections. Just before the Boworadet rebellion a large number of *tambon* representatives had been elected, and these, as representatives of the general populace, proceeded with the choosing of seventy-eight Assembly members. Among the chosen were many retired government officials (eight of them of high rank), three journalists, two professors, and three men who had played a key role during Siam's first abortive coup just over twenty years earlier. Another seventy-eight members were appointed by the king, among them forty-five army officers and five from the navy.[34]

After the insurrection had been repressed, the king's prestige seemed to have suffered. When the revolt broke out, Prachāthipok, at his Huahin palace, was warned by *phrayā* Phahon that the rebels had reached the aerodrome, that the government had proclaimed martial law, and that the army intended to stand firm. At the same time Phahon reiterated his loyalty to the king.[35] The king answered that he regretted the strife and civil disturbances, and this message played a role in the propaganda battles between the Bangkok regime and the rebels. During the days following the king's telegram to Phahon, it became clear that apart from the Ayutthayan and Nakhon Ratchasima troops mentioned by Phahon, many other provincial garrisons were involved, including the one at Phetburi, not far from Huahin. It is not clear whether the king was motivated by fear of being captured by rebels or by the wish to avoid having to make further choices between Phahon and Boworadet, but the fact remains that at the height of the fighting the king and queen took refuge in Songkhla, near the Malay border. The king's withdrawal from the scene when there was a crucial battle going on near Bangkok was interpreted by the victorious party as a sign that he had failed to do his duty; by refusing to throw his full support behind the government forces he had undermined his credibility.[36]

One of the first items to be discussed in Siam's first half-elected Assembly was the king's plan for another lengthy visit overseas for further medical treatment. It was widely felt that the king's proposed travel was ill-timed, and the government offered to invite the world's best ophthalmologists to come to Siam rather than let the king make the strenuous journey. Prachāthipok insisted, however, and in January 1934 he left for Europe. On the way he stopped at Belawan, Sumatra, where he was met by a large gathering of exiled Siamese, including his uncles Damrong and Sawat, his half-brothers Boriphat and Burachat, and the former prime minister *phrayā* Manopakōn.[37] Early in 1934 the king and his party arrived at Marseilles and went for a while to Paris, and later to London. From Europe he kept up a regular correspondence with the Bangkok government, increasingly demonstrating his dissatisfaction with the manner in which Siam was governed. He protested against measures that whittled away the few remaining royal prerogatives, safeguarded in the constitution, and suggested some changes that would make the king's position more significant. When his suggestions were not heeded, he threatened to abdicate. In November 1934 a special government mission was sent to England to negotiate Prachāthipok's return. The rift between king and government could not be bridged, however, and on 2 March 1935 the king formally abdicated.[38]

As Prachāthipok had no children, the committee considering the succession decided to turn to another branch of Čhulālongkǫn's offspring. They proposed Prachāthipok's nephew, Anǫn Mahidon, the eldest son of *čhaofā* Mahidon, as the new king. Anǫn Mahidon was still a young boy at school in Lausanne. A council of regents was therefore appointed to act for him.

The Seventh Reign had lasted less than a decade, a time during which the king had presided over the dismantling of the system that had placed him on the throne. Prachāthipok had been a kind, sincere, and diligent king. In his own mild way he had stimulated debate and encouraged a fundamental reassessment of the state system. He had done this at a time when there were serious economic fluctuations in the nation causing widespread hardship. While the king was aware of the new forces in Siamese society and was more open-minded than his predecessor regarding different approaches to sharing responsibility, it was his personal tragedy that he was easily swayed by any well-argued opinion and that he lacked the measure of decisiveness needed to lead the nation in a new direction.

## The Creation of a Stable Government

In Prachāthipok's abdication speech he accused *phrayā* Phahon and his party of having no regard for democratic principles, of employing methods of administration incompatible with individual freedom and the principles of justice, of ruling in an autocratic manner and not letting the people have a real voice in Siam's affairs. As an idealistic democrat, the former king had some grounds for complaint. The Executive Committee and Cabinet did not seem eager to develop an atmosphere of debate or to be guided by resolutions of the Assembly. In 1934 a Press Act came into effect forbidding the publication of material detrimental to public order or undermining morals, and this law was strictly applied. All publications had to be submitted for censorship, and the government Press Bureau dictated what items of news were allowed to appear. Similarly, all speeches over the radio were subject to censorship.[39]

Military officers had toppled Manopakọn's government, and the military gained considerable influence in the nation's decision-making processes. This is apparent in the generous budget allocations for military spending. By 1935 some 27 per cent of the total ordinary expenditure went on defence, and this was to increase in the years to follow.[40] The drive to democratize from below, by setting up local government councils with independent funds derived from local taxes, a key project in Prachāthipok's plan to educate the Siamese in the handling of political power, was actually slowed down by the form of the legislation implementing it in 1934. Although the law provided for the creation of municipal councils and election of local councillors, the central authorities reserved the right to appoint all office-bearers and thus retained effective control.[41]

Yet *phrayā* Phahon probably did not regard himself as an autocratic ruler. He presided over a cabinet that could be considered representative of various different groups and opinions. It contained not only those who were firmly linked with the army and the navy but also men who were sponsored by different sections of society. The most notable non-military face in the cabinet was *luang* Pradit, who in February 1934 was formally declared to be free of the "stigma of communism" which had been imputed to him at the time of his controversial economic plan,[42] and who soon afterwards was appointed as Minister of the Interior. Another representative of the "intellectuals", *phra'* Sarasat, became

Minister of Economic Affairs, but his opinions were so much at variance with those of the military that he was dropped in September 1934 during the first cabinet crisis.[43]

In the years to follow, the influence of the military remained such that its hand can be seen in many of the decisions made at cabinet level. In the five years between 1933 and 1938 Siam's army, navy, and air force were equipped as never before. The navy, which had in 1932 a small number of rather outdated vessels, was augmented by twenty-four modern warships, built in Italy and Japan. The army was expanded to thirty-three battalions and boasted an armoured division and three sections of artillery. The air force had two hundred warplanes of the most modern American type. This investment in offensive weaponry caused some concern in the region, especially in French Indo-China.[44]

## Japan

Siamese leaders had long had an image of Japan as a major Asian country which was managing its own affairs and thus countering the myth, current in the colonies, that Asian peoples were incapable of ruling themselves. It was not until after 1932, however, that this general feeling was translated into measures that rapidly brought about fraternization between the two countries. The pro-Japanese attitudes of Siam's rulers were dramatically demonstrated in 1933 when the League of Nations passed a censure motion against Japan's invasion of Manchuria and Siam was the sole nation abstaining. At the same time, Siam was receiving a share of the rapidly expanding Japanese exports to South-East Asia. During 1934 there were official trade negotiations between Siam and Japan, giving rise to rumours that a secret military alliance between the two countries was being drafted and that the Japanese were proposing to build a canal through the Isthmus of Kra.[45] During 1935 the first groups of young Siamese officers arrived in Japan to complete their training in the Japanese army.

One of the strongest supporters of closer relations with Japan was Siam's Defence Minister, *luang* Phibūnsongkhrām, whose personal views were frequently expressed in articles published by the Defence Ministry, in which he noted Siam's need for a strong leader in these days of "nation building" and world crisis, much as "an animal herd needs its leader".⁴⁶ Phibūnsongkhrām was attracted by the effective and quite popular movements in Japan, Turkey, and Italy, where large numbers of people inspired by national goals managed to perform seemingly impossible tasks. Clearly influenced by these foreign examples, Phibūnsongkhrām encouraged the development of a system of military training for Siamese youth. In 1935 he set up the *Yuwayon* movement, to complement the less-militant Scouts. Dressed in smart, attractive uniforms, the *Yuwayon* boys trained voluntarily for two or three hours a week.⁴⁷ In September 1938 the movement comprised some six thousand boys, and it was decided to set up a section for schoolgirls.⁴⁸

## The Civilian and Military Factions

*Phrayā* Phahon was Prime Minister from 1933 to 1938. He remained the only one of the senior officers who had led the 1932 coup to maintain an executive position. *Phrayā* Songsuradēt, who had in 1933 been outwitted by *luang* Phibūnsongkhrām, refused to return to active politics, though reputedly he was once offered a cabinet post and later sounded out for the prime ministership.⁴⁹ Phahon presided over a cabinet in which two rather different groups were represented. One was the "young military clique", led by Phibūnsongkhrām; the other was the "civilian faction", with Pradit as its leader. The military faction's strength was reflected in many of the cabinet decisions, but at the same time Pradit was given the opportunity to implement some of his ideas. Thus, in 1934, as a result of Pradit's planning and preparations, the Law School was detached from Čhulālongkǫn University to become the nucleus of a new tertiary institute, Thammasāt University. Here the emphasis was to fall on political and social science, and it was in this institution that Pradit hoped to be able to train large numbers of young Siamese in critical analysis of aspects of society.

Before Thammasāt University even opened its doors, more than seven thousand applications for enrolment were received.[50]

Although the two faction leaders pursued quite different goals, one attempting to raise the defence budget and the other wanting to spend more on the people's general education, and one quite attracted by fascism and the other by socialism, they were at that time quite friendly with each other. As far as possible, each allowed the other scope to develop the nation. They had co-operated since their student days in France, and while they both held senior cabinet posts they could afford a measure of generosity. Siam had weathered the international economic crisis rather well, and between 1933 and 1938 budget expenditure rose dramatically.[51]

*Phrayā* Phahon maintained a fairly neutral stance with respect to any move towards fascism or socialism. Not all citizens remained as uncommitted and aloof. Phibūnsongkhrām came to be regarded as the most likely candidate for leadership of a fascist Siam, and in February 1935 he was the victim of an assassination attempt. Though shot in the neck and shoulder, Phibūnsongkhrām escaped serious injury. In August of that year the police discovered an army plot for another coup. Fifteen officers were arrested and their leader condemned to death.[52] In mid-1937 Phibūnsongkhrām was seriously embarrassed by members of the Assembly asking questions regarding the sale of the land that had been in the king's possession. A list of people who had bought these lands at a very low price was published; among them was the Defence Minister. Eventually the lands were returned. In 1938 the tension between Assembly and cabinet grew much worse. *Luang* Wichitwathakǭn, the Director-General of the Department of Fine Arts, had publicly made anti-Chinese statements. Members of the Assembly demanded an inquiry, and eventually the offensive remarks were publicly retracted. When the budget came up for discussion, a sizable number of Assembly members insisted that they ought to exert full control over it. Cabinet and Assembly could not solve the ensuing conflict. Eventually it was decided to dissolve the

Assembly, which since its reconstitution in 1937 had proved too hostile to the executive, and call for new elections.

*Phrayā* Phahon, who had often indicated his distaste for the political arena, announced that he would no longer be willing to serve as Prime Minister. Therefore, the first major task of the new half-elected–half-appointed Assembly was the choosing of Phahon's successor. Phibūnsongkhrām was the candidate sponsored by most of the military. In late 1938 his enemies organized two further attempts on his life, but both the shooting and the poisoning failed to remove him from the scene, and in December 1939 he was elected Prime Minister.

## The Military Regime

Phahon's resignation and Phibūnsongkhrām's rise to power marked a distinctive change in Siam's government. The new Prime Minister emulated Phahon in that he maintained Pradit and various other liberals in the cabinet. However, the chief ministries were given to his personal army friends, and Phibūnsongkhrām at first retained his old Defence portfolio. Within a month of coming to power, there were rumours of widespread discontent with the new government. Phibūnsongkhrām ordered a large number of arrests. Some members of the royal family, Assembly members, and some of Phibūnsongkhrām's army rivals were charged with treason. After a speedy court-martial, eighteen were found guilty and executed, another twenty-six were condemned to life-imprisonment, and others, including *phrayā* Songsuradēt, were exiled.[53]

The young King Anọn Mahidon had meanwhile come of age, and late in 1938 he had returned to Siam. However, in January 1939 he returned to Europe, probably because there was no significant role for him at that particular time. The new government had dismissed many royalist officials, and the Ministry of the Royal Household had been downgraded to a simple Bureau.

An outspoken critic of the autocratic regime was ex-King Prachāthipok. In 1939 he was officially accused of having misappropriated some six million *baht*. The subsequent court procedures were not yet concluded when Prachāthipok died in May 1941. Eventually he was declared guilty, and his Siamese possessions were confiscated. The government decided to prohibit any display of Prachāthipok's image.

Phibūnsongkhrām's ideas about leading the nation became visible in a series of measures which were intended to stimulate pride in the nation, in its military might, and in its leader. In 1939 the name Siam was dropped in favour of Thailand.[54] This name change was part of a campaign to foster values that would be recognized as "cultured" in the international world: "We must be as cultured as other nations otherwise no country will come to contact us. Or if they come, they come as superiors. Thailand would be helpless and soon become colonised. But if we were highly cultured, we would be able to uphold our integrity, independence, and keep everything to ourselves."[55]

A government-sponsored programme to create a new, civilized Thailand began. During the latter half of 1939 six "cultural mandates" were announced by the Prime Minister's office. They dealt with the name of the country, warned the people against endangering the nation's security, abolished the names for regional groups of Thais, stipulated paying respect to national flags and the anthem, advocated the use of locally made consumer goods, and proclaimed the new words of the national anthem.[56] Almost every night the government policies were discussed over the radio by two fictitious characters, Man and Khong, whose dialogues were designed and often directed by the Prime Minister himself.[57]

Another six cultural mandates followed between March 1940 and January 1942. They stressed the need to work hard, announced a minor change in the national anthem, emphasized the unity underlying all Thai dialects, told the populace that they should be decently dressed in public, presented a healthy daily routine of work and relaxation, and asked all Thais to be quick to assist aged people or invalids. Naturally, the unprecedented interference with regard to private habits met with some resistance. The proclamation that loose shirt-tails, or lack of a shirt, was not proper and not in accordance with cultured Thai behaviour must have been greeted in some circles with disbelief. However, in October 1940 the National Cultural Development Act was promulgated, in which it became the duty of all Thai people to comply with the aspirations of the national culture and to foster and promote national progress.[58] Orderliness in dress, good etiquette, efficient use of time, and an appreciation of Thai culture could be enforced, and people convicted of disobeying the law could be fined. In 1941 it became unlawful among other things to make unnecessary noise, to use improper language, or to ridicule those who attempted to promote national customs.[59] In the same year a campaign was launched to persuade people to wear hats in public.[60] The nationalistic programme also encompassed the fine arts. Fiercely nationalistic plays were sponsored by the government. Often these depicted a glorious past when Thai warriors fearlessly gained freedom for the country, defended their honour, or sacrificed themselves.[61] Patriotism was taught in schools and was a recurrent theme in song and dance.

## The Confrontation with France

In August 1939, when political tension in Europe was high, the French government proposed to Phibūnsongkhrām that France and Thailand should conclude a mutual non-aggression pact.[62] In reply to this overture, the Thais suggested that the two countries negotiate a border revision by which the position of various islands in the Mekong River would be reconsidered. The French minister at Bangkok and his superiors in Paris were sympathetic to the Thai requests, and when the pact was signed in June 1940 the Thais expected a high-level committee to look into the border question. The Thais had some hopes that the French enclaves on the west bank of the Mekong opposite Luang Prabang and Pakse, which had been ceded to France in 1904, would be returned. Before the end of that month, however, Paris was seized by German forces and the burden of the negotiations thus fell upon the French rulers of Indo-China, men committed to the idea of maintaining the French presence and resisting Thai encroachment.

In August 1940 Phibūnsongkhrām sounded out what German, Italian, British, American, and Japanese reactions would be to Thailand recovering territories formerly lost to Indo-China. The British and American governments were not encouraging, the German and Italian views were firmly in favour of the idea, while the Japanese saw the overtures as a good opportunity to draw Thailand in a much closer relationship. When all attempts to gain territorial concessions from the French seemed to fail, Phibūnsongkhrām proceeded to respond favourably to the Japanese offers of friendship, and in late September he let the Japanese diplomats know that he wished to join the Japanese camp. On 1 October 1940 he expanded on this and told the Japanese naval attaché that Japanese troops would be permitted to cross Thai territory if necessary and that he would consider supplying such troops. This agreement was a carefully guarded secret, and Phibūnsongkhrām did not discuss the matter in cabinet.

While these secret negotiations were taking place, great publicity was being given to alleged French border violations. Throughout October and November there were reports of French aeroplanes entering Thai airspace and of reputedly unprovoked acts of aggression against Thai citizens. On 28 November two bombs were dropped on the north-eastern town of Nakhon Phanom. Thai planes retaliated by bombing Thakhek and Savannakhet, towns on the French side of the Mekong River. From then on acts of military aggression became commonplace.[63] Early in January 1941 the French were reported to have attacked Aranyaprathet, near the Cambodian border, and this gave Phibūnsongkhrām the excuse to launch a large-scale invasion of French Indo-Chinese territory. After three weeks the Thai armies had taken not only the disputed enclaves on the western side of the Mekong River but also a large stretch of Cambodian territory. As early as November 1940 Japan had offered to arbitrate in the dispute,[64] and on 21 January 1941 great pressure was brought upon the French to accept Japan's intervention. Protracted negotiations took place on a Japanese cruiser off Saigon and in Tokyo, and in March 1941 an agreement was reached. Thailand was permitted to keep almost all occupied land. The Thai military incursion had thus paid off handsomely.

The whole conflict and its outcome eminently suited the nationalistic propaganda machinery. Thai troops had valiantly crossed the border and put the enemy to flight. Regions inhabited by members of the great Thai race had been liberated from a colonial regime and become part of Thailand. The Prime Minister, a dapper and handsome military figure, was photographed at the battle front, courageously facing the enemy. For the first time in living memory, Thai troops had been able to shoot and capture European troops with inpunity. There was widespread popular support for Phibūnsongkhrām's decision to press for border readjustments, and during much of 1941 he basked in a feeling of being truly the nation's leader. As if to celebrate the occasion, he promoted himself to field marshal, skipping the ranks of lieutenant-general and general.

Between May and December 1941 Phibūnsongkhrām and his cabinet remained publicly committed to strict neutrality, but gradually the Japanese managed to strengthen the links between the two countries. Japan was permitted to borrow ten million *baht*, and then another twenty-five million to purchase Thai produce such as rubber. During the last months of 1941, however, a Japanese invasion was widely expected, and the Thai government, while reiterating its neutral stance, sought to strengthen its military position by requesting planes, arms, and ammunition from Britain and the United States. The British sent some field guns and aviation fuel, but the Americans were still considering a loan to Thailand when war broke out.[65] On 7 December 1941 the Japanese ambassador requested permission for Japanese troops to pass through Thailand into Burma and Malaya. Phibūnsongkhrām was not in Bangkok at that time, and the cabinet had not come to a decision when the invasion began. Thai troops resisted some of the invaders, but at noon on 8 December the Prime Minister, who had hastily returned to discuss the matter in cabinet, announced an immediate cease-fire. Less than a fortnight later, on 21 December, Japan and Thailand signed a formal treaty of alliance. As he had already indicated in November 1940, Phibūnsongkhrām had opted for Japan's "New Order", hoping that the Siamese would be a leading force in the new configuration being created.

# Notes

1. The 1925 cabinet is listed in Charnvit Kasetsiri, "Each Generation of Elites in Thai History", *Journal of Social Science Review* 1, no. 1 (1976): 219-20; and that of 1926 can be found in B.A. Batson, "The End of the Absolute Monarchy in Siam", pp. 241-43.
2. The need for reduction in numbers of administrators had been recognized for some time (see the *Straits Times*, 3 December 1925).
3. The king's exact words can be found in B.A. Batson, ed., *Siam's Political Future: Documents from the End of the Absolute Monarchy*, p. 21. Much of the information on the events between 1925 and 1932 has been found in Batson's works; in "Nāisuchindā", *Phrapokklāo Kasat Nakprachāthipatai*; and in Sonthi Techānan, ed., *Phaenphathanā Kānmū'ang pai Sū Kānpokkhrǫng rabǫp Prachāthipatai tām Naew Prarātchadamri khǫng Phrabātsomdet Phrapokklāočhaoyūhua (Ph.S. 2469-2475)*.
4. Batson, "End of the Absolute Monarchy", p. 76.
5. Ibid., p. 74.
6. F.B. Sayre, an American, had been Siam's Adviser in Foreign Affairs in 1924 and 1925. He had been largely active in the negotiations for revision of treaties with European countries, negotations he had successfully concluded and which had assisted greatly in boosting not only the self-esteem of senior Siamese administrators but also the state's income by allowing an increase in import duty.
7. For details, see Batson, *Siam's Political Future*, pp. 13-41.
8. Batson, *Siam's Political Future*, p. 48; Sonthi Techānan, *Phaenphathanā Kānmū'ang*, p. 165.
9. Sonthi Techānan, *Phaenphathanā Kānmū'ang, passim*.
10. See the king's statements of April 1931, as reported in the *New York Times*, reprinted in Sonthi's book, pp. 103-8.
11. For details, see Nāisuchindā, *Phrapokklāo*, pp. 136-219.
12. Prince Boworadet was one of the grandsons of King Mongkut, a son of Prince Narēt. In 1929 the king honoured Boworadet by raising him from *mǫmchao* to *phra'ǫngchao* status.
13. See, for example, H.Ch.G.J. van der Mandere, "Het tegenwoordige Siameesche Koninkrijk", *De Indische Gids* 51, pt 2 (1929): 919-36; and J.G. Loohuis and L.D. Petit, ed., *Siam: Muang-Thai*. Petit's contribution on architecture was reprinted as *Siameesche Bouwkunst*.
14. In his typically unassuming manner, the king wrote to a close relative who had tried to dissuade him from going to the United States: "I am very keen on America unless it is an impossibility" (see Batson, "End of the Absolute Monarchy", p. 211).
15. Apparently ministers of state had their salaries cut by 10 per cent, senior civil servants by 7 per cent, and all lower salary earners by 5 per cent (see *La Revue du Pacifique* 11 [1932]: 447).
16. See Batson, "End of the Absolute Monarchy", pp. 224-29.
17. Ibid., p. 248.
18. Photographs of the military parade have been published in Nāisuchindā, *Phrapokklāo*, opp. p. 276.
19. The full text appears in Batson, *Siam's Political Future*, pp. 86-89.
20. Chula Chakrabongse, *The Twain Have Met*, p. 156.
21. Batson, *Siam's Political Future*, p. 92.
22. Batson, "End of the Absolute Monarchy", pp. 159 and 282.
23. Opinions vary greatly regarding the forces that led to the coup. See, for exam-

ple, V. Thompson, *Thailand, the New Siam*, pp. 64-65; B.A. Batson, in his review of Thawatt's book, *JSS* 61, pt 2 (1973): 193-95; and the references from the *Bangkok Times*, cited in Batson's "End of the Absolute Monarchy", pp. 293-94. See also R. de Lapomarède, "The Setting of the Siamese Revolution", *Pacific Affairs* 7 (September 1934): 251-59, and other contemporary documents, such as those published in Prīdā Wacharāngkūn, *Phrapokklāo kap Rabǫp Prachāthipatai*, pp. 96-99. A most fanciful account, in which he assigns a major role to himself, is given by Phra Sarasas in *My Country Thailand*, pp. 223-31.

24.   A detailed account can be found in Thawatt Mokarapong, *History of the Thai Revolution: A Study in Political Behaviour*. Various personal reminiscences can be found in Thak Chaloemtiarana, ed., *Thai Politics: Extracts and Documents, 1932–1957*, pp. 4-93.

25.   Chula Chakrabongse, *The Twain Have Met*, p. 161.

26.   Prīdā Wacharāngkūn, *Phrapokklāo*, p. 130.

27.   *Phrayā* Prasoetsongkhrām (acting, Defence), *čhaophrayā* Wongsānupraphan (Agriculture and Commerce), *phrayā* Chāsaenbodī (Interior), *phrayā* Pramuanwichāphūn (acting, Public Instruction), *phrayā* Sīwisānwačhā (Foreign Affairs), *phrayā* Manopakǫn (Finance), and *phrayā* Thēpwithūn (Justice).

28.   *La Revue du Pacifique* 11, no. 8/9 (August–September 1932): 576.

29.   The text, translated from the Siamese, appears in K.P. Landon, *Siam in Transition*, pp. 260-302. For an analysis and background see P. Fistié, *Sous-développement et utopie au Siam, le programme de réformes présenté en 1933 par Pridi Phanomyong*.

30.   Landon, *Siam in Transition*, p. 307. The text of the minutes of a meeting in which the plan is discussed appears on pp. 303-18. The Siamese original is reprinted in Nāisučhindā, *Phrapokklāo*, pp. 321-37.

31.   The names of four foreign advisers — two American, one French, and one English — are mentioned in *La Revue du Pacifique* 12 (1933): 507.

32.   Documents regarding the Boworadet uprising can be found in Nāisučhindā, *Phrapokklāo*, pp. 506-28. A short account is given in Landon, *Siam in Transition*, pp. 36-39. See also B.A. Batson's review of Chai-Anan Samudvanija, *14 tula*, in *JSS* 63, pt 2 (1975): 386-91.

33.   The most prominent member of the royal family, and critic of the government, to leave the country not long after the Boworadet rebellion was Prince Damrong.

34.   *La Revue du Pacifique* 13, no. 2 (February 1934): 122-24.

35.   The text of the telegram is given in Landon, *Siam in Transition*, p. 38.

36.   Batson, "End of the Absolute Monarchy", pp. 307-10.

37.   Landon, *Siam in Transition*, p. 253, where an article from the *Bangkok Times*, 27 January 1934, on the reunion is reprinted.

38.   The abdication statement is reprinted in Batson, *Siam's Political Future*, pp. 101-2; and the government's official reaction in Thak Chaloemtiarana, *Thai Politics*, pp. 238-40.

39.   For details, see Landon, *Siam in Transition*, pp. 49-50.

40.   J.C. Ingram, *Economic Change in Thailand 1850–1970*, pp. 192-93; and Landon, *Siam in Transition*, pp. 54-55.

41.   Thompson, *Thailand, the New Siam*, p. 254.

42.   Landon, *Siam in Transition*, pp. 319-23; provides the text of the investigating committee.

43.   *La Revue du Pacifique* 13 (1934): 565-67.

44.   *De Indische Gids* 61, pt 1 (1939): 467-68.

45.   See, for example D.F. van Wijk's article in *Onze Stem* of October 1934,

reprinted in *De Indische Gids* 57, pt 1 (1935): 76-77; and Thompson, *Thailand, the New Siam*, pp. 129-33.

46. Charnvit Kasetsiri, "The First Phibun Government and Its Involvement in World War II", *JSS* 62, pt 2 (1974): 35.

47. Phibūnsongkhrām's love for attractive uniforms is well documented in "Withētkaranī", *Sārakhadī Prawatisāt Thāngkānmu'ang Thai, Hētkān Thāngkānmu'ang 43 Pī Haengprakǭp Prachāthipatai*, pp. 53-57.

48. Thompson, *Thailand, the New Siam*, pp. 308-9.

49. The offer of a cabinet post is mentioned in *La Revue du Pacifique* 13 (1934): 567, and the 1938 request to consider the prime ministership is mentioned in H. Manzooruddin Ahmad, *Thailand, Land der Freien*, p. 238.

50. Thompson, *Thailand, the New Siam*, p. 785.

51. Ingram, *Economic Change*, p. 329. For a contemporary account of Siam's economic situation, see "L'activité économique du Siam", *La Revue du Pacifique* 15 (1936): 69-73.

52. Ahmad, *Thailand, Land der Freien*, p. 231.

53. Charnvit Kasetsiri, "The First Phibun Government", p. 36.

54. In the local vernacular, the name of the country was changed from Sayām to Mū'ang Thai. The change became effective on 24 June 1939, the seventh anniversary of the 1932 coup.

55. From the minutes of the cabinet meeting, 30 August 1939, as cited in Thamsook Numnonda, "Pibulsongkram's Thai Nation-Building Programme during the Japanese Military Presence, 1941-1945", *Journal of Southeast Asian Studies* 9, no. 2 (September 1978): 234.

56. For the text in translation, see Thinaphan Nakhata, "National Consolidation and Nation-Building (1939-1947)", in Thak Chaloemtiarana, *Thai Politics*, pp. 245-50.

57. Charnvit Kasetsiri, "The First Phibun Government", p. 39. Several of the dialogues have been published in Thak Chaloemtiarana, *Thai Politics*, pp. 260-316.

58. Prince Wan Waithayakon, "Thai Culture", *JSS* 35, pt 2 (1944): 140.

59. Thak Chaloemtiarana, *Thai Politics*, p. 258.

60. Prem Chaya and Alethea, *The Passing Hours: A Record of Five Amazing Years*, taken from the weekly features in the *Bangkok Chronicle* between 1941 and 1945. The entry for 23 July 1941 refers to the hat campaign.

61. Some extracts of plays are given in Thak Chaloemtiarana, *Thai Politics*, pp. 317-22.

62. The details of the treaty negotiations and Phibūnsongkhrām's secret alliance with Japan can be found in E.T. Flood, "The 1940 Franco-Thai Border Dispute and Phibun Songkhram's Commitment to Japan", *Journal of Southeast Asian History* 10, no. 2 (1969): 304-25.

63. Some partisan accounts are given in M. Sivaram, *Mekong Clash and Far East Crisis: A Survey of the Thailand-Indochina Conflict and the Japanese Mediation*; and *luang* Vichitr Vadakarn, *Thailand's Case*. A detailed account is also given in *phon'ēk* Nēt Khēmayothin, *Ngān Tai Din khǭng Phan'ēk Yothi* 3, pp. 65-120.

64. See the editorial comment by J.G. Keyes in Direk Jayanama, *Siam and World War II*, p. 40.

65. J.V. Martin, "Thai-American Relations in World War II", *Journal of Asian Studies* 21 (1963): 459.

# Glossary

*abhiseka* (Sanskrit). Anointing, consecrating, with particular reference to the inauguration of a king.

*at*. Old copper coin, one sixty-fourth of a *baht* in value.

*baht*. Siamese monetary unit. The name is derived from the *baht* unit of weight, 15 grams, which was its original weight in silver.

*biawat*. Sum of money the Siamese king used to give to his ranking officers.

Čhakrī. Traditional honorific name given to the head of the Mahātthai. Since the founder of the present dynasty once occupied that position, that dynasty is often referred to as Čhakrī dynasty.

*čhamū'n*. Military title indicating officer rank in the Mahātlek, also known as *čhaomū'n*.

*chang*. Unit of money and weight, corresponding to 80 *baht* or 1.2 kg.

*čhāngwāng*. Senior palace official; title of an officer in the Mahātlek.

*čhao*. Ruler, chief.

*čhāo*. Prince, the class of noblemen.

*čhaočhǭmmāndā*. Title indicating the king's concubine who has given birth to a child fathered by the king.

*čhaofā*. Title of a prince of the highest rank.

*čhaokrom*. Head of a department.

*čhaomū*. Leader of a small band of soldiers, comparable to corporal.

*čhaomŭ'ang.*  Ruler of a city or country.

*čhaomŭ'n.*  See *čhamŭ'n.*

*čhaophayā.*  Highest rank of conferred nobility; during the Bangkok period usually spent *čhaophrayā.*

*čhēdī.*  Sacred mound; memorial edifice.

*fu'ang.*  Unit of money and weight, corresponding to one-eighth of a *baht*, at present obsolete.

*hāp.*  Unit of weight, equivalent to 60 kg.

Jatakas.  Collection of stories of previous births of the Buddha; in the Buddhist canon there are 547 Jataka stories.

Kalāhom.  Ministry of Defence.

Kathin.  Annual religious ceremony, following the rainy season, during which robes are presented to some of the Buddhist monks.

*khun.*  Title of respect; during the Bangkok period it was one of the lower ranks of the conferred nobility.

*khunnāng.*  Term denoting the general class of the conferred nobility.

Khotchasī.  Mythical animal representing a lion with an elephant's trunk, found on the seal of the Kalāhom.

*krom.*  Department, bureau; an element in conferred titles for royalty.

*kromakhun.*  Conferred title for royalty, higher than *kromamŭ'n.*

*kromaluang.*  Conferred title for royalty, higher than *kromakhun.*

*kromamŭ'n.*  Conferred title for royalty.

*kromphra'.*  Conferred title for royalty, higher than *kromaluang.*

*kromsomdetphra'.*  The highest conferred title for royalty.

*kūp.*  Large hood, providing shade, found on ceremonial boats; a howdah.

*liang.*  To raise, bring up; to look after (someone else's) child.

*luang.*  Title of conferred nobility, higher than *khun.*

Mahā Uparāt.  Literally "Great Viceroy", the official rank of the occupant of the Front Palace, traditionally the highest office in Siam, second only to that of the king. Often referred to as Uparāt.

Mahātlek.  Corps of Royal Pages.

Mahātthai.  Department of Civil Affairs; since the Fifth Reign the name of the Ministry of the Interior.

*mǫmčhāo.*  Title of a member of royalty who is in the grandchild generation of royal descent, or treated as such.

*mŭ'ang.*  City; country.

*mŭ'n.*  One of the lower ranks of the conferred nobility, during most of the Bangkok period obsolete.

*nāi*.   Master, owner, boss.

*nāimuat*.   Chief or leader of a section.

*niphān* (Sanskrit: *nirvāna*).   State of salvation when an individual is released from the cycle of rebirth.

*parien*.   High grade of Buddhist religious instruction.

*phayā*.   High rank of conferred nobility, during most of the Bangkok period also known as *phrayā*.

*phonlaru'an*.   Civilians, as opposed to *thahān*.

*phra'*.   Rank of conferred nobility, higher than *luang*, but lower than *phayā (phrayā)*.

*Phra'rātchaphithī boromaphisēk*.   Elaborate ceremonies of anointnment and elevation to the status of absolute king.

Phra' Thammasāt (Sanskrit: *dharmaśāstra*).   Body of laws, jurisprudence.

*phrai*.   Commoner, freeman.

*phrai luang*.   Commoner, for corvée duties assigned to one of the king's departments.

*phrai som*.   Commoner, for corvée duties assigned to a private individual other than the king.

Phrakhlang.   The Treasury, traditionally also in change of Foreign Affairs.

*phrayā*.   See *phayā*.

*prāng*.   Tall religious monument with rounded top.

*rai*.   Square surface measure equal to 1,600 square metres.

*rātchakhana*.   Highest honorific title a Buddhist monk may receive.

*saktinā*.   Elaborate system of degrees of rank expressed by numbers of *rai* in land.

*salu'ng*.   Unit of money and weight, corresponding to one-fourth of a *baht*.

*samanokhrua*.   Census of the Siamese populace, occasionally held during the Ayutthaya period.

*samian*.   Scribe.

Sangha.   The brotherhood of Buddhist monks and novices.

*sārawat*.   Assistant superviser.

Satsadi.   Department of Registration, also known as Suratsawadī.

Sēnā.   Officer attached to the Department of Lands.

Sēnābodī.   Ministerial committee, corresponding to a cabinet.

*sodāban*.   Person who has entered the stream of wisdom. It is believed that a true *sodāban* will not have more than seven rebirths before reaching the blissful state of *niphān*.

*somdet*.   An adjective meaning "high, excellent", part of some exalted titles.

Suratsawadī.  See Satsadī.

*tambon.*  District.

*thahān.*  Military men, soldier, as opposed to *phonlaru'an.*

*tham khwan.*  Ceremony to restore or reinforce the "vital power" of a person, animal, or venerated object.

*thanāi.*  Legal counsellor.

*thang.*  Capacity measure equal to 20 litres.

*thawāi tua* (literally).  "To present one's body", to be presented to the king.

Tai.  Name designating the broad linguistic category of Tai-speaking peoples, of which the Thai are the branch situated in central Thailand.

Thai.  Word with which the people inhabiting central Thailand traditionally have indicated themselves; during the days of heightened nationalism it became (wrongly) equated with a similar-sounding word meaning "free".

Thā (literally).  "Landing place; ships' berth", name of a subdivision of the traditional Siamese Treasury.

*thāt.*  Class of slaves.

Traiphūmikhāthā.  Sacred work on the "Three Worlds", versions of which were known in Siam as early as the fourteenth century. It has provided the Siamese with a framework with which to view the universe and the role humans play in it.

Uparāt.  See Mahā Uparāt.

Wang Nā.  The "Front Palace", traditionally the residence of the Mahā Uparāt.

*yā.*  Rank of conferred nobility used in Ayutthaya times, obsolete during the Bangkok period.

Yokrabat.  Legal officer appointed by the king and attached to a provincial centre.

# Reference Bibliography

Only publications mentioned in the notes are listed. The bibliography incorporates the abbreviations used; immediately after the abbreviation the full reference is given. Only in a few instances, when they are repeatedly cited for primary source material, are periodicals listed here, together with the dates of the issues consulted. Thai names are listed under the "first name".

Abha Bhamorabutr. *A Short History of Thailand*. Bangkok: Department of Corrections Press, 1979.

Adey Moore, R. "An Early British Merchant in Bangkok". *JSS* 11, pt 2 (1914–15): 21-39. Kraus Reprint, 1969.

Ahmad, H. Manzooruddin. *Thailand, Land der Freien*. Leipzig: W. Goldmann, 1943.

Akin Rabibhadana. *The Organization of Thai Society in the Early Bangkok Period, 1782–1873*. Data paper no. 74, Southeast Asian Program. Ithaca, N.Y.: Cornell University, 1969.

Alabaster, H. *The Wheel of the Law*. London: Trubner, 1871. Republished by Gregg International, 1971.

Amat, R.d', and R. Limuzin Lamothe, eds: *Dictionnaire de biographie française*, vol. 10. Paris: Libraire Letouzey, 1967.

Amǫn Darunrak. *Dusit Thānī*. Bangkok: National Library, 1970.

*Bangkok Calendar*. Annual, edited by D.B. Bradley. Bangkok, 1859–72.

Batson, B.A. Review of Thawatt Mokarapong, *History of the Thai Revolution: A Study in Political Behaviour. JSS* 61, pt 2 (1973): 186-96.

_____, ed. *Siam's Political Future: Documents from the End of the Absolute Monarchy.* Data Paper no. 96, Southeast Asia Program. Ithaca, N.Y.: Cornell University, 1974.

_____. Review of Chai-Anan Samudvanija, *14 Tula: Khana Ratsadan kap Kabot Bowaradet. JSS* 63, pt 2 (1975): 386-91.

_____. "The End of the Absolute Monarchy in Siam". Ph.D. dissertation, Cornell University, 1977.

Battye, N.A. "The Military, Government and Society in Siam, 1868-1910: Politics and Military Reform during the Reign of King Chulalongkorn". Ph.D. dissertation, Cornell University, 1974.

Blankwaardt, W. "Notes upon the Relations between Holland and Siam". *JSS* 20, pt 3 (1927): 241-58.

Blofeld, J. *King Maha Mongkut of Siam.* Singapore: Asia Pacific Press, 1972.

Bock, C. *Temples and Elephants: The Narrative of a Journey of Exploration Through Upper Siam and Lao.* London: Sampson Low, Marston, Searle and Rivington, 1884.

Bowring, Sir John. *The Kingdom and People of Siam.* 2 vols. Oxford in Asia Historical Reprints. Kuala Lumpur: Oxford University Press, 1977.

Bradley, W.L. "Prince Mongkut and Jesse Caswell". *JSS* 54, pt 1, (1966): 29-41.

_____. "The Accession of King Mongkut". *JSS* 57, pt 1 (1969): 149-62.

Bristowe, W.S. *Louis and the King of Siam.* London: Chatto and Windus, 1976.

Brown, I. "British Financial Advisers in Siam in the Reign of King Chulalongkorn". *Modern Asian Studies* 12, no. 2, (1978): 193-215.

_____. "Siam and the Gold Standard, 1902-1908". *Journal of Southeast Asian Studies* 10, no. 2 (1979): 381-99.

Bruijn Kops, G.F. de. *Statistiek van den Handel en de Scheepvaart op Java en Madura.* 2 vol. Batavia: Lange & Co, 1857-58.

*Burney Papers, Bangkok 1910-1914, The.* 5 vols. Reprinted by Gregg International, 1971.

Caron, F., and J. Schouten. *A True Description of the Mighty Kingdoms of Japan and Siam,* with introduction, notes and appendixes by C.R. Boxer. London: Argonaut Press, 1935.

Cartwright, B.O. "The Huey Lottery". *JSS* 18, pt 3 (1924): 221-39.

Chaen Patčhusānon and Sawat Čhanthanī, eds. *Kǫraniphiphāt rawāng Thai kap Farangset lae Kānrop thī Pāknām Čhaophrayā samai r.s. 112.* Bangkok: Kromyuthasu'ksāthahānru'a, 1967.

Chaloem Yongbunkoet. *Thonabat Thai.* Bangkok: Thaikasoem, 1961.

Chaloem Yuwiengchai. "Prawatisāt Nakhǫn Sī Thammarāt samai Krung Thonburī". Rāingānkānsamanāprawatisāt Nakhǫn Sī Thammarāt, Nakhǫn Sī Thammarāt Withayalaikhrū, *Prawatisāt Nakhǫn Sī Thammarāt,* Krungsayāmkānphim, 1978, pp. 218-68.

Chandler, D.P. "Cambodia's Relations with Siam in the Early Bangkok Period: The Politics of a Tributary State". *JSS* 60, pt 1 (1972): 153-69.

Chandran, J. *The Contest for Siam 1889-1902: A Study in Diplomatic Rivalry.* Kuala Lumpur: Penerbit Universiti Kebangsaan Malaysia, 1977.

*Čhaofā Thammathibēt, Phraprawat lae Phraniphon bot Rǫykrǫng*: Bangkok: Bannakhan, 1973.

Charnvit Kasetsiri. "The First Phibun Government and Its Involvement in World War II". *JSS* 62, pt 2 (1974): 25-88.

_____. "Each Generation of Elites in Thai History". Translated by Chantima Ongsuruksa. *Journal of Social Science Review* 1, no. 1 (1976): 189-226.

Chatthip Nartsupha and Suthy Prasartset, eds. *Socio-economic Institutions and Cultural Change in Siam, 1851-1910, a Documentary Survey.* Southeast Asian Perspectives no. 4. Singapore: Institute of Southeast Asian Studies, n.d.

_____. *The Political Economy of Siam, 1851-1910.* Bangkok: The Social Science Association of Thailand, n.d.

_____, Suthy Prasartset, and Montri Chenvidyakarn, eds. *The Political Economy of Siam, 1910-1932.* Bangkok: The Social Science Association of Thailand, 1978.

Chen, Chingho A. "Mac Thien Tu and Phrayataksin: A Survey of their Political Stands, Conflicts and Background". *Proceedings, Seventh IAHA Conference, 22-26 August 1977, Bangkok* vol. 2, pp. 1534-75. Bangkok: Chulalongkorn University Press, 1979.

*Čhotmāihēthōn, chabap Phrayā Mūnlathonrak.* Bangkok: Sophānaphiphathanākǫn, 1921.

*Čhotmāihēt Phrarātchakitrāiwan nai Phrabātsomdet Phračhunlačhǫmklāo Čhaoyūhua Pī Thǫ Čhunlasakarāt 1241.* Bangkok: Cremation volume for Phra' Patiwētwisit (Sāi Lēkhayanon), 1970.

*Čhotmāihēt Ratchakān thī Sǭng, C.S. 1173.* Bangkok: Munlanithi-phraboromarāchānuson Phrabātsomdetphraphuthaloet-lānaphālai nai Phraboromarāchūpakam, 1961.

*Čhotmāihēt ru'ang Ballestier Thūt Amērikan khaomā nai Rat-chakān thī Sām mu'a pī čhǭ Ph.S. 2393. PP,* vol. 35 (1969), pp. 3-71.

Christian, J.L. "The Kra Canal Fable". *Amerasia* 1 (February 1938): 559-63.

Chula Chakrabongse, Prince. *Lords of Life: A History of the Kings of Thailand.* London: Alvin Redman, 1967.

_____. *The Twain Have Met, or An Eastern Prince Came West.* London: Foulis, 1956.

Čhunlačhǭmklāo čhaoyūhua, *phrabātsomdetphra'. Phrarātchahat-lēkhā mu'a Sadetphrarātchadamnoen Praphāt Yurōp Ph.S. 2440.* 2 vols. Bangkok: Khurusaphā, 1962.

Coedès, G. *The Making of South East Asia.* Translated by H.M. Wright. London: Routledge & Kegan Paul, 1967.

_____, ed. "The English Correspondence of King Mongkut". *JSS* 21 (1927), pt 1: 1-35, pt 2: 127-77; 22 (1928), pt 1: 1-18.

_____, and C. Archaimbault. *Les trois mondes (Traibhūmi Brah Rvaṅ).* Publications de l'École Française d'Extrême-Orient, vol. 89. Paris: École Française d'Extrême-Orient, 1973.

Collet, O.J.A. *Étude politique et économique sur le Siam moderne.* Brussels: Hayez, 1911.

Collis, M. *Wayfoong, the Hongkong and Shanghai Banking Cor-poration.* London: Faber and Faber, 1965.

Cosenza, M.E., ed. *The Complete Journal of Townsend Harris.* New York: Japan Society, 1930.

Cowan, W.L. "The Role of Prince Chuthamani in the Moderniz-ing of Siam and His Court Position During the Reigns of Rama III and Rama IV". *JSS* 55, pt 1 (1967): 41-59.

Crawfurd, J. *Journal of an Embassy to the Courts of Siam and Cochin China.* Oxford in Asia Historical Reprints. Kuala Lumpur: Oxford University Press, 1967.

*Crawfurd Papers, The.* Bangkok: Vajiranana National Library, 1915. Reprinted by Gregg International, 1971.

Crosby, Sir Josiah. *Siam: the Crossroads.* London: Hollis and Carter, 1945.

Cucherousset, H. *Quelques informations sur le Siam.* Hanoi: Éditions de l'Éveil Économique, 1925.

Curtis, L.J. *The Laos of North Siam.* London: Fleming H. Revell, 1903.

Damrong Rātchanuphāp, *kromphra'. Phrarātchaphongsāwadān*

*Krungratanakōsin Ratchakān thī Sǫng.* 2 vols. Bangkok: Khurusaphā, 1952.

———. *Phongsāwadān Ru'ang Thai Rop Phamā. PP,* pt 6, vols. 5 and 6. Bangkok: Khurusaphā, 1963.

———. *Tamnānwangnā, PP,* pt 13, vol. 11, pp. 1-176. Bangkok: Khurusaphā, 1964.

———. *Phrarātchaphongsāwadān Krungratanakōsin Ratchakān thī Hā.* Bangkok: Cremation Volume for Chayan Phlāchīwa, 1964.

DC First R — Čhaophrayā Thiphākǫrawong. *The Dynastic Chronicles Bangkok Era, the First Reign.* Edited by Thadeus and Chadin Flood. Vol. 1. Tokyo: The Centre for East Asian Cultural Studies, 1978.

DC Fourth R — Čhaophrayā Thiphākǫrawong, *The Dynastic Chronicles Bangkok Era, the Fourth Reign.* Translated by Chadin Flood. 5 vols. Tokyo: The Centre for East Asian Cultural Studies, 1965-74.

de la Loubère, S. *The Kingdom of Siam.* Oxford in Asia Historical Reprints. Kuala Lumpur: Oxford University Press, 1969. Reprint of 1693 edition.

de Schaek, I. *S.A.I. le grand-duc Boris de Russe aux fêtes du Siam pour le couronnement du roi.* Paris: Plon, 1914.

Dhani Nivat, *kromamū'n.* "The Reconstruction of Rama I of the Chakri Dynasty". *JSS* 43, pt 1 (1955): 21-48.

———. "The Age of King Rama I of the Chakri Dynasty". *JSS* 46, pt 1 (1958): 51.

———. "The Inscriptions of Wat Phra Jetubon". In *Collected Articles by H.H. Prince Dhani Nivat Kromamu'n Bidayalabh Brdihyakorn,* pp. 5-28. Bangkok: The Siam Society, 1969.

———. "King Rama VI's Last Work". In *Collected Articles by H.H. Prince Dhani Nivat Kromamu'n Bidayalabh Brdihyakorn,* pp. 121-27. Bangkok: The Siam Society, 1969.

Dilock, Prinz von Siam. *Die Landwirtschaft in Siam: Ein Beitrag zur Wirtschaftsgeschichte des Königreichs Siam.* Tübingen: Laupp'schen Buchhandlung, 1907.

Direk Jayanama. *Siam and World War II.* Translated and edited by J.G. Keyes. Bangkok: The Social Science Association of Thailand, 1978.

Engel, D.M. *Law and Kingship in Thailand During the Reign of King Chulalongkorn.* Michigan Papers on South and Southeast Asia, no. 9. Ann Arbor: The University of Michigan, Center for South and Southeast Asian Studies, 1975.

Eulenberg-Hertfeld, P. zu, ed. *Ost-Asien 1860-1862 in Briefen des Grafen Fritz zu Eulenberg.* Berlin: Mittler, 1900.

Finlayson, G. *The Mission to Siam and Hue, the Capital of Cochin China, in the Years 1821-2*. London: John Murray, 1826.

Fistié, P. *Sous-développement et utopie au Siam, le programme de réformes présenté en 1933 par Pridi Phanomyong*. The Hague: Mouton, 1969.

Flood, E.T. "The 1940 Franco-Thai Border Dispute and Phibun Songkhram's Commitment to Japan". *Journal of Southeast Asian History* 10, no. 2 (1969): 304-25.

Frankfurter, O. "The Mission of Sir James Brooke to Siam". *JSS* 8, pt 3 (1911): 19-33.

_____. "The Unofficial Mission of John Morgan, Merchant, to Siam in 1821". *JSS* 11 (1914-15): 1-8.

Gerini, G.E. "Trial by Ordeal in Siam and the Siamese Law of Ordeals". *Asiatic Quarterly Review*, April 1895, pp. 415-24, and July 1895, pp. 156-75.

_____. "Shan and Siam". *Imperial and Asiatic Quarterly Review*, 1898, pp. 145-63.

_____. "Historical Retrospect of Junkceylon Island". *JSS* 2, pt 2, (1905): 1-141.

_____. *A Retrospective View and Account of the Origin of the Thet Mahâ Ch'at Ceremony*. Bangkok: Sathirakoses-Nagapradipa Foundation, 1976. Reprint of the 1892 edition.

Gervaise, N. *The Natural and Political History of the Kingdom of Siam*. Translated by H.S. O'Neill. Bangkok: Siam Observer Press, 1928.

Gesick, L.M. "Kingship and Political Integration in Traditional Siam, 1767-1824". Ph.D. dissertation, Cornell University, 1976.

Giles, F.H. "A Critical Analysis of Van Vliet's Historical Account of Siam in the 17th Century". *JSS* 30 (1938), pt 2: 155-240, pt 3: 271-380.

Goldman, M.F. "Franco-British Rivalry over Siam, 1896-1904". *Journal of Southeast Asian Studies* 3, no. 2 (1972): 210-28.

Graham, W.A. *Siam: A Handbook of Practical, Commerical, and Political Information*. 2 vols. 3rd ed. London: Moring, 1924. Originally published in 1912.

Greene, S. "King Wachirawut's Policy of Nationalism". In *In Memoriam Phya Anuman Rajadhon, Contributions in Memory of the Late President of the Siam Society,* ed. Tej Bunnag and M. Smithies, pp. 251-59. Bangkok: The Siam Society, 1970.

Griswold, A.B. "King Mongkut in Perspective". *JSS* 45, pt 1 (1957): 1-41.

_____. "The Rishis of Wat Pho". *Felicitation Volumes of South-*

*east-Asian Studies Presented to His Highness Prince Dhanivat Kromamun Bidyalabh Bridhyakorn,* vol. 2, pp. 319-28. Bangkok: The Siam Society, 1965.

Guehler, U. "A Letter by Sir Robert H. Schomburgk H.B.M.'s Consul in Bangkok in 1860". *JSS* 37, pt 2 (1949): 149-54.

Gutzlaff, K. *Verslag van een Driejarig Verblijf in Siam, en van eene. Reize langs de Kust van China naar Mantchou-Tartarije.* Rotterdam: Wijt & Zonen, 1833. The English version was published under the title "Journal of a Residence in Siam and of a Voyage along the Coast of China to Mantchou Tartary" in the *Chinese Repository* 1 (1832): 16-25, 45-64, 81-99, 122-40, 180-96.

Hirshfield, C., "The Struggle for the Mekong Banks, 1892-1896". *Journal of Southeast Asian History* 9, no. 1, 1968, pp. 25-52.

Homan van der Heide, J. "The Economical Development of Siam During the Last Half Century". *JSS* 3, pt 2 (1906): 74-101.

Htin Aung, Maung. "Three Unpublished Papers by Harvey, Introduced, Explained and Commented Upon". *Journal of the Burma Research Society* 58, pt 1 (1975): 1-52.

Ingram, J.C. *Economic Change in Thailand 1850-1970.* Stanford, Cal.: Stanford University Press, 1971.

Ishii, Yoneo. "A Note on Buddhist Millenarian Revolts in Northeastern Siam". *Journal of Southeast Asian Studies* 6, no. 2 (1975): 121-26.

————, Osamu Akagi, and Shigeharu Tanabe. *An Index of Officials in Traditional Thai Governments, vol. 1, pt 1,* discussion paper no. 76. Kyoto: The Center for Southeast Asian Studies, 1974.

Johnston, D.B. "Opening a Frontier: the Expansion of Rice Cultivation in Central Thailand in the 1890's". *Contributions to Asian Studies* 9 (1976): 27-44.

Jones, R.B. *Thai Titles and Ranks, Including a Translation of Traditions of Royal Lineage by King Chulalongkorn.* Data Paper no. 81, Southeast Asia Program. Ithaca: Cornell University, 1971.

*JSS — The Journal of the Siam Society,* 1904 to the present. (Between 1942 and 1944 the journal appeared under the title *Journal of the Thailand Research Society).*

Kanlayā Čhunnuan, comp. *Čhaophrayā Aphairātchāsayāmānukūnkit (Khutsatāp Rolin Yakhmin).* Bangkok: Krom Sinlapākǫn, 1972.

*Kāntāēngtangkhunnāngthai nai samai Ratchakān thī Hā.* Bangkok: Kǫnghǫčhotmāihēthaengchāt Krom Sinlapākǫn, 1978.

Kemp, J. *Aspects of Siamese Kingship in the Seventeenth Century.* Bangkok: Social Science Association Press of Thailand, 1969.

Khana Kammakān Fū'nfū Būrana Khāi Bāng Račhan. *Wīrachon Khāi Bāng Račhan.* Bangkok: Rongphim Kānsāsanā, 1966.

Ki Thanit. *Prawat Khana Song Thai kap Thammayutprakān.* Bangkok: Thamrat, 1975.

Kiernan, V.G. "Britain, Siam and Malaya: 1875-1885". *Journal of Modern History* 27, no. 1 (March 1956): 1-20.

Koenig, J.G. "Journal of a Voyage from India to Siam and Malacca in 1779". *Journal of the Straits Branch of the Royal Asiatic Society,* no. 26 (January 1894), pp. 58-201; and no. 27 (October 1894), pp. 57-133.

*KTSD — Kotmāi Trā Sām Duang.* 5 vols. Bangkok: Khurusaphā edition, 1963.

*L'Asie Française — Bulletin Mensuel du Comité de l'Asie Française.* Paris: Comité de l'Asie Frančaise, 1910-1917.

*La Revue du Pacifique* — monthly, May 1922-March 1937.

Landon, K.P. *Siam in Transition.* New York: Greenwood Press, 1939.

_____. *The Chinese in Thailand.* New York: Institute of Pacific Relations, 1941.

Lapomarède, R. de. "The Setting of the Siamese Revolution". *Pacific Affairs* 7 (September 1934): 251-59.

Leonowens, A.H. *The English Governess at the Siamese Court; Being Recollections of Six Years in the Royal Palace at Bangkok.* London: Trubner, 1870.

_____. *The Romance of the Harem.* Philadelphia: Porter and Coates, 1872.

Lindenberg, P.P. "The Early Postal History of Thailand". *Journal of the Thailand Research Society* 35, pt 1 (1944): 77-94.

Lingat, R. *L'esclavage privé dans le vieux droit siamois.* Paris: Éditions Domat-Montchrestien, 1931.

_____. "La vie réligieuse du roi Mongkut". *The Siam Society Fiftieth Anniversary Commemorative Publication,* 1, pp. 18-37. Bangkok: The Siam Society, 1954.

_____. "Les suicides réligieux au Siam". *Felicitation Volumes of Southeast-Asian Studies Presented to His Highness Prince Dhaninivat Kromamun Bidyalabh Bridhyakorn,* vol. 1, pp. 71-75. Bangkok: The Siam Society, 1965.

Loohuis, J.G., and L.D. Petit, eds. *Siam; Muang-Thai.* The Hague: Het Genootschap "Nederland-Siam", 1931.

Low, J. "On the Government of Siam". *Asiatic Researches* 20, pt 2 (1836): 245-84.

_____. "On the laws of Mu'ung Thai or Siam". *The Journal of the Indian Archipelago and Eastern Asia* 1 (1847): 327-429.

McFarland, G.B. *Thai-English Dictionary*. Stanford: Stanford University Press, 1954. First printed in 1944.

McGilvary, D. *A Half Century Among the Siamese and the Lao*. New York: Fleming H. Revell, 1912.

MacGregor, J. *Through the Buffer State: A Record of Recent Travels through Borneo, Siam, and Cambodia*. London: White, 1896.

Mandere, H.Ch.G.J. van der. "Het tegenwoordige Siameesche Koninkrijk". *De Indische Gids* 51, pt 2 (1929): 919-36.

Manich Jumsai, M.L. *King Mongkut and Sir John Bowring*. Bangkok: Chalermnit, 1970.

_____. *Popular History of Thailand*. Bangkok: Chalermnit, 1972.

_____. *Prince Prisdang's Files on His Diplomatic Activities in Europe, 1880-1886*. Bangkok: Chalermnit, 1977.

Martin, J.V. "Thai-American Relations in World War II". *Journal of Asian Studies* 21 (1963): 451-67.

Moffat, A.L. *Mongkut, the King of Siam*. Ithaca, N.Y.: Cornell University Press, 1961.

Mongkut, King of Siam. "Brief Sketches of Siamese History, Facts from H.S.M. the late King Phra Chaum Klau in 1850". *Siamese Repository*, 1869, pp. 254-67. Also appeared in the *Chinese Repository*, 1851 and in Bowring, *The Kingdom and People*, vol. 2.

_____. "The English Correspondence of King Mongkut". See under G. Coedès, ed.

Montri Umavijani. *A Poetic Journey Through Thai History*. Bangkok: privately published, n.d.

Murdoch, J.B. "The 1901-1902 'Holy Man's' Rebellion". JSS 62, pt 1 (1974): 47-66.

Ñāṇamoli, The Venerable Thera, trans. *The Pāṭimokkha, 227 Fundamental Rules of a Bikkhu*. Bangkok: Maha Makut Academy, 1966.

"Nāisuchindā". *Phrapokklāo Kasat Nakprachāthipatai*. Bangkok: Samnakphim Sayām, 1976.

Neale, F.A. *Narrative of a Residence in Siam*. London: Office of the National Illustrated Library, 1852.

Neon Snidvongs. "Siam's Relations with Britain and France in the Reign of King Mongkut, 1851-1868". Ph.D. dissertation, University of London, 1961.

Nēt Khēmayothin, *phon'ēk*. *Ngān Tai Din khōng Phan'ēk Yothi*. 3 vols. Bangkok: Kasoembannakit, 1967.

Notton, C., trans. *The Chronicle of the Emerald Buddha*. Bang-
kok: Bangkok Times Press, 1933.
———, trans. *La vie du poète Sounthone-Bhou*. Limoges:
Rougerie, 1959.
O'Kane, J., trans. *The Ship of Sulaimān*. Persian Heritage series
no. 11. New York: Columbia University Press, 1972.
Owen, N.G. "The Rice Industry of Mainland Southeast Asia,
1850-1914". *JSS* 59, pt 2 (1971): 75-143.
Pallegoix, A. *Description du royaume Thai ou Siam*. 2 vols.
Farnborough: Gregg International, 1969. Reprinted from the
1854 edition.
Pavie, A. *Eine friedliche Eroberung, Indochina 1888*. Vienna:
Buchgemeinschaft, n.d. Translated from the French edition
of 1947 by S. Pruvost-Seguin.
Pensri (Suvanij) Duke. *Les relations entre la France et la Thailande
(Siam) au XIXe siècle d'après les archives étrangères*.
Bangkok: Chalermnit, 1962.
*Periodicals and Newspapers Printed in Thailand between
1844-1934, a Bibliography*. Bangkok: Department of Fine
Arts, 1970.
Petit, L.D. *Siameesche Bouwkunst*. Mouseion-reeks, no. 3.
Amsterdam: Van Munster, n.d.
*Photčhanānukrom Chabap Rātchabanthitsathān*. Bangkok:
Rātchabanthitsathān, 1950.
*Phrarātchaniyom nai Phrabātsomdet Phramongkutklāo Čhao-
yūhua*. Bangkok: Cremation volume for Nāng Čharatsi
Sučharitkun, 1971.
Piyachat Pitawan. *Kānyokloekrabopphrai nai Ratchasamai
Phrabātsomdetphra' Čhulačhǫmklāo rawāng Ph.S.
2411-2453*. Bangkok: Mūnlanithikhrongkāntamrā
Sangkhomsāt lae Manutsayasāt, 1980.
*PKRt Sām — čhaophrayā* Thiphākǫrawong. *Phrarāt-
chaphongsāwadān Krungratanakōsin, Ratchakān thī Sǫng*.
Bangkok: Khurusaphā, 1961.
*PKRt Sǫng — čhaophrayā* Thiphākǫrawong. *Phrarātchaphong-
sāwadān Krungratanakōsin, Ratchakān thī Sǫng*. Bangkok:
Khurusaphā, 1961.
*PP — Prachum Phongsāwadān*. The collected chronicles of Siam,
a multi-volume series published between 1961 and 1970.
Where I have consulted other versions than this recent
Khurusaphā edition, these are mentioned separately.
Prachoom Chomchai, ed. and trans. *Chulalongkorn the Great*.
East Asian Cultural Studies Series, no. 8. Tokyo: The Centre
for East Asian Cultural Studies, 1965.

Pradit Kraiwong. *Tāksin Mahārāt*. Bangkok: Pramuanson, 1965.

*Prāp Ngiew Ton Thī 1, PP*, pt 75. Bangkok: Cremation volume for mǫm Yu'an Thǫngyai na Ayutthaya, 1974.

*Prawatkitčhakānthahān samai Krungratanakōsin*. Bangkok: Cremation volume for *phan'ēk phrayā* Damkoengronaphop (That Pathāmanon) and *nāngsāw* Phian Pathāmanon, 1967.

Prayut Sitthiphan. *Phramahāthīrarātčhao*. Bangkok: Sayām, 1972.

Prem Chaya and Alethea. *The Passing Hours: A Record of Five Amazing Years*. Bangkok: Chatra Books, 1945.

Prīdā Wacharāngkūn. *Phrapokklāo kap Rabǫp Prachāthipatai*. Bangkok: Phranakhǫn Printers, 1977.

*Programme of the Coronation of His Majesty Vajiravudh, King of Siam*. Bangkok, 1911.

Prungsī Wanliphōdom. "Phraprāng Wat Arunrātchawārām". In *Chaloem Phrakiet Phrabātsomdet Phraphuthaloetlā*, pp. 41-51. Bangkok, 1978.

Rātchaburīdirēkru't, *kromaluang*. *Kotmāi Lem 1*. Bangkok: Cremation volume for *phanahua phonthō* Amphǫn Sīchaiyan, 1970.

*Rātchasakunwong*. Bangkok: Cremation volume for *nāi* Sanan Bunsiriphan, 1969.

Rajaretnam, M. *Thailand's Kra Canal: Some Issues*. Research Notes and Discussions Paper no. 8. Singapore: Institute of Southeast Asian Studies, 1978.

Ramsay, J.A. "The Development of a Bureaucratic Policy: the Case of Northern Siam". Ph.D. dissertation, Cornell University, 1971.

Reynolds, C.J. "The Buddhist Monkhood in Nineteenth Century Thailand". Ph.D. dissertation, Cornell University, 1973.

———, ed. and trans. *Autobiography: The Life of Prince-Patriarch Vajirañāna of Siam, 1860–1921*. Athens, Ohio: Ohio University Press, 1979.

Reynolds, E.E. *Baden-Powell: A Biography of Lord Baden-Powell of Gilwell*. 2nd ed. London: Oxford University Press, 1957.

Rian Sīchan and Nēt Phūnwiwat. *Kabot r.s. 130 (Kānpatiwat khrang rāēk khǫng Thai)*. 5th printing. Bangkok: Khamphī, 1976.

Riggs, F.W. *Thailand, The Modernization of a Bureaucratic Polity*. Honolulu: East-West Center Press, 1966.

Roberts, E. *Embassy to the Eastern Courts of Cochin-China, Siam and Muscat during the years 1832-3-4*. New York: Harper & Brothers, 1837.

Rong Syamananda. *A History of Thailand*. 2nd ed. Bangkok: Thai Watana Panich, 1973.

Rosenberg, K. *Nation und Fortschritt: Der Publizist Thien Wan und die Modernisierung Thailands unter König Culălongkǫn (r. 1868–1910)*. Hamburg: Mitteilungen der Gesellschaft für Natur- und Völkerunde Ostasiens (OAG), vol. 78, 1980.

Saengsom Kasēmsi, *mǫmrātchawong*, and Wimon Phongphiphan, comp. *Prawatisāt Thai Samai Ratanakōsin Ratchakān thī Nu'ng thu'ng Ratchakān thī Sǫng*. Bangkok: Khanakammakān Chamra Prawatisāt Thai Samnak Nāyokrathamontri, 1980.

Saint-Hubert, C. de. "Rolin-Jaequemyns (Chao Phya Aphay Raja) and the Belgian Legal Advisers in Siam at the Turn of the Century". *JSS* 53, pt 2 (1965): 181-90.

Sarasas, Phra. *My Country Thailand (Its History, Geography and Civilisation)*. Tokyo: Maruzen, 1943.

Sarasin Viraphol. *Tribute and Profit: Sino-Siamese Trade 1652–1853*. Cambridge, Mass.: Harvard University Press, 1977.

SarDesai, D.R. *British Trade and Expansion in Southeast Asia, 1830–1914*. New Delhi: Allied Publishers, 1977.

Senn van Basel, W.H. *Schetsen uit Siam*. Amsterdam: J.H. de Bussy, 1880.

*Siam Repository* — Bangkok: quarterly, 1869–74.

Sithi-Amnuai, P. *Finance and Banking in Thailand: A Study of the Commercial System, 1888–1963*. Bangkok: Thai Watana Panich, 1964.

Sivaram, M. *Mekong Clash and Far East Crisis: A Survey of the Thailand-Indochina Conflict and the Japanese Mediation*. Bangkok: Thai Commercial Press, 1941.

Siworawat, *luang*. Phongsāwadān Mu'ang Phathalung. *PP*, vol. 12, pt 15. Bangkok: Khurusaphā, 1964.

Skinner, G.W. *Chinese Society in Thailand: An Analytical History*. Ithaca, N.Y.: Cornell University Press, 1957.

Small, L.E. "Historical Development of the Greater Chao Phya Water Control Project: An Economic Perspective. *JSS* 61, pt 1 (1973): 1-24.

Smith, B.A. "The King of Siam". *The Contemporary Review* 71 (January–June 1897): 884-91.

Smith, H.B. "Historic Proposals for a Kra Canal: Their Impact on International Relations in Southeast Asia with Emphasis on British Perspectives". *Asian Profile* 3, no. 1 (February 1975): 43-58.

Smith, M. "The Families of the Kings of Siam of the House of

Chakri". *Annals of Eugenics* 12 (1943–45): 151-57.

_____. *A Physician at the Court of Siam*. London: Country Life, 1947.

Smith, M.J. "Taksin the Savior of Siam". *Sawaddi*, March–April 1968, pp. 18-20 and 29-31.

Smith, R.B. *Siam or the History of the Thais, from 1569 A.D. to 1824 A.D.* Bethesda, Maryland: Decatur Press, 1967.

Somathat Thēwēt. *Čhaofā Čhuthāmanī*. Bangkok: Phrae Phithaya, 1970.

*Somdetphraboromōrotsāthirāt Sayāmmakutrātchakumān.* Commemoration volume at the Installation of Crown Prince Mahāwachirālongkǫn, 18 December 1972. Bangkok: *krom* Sinlapākǫn, 1972.

Sonthi Techānan, ed. *Phaenphathanā Kānmū'ang pai Sū Kānpokkhrǫng rabǫp Prachāthipatai tām Naew Phrarātchadamri khǫng Phrabātsomdet Phrapokklāočhaoyūhua (Ph.S. 2469-2475).* Bangkok: Kasētsāt University, 1976.

*Souvenir of the Siamese Kingdom Exhibition at Lumbini Park B.E. 2468, The.* Bangkok: Siam Free Press, 1927.

Sternstein, L. "From Ayutthaya to Bangkok". *Hemisphere* 17. no. 11 (November 1973): 14-21.

Stockmann, H. *Muay-Thai: The Art of Siamese Un-armed Combat.* Bangkok: Duang Kamol, 1979.

Stoughton, E.W. "The Opium Trade — England and China". *Hunt's Merchants' Magazine* 2 (1840): 394-413.

*Straits Times.* I have consulted issues between 1854, when it appeared as a weekly, *The Straits Times and Singapore Journal of Commerce,* and 1926 when it was a daily, the *Straits Times.*

Stransky, J. *Die Wiedervereinigung Thailands unter Taksin, 1767-1782.* Hamburg: Gesellschaft für Natur- und Völkerkunde Ostasiens, 1973.

Tanabe, Shigeharu. "Historical Geography of the Canal System in the Chao Phraya River Delta". *JSS* 65, pt 2 (1977): 23-72.

Tarling, N. "Siam and Sir James Brooke". *JSS* 48, pt 2 (1960): 43-72.

_____. "The Mission of Sir John Bowring to Siam". *JSS* 50, pt 2 (1962): 91-118.

_____. "Harry Parkes' Negotiations in Bangkok in 1856'. *JSS* 53, pt 2 (1965): 153-80.

_____. "The Bowring Mission: The Mellersh Narrative". *JSS* 63, pt 1 (1975): 105-26.

Tej Bunnag. *The Provincial Administration of Siam, 1892-1915:*

*The Ministry of the Interior under Prince Damrong Rajanubhab.* Kuala Lumpur: Oxford University Press, 1977.

Terwiel, B.J. "The Tais and Their Belief in Khwans". *South East Asian Review* 3, no. 1 (1978): 1-16.

———. *Monks and Magic: An Analysis of Religious Ceremonies in Central Thailand.* Scandinavian Institute of Asian Studies Monograph Series no. 24. 2nd ed. London: Curzon Press, 1979.

———. "Tattooing in Thailand's History". *Journal of the Royal Asiatic Society,* 1979, pt 2, pp. 156-66.

———. *The Tai of Assam and Ancient Tai Ritual.* Vol. 1, *Life-cycle Ceremonies.* Gaya: Centre for South East Asian Studies, 1980.

Thaemsuk Numnon. "Khabuankān r.s. 130". *Wārasān Thammasāt* 8, pt 2 (October–November 1978): 2-29.

———. See also Thamsook Numnonda.

Thak Chaloemtiarana, ed. *Thai Politics: Extracts and Documents, 1932-1957.* Bangkok: The Social Science Association of Thailand, 1978.

Thamsook Numnonda. "The Anglo-Siamese Secret Convention of 1897". *JSS* 53, pt 1 (1965): 45-60.

———. "Pibulsongkram's Thai Nation-Building Programme during the Japanese Military Presence, 1941-1945. *Journal of Southeast Asian Studies* 9, no. 2 (September 1978): 234-47.

———. See also Thaemsuk Numnon.

Thawatt Mokarapong. *History of the Thai Revolution: A Study in Political Behaviour.* Bangkok: Chalermnit, 1972.

Thinaphan Nakhāta. "National Consolidation and Nation-Building (1939-1947)." In Thak Chaloemtiarana, ed., *Thai Politics,* pp. 243-562.

Thiphākọrawong, *čhaophrayā.* See *DC First R, DC Fourth R, PKRt Sām* and *PKRt Sọ̄ng.*

Thompson, V. *Thailand, the New Siam.* New York: Paragon Book Reprint, 1967.

Turton, A. "Thai Institutions of Slavery". In *Asian and African Systems of Slavery,* ed. J.L. Watson. Oxford: Blackwell, 1979.

Turpin, F.H. *Histoire civile et naturelle du royaume de Siam.* Paris: Costard, 1771.

———. *History of the Kingdom of Siam.* Translated by B.O. Cartwright. Bangkok: American Presbyterian Mission Press, 1908.

Udom Poshakrishna. "Geschichte der Chirurgie in Thailand, 1828-1922". *JSS* 51, pt 1 (1963): 59-73.

Vella, W.F. *Siam Under Rama III.* Locust Valley, N.Y.: Augustin, 1957.

———. "Siamese Nationalism in the Plays of Rama VI". Paper presented at the 28th International Congress of Orientalists, Canberra, 1971. Mimeographed.

———. *Chaiyo!: King Vajiravadh and the Development of Thai Nationalism.* Honolulu: The University Press of Hawaii, 1978.

Vichitr Vadakarn, *luang. Thailand's Case.* Bangkok: Thai Commercial Press, 1941.

Vickery, M. Review of *Thai Titles and Ranks*, by R.B. Jones. *JSS* 62, pt 1 (1974): 158-73.

———. "A Note on the Date of the Traibhūmikathā". *JSS* 62, pt 2 (1974): 275-84.

———. Review of Yoneo Ishii et al. *An Index. JSS* 63, pt 2 (1975): 419-30.

Vincent, F. *The Land of the While Elephant.* London: Sampson Low, Marston, Low and Searle, 1873.

Wales, H.G.Q. *Siamese State Ceremonies: Their History and Function.* London: Bernard Quaritch, 1931.

———. *Ancient Siamese Government and Administration.* New York: Paragon Book Reprint, 1965. A reprint of the 1934 edition.

———. *Supplementary Notes on Siamese State Ceremonies.* London: Bernard Quaritch, 1971.

Waley, A. *The Opium War through Chinese Eyes.* London: Allen and Unwin, 1958.

Wan Waithayakon, Prince. "Thai Culture". *JSS* 35, pt 2 (1944): 135-45.

Weiler, L. *Anfang der Eisenbahn in Thailand.* Bangkok: Chalermnit, 1979.

Wells, K.E. *History of Protestant Work in Thailand, 1828–1958.* Bangkok: Church of Christ in Thailand, 1958.

Wenk, K. "Ein Lehrgedicht für junge Frauen — Suphāsit sǫn ying — des Sunthǫn Phū'. *Oriens Extremus* 12, pt 1 (1965): 65-106.

———. *The Restoration of Thailand Under Rama I, 1782–1809.* The Association for Asian Studies Monographs and Papers, no. 24. Tucson: University of Arizona Press, 1968.

———. *Phali Lehrt die Jungeren — Phālī sǫn nǫng.* Hamburg: Gesellschaft für Natur- und Völkerkunde Ostasiens, 1977.

Wilson, C.M. "State and Society in the Reign of Mongkut, 1851–1869: Thailand on the Eve of Modernization". Ph.D. dissertation, Cornell University, 1970.

Wira Wimoniti. *Historical Patterns of Tax Administration in Thailand*. Bangkok: Institute of Public Administration, Thammasat University, 1961.

"Withētkaraní". *Sārakhadī Prawatisāt Thāngkānmu'ang Thai, Hētkān Thāngkānmu'ang 43 Pī Haengprakōp Prachāthipatai*. Bangkok: Ruamkānphim, 1975.

Wood, W.A.R. *A History of Siam, from the Earliest Times to the Year A.D. 1781*. Bangkok: The Siam Barnakich Press, 1933.

Wook Moon, J. "United States Relations with Thailand: The Mission of Townsend Harris". *Asian Profile* 1, no. 2 (1973): 355-63.

Wuthichai Mūnsin. *Kānpatirūpkānsu'ksā nai Ratchakān thī 5*. Bangkok: Samākhom Sangkhomsāt haeng Prathēt Thai, 1973.

Wyatt, D.K. "Siam and Laos, 1767–1827". *Journal of Southeast Asian History* 4, no. 2 (September 1963): 13-32.

_____. "Samuel McFarland and Early Educational Modernization in Thailand, 1877–1895". *Felicitation Volumes of Southeast-Asian Studies Presented to His Highness Prince Dhaninivat Kromamun Bidyalabh Bridhyakorn*, vol. 1, pp. 1-16. Bangkok: The Siam Society, 1965.

_____. "Family Politics in Nineteenth Century Thailand". *Journal of Southeast Asian History* 9, no. 2 (1968): 208-28.

_____. *The Politics of Reform in Thailand: Education in the Reign of King Chulalongkorn*. New Haven, Conn.: Yale University Press, 1969.

_____. "King Chulalongkorn the Great: Founder of Modern Thailand". *Asia*, supplement no. 2, 1976.

# Index

Administrative reform, 75-76, 77-80, 222-23, 252-55, 270, 320-21
Adoption, 36
Ahānbǫrirak, *phrayā*, 222
Alaungpaya, king of Burma, 30-32, 34
Amarintharāmāt, *kromsomdet*, 107
Amātayakun family, 221, 231
Angthong, 104, 200
Annam, 50, 137, 249, 256-57. *See also* Vietnam
Annual fleet, 52, 135-36
Anǫn Mahidon, king of Siam, 337, 342
Anuraksongkhrām, *kromakhun*, 62-63, 71-72, 85
Anurakthêwêt, *kromphra'*, 75, 92. *See also* Suriya Aphai
Anuwong, *čhao*, 130-31
Aphaiphānit, *luang*, 109
Aphaiphuthon, *čhaophrayā*, 120
Army recruitment, 215, 233-35, 270-71
Assam, Burmese invasion of, 129
Aubaret, I.N., 186-88
Ayutthaya: abandonment, 50, 66-67 n 19; Bangkok's paradigm, 73-74, 92, 95; fall of, 29-35; involvement in rebellion, 334, 336; political sphere, 10-11; region, 75, 104, 106, 119; royal excursion to, 334, 336

Balastier, Joseph, 153-54
Bamrāp, *kromphra'*, 234. *See also* Mahāmālā
Bamroe Rāchaphaethaya, *phrayā*, 140
Bangkok: construction of, 77-78, 87; development, 299; region, 100, 102, 104-106, 119
*Bangkok Calendar*, 185
*Bangkok Press*, 186
*Bangkok Summary*, 198
Bāng Račhan, stockade, 39, 65-66 n 4
Battambang, 229, 259, 260, 278
Bengal, 112
Betel, ritual use of, 2, 11
*Biawat*, 8-9, 91, 131, 137, 218
Boat races, 91, 308
Bodawpaya, king of Burma, 81, 82, 92, 121
Boriphat, *čhaofā* (Prince Nakhon Sawan), 290, 291, 293, 296, 305, 320, 321-25, 331
Boworadet, *phra-ǫngčhao*, 325, 326, 330, 334-36
Bowring treaty, 172, 174-79, 185, 196-98, 199
Bǫdindechā, *čhaophrayā* (Sing Singhasēnï), 134, 137, 143, 150, 152, 241. *See also* Nikorabadin; Rāchasuphāwadï

Bǫromakōt, king of Siam, 29-30, 32, 37, 70
Bradley: and Rama IV, 163, 169; the diarist, 138, 180, 184, 202, 220; the medical doctor, 175; the missionary, 204 n 20; the printer, 143
British relations: with Burma, 129, 249, 262-63; with France, 262-63; with Siam, 122, 129-30, 147-48. *See also* Siam and Britain
Brooke, Sir James, 154
Buacham, 105
Buddhist order. *See* Sangha
Bunlong family, 214
Bunmā, general, 43, 50, 56, 62-63, 71-72, 74. *See also* Uparat under Rama I
Bunnāk family: and Bowring treaty, 175; and Rama IV, 166, 189; and Rama V, 217, 230, 231, 235; appointments, 214, 221, 283; divisions, 234, 240-42; honours, 166-67
Bunnāk, *nāi,* 75
Bunyarathaphan family, 213
Būranasiri family, 221
Burmese: invasions, 29-35, 39, 40, 50, 51, 81-85, 111; relations with Britain, 129, 249, 262-63; relations with Siam, 112; prisoners of war, 106, 110-11; Sangha, 141
Burney, Henry, 129-30

Cambodia: asserting independence, 122, 132; expedition to, 50, 71, 137, 146; French protectorate, 186-87; Siamese vassal, 11, 96
Cambodian: labour force, 77, 106; troops, 89
Canal construction, 128, 132, 168, 228, 239, 274
Cannon: casting, 130; use of, 33
Caswell, Jesse, 150
Censorship, 338
Census, 17, 100-101, 103, 107. *See also* Tattooing drive
Chachoengsao, 104, 150
Chaibadan, 105
Chainat, 104, 119, 274
Chaiya, 119
Chakraphong, *čhaofā,* 277, 291, 293, 296, 305, 313-14
Champassak, 11

Chana, *luang,* 75
Chandler, J.H., 176
Chanthaburi, 38, 39, 102, 137, 260, 273
Chao Phraya River: at Bangkok, 72-73, 168; at Chainat, 274; at Thonburi, 40; mouth of, 130, 147, 258, 266
Chiang Mai: Ayutthayan influence in, 11; Burmese influence in, 30, 50, 52, 81, 86, 92; in ruins, 83; relation to Siam, 85, 102, 170, 171; Siamese influence in, 229, 253, 267, 272-73, 324; Taksin's attacks upon, 47, 51
Chiang Rai, 102, 324
Chiangrung, 170
Chiang Saen, 83, 86, 324
Chiangtung expedition, 170-72, 173
China, relations with Siam, 52, 62, 85, 109-10, 113-14, 138
Chinese: and opium, 144-45; and Siamese, 259, 282-83, 323, 341; immigrants, 114, 116, 136; labour, 131, 132, 133, 168, 264; poll tax, 116, 200, 215; secret societies, 149, 241; strike, 282-83; tax farmers, 267; under Taksin, 38
Cholera, epidemic, 110-11, 151-52
Chonburi, 38, 104
Chuang Bunnāk. *See* Sīsuriyawong
Chumphon, 83, 119, 153
Chun Bunnāk. *See* Samoečhairāt
Chūtō family, 221
Civilian ranks, in *saktinā* system, 5, 7, 13, 15, 38. See also *Phayā*
Clarke, Sir Andrew, 226
Cochin-China, 114, 137, 186. *See also* Vietnam
Coins: debasing the *baht,* 279-80, 309; flat shape, 180, 195; introduction of new, 213; shortage of, 180
Commoners' ranks. *See* Civilian ranks
Corruption, suppression of, 61, 250, 341
Corvée: abolition of, 251-52, 265, 270; general system, 17-18, 24; during the First Reign, 84, 96; during the Second Reign, 101, 116; during the Third Reign, 132; during the Fourth Reign, 181, 201-202; during the Fifth Reign,

214, 220, 235; some exemptions, 116
Cotton, manufacture, 197
Coup d'état: suspected, 179, 211-12, 305; abortive, 296-99, 334-35; attempted, 93, 99; successful, 75, 330-32
Crawfurd, Sir John, mission of, 112-19, 135, 197
Crown prince, 251, 261, 266, 278. *See also* Succession to the throne
Cultural Mandates, 343-44
Currency. *See* coins
Čhakčhētsadā, *kromaluang,* 94
Čhakri, *čhaophrayā,* head of *krom* Mahātthai, 7, 9, 36, 55, 71
Čhamū'n, *rank,* 5
Čhāngwāng, 167
Čhanthaburi, prince, 279, 320. *Also known as* Prince Kitiyākǫn
Čhaochǫmmāndā, 4
Čhāo, 16
Čhaofā, title, 3, 25 n 13, 74
Čhaomū'ang, 10
Čharūn, *phra'ǫngčhao,* 322, 329
Čhētsadābodin, *kromamū'n,* 108, 111, 112, 115, 120, 127. *See also* Rama III
Čhiraprawat, *kromaluang,* 270
Čhoem Saengchūtō, 233, 252. *See also* Waiworanāt; Surasak
Čhulālongkǫn, *čhaofā,* 184, 189-90, 195, 210. *See also* Čhulālongkǫn, king of Siam
Čhulālongkǫn, king of Siam: accession, 210-12; ceremonial role, 216-17; travels, 217-18, 219, 267-68, 277-78; and education, 219, 268-69; and Palace Incident, 223-27; and Phra' Prīchā, 231-32; and Bunnāks, 230, 241-42; reform measures, 222-23, 252-54, 268-69; health of, 260-61, 267, 277, 283; accomplishments, 282, 283, 284
Čhuthāmani, *čhaofā,* 115, 127. *See also* Itsarēt; Phra' Pinklāo

Dalang, 92
Damrong Rātchanuphāp, *kromphrayā*: career, 252, 261, 264, 311, 320; travel, 254; as Minister of the Interior, 268, 269; and education, 270; on the constitution, 323; in exile, 336; as historian, 4, 37

Debt bondage, 18-19, 100, 116-17, 214. *See also* Slavery; Slaves
Dēchādisǫn, *kromsomdetphra',* 165, 183. *See also* Dētadisǫn
Decorations: Mongkut's request for, 182; new system of, 238-39
Decree. *See* Edict
Dētadisǫn, *kromakhun,* 155. *See also* Dēchādisǫn
Dilok, *kromamū'n,* 305
Directions of the compass, ritual function of, 3
Dit Bunnāk. *See* Phrakhlang of the Third Reign; Elder Somdet
*Dusit Samit,* 308
*Dusit Thāni,* 307-309

Economic crisis, 309-10, 326-28
Economic development, 196-98
Edict: on gambling, 49, 78-79; on tattooing, 50-51, 100; on combatting cholera, 111; on litigation, 100; on prisoners, 100; on corvée, 101; legal basis for, 93-94
Education reform, 219, 228, 264, 268-69, 340-41
Ekathat, king of Siam, 29-32, 37, 41, 70
Elder Somdet (Dit Bunnāk), 166, 175, 221, 241. *See also* Phrakhlang of the Third Reign
Elephant: in warfare, 15, 31, 33-34, 172; white, 121, 137, 176
Emerald Buddha, temple of the, 80, 81, 95, 296. *See also* Wat Phrakaew
Etiquette, 168, 343-44
Exhibition, national, 239, 311, 313

Fāng, Phra', 39, 43, 46, 47, 48
Finlayson, George, 118-19, 136, 145
First Foot Guard, 233-35, 248
Food shortage, 45, 47, 81, 83, 84, 134, 309. *See also* Rice
Foreign advisers, 261, 264, 272, 274-75, 278-80, 307, 311, 322-23, 327
Fortress, 172, 258-59
France: relations with Siam, 185-88, 229, 248, 267; and liquor licences, 236; and the Kra Canal, 237-38; confronting Siam, 256-63
Front Palace. *See* Wang Nā; Uparāt

Gambling: decree on, 49, 67-68 n 40,

89-90; prohibition for civil servants, 78-79; state lottery, 131; tax on, 199; abolition of, 220, 253
Gold mine, 136
Guard, royal, 2-3
Gutzlaff, Karl, 133-34, 136, 142

Harris, Townsend, 177, 205 n 56
Ha Tien, 50, 59, 137
Hillier, C.B., 178-79, 181
Họ gangs, 230, 247-48, 257
Hsinbyushin, king of Burma, 31, 52
Huahin, 331, 333, 336
Hunter, Robert, 134, 138-39, 147-49, 152, 157, 174

In, *mü'ang*, 104
Inao, 92
Income of princes: during Ayutthayan times, 3; during the First Reign, 91; during the Fourth Reign, 164. See also *Biawat*
Insignia of rank, 7, 11
Inthaphat, 93
Inthra Aphai, *phra'*, 108
Isthmus of Kra, 89, 237-38, 278
Itsarēt, *kromakhun*, 127, 142, 150, 155-56, 163-65. *See also* Čhuthāmani; Phra'Pinklāo

Java, 198, 236, 324
Johore, 121

Kalāhom, *krom*, 7, 76, 102, 120, 136, 200, 254
Kamphaeng Phet, 10, 102, 105, 119
*Kanchā*, use of, 145
Kanchanaburi, 82, 105, 119
Kanlayānmit family, 221, 222, 254
Kasēt, *krom. See* Nā
Kathin robe giving, 95, 217
Kawila, *phrayā*, 83, 86, 92, 93
Kawilōrot, 229
Kedah, 109, 121-22, 145, 278
Kelantan, 114, 121, 278
Kham Bunnāk. *See* Rawiwong; Thiphākọrawong
Khamphran, 105
Khochasēnā family, 221
Khorat plateau, 39, 263
Khridet family, 221
*Khunnāng*, 13-14, 16, 212
*Kitchānukit*, 192
Kitiyākọn. *See* Čhanthaburi

Knox, Fanny, 231-32
Knox, Sir Thomas, 225, 231-32
Kōt, *krom. See* Phrakhlang
*Kotmāi Lilit*, 94
*Kotmāi Trā Sām Duang*, 94
*Krom* ranks, 4-5, 12, 17, 75, 134, 163, 166

Lamduan, 93
Lampang: under Kawila, 83, 86; semi-independent, 102; under Siamese umbrella, 170, 267, 324; during the Shan rebellion, 272
Lamphun, 102, 170, 171, 267
Land ownership, 106-107
Laotian: principalities, 30, 56, 88; labourers, 77, 106; troops, 89, 137; slaves, 131
Law: of inheritance, 90, 93-94; of compensation, 14-15; of Civil Hierarchy, 5; reform, 280-81
Lebon, Mgr, 55, 57-58, 60
Leonowens, Anna, 190-92
Lomsak, 170
Lopburi, 104
Lottery. *See* Gambling
Luang Prabang: relations with Ayutthaya, 11; relations with Bangkok, 229, 230, 256, 273; and Họ troops, 248; relations with the French, 249, 256, 257, 273

McFarland, Samuel, 228
Maeklong River, 43, 133
Mahābharata, 92
Mahāchāt preaching, 95
Mahā Dā movement, 59
Mahākasatsu'k, *čhaophrayā*, 62-63, 71-72. *See also* Rama I
Mahāmālā, *čhaofā*, 212, 234. *See also* Bamrāp
Mahāsēnā, *čhaophrayā*, 120-21
Mahāthirāt, *phrayā*, 83
Mahātlek: organization, 5-6, 20-21, 36, 78, 103; and oath of allegiance, 80; under Čhulālongkọn, 217, 220, 221, 225
Mahātthai, *krom*: organization, 7, 15, 76, 103, 230; hierarchical position of, 120; and taxation, 200; abolition, 254
Mahāvangsa, 92
Mahāyothā, *čhaophrayā*, 132
Mahēsuan, *kromamū'n*, 189

Mahinthon, *čhaophrayā,* 251
Mahit, *kromamū'n,* 261
Malacca, 114, 121
Malay Peninsula, 84, 266
Mandalay, 249
Manopakǫn, *phrayā,* 332, 333, 336
Manoram, 104
Martaban, 88
Mattoon, Stephen, 178
Mekong River, 256-57, 260, 262-63,
   273, 344, 345
Mergui, 30, 34, 88
Mindon, king of Burma, 170-71
Mitchell-Innes, A., 264-65
Mon, 87, 88-89, 106, 131
Money. *See* Coins
Mongkut, *čhaofā:* place at the court,
   107-108; joins Sangha, 121,
   140-41; and missionaries, 149;
   right to the succession, 115, 128,
   156, 162-63. *See also* Mongkut,
   king of Siam
Mongkut, king of Siam: appoint-
   ments, 165-66; and Bowring treaty,
   172-79; and missionaries, 173-74;
   ceremonial role, 181-83; conflict
   with Aubaret, 186-88; and
   Sīsuriyawong, 179, 187-89; and
   astronomy, 192-95; and the
   Siamese language, 204 n 35; as
   historian, 65 n 11
Monthienbān, *krom,* 7
Montigny, Ch. de, 177
Morgan, John, 112
Mū'ang, *krom,* 8, 75, 100, 167, 200

Nā, *krom,* 8, 22, 75, 101-106, 200,
   254
*Nāi,* role of, 17, 23, 51
Nakhon Chaisi, 104, 257, 296
Nakhon Nayok, 104, 200
Nakhon Pathom, 182
Nakhon Ratchasima, 10, 39, 52, 63,
   119, 253, 270, 271, 334, 336
Nakhon Sawan, 104, 105, 334
Nakhon Sawan, *kromakhun. See*
   Boriphat
Nakhon Si Thammarat, 10, 40, 44,
   46, 69 n 69, 145
Nakhon Thai, 10
Name: on golden plate, 2, 166, 167;
   of kings, 164, 303-304; of
   members of the populace, 300-301;
   of Siam changed to Thailand, 343

Nan, 102, 170, 267
Narāi, king of Siam, 4
Narathip, *kromphra',* 255
Narēt, *kromphra',* 264
Narit, *kromphrayā,* 252, 255, 264,
   311, 320
Nationalism: Wachirāwut style; 299-
   304; Phibūnsongkhrām style,
   339-40, 343-44
Naungdawgyi, king of Burma, 31
Negri Sembilan, 121
Nikorabadin, *čhaophrayā,* 167. *See*
   Rāchasuphāwadi; Bǫdindechā
Nirāt poetry, 92
Nok, *nāi,* 109
Nongkhai, 253, 256
Nonthaburi, 104, 106

Oath of allegiance, 2, 9-10, 21, 53-
   55, 296
Opium: trade, 112, 148, 149; suppression, 143-45; state monopoly,
   168-69; medicinal use of, 178

Pages, corps of. *See* Mahātlek
Pahang, 114, 121
Paknam, 172, 258-59
Pallegoix, Mgr A., 54, 141-42
Paramānuchitchinōrot, *kromsomdet-
   phra',* 165, 182
Parkes, H.S., 175, 176-77
Pathiu, 119
Pattani, 10, 84, 114
Patthalung, 10, 119
Penang, 110, 114, 122
Perak, 121, 122
Perlis, 278
Phahon, *phrayā* (Phot Phahonyo-
   thin), 330, 333-36, 337, 341-42
Phānuphantuwong, *kromphrayā.*
   *See* Phānurangsi
Phānurangsī, *čhaofā,* 240, 252, 255,
   261, 311, 320, 324
Phānuwong, *čhaophrayā* (Thuam
   Bunnāk), 213, 223, 234, 237
Phat, *khun,* nāi Akǫn, 36
Phātsakǫrawong, *phrayā* (Phon
   Bunnāk), 221, 222, 233, 242, 255,
   268
*Phayā* and *phrayā* title, 6-7, 9, 66
   n 8, 74
Pheng, *luang,* 39
Phetburi: warfare in, 31, 37, 81, 111;
   and King Mongkut, 182; woodcut-

ters in, 201; sugar industry
around, 202; manpower in, 234;
and rebellion, 334, 336
Phetchabun, 10, 102, 105
Phibūnsongkhrām, *luang* (Plaek
Khittasangkha), 330, 333, 334,
335, 339-40, 342-46
Phichai, 47, 50, 102, 105
Phichit, 105
Phimai, 39
Phiphatkosa, *phrayā*, 91. *See also*
Sorawichit
Phiphitphubēn, *kromphra'*, 155, 183
Phisētsisawat, *kromaluang*, 183
Phithakmontrī, *kromaluang*, 128
Phithayalāp, *kromakhun*, 264
Phitsanulok: as seat of power, 10,
39, 71, 102; battles around, 43-44,
52; taxation, 105, 200; royal
travel, 324
Phonlathēp, *phrayā*, 8, 84, 99, 102,
167
*Phračhaolānthoe*, in *saktinā* system,
12
Phrae, 102, 170, 267, 272, 324
*Phrai*, 16-19, 50-52, 77, 90, 100-101,
116-17
*Phrai luang*, 24, 84, 101, 117, 132,
214, 251-52, 265
*Phrai som*, 84, 214, 233, 251-52, 265
*Phrai suai*, 24, 123, 136
Phrakhlang, *čhaophrayā*, 57-58, 112,
137, 143, 145, 146
Phrakhlang, *čhaophrayā*, of the
Third Reign (Dit Bunnāk), 150,
153, 155, 163, 166. *See also* Elder
Somdet
Phrakhlang, *krom*, 8, 9, 76, 102,
133, 254
Phra'nakhonbān, *krom*. *See* Mū'ang
Phraphetrāchā, king of Siam, 113
Phra'Pinklāo, Second King during
the Fourth Reign, 164-65, 183,
185, 188, 212, 218, 223. *See also*
Čhuthāmanī; Itsarēt
Phra'Sadet, 9
*phrayā*, title. See *Phayā*
Phrom, 104
Phuket, 230
Phutharaphai, *čhaophrayā*, 212, 223
Phūtharēt, *kromamū'n*, 234
Plaek Khittasangkha. *See*
Phibūnsongkhrām
Phon Bunnāk. *See* Phātsakǫrawong

Phutthaimat. *See* Ha Tien
Phūwanēt, *kromaluang,* 183
Portuguese, 86, 109
Postal service, introduced, 239-40
Pračhak, *kromamū'n,* 248
Prachāthipok, king of Siam: early
career, 314, 319-20; style of
government, 320-22; travels,
324-26; health, 325-26, 336-37; and
democracy, 331, 335-38, 342-43; in
exile, 337, 343; abdication, 337;
death, 343
Prachinburi, 104, 105, 119, 231, 334
Praditmanutham, *luang. See* Pridī
Prayūn Phamonmontri, 330
Pričhā, *phra',* 230-32
Pridī Phanomyong, 321, 329-33, 338,
340, 342
Princely ranks. See *Krom* ranks
Printing, 134, 138, 143, 193, 195
Pritsadāng, *mǫmčhao*, 236
Privy Council, 222-23, 227, 228, 323,
331
Procession, 2, 111, 165, 295
Prostration, before the king, 2-3, 60-
61, 76, 220, 239

Queen: elevated to Regency, 266;
income during Ayutthayan times, 3

Rāchasuphāwadī, *phrayā*, 134, 166,
167. *See also* Nikorabadin;
Bǫdindechā
Railway construction, 263-64, 266,
273, 278, 279, 299-300, 328
Rakronarēt, *kromaluang*, 143, 151
Rama I, king of Siam: accession, 71-
72; as reformer, 76; tension with
Uparāt, 77, 91-93; second anointment, 80-81; as law maker, 93-94;
predilection for ritual, 94-96
Rama II, king of Siam: accession,
99-100; measures by, 100-108; appointments made by, 107; foreign
policy, 109; literary projects, 110;
style of government, 112, 121-23;
as trader, 115, 123
Rama III, king of Siam: accession,
127-28; attitude towards missionaries, 152; actions to combat
epidemic, 151-52; and reform of
the Sangha, 156; death, 155-56
Rama IV. *See* Mongkut, king of
Siam

Rama V. *See* Čhulālongkǫn, king of Siam
Rama VI. *See* Wachirāwut, king of Siam
Rama VII. *See* Prachāthipok, king of Siam
Rama VIII. *See* Anǫn Mahidon, king of Siam
Rāmanwong, *phrayā*, 62
Rāmāyana, 92
Rangoon, 88, 169
Ranong, 230
Ratanabǫdin, *čhaophrayā* (Rǫt Kanlayānmit), 254
Ratburi: Burmese occupation of, 31, 43, 52, 81-83; taxation, 105, 200; canal link with Bangkok, 132; Sīsuriyawong's abode, 225, 234; manpower in, 234, 235, 270; Chinese riot in, 257
Rātchaburidirēkru't, *kromaluang*, 264, 296
Rātcharin, *phra'*, 71. *See also* Mahākasatsu'k; Rama I
Rātchawǫranakun, *phrayā*, 222
Rattanamuni, Phra', 57
Rawiwong, *čhaophrayā* (Kham Bunnāk), 183, 200. *See also* Thiphākǫrawong
Rayong, 38, 46, 119
Regalia, 2, 80
Registration of the populace, 24. *See also* Satsadī
Rice: price of, 81, 134, 273-74, 326-27; distribution, 45, 47; and irrigation, 273-74. *See also* Food shortage; Taxation
Right and left side, division, 6, 26 n 22
Roberts, Edmund, 127, 134, 135-36, 196
Rolin-Jaequemyns, Gustave, 261, 265
Rǫt Kanlayānmit. *See* Ratanabǫdin
Royal names. *See* Name of kings

Saeng, *nāi. See* Thipphakosa
Saigon, 114
Sai Han, 92
Sāi Sanitwong, *mǫmčhao*, 233, 252
Sakdiphonlasēp, *kromamū'n*, 112, 127, 151

Sakhonburi, 104
*Saktinā* system, 11-16, 107, 116, 213, 218, 221
*Samian,* 15
Samlok, 104
Samoečhairāt, *čhaomū'n* (Chun Bunnāk), 230
Samut Prakan, 104, 105, 110
Samut Songkhram, 71
San, *mū'ang,* 104
San, *phrayā,* 61-63
Sangha: members administering oath, 10; in confrontation with king, 60-61; identification cards, 77; revised Buddhist texts, 88; rules of the, 48-49, 67 n 33; as refuge, 30-31; under Rama I, 76, 79
Sanphasit, *kromakhun,* 271
Saowaphā, queen of Siam, 266, 291, 314
Saraburi, 56, 104, 106, 131, 200, 334
Sarasat, *phra',* 338
Satsadī, *krom,* 17, 23-24, 78
Sawangkhaburi, 39, 40, 43, 47-48, 65, 102
Sawankhalok, 10, 105
Scouting movement. *See* Wild Tiger Corps
Selangor, 121
*Sēnā,* 101, 104
*Sēnābodī,* 227, 230, 232, 233, 234, 252
Sēnānurak, *kromaluang,* 99-100, 165
Sēnāthibēt, *čhaophrayā,* 112
Seng, secretary to the British consul, 178-79
Shan rebellion, 272
Shan States, 30, 170
Ship building, 135, 139, 146-47, 160 n 68, 163, 176, 180
Siam: and Sri Lanka, 109, 110; and Laos, 256-57; and Britain, 122, 147-48, 154-55, 182-83, 186-87, 236-38, 257; and France, 236-38, 249, 256-61, 271-72, 277-78, 344-46; and United States, 109, 112-13, 153-54, 258; and Germany, 304-305, 307, 312; and Japan, 338-40, 345-46

Siam Land, Canals and Irrigation Company, 255, 263, 274
*Siam Observer*, 302
Singapore: and trade, 112, 114-15, 154-55, 198; and Siamese printing press, 134, 138; and opium, 144; and royal travel, 217, 219, 324
*Singapore Free Press*, 163
*Singapore Straits Times*, 163, 186
Singburi, 104
Singhasēnā family, 214, 221, 241
Sing Singhasēnā. *See* Bọdindechā; Nikorabadin; Rāchasuphāwadī
Singu, king of Burma, 56
Sīphiphat, phrayā (That Bunnāk), 130, 153, 166. *See also* Younger Somdet
Sīsọrarak, *čhamū'n*, 167
Sīsurēn, *kromamū'n*, 108
Sīsuriyawong *čhaophrayā* (Chuang Bunnāk): career, 155, 167, 183, 200, 211-13; travel, 171, 228; role in making Bowring treaty, 173-76; relation with Rama IV, 179, 187-89; and modernization, 168, 185, 195, 223; during the Regency, 215, 219; and the Palace Incident, 224; relation with Rama V, 234-35, 241-42, 266; general assessment of role, 240-42
Sithammathirāt, *phrayā*, 8, 83
Slavery: rules, 79; abolition, 220, 222, 239
Slaves: class of, 16, 19; through debt, 100, 116-17, 214; runaway, 123
Smallpox: epidemic, 82; inoculation, 143, 299
*Sodāban*, 57, 60-61, 76
Songkhla, 84, 145, 200, 336
Songsuradēt, *phrayā* (Thēp Phanthumasēn), 330, 333, 335, 340
Sorawichit, *luang*, 71, 75, 91. *See also* Phiphatkosa
Sport: boxing, 87-88; boat racing, 91, 308; football, 303, 312; various, 303, 312
Sri Lanka, 109, 110
Steam engines, 176, 184-85, 195, 197
Suan Kulap school, 303
Succession: rules of, 1-2, 25 n 4, 291, 313-15; considerations on, 155-56, 210-11; struggle, 30. *See also* Crown prince

Sugar: trade figures, 113, 147, 196-97; and taxation, 148-49, 150-51, 202, 203
Sukhothai, 102, 105, 119
Sunthǫn Phū, *phra'*, 110, 124-25 n 23
Suphanburi, 31, 34, 104
Sura, *luang*, 75
Surasak, *čhaophrayā*, 255, 272. *See also* Choem Saengchūtō; Waiworanāt
Surasī, *čhaophrayā*, 62
Suratsawadi, *krom. See* Satsadī
Surawongwaiyawat, *čhaophrayā* (Won Bunnāk), 213, 234, 237, 242, 251, 252
Suriya, *phrayā*, 279
Suriya Aphai, *phrayā*, 63, 71-72, 75. *See also* Anurakthēwēt
Suriyawongkosā, *phrayā*, 115

Tak, *mū'ang*, 37, 51, 81
Tāk, *phrayā. See* Taksin
Taksin, king of Siam: youth, 35-37; early career, 37-38; conqueror of Siam, 40-49; protector of the people, 41; and Buddhist monks, 44-49; and Catholic missionaries, 53-55; administration, 53-63; execution, 63; relation with southern region, 69 n 69; cremation, 80
Talapoin, origin of the word, 68 n 53
Tattooing: decree, 50; drive, 77, 100, 153, 181, 214, 235
Tavoy, 30, 32, 34, 43, 85, 87-89
Taxation: general, 22-23, 118, 123, 151, 198-202, 264-65, 327; on fruit trees, 23, 101, 199; on rice land, 22, 101, 106, 117, 198, 222, 265; on alcohol, 22, 119, 136, 199; on salt, 128; on bamboo, 134; on teak logs, 134; on sugar, 148-49, 150-51, 202, 203; on gambling, 199; evasion, 61
Teak, 134, 136, 147, 149
Telegraphy, 239, 271
Tenasserim, 11, 30, 34, 88
Thā, *krom*, 8, 76, 102, 200
Tha Chin River, 131
Thailand, name change from Siam to, 343
*Tham khwan* ceremony, 105-106
Thammapurohit, *phrayā*, 92
Thammasāt, *luang*, 94

Thammasāt, Phra', legal code, 1
Thammasāt University, founding, 340-41
Thammāthikǫn, *čhaophrayā*, 167
Thammathibēt, *čhaofā*, 29
*Thammayutikanikāya*, 142
*Thanai*, 15, 214
Thāramāthibodī, *phayā*, 7
Tharong, 105
Thāt. *See* slaves
That Bunnāk. *See* Sīphiphat; Younger Somdet
Thatsanai Mitphakdī, 330
*The King and I*, 191
Thēpharirak, *kromaluang*, 94
Thēp Phanthumasēn. *See* Songsuradēt
Thēpphiphit, *kromamū'n*, 29, 30, 34, 39, 41, 44
Thēpwǫračan, *phrayā*, 229
Thēwan, *phra'ǫngčao*, 234, 236. *See also* Thēwawong
Thēwawong, *kromphrayā*, 254, 256, 258, 261, 264, 304, 311
Thēwētwacharin, *kromaluang*, 212
Thibaw, king of Burma, 249
Thienwan, 185, 276
Thiphākǫrawong, *čhaophrayā* (Kham Bunnāk), 188-89, 193, 213. *See also* Rawiwong
Thipphakosa, *phrayā*, 75
Thonburi, 40, 41, 44, 50, 65, 72, 73
Thǫng Duang, general, 56, 62, 70-71. *See also* Rātcharin; Mahākasatsu'k; Rama I
Thǫng-In, 93
Three Pagoda Pass, 81
Thuam Bunnāk. *See* Phanuwong
To Bunnāk, 235
Tomlin, Jacob, 133
*Traiphūmikhāthā*, 141, 192, 193
Trat, 102
Trengganu, 113, 121, 278
Trial by ordeal, 21, 46-49
Turpin, F., 44-47
Typhoid fever, 45

Ubon Ratchathani, 252, 271, 334
Unarut, 92
United States. *See* Siam and United States
Uparāt, Mahā: the office, 1, 3, 25 n 11, 163, 166, 189-90; *saktin*ā, 12;
under Rama I, 73, 74, 76, 82, 86-87, 91-93, 94; under Rama II, 99-100, 108, 115, 128; under Rama III, 128; under Rama IV, *see* Phra'Pinklāo; under Rama V, *see* Wichaichān
Uthai Thani, 104
Uthumphǫn, king of Siam, 29, 32, 70

Vientiane, 119, 130-32, 229-30, 248
Vietnam: cholera in, 111; and Cambodia, 122, 137, 146, 148-49, 186, 247; and Siam, 122
Vietnamese, prosecuted, 59

Wachirāwut, king of Siam: when crown prince, 261, 277, 278; accession, 290; coronation, 294-95; style of government, 299-302; as author, 301-303, 312-13; general assessment, 315-16
Wachirayān, *kromphrayā*, 268, 269
Wachirunhit, *čhaofā*, 251
Waiwǫranat, *čhamū'n*, 5, 168
Waiwǫranāt, *čhamū'n* (Čhoem Saengchūtō), 248. *See also* Surasak
Wang, *krom*, 7-8, 75, 254
Wang Nā, 3, 73, 103
Wannarāt, Phra', 57
Warfare, traditional, 32-35
Wat Bowoniwēt, 140-42, 268
Wat Bangyiru'atai, 80
Wat Chaeng, 109, 110, 125 n 36
Wat Kōsawat, 36
Wat Pho. *See* Wat Phra Chetuphon
Wat Phra Chetuphon, 139, 140, 153
Wat Phrakaew, temple of the Emerald Buddha, 238, 239, 296
Wat Saket, 269
Wat Samorai, 140-42
Wichaichān, *kromakhun*, 189, 212, 223-27
Wild Tiger Corps, 291-94, 298, 312
Wisut, *phrayā*, 268
Women: in the court, 2, 4, 190; in Siamese society, 16, 27 n 45; and views on monogamy, 314
Won Bunnāk. *See* Surawongwaiyawat
Wongsathirāt, *kromaluang*, 165, 170-71, 175, 178, 183, 188
Wǫrasak, *kromakhun*, 189, 212, 213

*Yā* rank, in Ayutthayan times, 6-7
Yokrabat, 37, 70, 101
Yomarāt, 8, 9, 71, 83, 88, 136, 170-71
Yomarāt, *čhaophrayā*, of the Sixth Reign, 299, 310, 320

Younger Somdet (That Bunnāk), 166, 175, 178, 183. *See also* Siphiphat
*Yutthakot,* 253
*Yuwayon,* 340